GENERAL WILLIAM T. SHERMAN'S MARCH THROUGH GEORGIA and the CAROLINAS NOVEMBER 1864 – APRIL 1865

OTHER BOOKS BY BURKE DAVIS

Biography:

They Called Him Stonewall
Gray Fox: R. E. Lee & the Civil War
Jeb Stuart, the Last Cavalier
Marine! The Life of Lt. Gen. Lewis B. (Chesty) Puller, U.S.M.C. (Ret.)
The Billy Mitchell Affair
Old Hickory: A Life of Andrew Jackson

History:

To Appomattox
Our Incredible Civil War
The Cowpens-Guilford Courthouse Campaign
A Williamsburg Galaxy
The World of Currier & Ives (with Roy King)
The Campaign That Won America: The Story of Yorktown
Get Yamamoto
George Washington and the American Revolution

Novels:

Yorktown
The Ragged Ones
Whisper My Name
The Summer Land

For Children:

America's First Army
Heroes of the American Revolution
Black Heroes of the American Revolution
Biography of a Leaf
Biography of a Kingsnake
Mr. Lincoln's Whiskers

SHERMAN'S MARCH

SHERMAN'S MARCH

Burke Davis

Random House New York

 Published in the United States by Random House, Inc., New York, and simultaneously in Canada by Random House of Canada Limited, Toronto.

Library of Congress Cataloging in Publication Data

Davis, Burke, 1913–
Sherman's march.

Includes index.
1. Sherman's March to the Sea. 2. Sherman's March through the Carolinas. 3. Sherman, William Tecumseh, 1820–1891.
I. Title.
E476.69.D38 973.7'378 79-5550
ISBN 0-394-50739-8

Manufactured in the United States of America
2 4 6 8 9 7 5 3
First Edition

To Archie and Wayne
and the faculty of the New River War College

Contents

SHERMAN'S MARCH

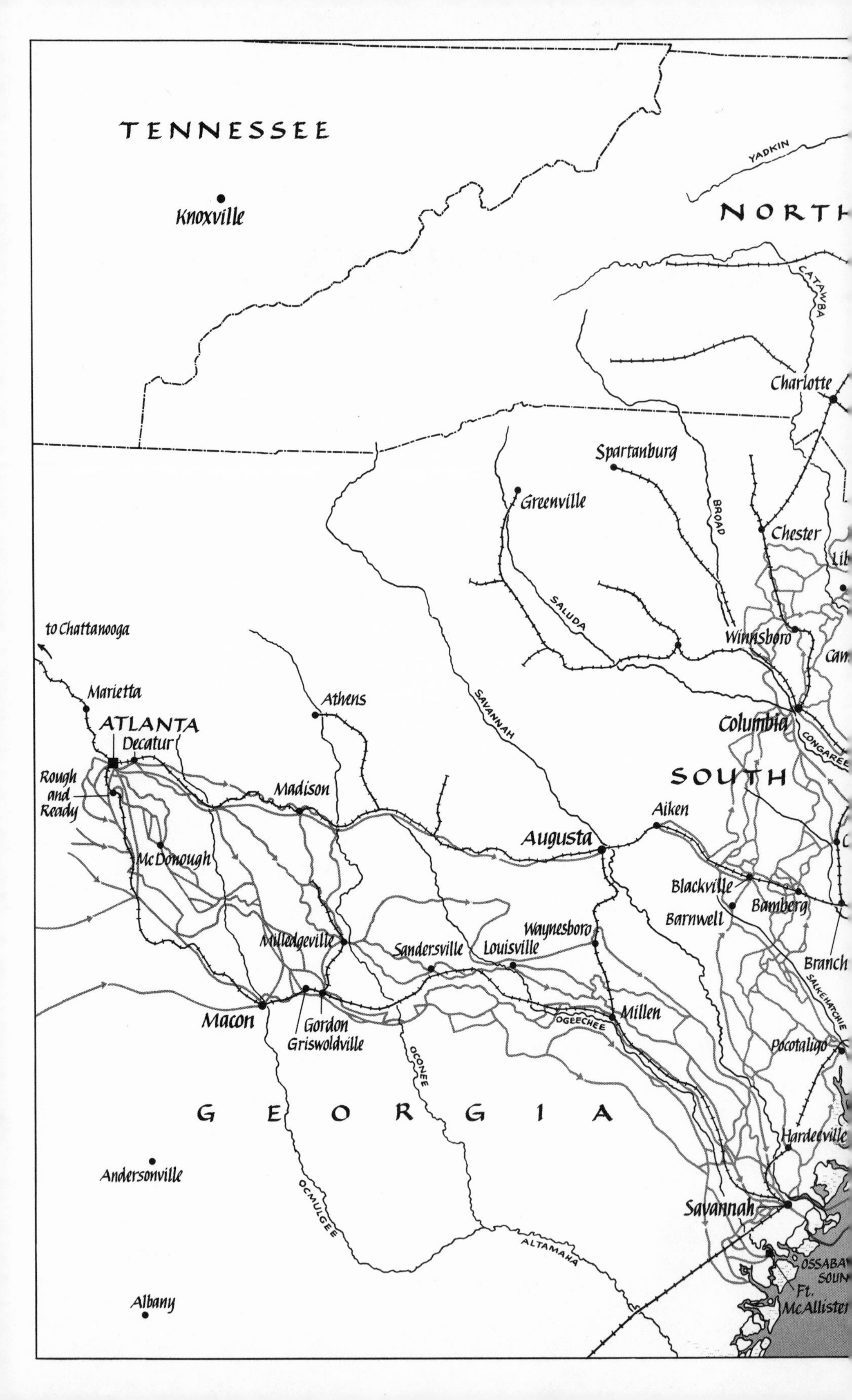

TENNESSEE
Knoxville
NORTH
YADKIN
CATAWBA
Charlotte
Spartanburg
Greenville
BROAD
Chester
SALUDA
Winnsboro
to Chattanooga
Marietta
Athens
SAVANNAH
Columbia
ATLANTA
Decatur
CONGAREE
Rough and Ready
Madison
SOUTH
Aiken
Augusta
McDonough
Blackville
Bamberg
Barnwell
Waynesboro
Milledgeville
Sandersville
Louisville
Branch
SALKEHATCHIE
Macon
Gordon
Griswoldville
OGEECHEE
Millen
OCONEE
Pocotaligo
GEORGIA
Hardeeville
Andersonville
OCMULGEE
Savannah
ALTAMAHA
Ft. McAllister
Albany

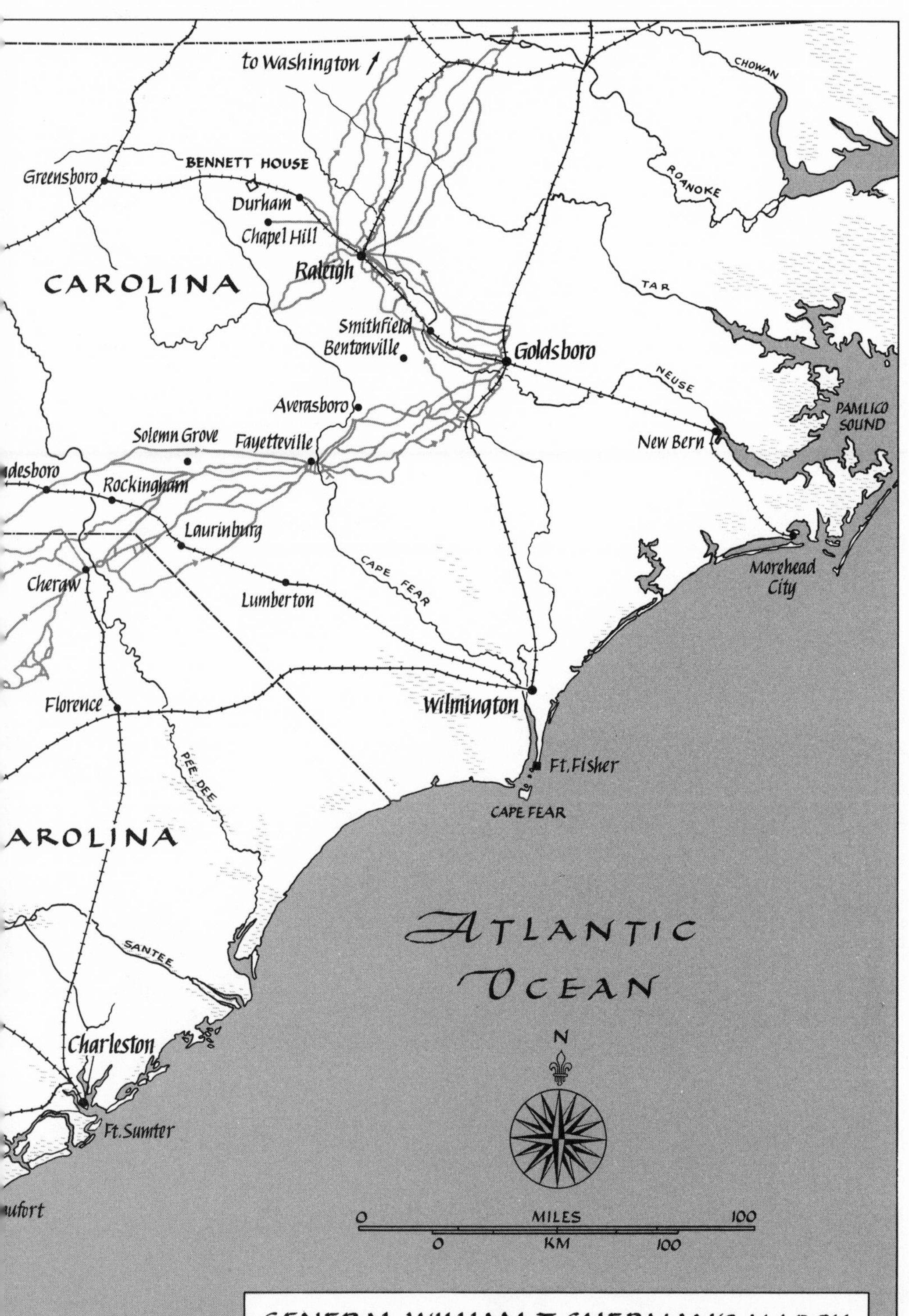

GENERAL WILLIAM T. SHERMAN'S MARCH THROUGH GEORGIA and the CAROLINAS NOVEMBER 1864 – APRIL 1865

I

"He believes in hard war"

From a window of a brick house on the hill a bearded face peered across the burning heart of Atlanta. It was a face incredibly wrinkled and furrowed, dominated by a ruddy scimitar of a nose and a broad mouth that writhed about the stump of a cigar as the tall man spoke to those in the room behind him.

General William T. Sherman glanced restlessly about, squinting toward a setting sun now obscured by smoke, to the courthouse and Masonic hall, still undamaged, into an inferno of blazing railroad shops, depots and factories, and along streets patrolled by Federal sentries who were under Sherman's orders to save churches and private homes.

Scorching heat pulsed against the columned mansion where Sherman made his headquarters, and in the growing darkness the glare lighted the countryside so brightly that soldiers in camps a mile from the city could read their letters from home. Exploding shells burst in the ruins of captured Confederate arsenals, shaking the house and rattling shrapnel against its walls.

It was November 15, 1864. Sherman's troops, some 62,000 strong, had already begun to evacuate the burning city. By the next morning they would be off on a thousand-mile foray through the heart of the reeling Confederacy that would leave a path of destruction eighty miles wide, pillage three state capitals, and bring an end to the war that had racked the nation for three years.

The general rubbed the thinning thatch of his hair upward with both hands, tugged at his blouse buttons, drummed the window sill with his fingers, seized the cigar, snapped furiously at its ashes and replaced it, puffing in a fury, shooting smoke from his mouth like pistol fire, as if it were the last cigar in the world. His soldiers had often seen him in such a state, picking nervously at himself with fluttering fingers. One of them said, "I never saw him but I thought of Lazarus."

The city that he had so recently captured seemed to Sherman a symbol of Confederate resistance. "Atlanta," he said abruptly. "I've been fighting Atlanta all this time. It's done more to keep up the war than any—well, Richmond, perhaps. All the guns and wagons we've captured along the way—all marked 'Atlanta.' " He was determined that the city would no longer serve as a major Confederate supply center. He had captured Atlanta on September 2, after one of the war's most brilliant campaigns, and six weeks later was now to leave it behind, ungarrisoned, to lead his troops on a march that was to bring him military immortality.

Sherman turned into the room, gesturing to his officers with his cigar-stump baton. "They've done so much to destroy us, we've got to destroy Atlanta—at least, enough to stop any more of that."

No one, not even the most devoted of his staff, could imagine that Sherman was on the threshold of fame tonight. He strode to the dining table and sank into a mahogany chair as awkwardly as if he were straddling a cracker box, his customary seat in the field. Sherman was a slight, almost frail figure of deceptively wiry strength.

He wore no badge of rank. His weather-stained blouse looked as if he had slept in it for three years of war; he wore a dirty dickey with wilted points, a faded gray flannel shirt, muddy brown trousers older than the memory of his most veteran staff officer, low-cut shoes rather than boots, and but one spur—the only general of either army who affected shoes and a single spur.

Sherman's headquarters would have done justice to a bandit chief. It traveled in a single wagon, including baggage for all clerks, aides and orderlies. "I think it's as low down as we can get," he said. He scorned elaborate equipment hauled along by comfort-seeking officers as "a farce—nothing but poverty will cure it." There had been only three aides, though two others had come recently, one of them Major Henry Hitchcock, a young Republican lawyer from St. Louis who was assigned to handle a correspondence that had begun to overwhelm the general: "Just tell 'em something sweet, Hitchcock—you know, honey and molasses."

Hitchcock had been completely won over by Sherman at their first meeting. Despite the general's eccentricities, the young lawyer found him "straight-forward, simple, kind-hearted, nay, warm-hearted . . . scrupulously just and careful of the rights of others." Above all, Hitchcock was impressed with Sherman's competence: "You may be sure of one thing—what he says he can do, he *can.*"

Tonight the general's meal was as simple as those of his interminable marches—hardtack, sweet potatoes, bacon and coffee. Sherman gnawed at a flinty piece of hardtack and began his familiar lecture on its virtues, halted to greet a dispatch-bearer, ripped open a message and barked out a reply. He talked of the enemy, of Southern women, of U. S. Grant and President Lincoln, heedlessly gulping his food, then returning to the smoldering cigar, still talking and laughing, giving orders, dictating telegrams, "bright and chipper," one of his generals noted. He cut short others who spoke and went on with his hurried comments, refusing to be interrupted. "I'm too red-haired to be patient," he had said. A war correspondent described him as he was at this moment: "He walked, talked or laughed all over. He perspired thought at every pore . . . pleasant and affable . . . engaging . . . with a mood that shifted like a barometer in a tropic sea."

The meal was ended by a regimental band from Massachusetts blaring beneath the windows in a serenade to the general, the brasses pealing incongruously above the explosions and roaring flames. Sherman listened briefly, lost interest and turned back to dispatch-bearers and officers who had come for orders. After a few lively military tunes the band played the "Miserere" from *Il Trovatore,* whose melancholy beauty, Henry Hitchcock thought, would forever remind him of this November night of roaring flames when Atlanta was destroyed and the army began its march to the sea.

Drunken Federal soldiers had been setting fires in the stricken city for several days, in defiance of Sherman's orders, but the official work of destruction had begun only when two Michigan regiments knocked down the massive stone roundhouse with improvised battering rams, placed powder charges under large buildings, and piled mountains of worn-out wagons, tents and bedding in the railroad depot, ready for the torch.

Sherman had ordered the city's destruction postponed until this night of November 15. A foundry, an oil refinery and a freight warehouse were burned first; the blazing depot square spread a storm of fire. The Atlanta Hotel, Washington Hall, dry-goods stores, theaters, the fire stations and jail, slave markets, went up in flames. A mine exploded in a stone warehouse. Old pine timbers burned with astonishing brilliance and flung brands in all directions. The sun shone blood red through a thickening cloud. The air for miles about was "oppressive and intolerable."

By night the burning city was "the grandest and most awful scene," with fires towering hundreds of feet into the sky. Hitchcock watched in fascination: "First bursts of smoke, dense, black volumes, then tongues of flame, then huge waves of fire roll up into the sky: Presently the skeletons of great warehouses stand out in relief against . . . sheets of roaring, blazing, furious flames . . . as one fire sinks, another rises . . . lurid, angry, dreadful to look upon."

The fires died down before midnight and the glare began to fade. Hitchcock saw that the courthouse and Masonic hall still stood. No private homes within view of headquarters had been burned—*but tomorrow,* he thought, *when the guards are gone, all would go up in smoke.* Already bands of drunken Federal soldiers raced through the streets on foot and horseback, smashing plate-glass windows, bearing huge loads of uniforms from army warehouses and selling them on street corners for any price they could get. Sherman's troops gathered before large buildings and "shouted and danced and sang while pillar and roof and dome sank into one common ruin." A bitter stench filled the night—odors of pine, tar, gunpowder, oil, charred meat and cloth, leather, carpets, feather beds, hot metal, burned privies, hospital sheds, hotels, drugstores, and from the streets themselves the sickening smell of dead horses and mules.

Some of Sherman's soldiers watched the sea of flames in dismay. Harvey Reid, a twenty-three-year-old Wisconsin schoolteacher in the XX Corps, wrote indignantly: "This destruction of private property in Atlanta was entirely unnecessary and therefore a disgraceful piece of business . . . the cruelties practiced on this campaign toward citizens have been enough to blast a more sacred cause than ours. We hardly deserve success." And Major James Austin Connolly, who rode near the head of an Illinois regiment, blamed Sherman himself for the needless destruction of the city: "He is somewhere nearby now, looking on at all this, and saying not one word to prevent it."

Major Connolly would have been surprised to learn that Sherman spent most of this night with his engineers in the streets trying to help save threatened houses. The general worked while his wagons, guns and troops were moving eastward from the city.

By dawn some two hundred acres of Atlanta lay in ashes. The only survivors were four hundred houses and a few larger buildings, most of them churches. Father Thomas O'Reilly of the Church of the Immaculate Conception, who had assembled a guard of Federal soldiers, saved his church and parsonage and nearby houses—as well as the city hall and St. Philip's Episcopal, Trinity Methodist, Second Baptist and Central Presbyterian churches.

Atlanta Medical College was saved by another resolute Confederate, Dr. Peter Paul Noel D'Alvigny, a French army veteran who hoodwinked the enemy. When his last patients were evacuated, Federal soldiers spread straw on the floors of the buildings, ready for the torch. D'Alvigny bribed hospital attendants to pose as patients, and protested to a Federal officer that he must have time to move his wounded.

"You have no patients. The place is empty, and it burns tonight with the rest of them. Those are my orders."

The doctor led him to an upper room where his hospital attendants lay groaning in a distressing display of helplessness. "All right," the bewildered officer said. "I'll give you until sunrise to get 'em out of here."

The last of the army was moving out by dawn, and the medical college survived, overlooked in the haste of departure.

In the last hours Federal soldiers looted the city in company with Confederate deserters and a few civilians who hurried in to pillage. The bluecoats robbed warehouses of uniforms, tobacco and whiskey, put on Confederate gray, stuffed their pockets with foot-long plugs of tobacco and drank the whiskey.

The XIV Corps, last to leave the city, began to move at sunrise, marching past a vacant lot where civilians crouched among piles of household goods they had snatched from the flames. Chaplain John Hight of the 58th Indiana carried a memory of women wringing their hands in agony, some of them praying aloud. "How far these people are deserving of pity, it is hard to tell."

Sherman left Atlanta at seven in the morning of November 16, riding his favorite mount, Sam, a blaze-faced little horse whose "horribly fast" walk was the dismay of his staff. The general was erect and vigorous in the saddle, like a gamecock, some of his men thought. His face was drawn with fatigue and half-concealed by a broad-brimmed hat jammed down over his ears, a formless black hat worn without braid or tassels. The sunlight revealed streaks of gray in the cinnamon beard. Sherman's cigar rolled constantly across his mouth, even as he talked with staff officers and his bodyguard of Alabama cavalry, waving and gesturing with his slender, feminine hands. His nose twitched as if the general were snuffling out the trail ahead, a relic of his long bouts with asthma; he had burned niter papers in his room for years, until the Southern climate had cured him. The general was watchful as he rode among his troops, missing nothing as he passed:

Illinois artillerymen breaking camp, furiously discarding surplus equipment, squabbling over hatchets, stewpans and coffeepots to be taken, each officer reduced to a gripsack and blanket and canvas tent "about the size of a large towel"; a Minnesota regiment stuffing the stringy flesh of freshly killed beeves into knapsacks, bellowing in protest, "Blue jerk! Thirteen dollars a month and blue jerk!"; quartermasters snatching stores from flames that had freshly sprung up, flinging boots, coats and trousers onto the passing column; the 86th Illinois infantry, its men calling in unison as they marched, "Split peas! Split peas!"—victims of a commissary officer who had no other rations left to him, men who knew they must cook the peas three hours tonight.

Whiskey had been issued and many had drawn double rations. Hosea Rood of Wisconsin saw these men begin as if they would reach the sea by nightfall: "They stepped high and long; they sang and made merry, and could not for the life of them see why the glorious march had not begun a long time before."

Every private seemed to know the army's destination, though Sherman's orders had told them little of what was to come: "It is sufficient for you to know that it involves a departure from our present base, and a long and difficult march . . ." They would carry few supplies, live off the country and "forage liberally." Soldiers were forbidden to enter houses along the route—though they might take food they saw in the open, crops and livestock and all else—and should plunder hostile rich Southerners rather than the poor. Able-bodied Negroes could be taken along, but not so many as to burden the columns. Enemy country was to be devastated only where the army met resistance by Confederate guerrillas.

The general had reassured the army that its passage through enemy country could be made safely: "All the chances of war have been considered and provided for, as far as human sagacity can. All he [Sherman] asks of you is to maintain that discipline, patience, and courage which have characterized you in the past; and he hopes, through you, to strike a blow at the enemy that will have a material effect in producing what we all so much desire, his complete overthrow . . ."

Recruits who cheered the general on the first day's march were quieted by veterans who had followed him for years: "He don't like it." But today, for some reason, Sherman seemed to welcome the cries of his troops. He waved and grinned when others called, "Guess Grant's waitin' for us at Richmond, Uncle Billy!" He passed within ten feet of a drunken soldier who scowled up at him, cursing the general with a steady vehemence. Sherman rode on as if he had heard nothing.

The general was an enigma to most of his troops. One soldier declared him "the most American-looking man I ever saw," but an Indiana officer who studied him closely said, "There are no outward signs of greatness. He appears to be a very ordinary man." War correspondents wrote: "All his features express determination, particularly the mouth . . . a very remarkable man such as could not be grown out of America—the concentrated quintessence of Yankeedom . . . He believes in hard war." And: "His eyes had a half-wild expression, probably the result of excessive smoking . . . He looks rather like an anxious man of business than an ideal soldier." A more thoughtful reporter from Cincinnati who had followed Sherman for hundreds of miles on his Southern invasion wrote: "Above all the men I have met, that strange face of his is the hardest to read. It is a sealed book even to his friends."

The general's pursuit of modesty was almost an obsession. He had recently replied to a prospective biographer, "Desire no notoriety. Have endeavored to escape the itching of fame." To a woman who requested a lock of his hair he replied that his hair was "too short to plait and too thin to spare from its natural office." Still, he was not without vanity. He suppressed an unflattering photograph that revealed too many of his wrinkles.

Only a few months earlier a hostile Northern press had threatened Sherman's career by charging that he was insane. Southern newspapers had begun to echo that theme in response to the general's introduction of total warfare—a destructive attack upon civilians. Sherman had already declared that the most humane way to end the war was to destroy the South's power to resist by cutting off supplies and manufacturing and by making the civilian's lot so miserable as to break the morale of Confederates at home and in the field.

The general sensed a subtle form of intoxication in the troops as they left the city today, an exhilaration he shared: "A feeling of something to come, vague and undefined, still full of venture and interest . . . a devil-may-care feeling pervading officers and men." He thought of the risks of his march: If he failed, the campaign would be condemned as "the wild adventure of a crazy fool."

Army bands played an odd medley this morning—"Farewell, Farewell, My Own True Love," "Oh, Jenny, Come Tickle Me," "When This Cruel War Is Over," and the general's favorite, "The Blue Juniata." Halts became frequent. Alonzo Brown of the 4th Minnesota said, "Ten minutes march and twenty minutes standstill, weight on the left leg and head under wing." Officers fell asleep in their saddles.

The general passed men in new uniforms wincing at every step in tight boots, and then ragged brigades just as they had come from the Georgia mountains and Atlanta trenches—veteran infantry mingling odors of sweat and urine, unwashed bodies, tobacco, whiskey and old boots with those of horses, mules and sun-bleached wagon canvas. The column swarmed with pets: A squirrel named Bun sat on his master's shoulder gnawing hardtack; Old Abe, the war eagle of a Wisconsin regiment, perched on a cannon; Minerva, the screech owl; a pet bear; scores of dogs, riding on saddles, wagons and caissons.

It was a lean army, stripped to the bone and ready for action. Sherman had sent his sick and wounded back to his old base in Tennessee. In the spare ranks remaining, many brigades had shrunk to regimental size. It was a rare regiment that could muster as many as three hundred of its original thousand men. The average company had only thirty men in ranks; files that had once been four abreast had become a single soldier. There were a few green recruits, including an overage victim in his fifties who had lied about his age to deceive a young woman and had been seized by draft officers—the butt of endless jokes by his companions.

Though there were many old men in the ranks, most of the soldiers were boys; thousands were under eighteen, too young to vote even in the recent election that had kept Abraham Lincoln in the

White House. "My little devils," Sherman called these teen-aged adventurers. Most of the army's colonels were under thirty, captains and lieutenants were in their early twenties. The six commanders of armies, corps and divisions averaged thirty-one years of age.

These troops were taller and stronger than the bluecoats of the Eastern armies, and were bearded, long-haired and tattered, men who marched with a rolling stride, Midwesterners, most of them, sons and grandsons of pioneer settlers of the country from Kentucky to Minnesota, of English, Irish and Scotch descent, with a sprinkling of Germans and Swedes. (Two regiments took their orders and got their band music in German.) Several Chippewa Indians marched with the 3rd Wisconsin.

Many of the troops bore deep resentment toward Negroes and "the agitators," whom they blamed for causing the war, for the virus of race prejudice was nationwide. They told rebel prisoners with grim earnestness, "I'd sooner shoot an Abolitionist than a Johnny, any day."

In all there were 218 regiments, most of them from the West. Ohio had 52 regiments, Illinois 50, Indiana 27, but there were others from Wisconsin, Michigan, Minnesota, Iowa, Missouri and Kentucky. Thirty-three regiments came from the East—New York, New Jersey, Pennsylvania, Connecticut and Massachusetts. One regiment of white Alabama Unionists rode with the cavalry—hill countrymen of fiercely independent spirit who owned no slaves and refused to side with the arrogant plantation owners of the low country.

Sherman had made no effort to reform these troops. He left them as he found them upon taking command, coolly efficient in battle and of free-and-easy discipline, inclined to treat their officers as if they were schoolteachers, bedeviling them with pranks and practical jokes. The affection of these soldiers for Sherman dated from the beginning of his command when he canceled dress reviews and reduced formality to a minimum, and it grew after he had led them in the slashing campaign into Georgia with a minimum of head-on fighting.

The troops traveled lightly, as if they were on an overnight reconnaissance rather than a march through the heart of the South. Each man carried a blanket wrapped in a rubber poncho slung over his shoulder, a haversack, a tin cup hung at the waist, a musket and a cartridge box with forty rounds of ammunition. "I doubt," said Private Theodore Upson, an Indiana farm boy, "if such an army as we have ever was got together before . . . all the boys are ready for a meal or a fight and don't seem to care which it is."

In this they were like most citizen soldiers, eager to escape discipline and control of officers, seeking adventure where they found it. Their families back home, like the nation at large, conceived of them as moral, honorable young Americans, ideal products of the world's most enlightened system of government. In fact, they were potentially cruel and heartless pillagers, many of whom awaited only the opportunity to plunder, burn and rape.

Sherman climbed a steep hill crowned by old entrenchments that encircled the city and overlooked a stark, scarred landscape as barren as the face of the moon, a vista of rifle pits hacked into red clay, earthworks bristling with rows of sharpened sticks and piled brush. Irregular ranks of graves marked the tides of Federal advances during the siege of Atlanta, with headboards made from cracker or ammunition boxes, the names of soldiers crudely scratched on one side and on the other "Pilot Bread" or "Watervliet Arsenal."

The general wheeled for a final glimpse of the city, where a black pall still rose from the ruins. He looked toward the distant village of McDonough and caught sight of a column of Howard's right wing, "the gun barrels glistening in the sun, the white-topped wagons stretching away to the south; and right before us the Fourteenth Corps, marching steadily and rapidly, with a cheery look and swinging past with a stride that made light of the thousand miles between us and Richmond." A passing band struck up "The Battle Hymn of the Republic," and the troops joined the chorus, their echo rolling through the hills: "Gloree, gloreee, halle-lujah!", a triumphant roar that Sherman was to remember for the rest of his life.

The general was moved by his departure: "We turned our horses' heads to the east. Atlanta was soon lost behind the screen of trees, and became a thing of the past. Around it clings many a thought of desperate battle, of hope and fear, that now seem like the memory of a dream." He was off on his march to fame.

Elsewhere, the war that had dragged on for three and a half years seemed to have degenerated into a stalemate. Far to the north, in trenches about Richmond and Petersburg, Virginia, the weary armies of U. S. Grant and Robert E. Lee faced each other in siege warfare that promised to be interminable. The Confederacy's strength was being sapped by the blockade of her ports and the effort to meet superior force on far-flung fronts, but her armies still in the field remained fiercely defiant.

The last Federal soldiers were still within sight when a growing horde of Confederate scavengers invaded Atlanta. Men, women and children swarmed among the smoking ruins, some from as far as a hundred miles away. They loaded iron, salt, bacon, sugar, coffee and hides into wagons, carts and carriages.

The Augusta *Constitutionalist* reported that "our country cousins" also ransacked vacant houses. One woman who tugged at a rope tied to a piano leg explained, "I found a mity nice table in thar and I'm trying to git it in my keart."

The Georgia militia general, W. P. Howard, on an inspection tour for Governor Joseph Brown, found two hundred and fifty loot-filled wagons in the city. Howard also reported "the crowning act" of villainy by Sherman's men, who had broken gravestones in the city cemetery, dragged bodies from vaults and replaced them with Federal dead.

But Atlanta's revival began with the bizarre scenes of pillage; within a month there would be an election for a new mayor and aldermen, who were to begin with $1.64 in the treasury. The post office, a newspaper, a grocery, a bar and a salt factory would open, and trains would be running again.

The irony of Confederates looting their ruined city on the heels of Sherman's departure seems to have escaped contemporary observers—but the universality of the impulse to vandalism under such circumstances was to become familiar to Americans in generations to come. The instinct to pillage when pillage was possible was not limited to Sherman's troops nor to the impoverished Southern civilians who scrabbled in the ruins to find the means for a new life.

2

"I can make Georgia howl!"

William Tecumseh Sherman, who was now on the brink of fame at forty-four, had been born February 8, 1820, in Lancaster, Ohio, the son of a State Supreme Court judge who died when the boy was nine and left him to be brought up by Thomas Ewing, a wealthy neighbor who was to become his father-in-law and an influential senator.

Through Ewing's influence Sherman went to West Point, where he graduated sixth in the class of 1840, despite so many demerits that he narrowly escaped expulsion. After thirteen years in the army, he married Thomas Ewing's daughter Ellen, left the service, failed at banking, real estate and law, and finally became superintendent of Louisiana Military Academy, where the approach of war found him at Christmas, 1860. The intensely patriotic Sherman loved the South, where he had formed many friendships, but was emotionally wracked by the collapse of the Union. His wife and five children were away for the holidays, and he was lonely and depressed, watching the country "melting away like a snowball in the sun."

Though he wished slavery did not exist, Sherman said, he "would not abolish or modify" it if he could—an opinion widely held at the time by whites both north and south. "All the Congresses on earth can't make the Negro anything else than what he is," Sherman said, remembering only the illiterate and repressed black slaves he had known in the South; there is no evidence that he had come in contact with educated Negroes. But though he believed in "the right of revolution," and had been a Southern sympathizer, Sherman felt that secession was absurd. He said firmly, "I will do no act, breathe no word, think no thought hostile to the government of the United States."

One night after South Carolina's secession from the Union, Sherman paced the floor of his Louisiana home, literally sobbing with anxiety, regaling his friend Professor David Boyd with an impassioned warning and prophecy:

"This country will be drenched in blood. God knows how it will end . . . Oh, it is all folly, madness, a crime against civilization. You people speak so lightly of war. You don't know what you are talking about. War is a terrible thing. You mistake, too, the people of the North. They are peaceable but earnest and will fight too . . . you are rushing into war with one of the most powerful, ingeniously mechanical and determined people on earth—right at your doors. You are bound to fail."

When Louisiana seceded, Sherman parted from his cadets in an emotional scene. Unable to say more, he placed his hand over his heart, blurted, "You are all here," and left. He was soon in Washington, where his brother John, a senator from Ohio, introduced him to Abraham Lincoln as a military expert recently arrived from the South.

"Ah. How are they getting along down there?" Lincoln asked.

"They think they're getting along swimmingly," Sherman said. "They're preparing for war."

"Oh, well," Lincoln said mildly. "I guess we'll manage to keep house."

Sherman was disgusted. He dismissed Lincoln as an unimaginative, provincial and partisan politician who lacked the vision to foresee approaching war. He railed at his brother and all Republican leaders: "You have got things in a hell of a fix, and you may get them out as best you can." He went to St. Louis, where he became president of a streetcar company at a salary of forty dollars per month. When war was declared, Sherman returned to the White House to volunteer, but to Lincoln's astonishment the intense Ohioan refused a commission as brigadier general and began as a colonel of regular infantry—so that he could win his stars without becoming a "political general" beholden to Lincoln's administration.

Sherman first saw battle at Bull Run, where he fell back in the Federal retreat with his regiment and shielded the army on its panic-stricken flight into Washington. He was one of the last Union officers to leave the Virginia field. A day or so later, when Lincoln came out to visit the army, a disgruntled captain called out, "Mr. President, I have a grievance. This morning I went to speak with Colonel Sherman and he threatened to shoot me."

Lincoln glanced at the grim-faced Sherman. "Threatened to shoot you?" He leaned forward and said in a stage whisper, "Well, if I were you I wouldn't trust him, for I believe he'd do it." The President's carriage rolled away amid the laughter of the troops.

Sherman had serious disciplinary problems; he found it impossible to halt the pillaging of his troops: "No curse could be greater than invasion by a volunteer army. No Goths or Vandals ever had less respect for the lives and property of friends and foes, and henceforth we ought never to hope for any friends in Virginia."

These were problems that would haunt him until the war's end, that he would never bring himself to resolve. Sherman's ambivalence in the matter of troop discipline stemmed from his conflicting beliefs that war must be made so terrible as to demoralize the enemy—and that troops should never be permitted to victimize the innocent and helpless.

Though he had protested that he wished to avoid high rank, Sherman found himself commanding general in Kentucky three months later, "in direct violation of Lincoln's promise." It was perhaps a result of this bizarre attitude that Sherman was soon contending fiercely with Midwestern politicians who sought to interfere in his command, with his undisciplined troops, and with newspaper reporters he regarded as enemy spies. The general's behavior was so unpredictable that vengeful newspaper correspondents, smarting under his rigid censorship, published false reports that the quixotic general was insane. General Henry Halleck, the popeyed commander of the Department of Missouri, sent Sherman home as "unfit for duty." The despondent Sherman said he would have committed suicide except for his children. One newspaper reported: "General Sherman, who lately commanded in Kentucky, is said to be insane. It is charitable to think so." Mrs. Sherman wrote Lincoln insisting that the sensitive and nervous general found the "cruel attacks" of the press unbearable and begging the President to transfer her husband to the East.

Instead, Sherman was rescued by Halleck himself, who sent him to Paducah, Kentucky, to serve under U. S. Grant, another obscure army veteran and refugee from civilian life whose reputation was under a cloud. Grant was said to be a hopeless alcoholic, but he won the first great Union victories in the West at Fort Henry and Fort Donelson and then commanded at Shiloh, where 100,000 men clashed in the first major battle between the Western armies. Grant won victory by the narrowest of margins, and Sherman's division played a decisive role on the bloody field, standing its ground stubbornly against waves of Confederate attacks while thousands of other Union troops huddled in fright beneath the bluffs of the Tennessee River.

Within a few days Sherman wore the twin stars of a major general, and high command became more palatable to him. He wrote his wife, Ellen: "I have worked hard to keep down, but somehow I am forced into prominence and might as well submit."

Sherman was in the field on the Western front when he was stricken by the death of his young son Willy, who had come with his mother to visit the general. Willy succumbed to typhoid fever and left his father grieving for "that child on whose future I based all the ambition I ever had." He resolved, he said, to cherish the boy's memory as "the cure for the defects which have sullied my character." A major reorganization of the Federal high command soon thrust Sherman into the eminence he had professed to dread: Lincoln called Henry Halleck, a born staff officer, to Washington as Chief of Staff. Grant, suddenly famous as the North's only victorious general, was transferred to Virginia as Commander in Chief of the armies—his first assignment to overcome Robert E. Lee and the Confederate Army of Northern Virginia.

Sherman was now left in command in the West, and with a burst of energy that revitalized his army, he organized an offensive against Atlanta from the Federal base at Chattanooga, Tennessee. He was beginning to develop his theory of total warfare that involved civilians as well as armies, resolved to "make war so terrible" that the rebels would never again take up arms. The Southern people, he said, though they "cannot be made to love us, can be made to fear us, and dread the passage of troops through their country."

This theme became almost an obsession with the compulsive Sherman. He declared that the people of the South bore "a collective responsibility," and that the war was not merely an armed uprising. "It is about time the North understood the truth," he wrote. "The entire South, man, woman and child, is against us." Even so, the complex man whose name was to symbolize the terrors of total warfare had a keen realization of the sufferings he was to impose upon the Southern people. He wrote his daughter Minnie, who was in school in Notre Dame, Indiana, lamenting his role: "Think of how cruel men become in war, when even your Papa has to do such acts. Pray every night that the war may end. Hundreds of children like yourself are daily taught to curse my name, and every night thousands kneel in prayer and beseech the Almighty to consign me to perdition."

In early May 1864, Sherman moved his army against General Joseph E. Johnston's strongly entrenched Confederates in mountainous terrain at Dalton, Georgia. Though Johnston was a master of defensive strategy, Sherman slipped past the rebel force, maneuvering his army of 100,000 with a mobility new to modern warfare, constantly enveloping the enemy, threatening Johnston's rear, artfully flanking and countermarching over a broad front, using roads as a network—shielding all the while the railroad in his rear that was his lifeline. He feinted and flanked his way southward, attacking only when a collision was unavoidable, and fought only one pitched battle, at Kenesaw Mountain, Georgia, where he lost 2,500 men in less than an hour. Within a week Sherman had flanked the position and was on his way to Atlanta. He drove his army relentlessly. To a quartermaster who was not sure he could keep the pace, Sherman barked, "If you don't have my army supplied, and keep it supplied, we'll eat your mules up, sir— eat your mules up!" He shocked a methodical engineer who asked for four days to replace a burned bridge: "Sir, I give you forty-eight hours or a position in the front ranks." It was not only Sherman's skill and energy that drove the army forward; he had explored the hills, valleys and streams in his path as a young officer twenty years before. "I knew more of Georgia than the rebels did," he said.

Sherman's leadership during this remarkable campaign was no longer that of the frustrated, erratic and reluctant officer of the early months of the war. As one of his officers said, "His eccentricities disappeared, his grasp of the situation was firm and clear, his judgment was cool and based upon sound military theory as well as quick practical judgment . . . His mind seemed never so clear, his confidence never as strong, his spirit never so inspiring, and his temper never so amiable as in the crisis of some fierce struggle."

Confederate troops were also bewildered by innovations in Federal military equipment during this campaign. For the first time, telegraphers were with the general, bringing him news from distant parts of the field. Engineers who marched ahead of the army made maps that were reproduced in the "dark wagons" of photographers and hurried to field officers. Wagons carried prefabricated bridges to throw across streams. A Confederate prisoner gaped as Sherman's canvas-covered pontoons were swung across a river by ropes: "Boys," he said, "anybody who could make a bridge out of them dog tents could beat us." Others praised Sherman's tactics: "You-uns swing around on your ends like a gate." "Sherman'll never go to hell. He'll flank the devil and make heaven despite the guards."

Johnston skillfully extricated himself from each position but was forced relentlessly backward into trenches along Peachtree Creek, where he settled to fight for Atlanta. Amid a public clamor for his removal, the proud and stubborn Johnston refused to reveal his plans to Jefferson Davis and was replaced by the erratic Kentuckian John Hood, who had lost an arm in Virginia, suffered a maimed leg at Gettysburg and now rode strapped into his saddle.

Hood attacked fiercely, and though he routed a Federal corps in front of his trenches and all but overwhelmed one of Sherman's wings near Decatur, was twice defeated with ruinous losses. Sherman cut Hood's last rail supply line in late August, but since he had neither destroyed the enemy army nor taken the city, victory seemed far away.

Atlanta, a symbol of Southern resistance, still held out after bloody assaults had been called off, and Union troops settled down for a siege. After three years of war and sacrifice, Northern civilians felt that the war would never end. Generals and Washington politicians had forecast final victory too often. The South had been penetrated by Union armies before, to little avail.

Despite Sherman's finesse, the campaign against Atlanta had cost 31,000 Federal casualties—against 35,000 Confederate. There was a rising tide of protest, heightened by reports of even more terrible casualty rolls in Grant's army in Virginia. The campaigns on both fronts seemed destined to drag on without decisive victory, as campaigns had done for three years. Abraham Lincoln was so depressed by the public mood, and so apprehensive of defeat in the presidential election just two months away, that he made secret plans to negotiate with the Democratic candidate, General George McClellan—hoping, he said, "to save the Union." McClellan, who had won and lost Lincoln's favor as commander in Virginia, promised voters that he would end the bloody stalemate by making peace with the South.

A short-lived boom for Sherman excited the Democratic National Convention in Chicago for a day or two. Sherman wrote Halleck, "Some fool seems to have used my name. If forced to choose between the White House and the penitentiary for four years . . . I would say the penitentiary, thank you." Sherman fumed over newspaper reports that he would deliver 99 percent of his army's votes to McClellan—"The invention of some knave," he said—but was even more incensed when McClellan wrote two friendly letters currying his favor, after having ignored him throughout the war.

After five weeks of siege, when Sherman cut the last Confederate rail line in severe fighting, the city was doomed. Hood evacuated Atlanta abruptly, and on September 2 Sherman moved his troops swiftly into the city. The Lincoln administration's crisis subsided overnight, and the nation abandoned itself to celebration. Sherman's terse telegram to Washington was greeted as the most welcome and dramatic news of the war to date: "Atlanta is ours, and fairly won." Streets of cities and villages throughout the North were thronged with celebrants, who sensed that the end of the war was in sight at last, and that sons, brothers and fathers would soon be coming home. The South had been severed—only Virginia and the Carolinas remained to support Lee's army in the field. Coupled with Admiral David Farragut's capture of Mobile, Alabama, and General Phil Sheridan's sweep of the Shenandoah Valley in Virginia, Sherman's feat "knocked the bottom out of the Chicago platform" of the Democrats and assured the reelection of Lincoln.

Atlanta headquarters were deluged with newspapers, letters and telegrams, all praising Sherman and his army. Lincoln offered the nation's gratitude and declared a day of thanksgiving; Henry Halleck declared the campaign was the most brilliant of the war; Grant said it would go down in history as "unsurpassed if not unequaled." The young historian Charles Francis Adams, who was serving with Grant before Richmond, choked back tears of emotion as he read Sherman's dispatch on the fall of Atlanta. The campaign, he said, had unrolled "like a sonorous epic . . . a poem." He ranked Sherman with Napoleon and Frederick the Great.

Sherman behaved as if he heard none of the chorus of acclaim. His staff saw that he was thinking of the months to come, and that he was not to be distracted. He was intent on delivering a final death blow to the South. Already he looked beyond the occupied city, across hundreds of miles to the Atlantic and then northward to Virginia, where the major Confederate army was intact and defiant.

Months earlier, at the opening of the spring campaign, Sherman's inspector general had asked what was to be done after the capture of Atlanta. Sherman whacked ashes and sparks from his cigar and said brusquely, "Salt water. Salt water." He had no intention of immobilizing his army by garrisoning the conquered city. He would evacuate its remaining civilians, destroy it as a communications center and supply base, and move on. He explained to Halleck that he must move out civilians or arrange to feed them: "If the people raise a howl against my barbarity and cruelty, I will answer that war is war and not popularity-seeking. If they want peace they and their relatives must stop war."

To Atlanta's Mayor James Calhoun and aldermen who protested that the evacuation would doom thousands of civilians to wander homeless through the winter, Sherman said his order was intended not to "meet the humanities," but to help end the war. His letter of justification was a fiery statement of his credo:

> You cannot qualify war in harsher terms than I will. War is cruelty and you cannot refine it. . . . You might as well appeal against the thunder-storm as against these terrible hardships of war. . . . We don't want your Negroes, or your horses, or your houses, or your land, or anything you have, but we do want and will have first obedience to the laws of the United States . . . if it involves the destruction of your improvements, we cannot help it . . . But, my dear sirs, when peace does come, you may call on me for any thing. Then will I share with you the last cracker, and watch with you to shield your homes and families against danger from every quarter.

To John Hood, who also denounced the "studied and ingenious cruelty" of the evacuation, Sherman replied: "God will judge us in due time, and he will pronounce whether it be more humane to fight with a town full of women and brave people at our back, or to remove them in time to places of safety among their own friends and people."

Hood responded with threats: "We will fight you to the death. Better die a thousand deaths than submit to live under you . . . and your Negro allies."

When this bitter exchange ended, Sherman completed his evacuation of Atlanta, removing 1,600 natives and refugees in preparation for destruction of the city.

A visiting Catholic bishop appeared at headquarters and found Sherman brooding over Confederate charges of his inhumanity: "To be sure," he said, "I have made war vindictively; war is war, and you can make nothing else of it. But Hood knows as well as anyone that I'm not brutal or inhuman."

Sherman persisted in his scheme to set off through the heart of the South. At every opportunity he pressed his plans upon Grant. He had now begun to think of Savannah as the key to his hopes: "The possession of the Savannah River," he wrote Grant, "is . . . fatal to southern independence. They may stand the fall of Richmond, but not all of Georgia . . . If you can whip Lee and I can march to the Atlantic, I think Uncle Abe will give us twenty days' leave of absence to see the young folks."

Though he trusted his friend Sherman, the orthodox Grant was slow to accept this bold plan. The Commander in Chief saw the breathtaking possibilities in the success of such a march, but hesitated over the dangers of the unprecedented abandonment of base to sweep through enemy country where little was known of Confederate defenses. Grant and Sherman exchanged telegrams over the prospect for several weeks as they considered other aspects of the strategic situation.

The Confederate President Jefferson Davis added to Sherman's determination to march to Savannah—and perhaps to Grant's resolve to approve it. Davis, though he was ill and aging, campaigned through Georgia in these days at a distance from occupied Atlanta, rousing small-town audiences with defiant oratory, urging civilians to a final sacrificial effort for Southern victory. He promised that Hood would soon strike Sherman's rear, and that the Yankee army would be harried like Napoleon through the Russian snows until at last Confederate flags floated over the Ohio. Sherman read this revelation of rebel plans in Georgia newspapers with amazement, saying that Davis had "lost all sense and reason," but as for Hood, he said, "Damn him, if he'll go to the Ohio River, I'll give him rations. Let him go north. My business is down south."

And Grant, when he read the dire predictions of Davis, commented wryly that Sherman might suffer the fate of Napoleon in the Russian winter, but added that Davis had failed to "make it clear who would furnish the snow."

But there were other officers, in Washington and on Grant's staff, whose fears peopled the Georgia countryside with Confederate forces of vast size. Ignorant of conditions in Georgia, and of the nature of Sherman's troops, these officers beseeched Grant to forbid the move from Atlanta. Few men in the armies, north or south, could foresee that the impending march was to become Sherman's unique contribution to the war, and to the modern science of war.

In preparation for his move, Sherman sent General George Thomas northward to Tennessee with a strong army, and when the aggressive and unpredictable Hood moved in the same direction with an equally strong force, Sherman followed with the main body of his army. He gave up the chase after a sharp clash with Hood at Allatoona Station, then confident that no decisive action was pending in Tennessee. Sherman telegraphed Thomas that he was turning back "to make a hole in Georgia," and asked only that Thomas hold Tennessee for three months so that he could strike the South a crippling blow.

Sherman telegraphed Grant: "Until we can repopulate Georgia, it is useless to occupy it, but the utter destruction of its roads, houses and people will cripple their military resources. . . . I can make the march and make Georgia howl!"

This show of confidence merely inspired fresh apprehension in Washington. The timid Halleck joined General Aaron Rawlins, Grant's chief of staff, in a plea to Lincoln, saying that Sherman was about to sacrifice his army.

Grant himself raised another objection: A coastal base to supply the army could not be prepared overnight. Sherman replied that his troops would need no supplies, and no base, as they went "smashing things to the sea." The still-skeptical commander had visions of catastrophe, probably implanted by Rawlins: "I believe . . . you would be bushwhacked by all the old men, little boys, and such railroad guards as are still left at home." It was only after he was certain that Hood's Confederate forces had returned far to the north, into Tennessee, where they were guarded by Thomas, that Grant's fears subsided. At last, after weeks of Sherman's supplications, Grant was persuaded. He advised Lincoln that he considered the planned march to be sound, and telegraphed Sherman: "On reflection I think better of your proposition. . . . I say, then, go on as you propose." Sherman's inflexible resolve had stood him in good stead once more.

Within a few days of granting permission for the march, Grant was visited by a clergyman in his camp near Richmond. Sherman was much on the commander's mind.

"Sherman is a most superior general," Grant said. "A good, kind man, too."

"But very unrelenting," the minister said, "in walking out the path marked for himself."

Grant smiled. "Yes," he said. "That is his character."

Thoughtful men outside the Confederacy shared an apocalyptic vision of the fate awaiting Sherman's army, surrounded in swamps and woodlands, fired on from fences and hedgerows, and bled to death by bands of Georgia guerrillas.

British observers were perplexed by the army's plunge into hostile country. The London *Times* commented that the mysterious expedition of Sherman, "on an unknown route against an undiscoverable enemy," had no parallel since Marlborough's disappearance into Germany to fight the battle of Blenheim. The editors were dubious of success. *The British Army & Navy Gazette* said, "He has done either one of the most brilliant or one of the most foolish things ever performed by a military leader." *The London Herald* declared: "The name of the captor of Atlanta, if he fails now, will become the scoff of mankind, and the humiliation of the United States for all time. If he succeeds it will be written on the tablet of fame . . ."

Since Abraham Lincoln feared the London press as a possible catalyst for British intervention in the war, such comments probably increased his reluctance to approve Grant's decision—but the President became almost boyishly enthusiastic once the march had begun.

Southern newspapers assailed Sherman on the eve of the march as an "Attila" and a "Judas Iscariot," declaring that his foray would lead him to "the paradise of fools." A Richmond minister struck a popular chord for Confederate partisans: "God has put a hook in Sherman's nose and is leading him to destruction." Even Henry Hitchcock was uneasy as he watched the general in final preparations: "This campaign will be no joke. . . . doubtless it will be death to those of us who fall into their hands."

Once Sherman had left Atlanta, only the laconic Abraham Lincoln seemed to be unconcerned for his safety and confident that the general knew the route to final victory: "I know what hole he went in at."

In fact, fears for the army's security were absurd. Georgia lay defenseless before Sherman's horde. The way was open to the east on both northern and southern flanks of the Federal movement. Virtually all able-bodied men over sixteen and under sixty were out of the state serving with their regiments. Even most of the planters who lived in the region were to flee as Sherman approached, leaving women, children and slaves to face the swarming bluecoats. To oppose Sherman's 62,000 disciplined troops, most of them hardened veterans, Georgia could muster but 13,000, most of whom were untested and untrained state militia. These meager forces were divided between Macon and Augusta, which were assumed to be threatened by Sherman. No other cities in eastern Georgia could boast garrisons of respectable size.

Sherman had already severed communications with the North; the railroad that had supplied his troops was torn up by his men for many miles outside the city. The lone telegraph line had been cut on November 12 without the gesture of a final telegram to Washington. He had sent his farewell message to Grant more than a week earlier, however, promising a paralyzing blow against Confederate resources: "This may not be war but rather statesmanship . . . If the North can march an army right through the South, it is proof positive that the North can prevail." This bore no hint of the terror and atrocities to come during the first passage of a large hostile army through the American countryside, victimizing helpless civilians.

It was to be a decade before Sherman offered a justification for his march: "When we took Atlanta . . . they were bound by every rule of civilized warfare to surrender their cause. It was then hopeless . . . But they continued the war, and I had a right, under the rules of civilized warfare, to commence a system that would make them feel the power of the government and cause them to succumb . . ."

Sherman warned Grant that he should not expect reports for weeks to come: "I will not attempt to send couriers back, but trust to the Richmond papers to keep you well advised." About a dozen reporters and artists for Northern newspapers and magazines were to make the march with the army, but they would be beyond the reach of telegraph lines until they reached the Atlantic. Sherman was at ease once communication with Washington was severed; no longer did he fear an order to abandon his march. He was now the supreme commander, at large in the field. Unlike most generals in the war, Sherman directed his troops with little delegation of authority. He had no patience with chains of command that interfered with his freedom of action, and so had left his chief of staff in Nashville, Tennessee, long ago. Officers of all services reported to him directly. Paper work was at a minimum. As one officer noted, the general kept his office in a pocket, from which papers were soon discarded.

Still, no important details escaped Sherman. One of his last letters before leaving Atlanta was to Admiral David Porter, commander of naval forces along the Atlantic Coast. Porter was told to expect the army to appear on the coast somewhere between Savannah and Hilton Head, South Carolina, "about Christmastime." His final letter was to his wife, begging that she not worry about him, even at reports of disasters. She was to remember that the only news she could have of him would come through rebel sources.

The moves of the army during the first day's march conformed to plans perfected two weeks earlier: The columns would move eastward over several parallel roads on a front about sixty miles wide, taking "so eccentric a course" as to baffle the enemy. Sherman felt that the rebels would defend Macon to the south of his course and Augusta to the north, if only as symbols, and he intended to drive between them toward Savannah. His army would march in two wings, the right—or southern wing—under the pious young Abolitionist Oliver O. Howard, "Old Prayer Book," who had lost an arm in the Virginia fighting. The left—northern—wing was led by Henry Slocum, a New Yorker who had survived a severe wound at Bull Run to command a wing in the victory at Gettysburg.

Five thousand cavalry would be concentrated first on the south, to screen Howard's infantry in the Macon region. The horsemen were led by Hugh Judson Kilpatrick, known as Kilcavalry and Little Kil, a hard-driving little dandy with luxuriant sideburns who had been sent down from Virginia by Grant.

The artillery carried sixty-five guns, each drawn by an eight-horse team. More than 25,000 horses and mules would pull wagon trains some twenty-five miles long—2,500 wagons and 600 ambulances. Each wing carried pontoon bridges long enough to span the widest rivers in its path. Despite plans to live off the country, the army carried a herd of 10,000 cattle. The troops were to march fifteen miles a day, breaking camp before dawn. Each brigade was to send out small foraging parties to gather provisions from farms as they passed.

The southern wing marched southeast from Atlanta, feinting in the direction of Macon; the northern wing moved on parallel routes through Decatur and Covington, posing a threat to Augusta. The wings were to approach each other near Milledgeville, Georgia's capital, one hundred miles east of Atlanta, and then, providing the way was open, move directly on Savannah. Sherman intended to turn where opportunity beckoned, if the capture of Savannah seemed impracticable. Though he had not shared details of his plan with Grant, Sherman intended to halt only briefly in Savannah and then turn northward to march through the Carolinas, destroying Robert E. Lee's last sources of supply for his Army of Northern Virginia.

A few days earlier Sherman had gone over a map with his generals, tracing a route through South Carolina to Columbia, thence northward to Goldsboro, North Carolina, a rail junction near the battlegrounds of Grant and Lee. "I believe we can go there," Sherman had said. "When we reach Goldsboro, Lee must leave Virginia, and he will be defeated."

Sherman had chosen his route after poring over census reports of farm production county by county so that he could lead his troops through the regions richest in provisions. "Georgia has a million inhabitants," he said. "If they can live, we should not starve." Grant expected such resourcefulness of Sherman: "He bones all the time while he is awake, as much on horseback as in camp or in his quarters."

Among Sherman's jubilant troops as the march began was at least one soldier who would have scoffed at Grant's appraisal: "Old Sherman's got the big head now. He's captured Atlanta and thinks he can go wherever he pleases."

3
"I'll have to harden my heart"

The army's columns snaked eastward from Atlanta in a pattern that was to become familiar during the epic march of five months. Their roads now converged and then diverged, the wings from twenty to forty miles apart, the outermost units frequently eighty miles apart.

Impromptu plans for Confederate defense of Georgia were already collapsing in Sherman's path. Lieutenant General Joseph Wheeler's decimated gray cavalry squadrons, attempting stands to the south and east of Atlanta, were swept aside by Kilpatrick's troopers in brisk, noisy skirmishes at East Point, Rough and Ready, Jonesboro, Stockbridge, Lovejoy and Bear Creek. Howard's wing pressed eastward toward the crossings of the Ocmulgee River. Lieutenant John S. Ash of the Georgia Hussars reported one of these Confederate disasters: "We were so completely run over that we were scattered in every direction, those of us who were not killed or captured."

Wheeler could do no more than fall back before overwhelming force, with little prospect of making a stand until the invaders reached the sea, where Savannah's extensive earthworks awaited.

Sherman himself planned to move between his columns as the march advanced. He began with Slocum's northern wing as it wound through Decatur and past Stone Mountain.

Sherman stopped for half an hour in Decatur, "a dilapidated village" of old houses around a courthouse square where Manuel, the general's cook, chased chickens in the yard of a large house until a woman emerged to scold him. She was quieted by Colonel Thomas

Baylor, the ordnance chief, who bought the flock for the outrageously high price of a dollar a head and left the woman with a benign memory of the mercurial Sherman, who exhibited such callousness in hundreds of later incidents as to be remembered in the South as the devil incarnate.

In the countryside into which Sherman's army now flowed, Georgia's civilians had begun to meet the invaders. Their reactions ranged from terror and dismay among the whites to hysterical joy among the blacks.

At nightfall young Martha Amanda Quillen watched from her home in Decatur as a line of flaming buildings approached: "As far as the eye could reach, the lurid flames of burning buildings lit up the heavens . . . I could stand out on the verandah and for two or three miles watch them as they came on. I could mark when they reached the residence of each and every friend on the road."

She heard "the eternal gab of the Yankee army" and saw outbuildings at each house burst into flames. "I heard the wild shout they raised as torch in hand they started for the next house." She calculated the distance the burners traveled in an hour and "ascertained almost to the very minute when the torch would be set to our own house"—but she was saved by Federal officers who made headquarters in her parlor. Though several torches were brought to the Quillen house, they were stamped out by guards.

Martha dreaded the coming of dawn: "I prayed that I might never see the destruction, the deep distress, the morn would reveal to me. That too has all passed, and lives only in memory; but no one I hope will ever expect me to love Yankees."

Men of the 129th Illinois Regiment who halted in the village that night taunted frightened women in the dark houses around them: "Why don't ye come and see who's here?" Campfires were built so close by that the frame buildings caught fire, and women and children dashed out, begging for mercy. Private William Grunert helped to put out the fires, but others were set so rapidly that several houses burned before guards drove the men away. When the regiment left the town at midnight, two of its men were shot from the darkness, but the column did not stop to defend itself. A chilly rain began to fall. It was a march Private Grunert did not forget: "We would have frozen, if the fence on both sides of our route had not been fired and burned by those ahead of us . . . the heat became so intense that our ambulance wagons had to take to the field. To fulfill Gen. Sherman's order to the letter, several cotton presses and gins and mills were fired during the night, and along the whole route to Atlanta the sky was red."

Sherman's troops soon learned that some women in their path were of indomitable spirit. One farm wife who stood on the porch of her shack with two small boys was hailed by a soldier who carried two of her chickens over his shoulder: "Don't you think we'll end the war soon, now?" She looked beyond him to the moving blue columns, and said quietly, "Our men will fight you as long as they live, and these boys'll fight you when they grow up."

Jesse Macy, a Quaker soldier of the 10th Iowa, met a defiant young woman on the porch of a mansion. "My husband is a captain in the Confederate army and I'm proud of it," she said. "You can rob us, you can take everything we have. I can live on pine straw the rest of my days. You can kill us, but you can't conquer us."

A few miles away a young woman who watched the army with her mother and sisters was hailed by a passing soldier: "Is your husband in the rebel army?"

"Of course."

"Was he conscripted?"

She spat scornfully. "No, sir! I wouldn't have a man if he had to be conscripted!"

Federal soldiers were often amazed at the extent of provincial prejudice and ignorance in the rural South.

An old woman by the roadside in Jonesboro stared at the soldiers in disbelief. "I swear," she said, "I can make out every last word they utter—they told me so many of you was foreigners I'd never understand the Yankee tongue."

In Conyers an old woman greeted soldiers with complete resignation: "I've run away from you six times, clear across the south, starting back in Kentucky. I don't care where you go next, I'm done running. I'm going to let you go first, maybe I'll follow."

Sherman spent the first night of the march at the roadside near the village of Lithonia, from where he could see the granite hulk of Stone Mountain, clearly outlined by the glow of fires that stretched for miles, like "an old-time Republican torch light procession . . . with burning houses, outhouses and fences." Several houses in the village were ablaze, the first such burning Sherman had observed on the march. There was no sign of the enemy, but on the flank nearby, beyond the general's sight, rebel guerrillas captured six men of the 3rd Wisconsin who strayed from camp.

Sherman slept little and was up early on November 17 watching a regiment tear up railroad tracks, a long line of men stooping to raise an entire section of ties and rails at once, overturning it, burning ties, heating the rails until they were red hot, twisting them into spirals or wrapping them around trees until they were useless—Sherman's neckties, the men called them. At every milepost artistic wrecking crews twisted the rails into the letters US, "to encourage the loyalty of those who might see."

Sherman rode toward the little town of Covington during the morning and came upon troops prowling about a farm, filling cups and canteens with sorghum syrup. It was the general's first glimpse of looting troops who were violating his orders on foraging. One soldier carried a ham impaled on a bayonet, dripping a chunk of honeycomb in one hand and drinking from a cup of sorghum. He grinned up at the general and shouted, "Forage liberally!" The staff and men on the roadside roared with laughter at this quotation from Sherman's field order, but the general scolded the looter: "Regular parties will forage for the army. Don't let me catch you at it again."

For all his menacing manner, the troops realized that he tacitly approved and word spread through the ranks. Henceforth few soldiers would honor Sherman's field orders despite their stern words:

> The army will forage liberally on the country during the march. To this end, each brigade commander will organize a good and sufficient foraging party, under the command of one or more discreet officers, who will gather, near the route traveled . . . whatever is needed by the command, aiming at all times to keep in the wagons at least ten days' provisions for his command, and three days' forage. Soldiers must not enter the dwellings of the inhabitants, or commit any trespass; but, during a halt or camp, they may be permitted to gather turnips, potatoes, and other vegetables, and to drive in stock in sight of their camp. To regular foraging-parties must be intrusted [*sic*] the gathering of provisions and forage, at any distance from the road traveled.

There was a sputter of gunfire as the vanguard rode into Covington, an exchange quickly forgotten and rather vaguely recorded by both sides. A local woman remembered only that "a quiet old farmer named Jones" took his stand on a street corner, armed with a shotgun, the only man within sight; when four Federal horsemen rode past, he blasted one of them from his saddle and was instantly shot down by the other troopers. The old man's body lay in the street for a long time. General Slocum's headquarters reported that a Federal soldier was killed here, and that "all dwellings in the neighborhood" were burned in retaliation. There was no mention of the death of the elderly Jones.

It was in Covington that the troops saw the first effects of their emancipation of slaves, and that Sherman sought to deal with the problems that created for his army. For the first time, too, the army heard the cries of greeting as saviors of the blacks, a chorus that was to echo throughout the thousand miles of their march—but was often to fade all too quickly.

Slocum's column closed ranks as it moved through Covington; flags were unfurled, bands played and Negroes rushed to the roadside, "simply frantic with joy," as Sherman said. "Whenever they heard my name, they clustered about my horse, shouted and prayed in their peculiar style, which had a natural eloquence that would have moved a stone." The general remembered a young black girl here who was caught up "in the very ecstasy of the Methodist 'shout,' hugging the banner of one of the regiments and 'jumping up to the feet of Jesus.' " A white-haired old man who gazed at Sherman shouted, "I have seen the great Messiah and the army of the Lord!"

Sherman singled out an old Negro man among those who crowded about the headquarters tents.

"Do you understand about the war?" Sherman asked. "Do you know it's almost over?"

"Yes, sir," the old man said. "I've been looking for the Angel of the Lord since I was knee-high. I know you say you's fightin' for the Union, but I 'spect it's all about slavery—and you're gonna set us free."

"Do all slaves understand that?"

"Sholy does."

"You must stay where you are," Sherman said, "and not load us up with useless mouths. You'd eat up all the soldiers' food. If we win the war, you're free. We can take along a few of the young, strong men—but if you swarm after us, old and young, feeble and helpless, you'll just cripple us."

Sherman was convinced that the old man spread his message and that it was carried ahead of the army by word of mouth. "It in part saved us from the great danger . . . of swelling our numbers so that famine would have attended our progress." Though his passage through Georgia was the first effective implementation of Lincoln's Emancipation Proclamation of 1863 for great numbers of blacks, Sherman sometimes seemed to be more anxious for the safety and mobility of his column than for the freedom of slaves. Now, as never before, thousands of Negroes were free to leave plantations on which they had been held captive for most of their lives. Not since the early days of Carolina and Georgia settlements—not since the 1620's, in fact—had the status of blacks in the South changed materially until Sherman's columns swept through the midst of the Confederacy. Since he had realized that black hordes would impede the columns and doom them to failure, Sherman had issued orders in Atlanta barring the elderly, the infirm and mothers with young children from joining the march. Only the able-bodied, capable of aiding the army's progress, were to be taken along. This decision may have been rooted in Sherman's own ideas of white supremacy—as some of his more enlightened officers were to charge.

In Sherman's wake, the village of Covington was plundered by a succession of regiments, some of whom preyed upon the slaves themselves. One black girl, a young servant of the Travis family, watching the soldiers pass, recognized some of her clothing in the arms of a soldier and found that her hut had been plundered. Her wails rang out over the noise of passing bands. A German soldier who had forced his way into the house turned to Allie Travis: "What's de matter wid dat Nigger?"

"Your soldiers," Allie said, "are carrying off everything she owns, and yet you pretend to be fighting for the Negro."

The servant was afraid to speak to the white soldiers, but when she saw a black infantryman wearing her newest hat, she dashed from the yard, shook her fists in his face and shouted, "Oh! If I had the power like I've got the will, I'd tear you to pieces."

Soldiers of the 2nd Minnesota who dug for booty in Covington turned up an unexpected domestic tragedy. In midafternoon the thirsty troops of this regiment formed a queue at a roadside spring and sprawled on the lawn of a farmhouse amid the litter of those who had gone before. Three or four women looked on from the porch of the house, rocking nervously.

A soldier of the leading company rose to his knees and inspected the freshly dug sod on which he had lain, probed with his ramrod and whooped. "Treasure, boys! Who's got a spade?" Others crawled about to help dig in the soft earth. Shovels thumped hollowly on a pine box.

The women on the porch were standing, anxious and excited. "Perhaps," one officer thought, "their money or silver spoons were in peril." But when the box was pried open a foul odor rose. A dead spaniel lay within. The lid was hurriedly replaced, the grave refilled and the sod pressed down. One of the women called, "It looks like poor Curly will get no peace. That's the fourth time he's been dug up today."

Dolly Sumner Burge, a young widow who was a native of Maine and a relative of the Abolitionist leader Charles Sumner of Massachusetts, was among the first of thousands of women to plead for Federal guards to protect her property—and to mourn their ineffectiveness. Dolly awaited the enemy on her plantation a few miles east of Covington, alone but for her nine-year-old daughter and her slaves. She obtained a guard at once from a sympathetic Federal officer, but soon learned that nothing could halt the swarming looters: "But like demons they rushed in! My yards are full. To my smoke-house, Dairy, Pantry, Kitchen and Cellar, like famished wolves they came, breaking locks and whatever is in their way."

Dolly appealed to her guard, but was told, "I cannot help you, Madam; it is the orders."

Soldiers drove away all the horses, even Old Dutch, her husband's buggy horse who had carried him for many years and had finally drawn him to his grave. Dolly especially mourned the loss of her young slaves, who were forced to follow the soldiers at bayonet point. One slave boy jumped into his bed and said he was sick, and another, a cripple, crawled under a cabin, but was dragged out and carried away.

The sleepless Mrs. Burge paced her bedroom floor all night while two guards slept before her fireplace. The rear guard trailed by the next morning, November 20, mild-mannered soldiers who asked only a bucket of water for boiling coffee. Dolly mourned, "Thus ended the passing of Sherman's army by my place, leaving me poorer by $30,000 than I was yesterday morning. And a much stronger Rebel . . ."

Defenseless women in the widening tracks of the army now encountered pillagers wherever they turned, for looting bands roamed out of control, already outnumbering Sherman's official foragers. The vandals halted at nothing.

A funeral was in progress far to Sherman's rear, in the village of Chamblee's Mill, where a blind mule drew a wagon over a rutted road toward Mount Carmel Cemetery, three miles away. Half a dozen women rode in the wagon with the coffin of a little boy, a son of the Owens family; the two Negro men who had made the coffin were now in the cemetery digging the grave.

The funeral party had halted to rest the old mule when a band of Federal horsemen clattered up, unhitched the blind animal and led it away.

The women began to wail, and Mrs. Owens threw herself across the coffin, sobbing, "Oh, God! What will we do?" Sixteen-year-old Rachel Chamblee stepped between the wagon shafts. "Come on," she said firmly. "We'll go ahead. You push and I'll pull."

For more than an hour, sweating in heavy homespun dresses, the women struggled toward the cemetery, where they arrived with begrimed faces and ruined clothing, and stood exhausted as the gravediggers buried the coffin. The thought of dragging the wagon back over the cruel road was too much for the women; they removed one of the wheels, concealed it in the woods and made their way homeward.

Far to the south of Sherman and the left wing, General Oliver Howard led his columns through the village of Hillsboro on November 19, and demonstrated to at least one distraught woman that his piety did not extend to the plight of civilians on the route of march. Mrs. Louise Cornwell had spent much of the day watching in helpless anger as Kilpatrick's cavalrymen drove off her livestock, stole her grain and beehives, and burned the cotton gin, its screw, a blacksmith shop and piles of precious cotton bales. In short, her fate was that of hundreds of other farm women in the region.

In the afternoon, when there was hardly a scrap of food left on the Cornwell place, General Howard and his staff appeared, demanding tea. Mrs. Cornwell and her women relatives managed to serve them, though it took the last of their food. Louise watched somberly as Old Prayer Book sat at her dining table bowing his huge head to ask a blessing. Through a window she saw the work of his men: "The sky was red from flames of burning houses."

The infantry passed her house for almost four days while Mrs. Cornwell huddled in the cold on her front porch by day, hoping to keep the men out of the house.

One band of soldiers ordered her to leave: "Get out and take all your younguns and niggers. We're gonna burn it down." She replied calmly, "If you burn our house you'll burn us too. We will not leave. You've taken everything we owned. Now burn us up if you will, for we will not get out."

They turned away, shamed by the woman's unexpected bravery.

Mrs. Cornwell's Hillsboro neighbors were victims of the first recorded senseless vandalism of the march. One family reported that soldiers bore antique silver trays and bowls from the house, nailed them to trees and used them for target practice.

On an adjoining farm Federal officers stopped and ordered dinner served to them, a meal so delicious that they kidnapped Aunt Dinah, the aged and enormously fat cook. A soldier hoisted Dinah aboard a mule's back, where she sat with ludicrous dignity, followed by the laughter of her family until she disappeared down the eastward road. Three hours later an indignant Dinah limped back home after she had tumbled from the mule and been abandoned by the troops.

Sherman, who usually seemed to be oblivious to the sufferings of civilians, surprised Henry Hitchcock by his expressions of concern. On the third night of the march the general, sitting silently before his campfire with Hitchcock, spoke suddenly of a woman who had begged him for a guard during the day's march, pleading for him to halt the theft of her livestock. Sherman had refused brusquely and ridden away. He now revealed to Hitchcock the depths of his feelings: "I'll have to harden my heart to these things. That poor woman today—how could I help her? There's no help for it. The soldiers will take all she has." He placed the blame upon Confederate leaders for the ravages by his troops: "Jeff Davis is responsible for all this." Sherman said that nothing could keep men from straggling and pillaging: "For the first two years of the war no man could have done more than I did to try and stop it. I personally beat and kicked men out of yards for merely going inside—it's hopeless."

Hitchcock concluded that Sherman had merely closed his eyes to the destruction. The major realized that strict discipline would not be easy to enforce, but he saw a way to control the troops: "I am sure that a Headquarters Provost Marshal, with a rigid system of roll-calls in every company required at every halt—severe punishment inflicted not only on men who straggle but also on officers who fail to prevent it . . . would go far to prevent these outrages."

Hitchcock added in his journal: "I am bound to say I think Sherman lacking in enforcing discipline. Brilliant and daring, fertile, rapid and terrible, he does not seem to me to carry out things in this respect." Still, Hitchcock was forced to agree with the general that the campaign must give Southern civilians a taste of the miseries of war and convince them of the hopelessness of the rebel cause: "I believe more and more that only by this means the war can be ended . . . It is a terrible thing to consume and destroy the sustenance of thousands of people, and most sad and distressing to see and hear the terror and grief and want of these women and children . . . But if that terror and grief and want shall help to paralyze their husbands and fathers who are fighting us . . . it is mercy in the end."

Sherman expressed to his wife something of the compassion he had felt toward the anonymous woman of this day's march. He wrote Ellen of his realization that he would be reviled in the South for years to come, and added: "I doubt if history affords a parallel to the deep and bitter enmity of the women of the South. No one who sees them and hears them but must feel the intensity of their hate. Not a man is seen; nothing but women with houses plundered . . . desolation sown broadcast, servants all gone and women and children bred in luxury, beautiful and accomplished, begging with one breath for the soldiers' rations and in another praying that the Almighty or Joe Johnston will come and kill us, the despoilers of their homes and all that is sacred."

The general was oddly incensed by the lack of understanding on the part of his female victims—as if he felt that Southerners one and all must have known of his prewar warnings and had deliberately rejected their wisdom: "Why cannot they look back to the day and hour when I, a stranger in Louisiana, begged and implored them to pause in their career, that secession was death, was everything fatal . . ."

He had recently responded to a young woman he had known long before in Charleston, South Carolina:

> Your welcome letter came to me amid the sound of battle, and as you say little did I dream when I knew you . . . that I should control a vast army pointing, like a swarm of Alaric, towards the plains of the South.
>
> Why, oh why, is this? If I know my own heart, it beats as warmly as ever toward those kind and generous families that greeted us with such warm hospitality in days long past . . . today were . . . there children . . . to come to me as of old, the stern feeling of duty would melt as snow . . . and I believe I would strip my own children that they might be sheltered.
>
> And yet they call me barbarian, vandal, and a monster . . .
>
> My heart bleeds when I see . . . the desolation of homes, the bitter anguish of families, but the very moment the men of the South say that instead of appealing to war they should have appealed to reason, to our Congress, to our courts, to religion, and to the experience of history, then I will say peace, peace; go back to your point of error, and resume your places as American citizens, with all their proud heritages. . . .
>
> I hope that when the clouds of anger and passion are dispersed, and truth emerges bright and clear, you and all who knew me in early years will not blush that we were once close friends . . .

4
"The most gigantic pleasure expedition"

Sherman's official foragers were absurdly inept in their first attempts at living off the country. The bands were poorly organized, and though the army had looted houses in earlier campaigns, it had never done so on such a scale nor under the necessity of providing for all.

Charles E. Belknap, an eighteen-year-old captain, led one party into the back country on the first day out of Atlanta and discovered its shortcomings. These men halted at the cabin of a poverty-stricken "cracker" where they spotted a few lean razorback hogs—but were forced to fight for them with other foragers from competing regiments. Belknap led them to more plentiful spoils at a nearby farmhouse, but just as his party was loading all the loot they could carry, a few Confederate cavalrymen appeared, whooping and firing. The enemy numbered no more than half a dozen, but to Belknap's disgust, "All the foragers of the corps took to the woods for safety; in their wild flight chickens were left orphans by the roadside. Hams, pickles, preserves and honey were cast aside." Some of these men hid in the woods for a day or two before they made their way back to their commands.

The young captain was called into a conference at brigade headquarters when he returned to camp, and was relieved when the foragers were reorganized and he was given command of an enlarged band of ninety men, who thereafter roamed the countryside on their stolen horses, practicing their exciting trade.

The army—and Confederates—were soon calling such men bummers, an expression derived from "boomers," Belknap theorized, since gunfire was endless wherever the infantry foragers went. In fact, the term seems to have come from the fecund German word *bummler,* for idler or wastrel; ten years before the war, "bummer" had come to mean tramp.

In any case, these men learned rapidly. Within the first week, when Sherman slowed the march to ten miles a day rather than the customary fifteen, the troops realized that their mission was to despoil the country, and they responded with enthusiasm. Foragers became bummers, and as such they were destined for infamy above all others in the army. Their striking appearance became legendary.

Major Sam Merrill of the 70th Indiana long remembered the first bummers who returned to his camp one night at sundown in a motley array of carts, wagons and carriages:

> At the head of the procession . . . an ancient family carriage, drawn by a goat, a cow with a bell, and a jackass. Tied behind . . . a sheep and a calf, the vehicle loaded down with pumpkins, chickens, cabbages, guinea fowls, carrots, turkeys, onions, squashes, a shoat, sorghum, a looking-glass, an Italian harp, sweetmeats, a peacock, a rocking chair, a gourd, a bass viol, sweet potatoes, a cradle, dried peaches, honey, a baby carriage, peach brandy and every other imaginable thing a lot of fool soldiers could take in their heads to bring away.

Charles Booth of the 3rd Division's 2nd Brigade had an equally vivid memory of the raiders who were, he said, "the life of the army":

> Imagine a fellow with . . . a plug hat, a captured militia plume in it, a citizen's saddle, with a bed quilt or table cloth . . . poor fellow! He has rode upon that knock-kneed, shaved-tail, rail-fence mule over 30 miles, has . . . passed through untold dangers, and all for his load . . . a bundle of fodder . . . three hams, a sack of meal, a pack of potatoes, a fresh bed quilt, the old mother's coffee pot, a jug of vinegar and a bed cord.

Once they had a taste of foraging, these men remained in the countryside, far from their units, day after day in order to avoid army discipline. Even when their wagons were fully loaded by noon they roamed plantations the rest of the day in quest of loot and excitement.

* * *

According to David Conyngham of the *New York Herald,* the army's best forager was a lank Tennessean by the name of Joe, a half-breed Cherokee. As he led a party of bummers across an open field one day, Joe abruptly jerked his bony horse to a halt.

"I'm damned if I don't smell hog," he said.

There was no sign of an animal in the field.

"Hell," said one of his companions, "let's ride on. We're too far from the army."

"Nary a step until I make sure," Joe said. "A fat hog would be a mighty good change from chicken and turkey."

"They's no damned hog here, let's git on."

A hog grunted and Joe dismounted to search the ground. He kicked at a hollow spot, and the men soon dug out a fat pig, cleverly buried in a cave roofed with boards and covered with earth. The animal was butchered on the spot and borne away behind Joe's saddle.

Most foragers raided farms in the spirit of carnival, heedless of the distress of victims. One band that found a few chickens under a house was assailed by a sobbing woman: "No! they're all we've got left. They've been coming by all day, stealing everything—but they said we could have those to keep my little ones alive!"

A soldier bowed and smiled. "Madam, we're going to suppress this rebellion if it takes every last chicken in the Confederacy." The little flock was borne away.

After two days of looting, the army had more food than it could possibly use, and tons of fresh supplies were piled along the roadsides to go to waste. It was inconceivable, in this rich harvest country, that the troops would ever go hungry. The roads were littered with corn and fodder, and especially sweet potatoes, gigantic yams from a miraculous crop. Soldiers marveled at potatoes so large that they "started from the ground" as they were dug. Colonel Charles D. Kerr claimed he saw one three feet long, and his men reported yams "so large you can sit on one end while the other end roasts in the fire."

No rations had been issued, and butchers had killed none of the cattle brought from Atlanta. Captain Charles Wills of the 103rd Illinois, in Howard's wing, said, "Our men are clear discouraged with foraging, they can't carry half the hogs and potatoes they find right along the road."

Wills noted in his diary: "This is probably the most gigantic pleasure expedition ever planned. It already beats everything I ever saw soldiering, and promises to prove much richer yet." The captain had one complaint: "I wish Sherman would burn the commissary trains, we have no use for what they carry, and the train only bothers us."

Chaplain J. E. Brant of the 85th Indiana wrote: "All in fine humor at the expense of the Confederacy . . . killing nobody but an occasional cavalryman and eating out the very foundations of the Confederacy." Chaplain George Bradley of Slocum's corps found the men more cheerful than he had ever known them: "I wouldn't have missed it for fifty dollars," one soldier said.

One officer who made a valiant attempt to control wasteful looting was General Jefferson C. Davis, whose name was not an asset in this endeavor; his troops joked endlessly about the general and his namesake, the Confederate president. General Davis had a reputation for leniency, but occasionally lost his temper and sought to punish men at random. One day he saw two soldiers emerge from a house with armloads of women's clothing, and was so outraged that he had them dressed in the finery and marched them behind wagons, bearing placards on their backs: STOLEN. Discipline was often to be enforced in this haphazard fashion, with soldiers singled out from thousands of fellow looters to serve as examples to the army. Such injustice served merely to further undermine discipline among troops whose basest instincts were aroused by constant temptations to loot and burn.

When General Davis threatened to shoot men who burned houses, a chaplain fumed: "Just think of shooting American soldiers for the benefit of rebels. No man who really loves our cause could issue such an order. If an officer desires to shoot our men, let him join the rebel army at once."

The army regarded Davis as a dangerous man, though he was one of Sherman's favorite officers. The Indianian was a veteran of the Mexican War who had spurned an appointment to West Point to remain on the frontier fighting Indians. The outbreak of the rebellion had found him at Fort Sumter, where he fired the first shot in response to the fateful Confederate cannonade that opened the war. More recently he had killed his superior, Major General William

Nelson, during an argument over some trivial personal matter. He had escaped prosecution.

General Howard, like Davis, also threatened to shoot looters and burners, but when a court-martial sentenced one of his men to death, he commuted the sentence to a term in the prison at Dry Tortugas, in Florida waters controlled by the Federal navy. General Osterhaus fined pillagers a month's pay; General Frank Blair imposed a fine of fifty cents for each cartridge fired unnecessarily, in hopes of preventing civilian deaths.

But nothing was to halt the depredation of the army's foragers. From first to last, stragglers, deserters, camp followers—and occasionally whole regiments—joined official foraging parties in their pillage of the countryside.

Sherman was delighted with the "abundance" of plunder in the rich country yet untouched by passing armies. "The skill and success of the men in collecting forage was one of the features of this march," he said. "Often I . . . was amused at their strange collections." A decade later, when he defended his reputation in his memoirs, Sherman justified the stripping of Georgia homes on the basis of actual need: "No army could have carried along sufficient food and forage for a march of three hundred miles; so that foraging in some shape was necessary."

The general believed— or later convinced himself—that his army was not unnecessarily harsh in its treatment of helpless women and children, though his raiders left countless miserable victims in their wake: "No doubt, many acts of pillage, robbery, and violence were committed by these . . . bummers; for I have since heard of jewelry taken from women, and the plunder of articles that never reached the commissary; but these acts were exceptional and incidental. I never heard of any cases of murder or rape . . ."*

However convenient Sherman's memory, or however irresponsible his troops seemed to their victims and to later Americans, it remained that the army's experience was unique in the nation's history, and that the compulsion to pillage to excess was well-nigh universal in the ranks. Both North and South had been penetrated by other invading armies, but never in this fashion, sweeping through

*Sherman later conceded, in a speech in Washington, that at least two cases of rape had been brought to his attention. Southerners claimed rapes were common indeed along the army's line of march, but such cases were seldom reported by victims.

domestic areas without opposition, neither seeking nor expecting to meet enemy forces. This mission to despoil was a far cry from the classic campaigns that climaxed in Gettysburg or Bull Run or Antietam or Shiloh. Rather than bloodshed and pain and terror, each day brought fascinating new scenes to Sherman's eager young troops, and most of them wished that the lark would have no end.

Now, as the columns moved deeper into the black belt, they were almost mobbed by thousands of wildly enthusiastic Negroes who thronged the roadsides. Virtually all of the slaves were illiterate, deeply religious and superstitious, and joyously aware that salvation had come.

Plantation hands flocked to see the columns pass. Theodore Upson, a twenty-year-old private of the 100th Indiana, said, "They are all looking for freedom but just don't seem to know what freedom means."

All along his route, "Massa Sherman" was followed by a roar of acclaim. One ecstatic black woman held a mulatto baby high so that it could see the general: "Dar's the man that rules the world!"

Sherman rode past the 33rd Massachusetts as the regiment moved through a horde of Negroes. Blacks clung to the general's stirrups, pressed their heads against the sides of his horse. "He's the Angel of the Lord!" Men, women and children hugged the soldiers, laughing, crying and sighing: "The day of Jubilo!"

Federal pranksters sometimes victimized credulous Negroes who eagerly sought Sherman. As the XIV Corps neared a village where a great crowd of blacks waited at a crossroad, an orderly came from the rear of the column. "General Sherman will soon be along," he said. "Look for a soldier in a red uniform, with a cocked hat and a feather in it. He's driving a carriage with a pair of mules."

The Negroes craned to look down the road, and when a forager came along in a captured Revolutionary uniform, they marched after him, singing hymns and hailing him as Sherman until someone told them the truth.

Twenty-year-old Corydon Foote, a Michigan drummer boy, was clasped by a Negro woman who shouted, "They tole us this here army was debbils from Hell, but praise the Lord, it's the Lord's own babes and sucklings!"

The advance of the 74th Ohio was particularly admired by Negroes. "Lordy!" one said in amazement, "they look just like our people, they ain't got no horns!" Another caught sight of the regiment's new American flag: "My God, did you ever see such a pretty thing!"

On another road the XVII Corps passed miles of Negroes who had perched on rail fences. A soldier shouted, "Boys, this is a review and there's the reviewing officer!" An old black man stood on a rail, bowing and receiving salutes. When a black boy rode up behind him on a mule and reported that an equally large army was marching nearby, the old man raised his arms and screamed, "Dar's millions of 'em—millions!" He turned to his neighbors in wonder: "Is dere anybody left up Noth?"

A few days later General John W. Fuller saw this old man hobbling along with the corps, hatless and barefoot, trying to keep pace with the troops.

"How far are you going, uncle?"

The old man stared in astonishment: "Why," he said, "I'se jined!"

Despite all efforts of Sherman and his officers, thousands of Negroes fell in behind the line of march, many of them women. The 17th Indiana was followed by "vast numbers" of black women with babies in their arms or clinging to their skirts who plodded mile after mile, grimly determined to escape the plantations for the unknown that lay ahead. An officer of the regiment saw two little boys, four or five years old, hidden in a wagon by a weary woman apparently too exhausted to continue but determined that they should ride to freedom. Some babies perched upon the backs of mules by their mothers tumbled off and were abandoned at the roadside, or drowned in streams and swamps. David Conyngham saw hampers borne by mules, "a black head with large staring eyes peeping out of a sack" on one side, balanced by a ham or a turkey on the other.

An Illinois artilleryman watched with pity and admiration as the growing caravan of blacks came on in the rear of the army "like a sable cloud in the sky before a thunder storm. They thought it was freedom now or never, and would follow whether or no . . . Some in buggies, costly and glittering; some on horseback, the horses old and blind, and others on foot; all following up in right jolly mood, bound for ease and freedom. Let those who choose to curse the negro curse him; but one thing is true . . . they were the only friends on whom we could rely for the sacred truth in Dixie. What they said might be relied on, so far as they knew; and they knew more and could tell more than most of the poor white population."

At night the camps roared with laughter and the songs of revivals and music halls. Negroes danced and sang, juggled, played banjos and fiddles and homemade drums, rattled bones and entertained troops in African tongues. Soldiers and black girls made love all about the camps, Conyngham noted. The most attractive young women rode by day in baggage wagons, where they led "luxurious lives" dressed in finery stolen from plantation homes and fed at the servants' mess: "It would be vexatious to the Grand Turk or Brigham Young if they could only see how many of the dark houris were in the employment of officers' servants and teamsters. I have seen officers themselves very attentive to the wants of pretty octoroon girls, and provide them with horses to ride."

One night Sherman sent officers into the country to bring in a Negro from the neighborhood. "I don't want a white man—I need some reliable information about roads and bridges." An intelligent old black man came for a long talk with the general. He was scornful of the rebels: "When the Yanks are far off, our people are very brave. They say the women and children could whip 'em—but when you come close, then how they does git up and dust."

The general gave the old man a message for the blacks of the neighborhood: "You're free . . . you can go when you like. We want men to come with the army if they choose to come, but we don't force any to be soldiers. We pay wages. But since you have a family you should stay here and all go together later.

"But don't hurt your masters or their families—we don't want that."

Sherman repeated this message frequently as the basis of his personal policy of liberation. He ignored U. S. Grant's suggestion that he "clean the country of Negroes and arm them."

Unlike Sherman, who had known slaves and masters during his years in the South, most of his young Midwestern soldiers gazed upon the strange world of central Georgia's plantation life in fascination. The more sensitive of them could realize how the intimacy of rural life and the repression of ignorant blacks had served to perpetuate the system and made possible the squelching of revolts for some two hundred years. The soldiers also noted indications of affection and kindness between whites and blacks, relationships which, even more than economic factors, preserved a sort of racial détente in this back country.

For all its horrors, the slave system had imposed a stability of sorts for whites and blacks of the region, a stability that was forever altered by the passage of Sherman's columns. Both races were to be thrust into new and uncertain times. Soldiers had opportunities to see many blacks who were prepared to embrace the new day—and others who clung to the past. Major Nichols found an elderly black couple in a farmhouse who symbolized the division. After the major had talked with them for a few minutes, the old woman rose, glared and pointed to her husband. She hissed with a scorn that bespoke a lifetime of anger and frustration: "How come you sittin' there? You s'pose I been waitin' sixty years for nothin'? Don't you see the door's open now? I'm goin', you hear? I'm gonna follow my child and go 'long with these people till I drop in my tracks."

Nichols was astounded by the transformation in the old woman, who had been sitting with a dull expression on her worn face: "A more terrible sight I never beheld. I can think of nothing to compare with it except . . . Meg Merrilies."

The northern wing of the army now approached the pleasant country market town of Madison, which, though it was to escape major damage, would nurse bitter memories of Sherman's men in the holiday mood.

Reveille sounded at four in the morning on November 17, and troops of the left wing broke camp in a rainstorm. Several brigades of the XX Corps spent the morning tearing up the railroad on the way to Madison while the rear guard beat off a few rebels who attacked the rear. Gunfire sputtered throughout the day as foragers shot barnyard fowl, hogs and cattle; men entered the town carrying chickens, turkeys, headless sheep, and on their bayonets, chunks of fresh pork complete with hide and hair.

General Slocum was met outside the town by the mayor and three others, who begged him not to burn the place, but the interview was brief and the general made no promises. The troops found this the most beautiful town they had seen in Georgia, a quiet village of stately houses and large trees. The season was late and gardens were filled with roses and dahlias. A band played and Negroes crowded about, timorously at first, but soon becoming friendly with the bluecoats. "Our master told us you had horns," one of them told William

Grunert of the 129th Illinois. "He said you'd make holes in our shoulders to hitch us to your wagons." The blacks pranced and sang with delight as the courthouse, depot and a slave pen, with its whips and paddles, were set on fire.

The wife of the local railroad agent came to plead with soldiers to spare the tiny office in her yard, but men threw open windows, tossed in flaming brands, and the small structure burned to the ground. The woman scolded her tormentors with unconcealed hatred. "I almost always have sympathy for the women," Private Horatio Chapman wrote, "but I did not much pity her. She was a regular Secesh and spit out her spite and venom against the dirty yanks and mudsills of the north."

A few houses and other buildings in the town were burned, or were, as Grunert noted, "demolished more or less."

The town's stores were pillaged by "vagabonds" from the rear of the army who flung bales of cloth and clothing, hardware and harness into the streets. Two soldiers bore off a large gilt mirror, tired of carrying it, and dashed it to the ground. Drunken soldiers lay on the streets of the town with wine bottles lying about them.

The *New York Herald*'s man described a scene in the parlor of a house of "a lot of bearded, rough soldiers capering about the room in a rude waltz, while some fellow was thumping away unmercifully at the piano, with another cutting grotesque capers on the top-board." The soldiers tired of this "grotesque saturnalia" and burned the piano.

About 4,000 men of the corps camped near the home of the High family for two days and nights. The frightened Mrs. High greeted them by flapping her father's old Masonic apron from the porch, shouting, "I'm a Mason's daughter and a wife of a Mason, give me protection." An officer posted a guard at the house. "Put out your light," he said, "and go to sleep, and you will not be disturbed."

The household was not molested until morning, when the aroma of fresh gingerbread attracted Federal soldiers, who entered the kitchen, took a few pieces and dropped coins into a tin pan. The black cook grew more excited as the troops came and went for hours, and the mound of coins grew until a last soldier snatched the remaining cakes, emptied the plate of coins and ran. The sobbing cook dashed after him, shouting, "Our boys wouldn't have done that way, for they has had *some raisin'* and has got *manners,* too."

The army left Madison "in rather good spirits," young Emma

High said. The rear guard stacked arms on a lawn on the edge of town, stripped hundreds of roses from flower gardens, and marched away with flowers in their muskets and woven into garlands about their hats.

On November 20 Sherman halted at noon at the farm of a Mrs. Farrar a few miles east of Madison. The farm wife was a pretty but slatternly woman who said her husband was in the Confederate army "from choice." She listened complacently to one of the general's lectures on the war guilt of the South and made little comment. Her slaves told Henry Hitchcock that Farrar was in Milledgeville helping to build breastworks. "They're gonna fight you over there," a Negro said. "They done been building forts and all for two years." The rumor was false. Despite the importance of the state capital and the presence of earthworks, the town was not to be defended.

The Negroes of this farm complained of Farrar's cruelty: "He whups us with strops, hand saws and paddles with holes cut in 'em —and then rubs salt in the wounds." They told the staff of a celebrated bloodhound on the next farm, an enormous red dog used to track down runaways. Nichols sent to have the dog killed, and when they heard a shot and a quavering howl the Negroes shouted in triumph.

For the rest of the march the army killed most dogs in its path, and sometimes carried the hunt to ludicrous extremes. One soldier snatched a poodle from a wailing mistress. "Leave my baby alone— she's all I've got!"

"Madam, our orders are to kill every bloodhound."

"She's no bloodhound—she's a house pet."

"Well, Madam, we can't tell what it'll grow into if we leave it behind." He disappeared with the dog under his arm.

Sherman's columns had now marched almost one hundred miles without revealing their destination to the Confederates. Food was still plentiful and plunder of the countryside continued daily. Though the troops were already out of control, civilians had suffered few of the atrocities which were in store for many who lived along the route, especially in South Carolina. Officers made fewer, and less effective, attempts to restore discipline as the march proceeded.

The commander was anxious to concentrate the wings of the army at Milledgeville and drive toward Savannah, but he continued to threaten Macon to the south, hoping to conceal his true objective until the last moment.

From great distances, and without knowledge of the situation on Sherman's rapidly changing front, Confederate leaders breathed defiance and implored Georgians to resist to the last man. From Mississippi the flamboyant Creole general, Pierre Gustave Toutant Beauregard, sent an appeal: "Arise for the defense of your native soil! . . . Rally around your patriotic Governor and gallant soldiers. Obstruct and destroy all the roads in Sherman's front, flank, and rear, and his army will soon starve in your midst."

The secretary of war, James Seddon, telegraphed from Richmond: "You have now the best opportunity ever presented to destroy the enemy . . . Georgians, be firm, act promptly, and fear not."

Georgia's congressmen urged: "Let every man fly to arms! Remove your negroes, horses, cattle and provisions and burn what you cannot carry. Burn all bridges, and block up the roads in his route. Assail the invader in front, flank and rear, by night and by day. Let him have no rest."

Such bravado had long since been exposed. Sherman's columns had swept forward rapidly, without meeting serious opposition in any quarter. Georgia was powerless to resist, it seemed. Joe Wheeler claimed that he had saved the small town of Griffin by making a stand there, but soon discovered that his enemy had merely veered off toward another objective. Wheeler's next report revealed the hapless state of Confederate defenses: "Enemy turning column shortest route to Macon. I have no orders regarding the holding of any city should enemy besiege or assault. Please give me wishes and intentions of Government, or send someone who knows the course they desire pursued."

Wheeler hurried into Macon to fight for the city, but though Kilpatrick's horsemen were so close on his heels that some of them rode into the trenches, they soon turned away, their feint complete. Howard's infantry was already crossing the Ocmulgee River, moving rapidly eastward. Wheeler was then impotent to do more than hang on Sherman's flank, picking off stragglers.

5
"We never wanted to fight"

Now, months too late, high-ranking Confederate officers began converging on Georgia in a desperate effort to save the state. Lieutenant General W. J. Hardee, the dean of American military scholars and author of a text on tactics used by both armies, took command in Macon. General Beauregard hurried in from his station in Mississippi. The veteran Gustavus W. Smith, a former New York City street commissioner, and General Joe Wheeler of the cavalry joined the imposing gallery of rebel leaders in Macon. General Braxton Bragg settled in Augusta, in the northeastern section of the state, with 10,000 rebel troops brought down from North Carolina.

And at dawn on November 22 a handsome officer in full dress uniform stepped from a train in Macon, drawing his cape against a sifting snow, an unexpected rarity in the Deep South. The officer was Lieutenant General Richard Taylor, son of the late President Zachary Taylor. The general, an urbane officer who had been educated in Europe and at Harvard and Yale, was a veteran of Robert E. Lee's army. He had come from his post in Montgomery, Alabama, under urgent orders from Lee. Taylor was to observe Sherman's movements, report on the invasion, and draw plans for the defense of Georgia.

The coterie of generals was joined by Georgia political leaders — Governor Joseph Brown; former Governor Howell Cobb, who had also served as speaker of the House of Representatives and secretary of the treasury; and Robert Toombs, a former U.S. senator and Confederate secretary of state.

Cobb greeted Taylor at the Macon depot in his role as commander of state militia.

Cobb proposed an immediate inspection: "We'll ride out and see the defenses. I've been up all night, working on them. The Yankees were only twelve miles away at noon yesterday."

Taylor shook his head. "There's no need to see the trenches, and I hope you'll stop your workmen and let all of them get warm by the fire—which is where I'm going to stay. Sherman's not coming here. If his advance was twelve miles away at noon yesterday, you'd have seen him last night," Taylor said. "He'd have come before you had time to finish the works or move your stores."

In fact, Sherman and his main body were now nearing the capital of Milledgeville, and the blue columns moved steadily onward, meeting no resistance; the only gunfire heard by most Federal troops on this day came from barnyards where animals were being slaughtered.

Taylor, who would have been a formidable opponent for Sherman under other circumstances, realized at once that Georgia's plight was hopeless, but he was unable to communicate with the distraught and inexperienced Cobb, who persisted in his plans to defend Macon to the death against Sherman's onslaught, which he supposed would come at any moment, even now.

Taylor saw that Cobb thought he was "a lunatic," but during breakfast, when a messenger brought word that the enemy had turned away, the delighted Cobb praised the general's wisdom and confessed that he knew nothing of military affairs, but was serving merely "from a sense of duty."

The governor was announced at that moment. Cobb laughed. "This is awkward," he said. "Brown's the only man in Georgia I won't speak to." But when the governor entered with several others, Cobb conferred with them on the emergency. With the governor came Generals Toombs and Smith. Since Toombs was contemptuous of regular army officers ("The epitaph of the Confederate Army will be 'Died of West Point,' " he said), there was a lack of enthusiasm as he conferred with Smith, who had taught at the military academy before the war.

There was a more obvious strain as Brown and Toombs confronted Joe Wheeler, of whom Toombs had said during Wheeler's recent cavalry raid into Tennessee, "I hope to God he will never get back to Georgia . . . His band consumes more than the whole army . . . and will accelerate the evil day."

A flurry of excitement swept Macon while the high command conferred in Cobb's mansion. Several members of the legislature, passing in flight from Milledgeville, were set upon zealous conscription officers under orders to put "every man in the trenches," and it was only after heated exchanges that the lawmakers convinced the volunteer officers that they were exempt by their own freshly enacted statute, and were released from arrest.

The emergency council of war at Cobb's house acted with dispatch: General Smith sent forward the little garrison of militiamen from Macon, hoping that it could pass Sherman's front to the east and then turn northward to reach Augusta in time to help defend that city. Wheeler's cavalry was ordered to screen the movement. Quite inadvertently, this green, badly organized little force blundered into a tragic little skirmish that passed as a battle in this campaign.

Gustavus Smith had rounded up some 3,700 Georgia militiamen, most of them boys or old men fresh from home. In all, there were seven small brigades, untrained and poorly armed, and led by an inexperienced brigadier, General P. J. Phillips. General Phillips had been drinking that day, so some of his men later recalled.

Smith sent Phillips toward the Federal line of march along the Georgia Central Railroad, under orders to avoid battle at all costs, since this tiny force could be overwhelmed if Howard turned upon it. But on November 22, when his advance met Federal pickets near the village of Griswoldville, Phillips saw that he greatly outnumbered the enemy outpost, and the temptation to strike was irresistible. Phillips rashly formed his troops for an assault. The line of gray militia moved out into an open field, stepping smartly with the valor of ignorance, anxious to close with the enemy. The militiamen seemed eager to emulate the reckless élan with which Confederate veterans had charged the slopes at Gettysburg little more than a year before.

General Oliver Howard, near the head of Sherman's southern column, had been uneasy during the day. He feared that the vulnerability of his wing would invite attack from the gathering Confederate home guard and precipitate a battle, which Sherman hoped to avoid. Since Howard's wagon trains had lumbered up the steep banks of the

Ocmulgee River, they had snaked along the army's southern flank, stretched out for forty miles, exposed to attack. Yesterday rebel cavalry had charged repeatedly against Kilpatrick, captured General Peter Osterhaus's chief of staff, and narrowly missed the Prussian himself, who was but a few yards away. Kilpatrick had burned most of Griswoldville—a soap and candle factory, a pistol and saber factory, the depot and several houses. Cavalry fights had crackled amid the greasy smoke clouds until dusk, when Little Kil's rear guard was driven out.

This morning Howard had ordered troops of the 1st Division to shield the column's passage through Griswoldville. This duty was assigned to veteran regiments from Indiana, Illinois, Iowa and Ohio, most of whose men were armed with deadly new Spencer repeating rifles. This guard unit was supported by two guns of a Michigan battery. The force of 1,500 was commanded by Charles C. Walcutt, a slender young brigadier from Ohio.

During the night Theodore Upson, the young private of the 100th Indiana, shared picket duty near Griswoldville with Uncle Aaron Wolford, the patriarch of his regiment.

Wolford had been an unfailingly cheerful companion and counselor to young men of his company, but tonight he was silent and depressed. "I feel like I ain't got long to live," the old man said.

Upson scoffed: "The war's almost over, we may not have another battle."

"I want you to promise you'll take care of my things," Wolford said. "Send 'em to my wife and write her all about me."

"Sure, Uncle Aaron, but don't worry, you've got along safe this far, you'll make it to the end."

"No. I've got a feeling my time has come." The old man could not be stirred from his somber mood, and was still grim-faced and apprehensive as his regiment filed into position with the flank guard.

Walcutt's troops settled at the edge of a woodland, threw up a light barrier of rails and logs and were cooking their noon meal, "not dreaming of a fight," when there was a rattle of musketry and pickets raced in. Captain Charles Wills looked across the field and was astonished to see, some six hundred yards away, "a fine line of Johnnies" coming toward him.

A second and then a third Confederate line moved into the field, coming on steadily—each of the lines as strong as Walcutt's waiting brigade. It was so quiet for a time that Major Asias Willison of the 103rd Illinois could hear rebel officers calling commands.

General Walcutt peered out at the enemy from behind a big pine tree, and though his men turned anxiously toward him, expecting the order to fire, he shouted only when the rebels were within two hundred and fifty yards. A heavy volley from his line tore the gray ranks, but still waves of attackers came on steadily, most of them bearing toward the Federal right. Walcutt shifted more men to that flank, but was knocked down by a shell burst before he had completed the move, painfully wounded in one leg. Colonel K. J. Catterson took command.

The veteran Federal infantrymen suspected by now that these rebels had never seen battle—they came on too bravely, heedless of exposure or losses. The Johnnies did not realize, even after seven charges, that they were being cut to pieces by repeating rifles. The Rebs also fired too high. Charles Wills estimated that ten of every dozen bullets fired by the green troops flew high overhead, but even so men had begun to fall in the Federal line.

During the hottest of the firing, Aaron Wolford of the 100th Indiana slumped at Theodore Upson's side. The boy put a hand on the old man's shoulder. "Uncle Aaron! Oh, Uncle Aaron!" He was dead.

The repeating rifles fired so rapidly that most regiments ran low on ammunition, and drummer boys were sent for more cartridges. Men calmly fixed bayonets and waited for the Confederates to leap the breastworks. The Johnnies were within fifty yards when the drummer boys came down the line, furiously opening boxes of cartridges. The heavy volleys rolled out once more.

The old men and boys in the gray lines lost their nerve at last. They dared not retreat across the broad field under the heavy fire, but when they saw a ravine fifty yards in front of the Yankee line, they charged furiously toward its cover. At that range Federal marksmen could hardly miss. Charles Wills was almost sickened by the sight of men falling, spines stiffened, arms outflung, faces contorted by shock and pain. Some Confederates reached the ravine, and a few of them scrambled to safety behind a screen of bamboo, gallberry bushes and briars. One of them, sixteen-year-old J. J. Eckles, sat down exhausted as soon as he was out of sight of the bluecoats. He unrolled the thick home-woven blanket he had carried over his shoulder, shook out some misshapen lead pellets, and counted twenty-seven bullet holes in the cloth.

Walcutt's men went out to the fallen rebels. Captain Wills, who had seen many battlefields littered with bodies, had never been so moved: "Old grey haired and weakly looking men and little boys, not over 15 years old, lay dead or writhing in pain. I did pity those boys . . . "

One boy lay quietly, looking up steadily at the bluecoats. "Water," he said. "Can you give me some water?" His chest was torn, the bloody breastbone protruding. The Federals saw the beating of his exposed heart.

"We never wanted to fight," one of the boys said. "The cavalry rounded us up and drove us in and made us march." Others told the same story: Wheeler's troopers had cleaned the Georgia countryside of every male who could carry a gun and herded them into battle, almost literally as prisoners.

The Federals took some of the wounded to ambulances in the rear and covered others with blankets taken from the dead. "I hope we will never have to shoot at such men again," Wills said. "They knew nothing at all about fighting, and I think their officers knew as little, or else certainly knew nothing about our being there."

Theodore Upson was another who never forgot the field: "It was a terrible sight. Someone was groaning. We moved a few bodies, and there was a boy with a broken arm and leg—just a boy 14 years old; and beside him, cold in death, lay his father, two brothers and an uncle." Upson and his friends carried the boy to their fireside and found a doctor for him.

The Indiana troops then buried their dead. Upson could not bear to think of tumbling Aaron Wolford's body into a common grave. There was no time to make a coffin, for the brigade would be moving by dawn. Theodore split a hollow sycamore log, laid Wolford inside and scratched his name, company and regiment into a rail to mark his grave. Upson gathered the old man's worn Testament, his watch and a few dollars to send to his wife, and wrote to Mrs. Wolford: "I told her what a good man he was, how much help he had been to all of the boys, how brave and faithful to duty he was, all that I could think of to tell her about him, I did." Upson burst into tears when he tried to describe Uncle Aaron's burial, and moved away from his companions to finish the letter: "I am afraid she will have hard work to read it, for I could not help blotting the paper."

Upson thought mournfully of the widow and her eight children: "I hope they will realize what a grand soul he had."

The rebels fell back toward Macon under orders from Gustavus Smith, whose anger was barely concealed in his official report on the "unfortunate accident"—the action had not crippled the enemy, and the heavy Confederate losses, especially in officers, could be "illy sustained."

The much-sobered General Phillips and his survivors returned to Macon at two in the morning of November 23, but were given little rest. They were soon off on a circuitous journey, southward to Albany, Georgia, by train, thence marching overland to Thomasville and on to Savannah as reinforcements for General Hardee, who was assigned to defend the city in case Sherman advanced that far. Even before these troops had boarded their cars in Macon, Joe Wheeler's cavalry was galloping past the Federal flank, bound for the crossings of the Oconee River. Wheeler was under orders to circle into Sherman's front and impede his progress wherever possible.

The twin wings of Sherman's army were now drawing closer together near Milledgeville. Howard's column was passing south of the city, and Slocum's men were to enter the capital itself. From Milledgeville, the army would push on to the east, still using a network of country roads. Sherman was still in a position to threaten the nervous General Bragg and his Augusta garrison, but the way to Savannah was open and lightly defended. Sherman did not yet realize that Hardee was concentrating his small force in Savannah to challenge him, but the knowledge would not have disturbed the commander of the powerful columns.

6
"Our degradation was bitter"

Shock waves of panic reached the tree-shaded village of Milledgeville well in advance of Sherman's approach. Mrs. Joseph E. Brown, the governor's wife, had already left the capital, which lay some thirty-five miles northeast of Macon. Mrs. Brown was, one woman noted, "pale and terror stricken, flying hither and thither, not knowing where to turn—fearing that the house would be burned over her head before morning."

One of the few women left in town, Anna Maria Green, daughter of the superintendent of the insane asylum, saw the legislature in action on November 19: "The scene at the State House was truly ridiculous, the members were badly scared, such a body of representatives made my cheeks glow with shame . . . " Anna had expected "cool, wise legislation," but instead the lawmakers passed an act drafting all men in Georgia— except legislators and judges—appropriated three thousand dollars for a train to hurry them out of danger, and adjourned "to the front . . . to meet again if we should live at such place as the Governor may designate." These men did not help to oppose the Federal columns, but hurried home to hide livestock and other valuables, or fled from Sherman's path.

Joseph Brown, Georgia's popular governor, had been a poor farm boy from the north Georgia hills who made his way to Yale law school and served four terms as a maverick governor. Brown had opposed wealthy planters and predatory bankers with a barrage of vetoes, fought for public schools and the struggling University of Georgia—and had defied Jefferson Davis throughout the war, insisting upon the state's right to conduct its affairs, military and civilian.

Now, as Sherman's troops approached, Brown went to the penitentiary in Milledgeville in search of recruits, offering pardons to 126 assembled convicts if they would join General Howell Cobb's militia. Only a handful of prisoners refused. Brown then joined the eastward flight by rail, with a carful of baggage— carpets, curtains, most of the furniture from the governor's mansion, even a cow and a supply of cabbage. Brown hoped to find refuge in Savannah.

The last Confederate train left Milledgeville late Saturday night, November 19, loaded with the remnants of central Georgia's manpower, a nondescript band of 460 men commanded by General Harry Wayne, who until a day or so earlier had busied himself with office duties as adjutant to Governor Brown. A former Federal officer, the commander was the son of U.S. Supreme Court Justice James M. Wayne, who was even now serving in Washington.

General Wayne's rebel band disappeared in the direction of Gordon, a remote rail junction a few miles south of the capital; from there, an east-west rail line led toward Savannah. The little train chugged off in a cloud of wood smoke and glowing sparks, bearing the paroled convicts, penitentiary and factory guards, an artillery battery, two militia companies, and the boy cadets of Georgia Military Institute, the oldest of whom were seventeen years old.

Behind them the capital's civilians prepared to meet the enemy. Anna Maria Green and her family drove into town from the insane asylum, past refugees with wagonloads of household goods, going "they scarcely knew where, some to plantations and some to the woods." They passed four wagons carrying state archives to the asylum. In the town excited people scurried about to conceal valuables. The Greens hid their family silver under the city reservoir. Slaves buried barrels of syrup. White women dug in their yards and gardens with spades to hide valuables, not only jewelry and silver, but also pieces of homespun cloth from which uniforms were to be made, home-knit socks and slabs of bacon.

Benjamin Jordan, a prosperous farmer who lived near town, found an ideal hiding place for his cash. He had several Negroes dig holes for new gateposts, and when they had gone to dinner, dropped in bags of gold and silver and covered them with fresh earth, ready for the posts. The blacks completed the work without a suspicion that treasure was buried below.

Miss A. C. Cooper waited in the capital, a young refugee from

Atlanta who would flee no farther: "The excitement increased, we could neither eat nor sleep. Scouts were sent out up this road, down that, across the country, everywhere the roads teemed with foam-flecked hard-run horses bestrode by tired, excited men . . . these scouts would ride into the village almost exhausted, and, not dismounting, take their food from the willing hands that would carry it out to them, then off again . . . dogs howled and yelped, mules brayed, Negro drivers swore, while Negro girls giggled."

In the dusk half a dozen riders trotted warily into town, cut telegraph wires, stole a few horses, inquired about rebel troops and disappeared. News of these troopers alarmed the Green family, now back at the asylum. Anna Maria tied a small bag of jewelry under her clothing and sat up most of the night, "terribly frightened."

There was a day of respite. Milledgeville waited throughout a bitterly cold and rainy Monday without a sign of the enemy. Townspeople comforted themselves with the thought that the mysterious riders had been deserters and not Sherman's vanguard.

Sherman, who was traveling slowly, was still a few miles outside Milledgeville when he halted at four o'clock and turned from the road, seeking shelter from an icy wind in a plum thicket. His orderly was at his heels with the general's saddlebags, loaded with precious cargo: a change of underwear, campaign maps, a bottle of whiskey and "a bunch of cigars." Sherman took a drink, lighted a cigar and crossed the field to a Negro cabin, where he was warming by a fire when he discovered that he was on one of the half-dozen plantations of Howell Cobb, one of the "head devils" of the Confederacy. He sent word to General Davis to "spare nothing"; fences and outbuildings burned all night.

Sherman discovered that many slaves were much less naïve than he had imagined, despite a lack of education imposed upon them by law. Touched by the sight of Howell Cobb's ragged Negroes, Sherman passed out to them food found on the plantation, calling to the hesitant blacks, "Come on! We're your friends. You needn't be afraid of us. All this is for you— corn, wheat, molasses."

A white-haired old man said, "You may be true, master. But you'll go away tomorrow, and another white man'll come here." Sherman ordered soldiers to take or burn everything of value that the Negroes would not take.

"Our White folks tol' us you would string us up, every one," a woman said. "They said you put black folks out front in the battles and killed 'em if they didn't fight. They said you threw women and children into the Chattahoochee River, and roasted 'em in the Atlanta fire."

One old man came to the cabin and peered at the general in wonder. "Is you Massa Sherman?" "I am, what do you want?" "Jest to know if it's so!" the old man said. "There'll be no sleep for dis nigger dis night."

General Harry Wayne and his little Confederate band, retreating from Milledgeville, had halted in the railroad village of Gordon, where Wayne turned over field command to Major F. W. Capers, the superintendent of the Georgia Military Institute. On Sunday, when his telegraph line to Macon was cut, Wayne ordered a train sent from Griswoldville for a retreat to the east. Wayne was seated on a hotel porch when a horseman dashed up to offer his services. The rider was a remarkable volunteer, twenty-year-old Rufus Kelly, a veteran who had lost a leg in Virginia and had returned to his Georgia home still full of fight. Kelly rode precariously, with a rifle and a crutch swung from his saddle, but volunteered to scout against the enemy. Wayne sent him forward.

Kelly reported a few hours later that the Yankees had left Griswoldville for Gordon, then whirled his mount and rode toward the enemy once more. Wayne and his officers felt that they could not defend Gordon against two Federal corps, and ordered the troops aboard the train. The battalion was ready to retreat when Kelly reappeared, his face flushed with anger. "What's this mean, General? Ain't you going to make a stand?"

Wayne leaned out the window. "Mr. Kelly, it's ridiculous to fight an army of a hundred thousand with five hundred men. I'm going back to the Oconee where we can defend the bridge."

"You goddamned white-livered cur!" Kelly shouted. "You tuck-tail son of a bitch—you ain't got a drop of blood in your veins."

As the train began to move he called to Wayne, "If you've got no manhood in you, by God I'll defend the women and children of Gordon!"

Wayne's last sight from the window of the moving train was of Kelly hunched over his rifle, firing at the approaching Federals from his saddle, "alone in all his glory." Enemy flanking columns turned aside and closed cautiously on Gordon. The boy had forced the XVII

Corps column to pause for almost an hour. As Kelly fled toward the woods, his horse stumbled, he tumbled from the saddle, lost his crutch and was captured.

It was late in the afternoon of November 22 when the vanguard of Sherman's left wing, the XX Corps, entered Milledgeville, and despite the bitter cold the color guards broke out flags and bands played; one of them switched to "Yankee Doodle" as it passed the capitol. Two regiments halted on Capitol Square for guard duty, the 3rd Wisconsin and the 107th New York. The New Yorkers ran their flag to the top of the capitol dome as troops cheered and bands played the national anthem. The troops were more excited than usual, since the city was not only the state capital, but also the largest town they had entered since leaving Atlanta. They had visions of spectacular loot in the houses of the town.

N. C. Barnett, the Georgia secretary of state, was almost the only official who had not joined the flight. He waited in his office until Federals rode across the square, then took the great seal and the newly passed acts of the legislature from the capitol and hid below the river bluff until dark. When the town was quiet Barnett made his way home, and with the aid of his wife, Mary, and their son, buried the seal under a brick pillar of the house. It was midnight when they finished.

Mary Barnett wrapped the documents and buried them in the pigpen. "I had four fine porkers in the pen, and I thought that the heat of their bodies would help to keep the papers safe."

Barnett made his escape at four in the morning, and his house, the great seal and the acts of the assembly survived.

The main body of Sherman's left wing entered Milledgeville early on November 23, parading through the main streets between rows of black faces along the crowded sidewalks. The soldiers yelped, "Come on! Come on, Sambo! Come on, Dinah!" A tall girl rushed into the column, hugging two men. "Yes, I'm gwine!" she cried. "But some of you's gotta marry me."

An old black woman shouted, "God bless you, Yanks! Come at last! God knows how long I been waitin'."

Another woman shouted, "Lawsy, Massas, I can't laugh enough! I'se so glad to see you."

The 70th Indiana saw a white shirt flapping atop a pole before a shanty at the edge of town, and a soldier shouted to a band of Negro women in the yard, "What's that for?"

"We wants to let you know we's surrendered."

General Slocum settled in the Milledgeville Hotel, and Sherman, who came with the XIV Corps later in the day, made headquarters in the governor's mansion. Both generals were besieged by people seeking protection for their homes. The commander found the rooms of the mansion bare except for a few pieces of heavy furniture. His staff improvised a dining table from planks placed across camp chairs. Sherman made his bed on the floor.

Dr. Thomas Fitzgerald Green, the asylum superintendent, was granted guards by Slocum, and the Green family lost only two mules, but twenty-one-year-old Anna Maria was overcome: "We were despondent, our heads bowed and our hearts crushed—the Yankees in possession of Milledgeville. The Yankee flag waved from the Capitol — Our degradation was bitter."

The girl's spirits rose during the day: "We knew it could not be long . . . we went through the house singing, 'We live and die with Davis.' How can they hope to subjugate the South? The people are firmer than ever before."

During the day some of the troops, most of them from the 3rd Wisconsin and 107th New York, staged a mock legislative session in the statehouse, a rowdy scene that attracted thousands of officers and men to the building.

Colonel J. C. Robinson of the 1st Division's 3rd Brigade was elected president and other officers were named, most of whom were kept busy laying out under the tables members who suffered from "bourbon fits," an ailment "rather prevalent among the honorable members." Theodore Davis, the *Harper's Weekly* artist, served as page.

Kilpatrick, who had been drinking heavily, told of a raid on a plantation cellar: "Though I am a very modest man that never blows his own horn, like other gentlemen whom I could name, I must honestly tell you that I am Old Harry on raids. My men, too, have strongly imbibed the spirit . . . I must confess that my fellows are very inquisitive . . . if perchance they discover a deserted cellar, believing that it was kindly left for their use by the considerate owner, they take charge of it. It sometimes happens, too, that they look after the plate and other little matters. Coming to my own particular raid, it was one of the handsomest and most brilliant affairs of the War."

"Mr. Speaker, a point of order!" A member reeled to his feet. "I believe it is the custom to treat the speaker."

"Yes," Kilpatrick said, "I believe it is the custom. I beg to inform this honorable body that I am going to treat the speaker." He pulled out a brandy bottle and drank. The chamber rang with cheers.

The committee returned, singing "We Won't Go Home until Morning," and opened a noisy debate on the state of Georgia. The body finally passed resolutions repealing the Ordinance of Secession as "highly indiscreet" and "a damned farce." A committee was appointed to whip Georgia back into the Union—Sherman's army. The mock session broke up in bedlam when soldiers rushed in shouting, "The Yankees are coming!" and the members fled in noisy imitation of the Georgia lawmakers.

The mood of the invaders then changed abruptly. Hundreds of enlisted men crowded among the officers, bent upon destruction.

Soldiers began looting the statehouse, "a very bad exhibition of a very lawless nature," Sergeant Fleharty said. Hundreds of books were flung out the windows onto the wet ground, where soldiers tramped over "choice literary and scientific works" and picked up those they wanted. One horseman deliberately rode through the crowd to let his horse trample the books. Captain Storrs saw soldiers pawing through a copy of Audubon's *Birds,* and bought a volume of Washington Irving's works from a bummer for a few cents. "It seems a pity that a guard could not have been placed," Storrs thought. Lieutenant Colonel Samuel Merrill, who thought it was "melancholy to watch the books disappear from the shelves," was reminded of the vandalism of the Arabs in the sacking of Egyptian treasures—but Merrill succumbed and stole one volume. The indignant Major James Connolly of Illinois saw officers and men carrying books away by the armful: "It is a downright shame . . . I am sure General Sherman will, some day, regret that he permitted this . . . " Lieutenant Alfred Trego of the 102nd Illinois, who stole a dictionary and a copy of Macaulay's essays, saw Sherman enter the library and look about briefly. "He looked pretty rough," Trego said.

Major Connolly said he could have taken a thousand dollars' worth of law books, but refused to touch them: "I should feel ashamed of myself every time I saw one of them in my book case at home. I don't object to stealing horses, mules, niggers and all such *little things,* but I will not engage in plundering and destroying public libraries."

The troops entertained themselves with a stack of unsigned Georgia currency—billions of dollars' worth, some of them thought, though it was "less valuable than coffee grains." The money was used to light pipes and kindle fires, and became stakes in fantastic poker games. Soldiers took "bushels" of the bills to women textile workers, who said they had not been paid for months. The women were briefly ecstatic over their fortunes in crisp thousand-dollar bills.

The state arsenal was emptied of its pathetic assortment of arms —muskets, antique rifles and shotguns, spears, short swords and Bowie knives. Many of the crude blades were taken by army butchers or carried off by infantrymen who wore them in their belts like the swords of officers for a few days. Ammunition from the magazine was hauled off and dumped into the Oconee River.

The last of the XX Corps approached the town in the late afternoon, guided by towering flames from the state penitentiary, which cast a glow across the countryside. The remaining inmates—women, it was reported—had set fire to the buildings and escaped. One of the prisoners, a convicted murderer, joined the corps, and at least one of the women convicts, a "hard case," put on a Federal uniform and entered the camp of the 33rd Indiana, where, as a local historian put it, she plied "an ancient trade."

Most of the 30,000 troops who were to pass through the town had already swarmed in and about Milledgeville, tramping through yards and gardens as if they were highways, stripping fences and outbuildings for fuel. Colonel Merrill saw that most women of the town smiled pleasantly even as soldiers rummaged through their houses. It was the older women who were defiant, and they were quieted by their daughters: "Please, Mamma, don't ra'r so!"

Sherman spared two large cotton warehouses in Milledgeville, one owned by a German and the other by a Georgian who had married a New Jersey woman. Sherman knew that they were worthless, but accepted bonds from these merchants certifying that the cotton would not be used for the Confederate cause. The general also spared a flour mill owned by one Hugh Treanor, an Irishman. These decisions, made on the spur of the moment, were typical of his arbitrary approach. In similar cases he frequently ordered cotton burned without ceremony, since it was clear to him that the precious commodity would be used by Confederates when he had passed on.

He was, of course, acutely aware that renewed Confederate activity sprang up in the wake of the passage of his isolated body of troops.

At least one instance of rape went unreported by the invaders in Milledgeville. Mrs. Kate Latimer Nichols, the twenty-seven-year-old wife of a Confederate army captain, was in bed with an illness on her farm outside the town, alone but for her servants and one Negro guard who stood duty at her door. Two Federal soldiers appeared, threatened to shoot the guard if he did not step aside, entered the room and raped Mrs. Nichols.

News of the incident, an unspeakable dishonor in this time and place, seeped out slowly. Anna Maria Green heard of it: "The worst of their acts was committed to poor Mrs. Nichols—violence done and atrocity committed that ought to make her husband an enemy unto death. Poor woman, I fear that she has been driven crazy." Mrs. Nichols was to die later in a mental institution.

Most women of the town had suffered increasing hardships during the war as inflation ravaged the Confederacy. Federal officers noted ruinous prices in the markets: Coffee was $18 a pound, tea unobtainable, both sugar and butter $7 a pound, ham and lard $4, flour and beefsteak $1. Jean cloth sold for $15 a yard.

In this setting, the feasting of Sherman's troops on Thanksgiving Day provided a bizarre scene—but it was to become even more memorable.

During the noisy celebrations about the campfires, a few ragged and cadaverous men appeared, stalking slowly toward the bluecoats. Silence fell in the streets. These were Federal veterans who had escaped the terrible prison pen at Andersonville, far away to the southwest. These men had come almost one hundred miles across enemy country into Sherman's track, evading rebel patrols and bloodhounds. They gazed with "wild animal" stares at the well-fed troops in their blue uniforms, and wept at sight of the American flag and the rich food. The aroma of roasting pork, beef and poultry had drawn them unerringly into the town.

Colonel C. D. Kerr noted that his troops were "sickened and infuriated" when they saw these men and realized how near death they were, having been starved like chained animals in the midst of plenty.

Other reports of Confederate brutality reached the army at Milledgeville: Gossips said Confederates had cut the throats of men captured near Macon; two of them had lived to tell the tale because the "Rebs had sliced their throats too far up."

There was another report that men from the columns who had been captured by Wheeler had been given a choice: death or taking an oath of allegiance to the Confederacy.

Sherman's army began moving out of Milledgeville on November 24. There were reports that the town was to be burned, but only the arsenal and magazine were destroyed, blown up in explosions that damaged churches in Capitol Square. The church interiors were already in ruins, most of the pews chopped up for firewood and the pipe organ of St. Stephen's Episcopal Church poured full of molasses.

Before nine o'clock the next morning, November 25, the last Federal brigade prowled through the town, rounded up stragglers and soon crossed the wooden toll bridge to the east bank of the Oconee. The bridge's owner, "a fat, dirty, lazy-looking citizen," begged officers not to burn the structure. He told Major Connolly that though he had never been more than five miles from the river, he had "allers bin for the Union and wus yet." He also protested that he was a Mason and deserved protection, in vain. Soldiers set fires on the bridge, and within ten minutes the roaring timbers began plunging into the river. The bluecoats disappeared.

A Milledgeville newspaper editor walked through the litter of papers in the streets in "a stillness almost Sabbath," and found the statehouse knee-deep in scattered papers, plastering cracked, windowpanes shattered: "A full detail of all the enormities . . . would fill a volume, and some of them would be too bad to publish. In short, if an army of Devils just let loose from the bottomless pit were to invade the country, they could not be much worse than Sherman's army."

The quiet was broken by the arrival of Wheeler's men. Anna Maria Green's heart "leaped for joy" when she saw them: "A few ragged men came riding up and bowed and brandished their pistols, the tears streamed from our eyes—strong men wept—God bless our soldiers, our poor suffering soldiers."

In Anna Maria Green's eyes the troopers were heroes—and her Negro servant, Harriet, was so moved by the sight of a barefoot Kentuckian that she gave him a pair of new shoes given to her the day before. "I can do better without them than you can," she said. Anna Maria wrote, "If the Yankees knew of that little incident

. . . they might feel a little less kindly to our servants than they pretend."

On Sunday, when she went to church at St. Stephen's and sat amid the wreckage with a tiny congregation, Anna Maria was outraged: "God will not permit desecration of his holy temple to go unpunished."

7
"I don't war on women and children"

A new phase of the march opened as Sherman's columns moved east of Milledgeville into swampy country drained by the Oconee and Ogeechee rivers and their myriad tributaries. It was a country of dark, sluggish streams that wound through waterlogged, moss-hung forests. The streams themselves were the last natural barriers between the army and Savannah, which lay some 125 miles eastward. In ten days the army had covered half of its route through Georgia, virtually without opposition. The route to the sea, it appeared, was still open. Sherman no longer gave serious thought to advancing on Augusta, but he now planned a final deception for the Confederates as he moved on toward his goal on the Atlantic.

Howard's southern wing, which was south of Milledgeville, advanced into the low country by approaching the Oconee some miles below the capital. Howard was to continue wrecking the railroad and was to cross the river and veer northward to approach Slocum's wing near Sandersville, a courthouse village some two days' march in advance.

Sherman now ordered Judson Kilpatrick to demonstrate against Augusta with all his cavalry, a raid of about sixty miles to the northeast. Since the southern flank was now well east of Macon, and out of danger from rebel concentrations there, Kilpatrick was free to shift his force across the army's front and move northward at once. By this move Sherman hoped to draw off Joe Wheeler's cavalry, to break the Augusta-Savannah Railroad—and to attempt the rescue of Federal prisoners from an improvised pen at the village of Millen.

Kilpatrick stowed his luggage in infantry wagons, stripped his troopers to "jockey weight," and slaughtered the weakest of his horses. Troopers threw blankets over the heads of five hundred animals, cracked their skulls with axes and left the carcasses on the plantation where they had camped, to the consternation of their host, who gazed about and said, "My God, I'll have to move."

Many infantrymen were happy to see Kilpatrick off on his raid, for his unpopularity in the ranks was notable even in an army in which traditional infantry-cavalry rivalries were intense. There was something absurdly theatrical about Kilpatrick—who was indeed an amateur thespian in civilian life. One officer said, "I could hardly look at Kilpatrick without laughing." Though he was a fearless soldier, the impetuous Little Kil was boastful and obnoxious, given to fanciful reports of his skirmishes. He was also one of the army's most devoted skirt-chasers.

Sherman clung to Kilpatrick despite all criticism. "I know he's a hell of a damned fool," the commander said, "but I want just that sort of man to command my cavalry on this expedition." Handicapped by a recent wound, Kilpatrick had ridden in a carriage in the first days of the march, accompanied by his fourteen-year-old nephew, whose school lessons he planned to hear nightly. Now, at last, Kilpatrick was on horseback once more and ready to return to his trade.

In his move across the army's front the cavalryman brushed resisting rebel bands from his path, including the small force General Harry Wayne had carried south from Milledgeville by train.

Wayne and his troops halted about fifteen miles south of the capital in the swamps bordering the Oconee River, where a railroad trestle spanned the dark stream. This ragtag little force settled into position, some 650 men and boys assigned to hold the lower crossings of the Oconee against Howard's wing, which was more than 30,000 strong. Wayne was under orders to defend the trestle "to the last extremity," since the railroad led eastward toward Savannah.

Uneasily aware of the inadequacy of his force, his lack of combat experience—and of the dangers of being flanked from either direction, Wayne turned over command to Major Capers. On the west bank of the river, where danger was greatest, Capers placed his cadets from the military academy, reinforced by a few mounted

Kentuckians. The rest of the troops, assorted units of Georgia Home Guards, paroled convicts and prison guards, settled along the east bank. A single cannon, mounted on a railroad flat car, overlooked the crossing from the rear.

The enemy appeared on the second day, a band of Kilpatrick's riders on their way to Augusta. The cavalrymen lost forty-five men to Wayne's stubborn ragamuffins, but when Federal guns came up and opened a noisy artillery duel, Wayne's convicts vanished to the rear. In the midst of this confusion there was an alarm from an outpost eight miles downstream, where Yankees were reported crossing at Ball's Ferry. Wayne's nervousness increased when Kilpatrick's men set the trestle on fire, and though Confederates beat out the flames, they could no longer hold the position, Wayne thought. He was soon in full retreat, but sent a soldierly report to Hardee in Savannah: "I have held the bridge to the last extremity."

By the next morning, when a pontoon bridge was firmly in place and Howard's wing was streaming over the river, the 55th Illinois went over swiftly, "noisily gay, keeping up an incessant roar, singing, shouting and imitating the cries of bird and beast." The men sang hymns as they passed through the swamps, and during a halt, their longest since leaving Atlanta, the regiment washed clothing, "for which there was certainly great need."

The troops saw their first Spanish moss, palmettos, sugar cane and magnolias; one soldier killed a coral snake and carried it along in a jar of whiskey. The advance emerged abruptly from the lowlands into a dry country of pine barrens, where farms were small and poor, with only an occasional field of dwarf corn growing in the midst of the woods. Foragers found that some of the corn ears were no more than six inches long. One farmer told an officer, "Some of my land averages five or six bushels an acre, and some of it don't average nothing." From tumbledown cabins sallow, sickly-looking women stared dully, surrounded by throngs of children—dirt-eaters, some of the soldiers said.

Despite the army's unopposed advance through this country, it was followed so closely by rebel cavalry that stragglers were snapped up at once. The 2nd Minnesota made a sixteen-mile night march out of Milledgeville and lost a fourteen-year-old drummer boy, one Simmers. Drummer William Bircher saw the boy stumbling, half asleep, and carried his blanket and drum for him, but still Simmers could not keep up with his regiment. "Let me rest," he said. "I'll sleep a few minutes and then follow." Bircher pulled him back into line and tried to keep an eye on him, but Simmers could not be found when the column halted for a rest. Bircher felt that he would never see him again.

Bircher's fears were well grounded. In retaliation against the invaders, Confederates had already opened a campaign of counter-terror. One of Wheeler's squadrons, a few miles in Sherman's front, came upon some bluecoat foragers looting a plantation in the pine woods. Major J. P. Austin, of the Confederate 9th Kentucky Cavalry, led his men in swift revenge. Austin stormed into the house, which he found "almost completely wrecked, an elegant mirror and other furniture smashed, the piano split open with an axe." Kindling was piled under the house, ready to be ignited.

A Federal soldier waited in one room, holding a young woman before him as a shield. Major Austin admired the frightened girl: "She stiffened herself, and with a look in her eyes such as Joan of Arc must have worn when she was going to the stake, exclaimed, 'Shoot through me and kill him.' " The Kentuckians surrounded the bluecoat, and one of them thrust a pistol over the girl's shoulder to shoot him through the head. Austin's men killed every forager in the party.

Other atrocities were reported this week. To the army's rear, not far from Milledgeville, an unknown Federal victim was being buried —a homesick seventeen-year-old from Iowa who was an early victim of the mounting campaign of terror waged between Sherman and his adversaries.

At least two hundred stragglers and deserters from the Federal columns had been captured between Atlanta and Milledgeville. These men were forced to take oaths of allegiance at gunpoint and were then dragooned into the rebel service as "galvanized Yankees." The reluctant turncoats had been herded into a camp and drilled for service—a recruiting technique resorted to by both sides during the war.

The seventeen-year-old Iowan had escaped from this camp one night, but was captured a few miles away and put on trial for treason to the Confederacy. His court-martial was unmoved by his pathetic defense: "I just wanted to see my mother." The boy was shot by a firing squad and buried beside the Oconee. Some months later his body was to be exhumed and returned to Iowa.

Sherman sought to deal firmly with Confederate guerrillas who came into his hands, but he made an unpromising start. Soon after crossing the Oconee, the commander was presented the case of the fierce young rebel Rufus Kelly, who was treated as a guerrilla though he had fought bravely and in the open, recklessly resisting overwhelming force at Gordon. Kelly had been riding in a Federal wagon for several days, closely guarded. He was hauled before a court-martial after the first day's ride. The trial was brevity itself. "Guilty of murder," a Federal officer said. The army then began a game of cat and mouse with Kelly.

A regimental band paraded about him several times, blaring "The Dead March." Kelly was told that he would be shot at sunrise and was led to headquarters, where Sherman questioned him about roads, rivers, swamps and bridges on the route to Savannah.

"Do you know you're going to be shot in the morning?" Sherman said.

"They told me. But I'm not guilty of murder. I shot in self defense. Anyway, General, a man can die only once."

Sherman paused, looking keenly at Kelly, then spoke to the guard: "See that the sentence of the court martial is carried out and have him shot in the morning." But he smiled quizzically as he said it, and Kelly appeared to take heart.

"The Dead March" was played again for Kelly the next morning and the morning thereafter, but he was not shot. Kelly was beginning to feel that the court-martial was "a farce" staged to frighten him, and almost wished for the firing squad: "I was sick of this Dead March business. It got on my nerves . . . "

The next night Kelly slipped from the wagon, crawled away from his inattentive guards and disappeared in a swamp, where he hid for two days and nights. He improvised a crutch and hobbled back to his father's farm near Gordon. He had been a captive only six days.

The small town of Sandersville, a hotbed of rebel resistance that was chosen by Joe Wheeler for his first attempted rear-guard action, was the scene of another Confederate atrocity.

Wheeler and his remaining Confederate veterans trotted into

the main street of Sandersville on the evening of November 25 and awaited the appearance of Sherman's vanguard.

From the yard of a nearby house, nine-year-old Ella Mitchell had a glimpse of Wheeler, "a very small, very erect man, dressed in grey, wearing a crimson sash and a large black plumed hat . . . "

Fightin' Joe Wheeler, now a few days past his twenty-eighth birthday, was said to be the youngest—and was probably the smallest —major general ever commissioned in America. He stood five feet five inches tall, and weighed 120 pounds "with a rock in each pocket and his hair combed down wet," as one veteran said. The miniature West Pointer was an unlikely warrior, courteous, dignified, and pompous, but an unsparing campaigner who rode farther and harder on less food than most of his troops. Sometimes, his men noted, he seemed to forget the war for hours on end as he rode with his column looking intently upward into the woods in search of a "bee tree"— honey was one of his passions.

Wheeler's staff could not recall that he ever laughed: "He buzzes about, taking himself and everybody about him frightfully in earnest . . . He'll fight; game as a pebble. But there's one trouble with Wheeler's valor. It overruns itself." As one of his officers said, he fought flies with the same ferocity that he fought the enemy. The boy general betrayed his intensity in every movement: "He never walks, he lopes . . . as restless as a disembodied spirit and as active as a cat . . . frank, fearless, outspoken to the verge of bluntness."

Wheeler was born near Augusta, Georgia, the son of a prosperous Northern merchant who had become bankrupt after twenty years in the South and returned to New England. Fightin' Joe had been educated in Connecticut, graduated near the bottom of his West Point class (his poorest grades were in cavalry tactics), and fought Indians on the Western frontier, where he won his nickname. The war brought rapid promotion to command of the cavalry of the Army of Tennessee, in which he became celebrated as a raider. Wheeler had never fought with a victorious army; in the long series of Confederate defeats from Shiloh to Atlanta, it was always Wheeler's reckless, undisciplined riders who covered the rear. The general was the author of *Cavalry Tactics,* a manual notable for its concept of the use of cavalry as mounted infantry.

Wheeler's bravery was unquestioned; he had led an infantry regiment through the slaughter at Shiloh, holding the unit's colors when others fell; once cornered by enemy cavalry on a bridge in

Tennessee, he jumped his horse fifteen feet into the swollen Duck River with fifty of his riders behind him, and led a dozen survivors to safety through the raging current and a hail of Federal bullets. In the Atlanta fighting he had once defeated Sherman's cavalry and captured General George Stoneman and more than five hundred of his men.

Wheeler's command drove the Federal advance from Sandersville after a brief skirmish and settled in the town for the night. This rare, if temporary, success inspired a Sandersville lynch mob to murder some of Wheeler's captives. A mob appeared near midnight —probably a band of Confederate troops—pushed aside the frightened guards, carried the Federal prisoners into a nearby field, and shot them down.

About three in the morning, Pincus Happ, one of the few able-bodied men left in Sandersville, went to the Mitchell home and asked Ella's father to help bury the dead Yankees. "Mother was afraid for father to go, he was so ill, but he went and took the two Negro men servants we had . . . the party buried the soldiers before dawn."

The Mitchell family was at breakfast when rifle fire broke out, Wheeler's men fled past at a gallop, and bullets spattered on the roof. Young Ella Mitchell saw that Yankees had come in force: "In a few minutes our house was filled with the surging mass. In a little while even the table cloth left, and the food disappeared in a second. Fences were torn down, hogs shot, cows butchered, women crying, children screaming, pandemonium reigned. Then the jail, court house, peoples' barns and a large factory that made buckets and saddle-trees were all ablaze . . . "

From a nearby house "L.F.J.," a sixteen-year-old war widow, watched the end of the skirmish between the bluecoats and Wheeler's men. She sat in a window with soldiers in battle line so close by that she could touch them. A Confederate soldier shouted into the room: "For God's sake, ladies, go into your cellar! Don't you know these bullets will kill you?" Since they had no cellar, the women huddled beside a chimney while bullets "rattled like hail-stones against the house."

One of the last rebel soldiers to leave town warned the women: "Take care of yourselves, ladies, we'll have to run. . . . Lock your doors, keep inside. If the Yankees come to the doors, unlock them and stand in them. Be sure to ask for a guard. Be polite, and you won't be mistreated, I hope. Good-bye. God bless you ladies . . . "

The young widow turned to see a blue column filling the Milledgeville road: "It seemed to me the whole world was coming. Here came the 'wood-cutters'— clearing the way before the army. Men with axes on their shoulders, men with spades, men with guns. Men driving herds of cattle— cows, goats, hogs, sheep. Men on horseback with bunches of turkeys, bunches of chickens, ducks and guineas swinging on both sides of the horse like saddle-bags. Then the wagons—Oh! the wagons—in every direction—wagons! wagons!"

Tents were pitched in the yard and garden, and soldiers "with hateful leers from their red eyes" sliced stolen hams on the porch, ransacked outbuildings of sugar, flour, salt, lard, syrup, grain and potatoes, and killed the cows.

Sherman had left his camp at six-thirty the morning of November 26 and was behind Slocum's lead brigade as it skirmished with Wheeler's cavalry into Sandersville. The troops fought through banks of fog so dense that some Federal cavalrymen formed on the flank of a waiting regiment, ready to join it in a charge, when they discovered the strangers were some of Wheeler's Texans, and were forced to flee. Rebels fired on the head of the column from the courthouse, street corners and behind houses, but fell back after a few rounds. Federal losses were one dead and eleven wounded. Confederate losses went unrecorded, but they were not inconsequential. As Sherman's lead files trotted into the village, officers of a Wisconsin regiment were forced to restrain some of their Chippewa Indians who were gleeful at the sight of Confederate dead in the street and thought it "a great waste of scalps" to bypass so many long-haired corpses.

With resistance in Sandersville at an end, Sherman entered and sent Hitchcock to the door of a large brick house, where his knock was answered by a Federal soldier who had broken in from the rear. A woman shouted from within the house: "I demand protection!" Hitchcock ordered the soldier to leave. "General Sherman's here now, Madam. You will be protected."

"I demand protection because General Sherman is a Catholic!"*

"Madam, it's a pity the Catholics in the South haven't acted so as to protect themselves." The still-invisible woman made no reply.

*Mrs. Sherman was a Catholic, but the general was not.

Sherman sat on the steps of the house, growling about the firing from the courthouse and the murder of his soldiers. He later spoke bluntly to the women of the house, a Mrs. Green and two relatives: "I'll protect you, but I'll give you no guard—and I'm going to burn this town." The general then went into the old woman's room, where he talked so entertainingly that Mrs. Green, who was "sharp" at first, "softened a good deal."

A Methodist minister came to intercede for the town's women and children. The men who had killed the Federal prisoners, he said, "were not Georgians, much less inhabitants of Sandersville and Washington County." The innocent, he said, should not be punished. Sherman heard him out and said mildly, "I don't war on women and children."

Sherman told the women, "Houses will not be burned, but the courthouse and stores will." He rode through town to his camp, just to the north, but left an officer behind to burn the courthouse and jail. There was no one to plead for the old landmarks—the courthouse, a handsome Greek Revival building of stuccoed brick, and the adjoining jail, where Aaron Burr had slept overnight on the way north to be tried for treason more than fifty years before. Soldiers also burned the railroad station at the nearby village of Tennille.

Sandersville provided another instance of the warm-hearted response of some Federal soldiers to the suffering of civilians. The widow "L.F.J." stood on her porch with a Federal guard as flames of the burning courthouse illuminated the village. The stench of garbage from Sherman's camps was intense, and smoke obscured houses just across the street. L.F.J.'s infant son wailed in his crib.

"Why does he cry so?" the soldier asked.

"He's hungry. For two days I've had nothing to eat, and I can't nurse him."

The young soldier's eyes filled with tears. "I'll be relieved soon," he said, "and when I draw rations this evening I'll bring them to you."

The guard brought flour and coffee, and with pans borrowed from the Federal camps, the cook produced biscuits and hot coffee. The young guard joined the family for its meager dinner.

Elsewhere in the army other soldiers revealed their compassion for their victims. Not far from Sandersville, in a poor, barren area, Captain Charles Belknap and his foragers found a surprise in a remote mud-chinked log cabin. The place appeared to be deserted, but in the dark room the soldiers found two small girls, one about three and the other five years old. They were so grimy that Belknap at first thought they were Negroes. They wore thin cotton dresses made from sacks with holes ripped out for the arms.

The troops found no trace of the parents. The little girls, as shy as young partridges, said only, "Mamma gone, Mamma gone." Hot food won their confidence, and they were soon prattling away to the soldiers, who built a fire, bathed the girls and washed and combed their hair. Belknap carried the children to neighboring cabins and tried to leave them, but was refused by one woman after another: "I've got a houseful of my own."

The bummers stole clothing for the little girls, and before night the motherless sisters had a complete wardrobe. A soldier from Michigan removed the cotton sacks from their thin bodies and dressed them in the best the countryside could afford.

The girls rode a pack mule all day, and when the party camped for the night, each of them slept in a soldier's arms, warm and dry despite a rainstorm. The two were turned over to the regiment the following night, and began their long ride toward Savannah on the backs of soldiers.

In his camp just outside Sandersville, the general had his first impression of Confederate reaction to his sweep through Georgia. Major Nichols of his staff had found some recent newspapers during the day, and amused his chief by reading forecasts of the army's doom.

The Augusta *Constitutionalist* urged Georgians to destroy everything of value in Sherman's path, and proclaimed that the Federal army was now vulnerable and might easily be cut to pieces: "The opportunity is ours. The hand of God is in it. The blow, if we can give it as it should be given, may end the war. . . . Sherman has many weary miles to march . . . It is absurdity to talk about his making a winter campaign with no communication with his Government. He is retreating—simply retreating . . . "

The *Savannah News* predicted the "utter annihilation" of Sherman's army at the hands of "an insulted and outraged people," all of whom would become guerrillas.

The *Columbus Daily Times* made a feeble joke about the treacherous swampy terrain in the path of the invaders: "Favorable *grounds* exist for checking the advance of Sherman towards Savannah—grounds soft and moist."

Sherman also read stories detailing his strength: "A St. Louis telegram states that Gen. Sherman's army in Georgia consists of . . . " It was clear that the rebels had learned of his strength through Northern newspapers before the army left Atlanta. Sherman growled: "I've a good mind to resign as soon as this campaign's over. It's impossible to carry on a war with a free press."

Henry Hitchcock saw that the general was not seriously disturbed by the editorial fulminations, and that he recovered swiftly from his irritation. Wheeler's prompt disappearance after the skirmish in Sandersville cheered Sherman. He now expected no serious opposition in Georgia. "Pierce the shell of the Confederacy and it's hollow," he said. "All hollow inside."

One of the first travelers to observe the devastating scope of Sherman's passage through the state was Eliza Frances Andrews, the daughter of a Washington County judge. Eliza crossed the desolate region in the immediate wake of the invading army. With three other women, she made the sixty-five-mile journey from the village of Sparta to Gordon, riding a few miles on a train that tilted and almost overturned on the rough tracks. A few miles beyond, where they hired seats on farm wagons bound for Milledgeville, the women overheard the doleful comment of a countryman: "Milledgeville's like hell; you kin get thar easy enough, but gittin' out again would beat the Devil himself . . . If them ladies ever gets to Gordon, they'll be good walkers. Sherman's done licked that country clean."

Eliza entered the track of the enemy at once: "About three miles from Sparta we struck the 'Burnt Country' . . . and then I could better understand the wrath and desperation of these poor people." She saw hardly a fence during her journey; grainfields were trampled flat, and carcasses of horses, cattle and hogs lined the road. Eliza sniffed frequently at a vial of cologne to overcome the stench. Hundreds of pillaged houses stood vacant with ruined doors and windows, yards littered, outbuildings in ashes. "Here and there" were blackened chimneys of burned homes.

Ragged Confederate soldiers thronged the road, so many that it was like passing through the heart of a great city. Hundreds of men squatted at the roadside gnawing raw turnips, meat skins and parched corn—the grain grubbed from the earth where Sherman's horses had left it.

There was a long wait for a ferry outside Milledgeville at the site of the burned toll bridge over the Oconee. Eliza then passed a field where Sherman's men had camped. Little of value was left on the campsite; tufts of cotton blew over piles of rotting grain and carcasses of cattle. Men were already ploughing in a corner of the field, preparing for spring crops.

When she reached Gordon, Eliza Andrews saw the most complete destruction in the "Burnt Country": "There was nothing left of the poor little village but ruins, charred and black as Yankee hearts." The depot was a ruin of smoked brick and crumpled tin, and rails were twisted around the trunks of trees. Several poor families were living in a locomotive and some railroad cars run off the track by Sherman's men. The embittered Eliza noted that the invaders, not content with general destruction, had taken revenge on innocent trees, "whose only fault was that they grew on southern soil."

8
"Even the sun seemed to hide its face"

On November 29, when they had been two weeks on the march, Sherman and his staff camped in a huge grove of pines. The general went to bed early, as usual, but dispatch riders came and went for hours, bearing news of his distant columns. Sherman dealt with each messenger promptly in his intense, brusque manner, then went back to sleep at once.

In the early hours of November 30, Henry Hitchcock heard someone poking at the dying embers of the campfire and saw the general, dressed in red flannel drawers and a woolen shirt under a ragged dressing gown, his bare feet thrust into slippers. "I always wake up at 3 or 4 o'clock," Sherman said, "and can't sleep again till after daylight. I like to walk through camp then. It's the best time to hear any movement at a distance."

Hitchcock thought the general was the most restless man in the army: He "never sleeps a night straight through, and frequently comes out and pokes around in this style, disregarding all remonstrances as to taking cold." The staff thought the general's neuralgia, which had settled in his right arm and shoulder, was the result of his night prowling.

Hitchcock knew Sherman made up his sleep with catnaps every day. "I heard a story about you, General—that a soldier saw you asleep one day near Atlanta and said, 'There's a Major General drunk while we have to fight . . . ' "

Sherman laughed. "It's true. It was a hot June day and I lay under a tree, tired out, with my face covered. I woke up and said,

'No, boys, not drunk, but I was up all last night, and need a little sleep.' "

Good news came to the commander during the night. Kilpatrick had raided within thirty miles of Augusta, burned a railroad bridge and driven Joe Wheeler's cavalry away after a sharp fight. Rebel cavalry had been pressing him daily, but all was well—there was no sign of Confederate infantry on that front.

An infantry brigade, pushed forward by Slocum in support of Kilpatrick, had taken a bridge over the Ogeechee without opposition. Though he had no word from General Jeff Davis, who was at the head of the XIV Corps, Sherman concluded that he should have reached the town of Louisville by now. "He must be there," Sherman told Hitchcock, "or otherwise Hardee would have stood and fought at the Ogeechee. We've flanked him out of that line." He was now confident that the army would reach the gates of Savannah without fighting a pitched battle. The first prize of his audacious campaign was within Sherman's grasp.

As Sherman guessed, Hardee was contenting himself with gathering a small force of Confederate defenders within Savannah itself, and with hurriedly improving old earthworks that guarded the city from the west. In Augusta, the timorous Braxton Bragg merely waited with his garrison of 10,000 troops. Sherman, who knew Bragg well, had no fear that the Confederate would emerge to challenge him. The commander was elated by prospects.

In truth, Kilpatrick had given Sherman a false impression, for his cavalrymen had been fighting for their very lives, and the bold stand of Joe Wheeler's wild riders on the Augusta front augured growing Confederate resistance. Kilpatrick had camped on the railroad near the village of Waynesboro on November 26 when, about midnight, Wheeler's troopers galloped over them, scattering pickets, leaping log barricades and terrorizing the sleeping Federals. Wheeler took many prisoners, fifty horses, several regimental colors, and numerous blankets and overcoats.

Kilpatrick had escaped because he was in a nearby house with some women. Little Kil barely avoided capture by leaping from the house with staff officers, leaving behind two handsome brown women who were the talk of the envious infantry. Kilpatrick recovered from "the folly of a misspent night" to lead his squadrons into a nightmare "skirmish" that bore little resemblance to the trifling incident he reported to Sherman.

Fighting continued throughout the day of November 27 as Kilpatrick fell back from one road barricade to another in some of the war's most furious cavalry clashes; galloping squadrons hurtled together with a ringing of sabers and crackling of pistols and carbines at point-blank range. The Confederates, convinced that the bluecoats were raiding against Augusta, fought ferociously to save the city.

Kilpatrick was saved by infantry hurried forward by General Slocum, a full division led by General Absalom Baird. Little Kil dismissed lightly the final hours of his trial: "I deemed it prudent to retire to our infantry."

Joe Wheeler told another story: "About 3 A.M. I sent Hume's division to gain the enemy's rear . . . I charged the enemy's . . . front with the balance of my command, driving the enemy from his fortified position . . . killing a great many who refused to surrender . . . the rout was complete."

Wheeler reported that he lost twelve of his Confederate buglers in the furious action—but that he had demoralized the entire Federal cavalry column, "capturing, killing and wounding nearly 200, and completely stampeding the entire force."

Major James Connolly, who had come up with General Baird and the Federal infantry, noted that Kilpatrick was in deeper trouble than he had acknowledged. Connolly was aroused late at night by one of Kilpatrick's officers, who came to plead for support: "They had been fighting day and night for the past three days; Wheeler's cavalry was all around them with a vastly superior force; they were out of ammunition, and men and horses were utterly worn out; Kilpatrick . . . had started him off at midnight to try and make his way to some infantry column and beg for support or they would all be lost."

Connolly soon had infantrymen on the way, without breakfast, the men growling complaints at having to save the skins of the notoriously inept cavalrymen. The infantry heard firing ahead and formed lines across their roadway. "In about ten minutes Kilpatrick's jaded cavalry hove into sight, skirmishing with Wheeler and retiring before him; but when they saw the line of blue coated infantry . . . they knew that they were saved, and sent up such shouts as never before were heard in these 'Piney Woods.' " The rebels fell back. Kilpatrick settled in Louisville for two days to rest horses and men.

Connolly could not conceal his contempt for Kilpatrick's riders, a prejudice he shared with most infantrymen: "These cavalrymen are a positive nuisance; they won't fight, and whenever they are around they are always in the way of those who will fight . . . Confound the cavalry. They're good for nothing but to run down horses and steal chickens."

On December 1 Sherman sent up orders that Kilpatrick was to attack Wheeler at every opportunity, and the running cavalry fighting erupted once more. Federal troopers and infantrymen, moving together toward Waynesboro, skirmished with Wheeler's men for miles.

On December 4 Kilpatrick finally drove off his tormentors by occupying Waynesboro after breaking Wheeler's line with the fire of new repeating rifles. In a final melee of charge and countercharge, the bluecoats pushed Wheeler's worn troopers eight miles out on the road toward Augusta, and the noisy little cavalry campaign in that quarter came to an end, to be echoed in the reports of Wheeler and Kilpatrick, each of whom claimed victory, as if their reputations were at stake in this obscure phase of Sherman's memorable march. Kilpatrick claimed that he had so crippled Wheeler that the rebel cavalry thereafter followed "discreetly" in Sherman's rear. Wheeler insisted that he had so "demoralized and defeated" Kilpatrick that he never again dared leave the protection of the infantry.

In any case, Sherman's entire force turned upon Savannah in the first week of December, leaving Wheeler to "protect Augusta"; within that city General Braxton Bragg continued to wait, isolated and helpless to use his troops. Sherman had survived the challenge without an hour's pause in the onward movement of his main columns.

On the roads in Sherman's immediate front, where foragers plundered their victims, some incidents revealed the brutalizing effects of war and lack of discipline. Some Federal soldiers took delight in torturing and bedeviling civilians in their path, confident that their crimes would never become known. The Canning family, on its plantation near the Ogeechee, met a few such men:

Nora M. Canning and her elderly husband met the invaders on November 28. The first men offered to pay for food, advised Mrs. Canning to move her meat indoors for safety, and helped to carry food in the house. "I began to think they were not so bad after all," Mrs. Canning said.

She was disillusioned swiftly when the band grew into a swarm of hundreds, and men pressed into the house through every door. The foragers now became bullies. "How long since the rebs passed here?" one of them asked. Mrs. Canning was silent.

"You goddam old bitch, why don't you answer me?"

"Don't you know Southern women know no such persons as 'Rebs'?" another soldier said.

"Then will you please tell me, ma'am, how long since the last Confederate soldier passed here?"

"General Wheeler's men have been passing for several days, and some of them went by this morning. I expect they're waiting for you down in the swamp."

The soldiers now became threatening, and some of them carried old Mr. Canning to the swamp. "We just want you to show us where you hid the syrup," they said. When Canning said he could not walk so far, soldiers hoisted him onto a mule and led the old man from sight.

Three soldiers dragged Canning from the mule. "Now, old man, where's your gold?"

"I've got none. I just came down here for a short stay. All our money's at home in the bank."

"That tale won't do. Your wife went to Macon and brought it down, a whole trunkful of gold and silver. Your nigger man said he could hardly lift it. Now, where's it at?"

"No," he said. "You're wrong. I have none."

They tied a rope around his neck and swung him from a tree limb until he was almost unconscious, then lowered him to earth and demanded the gold.

The old man shook his head. "I have none, you must believe me."

"You'll tell another tale before we're done." They raised him up once more, lowered him again and badgered him more fiercely. "Now, where's the gold, or we'll kill you. Your wife'll never know what became of you."

"I've told you the truth—I've got no gold." He croaked, "I'm an old man, and at your mercy. You can kill me, but I won't die with a lie on my lips. I've got no gold. I have a gold watch at the house, but nothing else."

"Swing the old rebel up again!" one of them said, and they lifted and then dropped him with greater force than ever. The old man lost consciousness. One of the soldiers said, "We like to have carried that game too far." When the old man had caught his breath, they propped him on his mule and carried him back to the house. Mrs. Canning was astonished when her husband turned to her and said, "Give them my watch."

"Why? They've no business with your watch."

"Give it to them and let them go," he said. "I'm almost dead." Mrs. Canning had the watch brought to them, and the looters went into the yard, where they forced the overseer's wife to lead them to the family's buried table silver.

The old man lay all night with "scorching fever," his tongue swollen and parched, his nose bleeding and a bloody liquid oozing from his ears. Mrs. Canning could give him no relief: "The Yankees had cut all the well ropes and stolen the buckets, so there was no water nearer than half a mile."

She was saved by a "rough-looking man from Iowa," a soldier who not only found a bucket and brought water, but gave her a few tablespoons of parched coffee and some brown sugar. "I never appreciated a cup of coffee more than I did that one," Mrs. Canning said.

When the army had gone, the Cannings looked out upon desolation: "We could hardly believe it was our home. One week before it was one of the most beautiful places in the state. Now it was a vast wreck. Gin-houses, packing screws, granary—all lay in ashes. Not a fence was to be seen for miles . . . the army had turned their stock into the fields and destroyed what they had not carried off. Burning cotton and grain filled the air with smoke, and even the sun seemed to hide its face."

Blacks and whites had fared alike. Canning had given his Negroes a month's provisions, hoping to save food, but they had been stripped of everything, even shoes from their feet.

A Negro woman complained: "What kind of folks is them Yankees? They won't even let the dead rest in their graves." She showed the Cannings the small coffin of a child she had buried a week or so earlier, dug up by the Federals and left on top of the ground "for the hog to root."

One Burke County woman whose farm was overrun was moved to take a unique personal revenge upon Sherman. Mrs. Gertrude Clanton Thomas was one of Georgia's rare women college graduates, widely read and intelligent and an outspoken opponent of slavery. She had written in her diary a few days earlier, "I don't know why

. . . but that man Sherman has interested me very much—perhaps it is . . . that all women admire successful courage and . . . a very brave man. Our enemy though he is, I can imagine that his wife loves him."

Now, in bitterness over her losses, Mrs. Thomas wrote a stinging letter to Ellen Sherman, repeating gossip she had heard in recent days.

> Mrs. Gen. Sherman:
>
> A few days since I read your husband's farewell telegram to you dated Atlanta. Will you believe it? For a moment I felt sorry for you, forgetting who you were and for what purpose he was coming among us, so my heart went out in womanly sympathy for you. Last week your husband's army found me in possession of wealth, tonight our plantations are a scene of ruin and desolation. You bade him Godspeed on his fiendish errand, did you not? You thought it a gallant deed to come amongst us where by his own confession he expected to find "only the shadow of an army," a brave act to frighten women and children! desolate homes, violate the sanctity of firesides and cause the "widow and orphan to curse the name Sherman for the cause" and this you did for what? To elevate the Negro race. Be satisfied Madame your wish had been accomplished. Enquire of Gen. Sherman when next you see him Who had been elevated to fill your place? . . . Did he tell you of the mulatto girl for whose safety he was so much concerned that she was returned to Nashville when he commenced his vandal march? This girl was spoken of by the Negroes whom you are willing to trust so implicitly as "Sherman's wife." Rest satisfied Mrs. Sherman and the apprehension of your northern sisters with regard to the elevation of the Negroes. Your husbands . . . are most of them provided with "a companion du voyage—" . . . I *will only add* that intensely Southern woman as I am *I pity you.**

Kilpatrick, racing ahead of the army once more, turned to his assignment to rescue Federal prisoners in the filthy pens at the crossroads settlement of Millen—where many survivors of the now abandoned Andersonville prison had been taken. The cavalry was too late. As his riders appeared on the banks of the Ogeechee, Kilpatrick saw the last of the prisoners being herded into boxcars by

*Whether Mrs. Thomas actually mailed this letter is uncertain. The original is in the Manuscript Division of the Duke University Library. The writer was unable to find other testimony that Sherman had a Negro mistress.

Confederates on the opposite side of the stream. These emaciated men were being shipped to other prisons, beyond the reach of Sherman.

Federal infantrymen who came up could only make an inspection of the miserable stockade in the pine woods where thousands of captured Federal soldiers had died. The first Federals found three corpses in the huts and buried them at the end of a long freshly dug trench that bore a crude board sign: 650 BURIED HERE.

The troops inspected everything closely, the hospital, the deadline, the "rather tasty" kitchen and ovens. "They kept at least 1,500 men here," one soldier said. Other estimates ran from 3,000 to 10,000.

Chaplain Bradley climbed to one of the guard posts and looked down on the huts and holes where prisoners had lived: "It made my heart ache . . . such miserable hovels, hardly fit for swine to live in."

He saw the shed where prisoners had been punished with stocks for seven men, "and they appeared to be well worn." Bradley heard men cursing Davis and the rebels as they left the place.

Captain Storrs of the 20th Connecticut, who drank some of the "very bad-tasting water" from the stream, thought the rebels had chosen the swampy site to hasten the deaths of prisoners from malaria: "I am afraid if the soldiers generally could visit this pen there would be no quarter given beyond here."

John Potter of the 101st Illinois wandered over the ground in a vain search for souvenirs: "It was the barest spot I ever saw. The trees and stumps and roots to the smallest fiber had been dug out for fuel, not a rag or a button or even a chip could be found."

Alex Downing, almost sickened by the sight of the pen, was one who helped to destroy it: "We burned everything here a match would ignite." Not long afterward, some of Slocum's men burned most of the village of Millen, including the hotel, depot and other buildings. They also burned a plantation house on the outskirts, and shot a pack of bloodhounds they found there.

In Washington this week there was growing anxiety for the safety of Sherman's army. Since the general had cut his telegraph line on November 12—three weeks earlier—the only news from the vanished columns had come through rebel newspapers, which claimed that the invaders faced starvation and must soon surrender. Lincoln beseeched Grant for news and reassurance, but the commander merely repeated his calm pronouncement that Sherman was in no danger, and that his army would reach the coast in due course.

Soon afterward Lincoln told some civilian visitors who asked about Sherman's army, "Grant says they're safe with such a general, and that if they can't get out where they want to, they can crawl back by the hole they went in at."

One day, in the midst of a conversation with the Pennsylvania Republican leader A. J. McClure, Lincoln said abruptly, "McClure, wouldn't you like to hear something about Sherman?" McClure turned eagerly and Lincoln laughed. "I'll be hanged if I wouldn't myself," he said.

Frank B. Carpenter, an artist who was at work on a portrait of the President, saw Lincoln forget himself when he was shaking hands with people at a crowded White House reception. Lincoln stared vacantly for a moment, then stirred and took the hand of a friend he had failed to recognize. "I'm sorry," he said. "I was thinking of a man down south."

The President addressed Congress on December 6, but though he said Sherman's march was the "most remarkable" news of the year from the fronts, he reported nothing of the army's progress and declined to speculate. To a crowd that gathered on the White House steps to serenade him that night, Lincoln made the same vague comment, then led the serenaders in three cheers for the general and his army.

The stoical Grant sometimes heard all too much of Sherman. A group of Republican politicians from Philadelphia who hoped to make Grant into a presidential candidate became so concerned for the general's future reputation that they went to Virginia to see him. Their spokesman said bluntly, "Sherman is absorbing all attention. He's thundering away in the heart of the rebellion. You alone do nothing. We've come to implore you to wake up."

Grant fumbled with matches and a cigar until he had gathered his thoughts, and then said quietly, "Sherman is acting by my order and I'm waiting on him. Just as soon as I hear that he's at . . . the seacoast I will take Richmond. If I were to move now, Lee would evacuate Richmond and I would have to follow him to keep him from jumping on Sherman . . . "

The general warned his visitors to keep his plan confidential, and said as an afterthought that "jealousy between General Sherman and me is impossible."

Grant sent Colonel A. H. Markland of the army's postal service southward with mail for Sherman's troops, and asked the colonel to call on Lincoln before he left. The President was in conference, but had Markland shown in at once and crossed the room to take his hand. "Well, Colonel, I got word from General Grant that you were going to find Sherman . . . Say to him, for me, whenever and wherever you see him, 'God bless him and God bless his army.' That is as much as I can say, and more than I can write."

The colonel saw with surprise that Lincoln's lips trembled and that tears stood in his eyes. The President called as Markland moved toward the door: "When I looked back he was standing like a statue where I had left him. 'Now, remember what I say. God bless Sherman and all his army.' "

9

"An inhuman barbarous proceeding"

The army was now well to the east of Macon and Augusta, with few signs of serious rebel opposition at hand, yet the pace of the march slowed perceptibly. The roads of the Georgia swamp country became softer and narrower, and the tidal streams deeper. Flimsy wooden causeways spanned the dark watercourses, and stream crossings were more frequent. Most exasperating of all to officers who sought to speed the march were the bands of black camp followers at the rear of each unit, hindering the progress of the army. Though many blacks who had joined in the early days of the march had grown weary and turned back homeward, more refugees streamed in from each plantation on the route. The newly liberated slaves began their trek with a resolve to find freedom in the distant North, beyond the reach of their masters.

General Jefferson C. Davis, the proslavery Indianian, had his own solution for the problem. On December 3, when his XIV Corps began crossing Ebenezer Creek on the northern flank of the advance, Davis ordered the blacks with his column to halt at the roadside and allow the troops to pass forward, ready to meet reported Confederate resistance in front. The Negroes ignored his order and traipsed along at their usual pace. Davis then moved his men ahead at the double-quick and left the blacks to the rear.

The creek, a brown swollen stream some one hundred feet wide, rose in the swamps near the village of Springfield, some thirty-five miles west of Savannah, and flowed north into the Savannah River. Confederates had burned a bridge to delay the army's passage, but

Colonel George Buell's 58th Indiana Regiment had worked all night to lay a pontoon bridge, and the troops began crossing soon after sunrise.

The corps, some 14,000 strong, approached over an old causeway closely screened on either side by forests of cypress and gum. More than 500 slaves, most of them women and children, were turned aside by guards at the end of the pontoon bridge and forbidden to cross.

General Davis watched the crossing for a time, his lean hawk's face half-concealed by a huge tufted beard and mustache. The profane and hot-tempered Davis, who had come up from the ranks, was determined that the blacks would no longer hamper the movement of his men and slow their march.

As Davis watched, chattering bands of Negroes, mostly women and children, appeared at the end of each division and were halted at the water's edge, where they were held under guard while troops, wagons and guns passed over the creek. The swamp about them was quiet, but officers told the blacks that there was fighting ahead and that they were being held back for their safety.

Soon afterward, when Davis had disappeared toward the front, soldiers suddenly cut loose the pontoon bridge and pulled it to the opposite bank, abandoning the blacks. The scene was recorded by the Indiana chaplain John Hight:

"There went up from that multitude a cry of agony." Women and children wailed, and men looked apprehensively to the rear, down the causeway through the impassable swamps, where, they feared, Wheeler's cavalry awaited them.

Someone shouted, "Rebels!" and as Hight watched, "They made a wild rush . . . some of them plunged into the water, and swam across. Others ran wildly up and down the bank, shaking with terror." Sympathetic soldiers on the far bank tossed logs and pieces of timber into the stream, and Negro men dragged them ashore and built a makeshift raft. Using a rope made of blankets, the blacks ferried dozens of women and children across the channel. The raft could carry no more than six at once, and sank several times. The raft had made numerous crossings when Private Harrison Pendergast of the 2nd Minnesota saw at least one hundred blacks waiting, "huddled as close to the edge of the water as they could get, some crying, some praying, and all fearful that the rebels would come before they could get over."

One husky Negro who could not swim plunged into the stream and flailed in a frenzy, head high and eyes rolling in terror until he reached the far bank. Others pressed after him, several of them women who carried babies in their arms, and were swept downstream and drowned. Federal troops who had returned to the rear cut down trees, and some Negroes splashed across by clinging to trunks and branches.

A few minutes later Confederate riders came into sight and opened fire on the Negroes, but soon wheeled away.

A Negro woman crossing on the raft stumbled into deep water. Her husband dragged her back aboard, and they reached the shore dripping and laughing. "I'd rather drown myself than lose her," the man said. Pendergast saw one old couple climb the bank to safety, having saved only the dripping garments they wore. The old man shouted: "Praise the Lord, we got away from them Rebels . . . We got troubles on our road but bless the Lord, it will be all right in the end."

A huge black man continued to yank the raft back and forth over the stream until the last Federal soldiers had disappeared.

A company of Wheeler's riders rode up a few minutes later and herded the stranded band of terrified blacks to the rear. Within a few days, so Wheeler reported, most of them had been returned to the owners from whom they had escaped. Emancipation for these survivors had been brief indeed.

The army's reaction to the heartless abandonment of these blacks was mild; few soldiers seem to have mentioned the incident in letters or diaries, but the resentment of a few liberal-minded witnesses was enough to brew a controversy and provoke criticism of General Davis and of Sherman himself.

Private Pendergast was outraged by the order by Davis, "who I presume considers himself a Christian." The Minnesotan expressed the resentment of many soldiers: "Where can you find in all the annals of plantation cruelty anything more completely inhuman and fiendish than this? Legree was an angel of mercy in comparison . . . this barbarous act has created a deep feeling against Davis in this division."

Pendergast hoped the incident would be reported to President Lincoln and that the general would lose his commission. Chaplain Hight was incensed: "Davis is a military tyrant, without one spark of humanity in his makeup. He was an ardent pro-slavery man before he entered the army, and has not changed his views since."

Major James Connolly could not contain his anger: "The idea of five or six hundred black women, children and old men being returned to slavery by such an infernal Copperhead as Jeff C. Davis was entirely too much . . . I told his staff officers what I thought of such an inhuman barbarous proceeding."

Connolly expected a reprimand from "his serene Highness," and perhaps loss of his brevet rank of lieutenant colonel, "for I know his toadies will repeat it to him, but I don't care a fig; I am determined to expose this act of his publicly."

Connolly wrote a letter of protest to the Senate Military Committee, ready to be mailed as soon as he reached the coast; he showed the letter to General Absalom Baird, who promised to write influential friends in New York and have Davis exposed in newspapers.

Sherman, who was not present, knew nothing of the incident at this time, and was to take no official cognizance of it until an outcry was raised in the North some weeks later.

The commander was riding with the advance of the XVII Corps of the northern wing this week on another road, but was not many miles from Ebenezer Creek when he discovered a new menace to the army's progress—a novel rebel weapon, buried "torpedoes." These were land mines, wicked explosive traps devised by the Confederate ordnance expert General Gabriel J. Rains after an earlier design by Samuel J. Colt.

It was a squad of the 1st Alabama Cavalry (U.S.) that set off the first explosions of these mines, a series of blasts that flung bodies of men and horses across a sandy roadway. The corps came to a halt.

Sherman moved to the head of the column and saw a dead horse in the road and several wounded men stretched beside a fence. One of the victims was a Lieutenant Tupper, a boy who gazed at the general from eyes glazed with shock and pain. Tupper's right foot had been torn off and a knee and one hand were badly mangled. "How long have you been in, son?"

"Three years, sir. My time had just expired last week." Hitchcock saw that Tupper's leg, "horribly torn and mutilated," was raw and bloody, with bone and muscle protruding and the knee shattered.

A squad of Confederate prisoners came up from the rear, ordered by General Frank Blair, the corps commander, to clear the road of the explosives. They begged Sherman for mercy.

"You can't send us out there to get blown up—in the name of humanity, General!"

"Your people put 'em there to assassinate our men," Sherman said. He pointed to Lieutenant Tupper. "Is that humanity?"

"It wasn't us, General. We don't know where the things are buried."

Sherman was unmoved. "I don't care a damn if you're blown up. I'll not have my own men killed like this."

One of the prisoners was sent back into his lines to ask that no more shells be buried in the roads, to save the lives of captives. The other rebels went gingerly out in front of the column, working with hands, picks and shovels until they had uncovered seven more torpedoes, some of them copper cylinders over a foot long, triggered to blow up at the slightest touch. The bluecoats looked on expectantly, as if hoping to see an explosion.

Hitchcock was infuriated. "Perhaps when we take Savannah the 1st Alabama Cavalry won't make somebody suffer for this! . . . These cowardly villains call us 'barbarous Yanks'—and then adopt instruments of murder in cold blood when they dare not stand and fight like men."

Skirmishing broke out in the woodlands ahead, and Sherman dismounted, handed his reins to an orderly, and disappeared before the staff noticed his movement. A few minutes later Hitchcock followed and found him waiting in a farmhouse where Lieutenant Tupper had been taken for treatment. Surgeons amputated the boy's leg.

During the afternoon Sherman came upon a wagon mired in a mudhole. One of the mules was belly-deep in the black muck, and a teamster flailed her with a blacksnake whip.

"Stop pounding that mule," the general said.

"Mind your own damned business."

"I tell you again to stop. I'm General Sherman."

"Hell, that's played out," the teamster said. "Every son of a bitch who comes along with an old coat and slouch hat claims he's Sherman."

Uncle Billy grinned and rode on.

Now, for the first time since the advance on Atlanta, there was an almost constant crackling of musket fire, and the infantry advanced but a few miles each day. Rebels had barricaded the roads with felled trees, and axes rang night and day as Sherman's Negro pioneers cleared the way. Still, resistance was not serious. Prisoners reported that a small division under General Lafayette McLaws was in the front, retiring steadily toward the Savannah trenches. Negroes who came into the line said, "Them rebs is arunning now. They talked mighty big at first and said it was just a nigger army acoming —but when they found out it was Sherman's they couldn't get away fast enough." The troublesome Confederate platform gun, last fired at the crossing of the Oconee, reappeared on its railroad car, running forward to fire a few rounds at the advancing blue column, then retreating from sight when Federal gunners appeared.

On December 10 Sherman rode to the front along the railroad cut and saw a rebel gun crew about eight hundred yards away.

"Scatter," he said. "They'll give us a shot." He was to remember the moment for years: "I saw the white puff of smoke, and watching close, caught sight of the ball as it rose on its flight."

An Illinois soldier was hypnotized by the cannonball: "It holds the gaze . . . it seems to be charged with a personal message. Its motion appears to be slow and deliberate . . . at first a small black blotch on the sky. It grows. It is as large as a tin cup —as a plate —a barrel. Now its immensity fills the entire field of vision, shutting out trees and sky."

A Michigan soldier thought the sound of the projectile was "like a steam engine starting: 'Wh . . . ew! . . . whh. . . . eew. . . . w-h-e-w!' . . . commencing slow and gradually growing faster and ending with a roar."

Sherman stepped aside, but a Negro who was crossing the tracks a few feet away was struck under the jaw by the richocheting ball and was decapitated. Someone threw a coat over the body and the officers ran for cover.

By now the invaders were in a difficult country where fresh trials lay ahead. The army's days and nights of feasting had ended abruptly when the columns entered the tidal swamp country between the Savannah and Ogeechee rivers. Plantations here were few, and those had been swept clean by cavalrymen of both armies. The fat farms of central Georgia, with rich harvests of corn, potatoes and fresh pork, were now tantalizing memories. Many of Sherman's infantrymen went hungry, since little surplus food from the foraging parties had been saved, and it was to be almost a week before supply trains caught up with the leading infantry in the sandy swamp tracks. Rations were still in the ponderous wagons, and the beef herd still brought up the rear, but men at the front suffered.

Illinois troops begged quartermasters for food, and when they were turned away, besieged the tents of colonels and generals, clamoring for rations and threatening to raid the supply wagons. They were issued rations for three days, ordered to make them last ten days. William Grunert of the 129th Illinois said: "More than one Illinoisian wished himself back to the fleshpots of Egypt."

Major Alfred B. Smith of the 150th New York was so moved when he saw his troops scratching in pine straw for grains of corn left by horses that he helped to feed the hungry men by dividing the few ears of corn issued for his own horse.

Private Francis Baker and his companions of the 78th Ohio had no rations except coffee for three days, and got little comfort from their colonel: "Well, boys, the only thing I can advise is to draw in your belt one more hole each day."

The column passed a few bony cattle that had wandered into a bog in search of forage, had sunk into the muck, too weak to move, and were finally drowned. Soldiers floundered into the swamp and "perched upon their dead bodies cutting chunks of meat." Sergeant Ed Smith of the 2nd Illinois artillery, an inveterate forager, solved his battery's meat shortage by killing a fat mule and dividing it among the appreciative gunners, who thought it was "the best of beef."

The column then entered the rice country, where the roads threaded past tidal marshes; but though enormous piles of harvested grain lay on every plantation, the troops went hungry until they learned to hull the rice.

One Iowa soldier, who hulled his rice by beating it with a bayonet and cleaning it by hand, protested that he spent one day getting enough rice for a meal, had a late supper, and went to sleep before he got hungry again. "Then in the morning I'm as hungry as a bitch wolf that's been in a snowdrift twenty-four hours." Men of the 3rd Wisconsin, who had no salt, seasoned their rice with gunpowder, an experiment they did not repeat.

The army lived on rice for more than a week—and for several days fed the grain to horses and mules. Captain Storrs, whose front-line Connecticut troops were shelled by rebel cannon almost daily, dug in with his men: "We played cards, laid low, and our diet was rice for breakfast, rice for dinner, rice for supper, and then more rice." The only other edible item in the regiment's headquarters baggage was mustard: "The guest who dined with us, if he declined rice, was simply given mustard."

Savannah now lay only a dozen miles ahead, its approaches guarded by marshes, rice fields and canals. Five causeways led through this watery wilderness like arrows converging upon the city—three wagon roads and two railroad lines. Sherman pushed his army nearer the city in slow, deliberate moves, and formed a siege line across these arteries in the form of an irregular crescent. The new position lay some four miles outside Savannah itself, and was occupied without serious resistance from the rebels, who watched from their own earthworks, a formidable system of forts and rifle pits protected by rows of sharpened logs and by flooded lowlands whose water level could be altered by raising and lowering floodgates in the rice fields. A frontal assault along this line was all but impossible.

The 4th Minnesota approached its position before these works apprehensively: "Swamp on either side, pines, cypress, live-oak and magnolia . . . a chilly mist is above and around us, which, rising from the low water of the swamp and canal, gives a spectral appearance to the long lines of blue-coats. After marching ten miles we halted. Ahead of us was a swamp and a rebel fort."

Confederate cannon fire drove the Minnesotans to earth, and they scraped out rifle pits where they lay all night in a cold rain, without fires or tents.

Captain Ephraim Wilson of the 10th Illinois, whose regiment was forced to wade a canal, remembered this as the worst night of the war: "We all plunged in and waded through, the water being like ice . . . up to our armpits . . . Our bones were fairly frozen and the marrow within them congealed."

When the men halted and built fires to thaw their frozen clothing, rebel guns opened on them with rounds of grapeshot. Fires were stamped out in a fury, "and the balance of the night we were compelled to dance around in our wet clothes to keep ourselves from freezing to death."

Men of the 58th Indiana, camped on a riverside rice plantation, saw Savannah in the distance—"a very beautiful city," they thought. These troops worked from dawn until late at night to make hundreds of fascines—huge bundles of bamboo and rice straw that were to be thrown into ditches and canals when rebel lines were stormed. Other regiments built tiny one-man rafts and carved paddles, ready to cross canals in front of enemy trenches.

At night, when firing ceased, troops heard the rattling of wagons in Savannah streets and the clang of church bells striking the hours.

The cavalry, as usual, ranged widely, and were now prowling several miles to the south of the siege line that enclosed the city by land. Kilpatrick's horsemen, loosed on the city's southern flank, began to prey upon the rich farmlands of Liberty County, yet untouched by war. The troopers overran the villages of Hinesville, Walthourville, Dorchester, and Midway, and at last a few of them reached Sunbury, a village of a dozen houses on the coast overlooking St. Catherine's Sound. Five-year-old James R. Morgan, who watched from a house, was summoned by a trooper: "Johnny, get me a piece of fire."

The boy brought a glowing coal from the fireplace of his home and watched the soldiers ride to Sunbury Church: "I wondered where they were going to build the fire. I knew the church had no chimney. I followed them to the church. They took rails from a fence nearby and built the fire under the stair steps. Soon the church was blazing."

This was a signal to gunboats anchored in Ossabaw Sound, vessels that anchored the next morning within sight of the most advanced Federal troops. The army had made its first contact with the U.S. fleet some two weeks in advance of the date Sherman had forecast in his message to Admiral Porter. Actual communication with the navy, however, must await the fall of Savannah or some of its outlying defenses— especially Fort McAllister, which dominated the Ogeechee, the only convenient deep-water approach to the city.

Cornelia Screven, a young widow with several children who met the enemy in the village of Dorchester, near Sunbury, discovered a good Samaritan who must have been the most tender-hearted man among the rude invaders.

At the sound of horsemen in her yard, Mrs. Screven opened her door and was pushed backward by a soldier who demanded her keys.

"I'm ordered to search the house for firearms."

"I have none."

"Give me your keys or I'll break down every door in your house."

Mrs. Screven gave up the keys, and the leader went up the stairs. Cornelia faced the others fiercely.

"I defy another man to put his foot on these steps. I've been promised protection, and I expect an officer any moment to guard my house." The leader ordered his men back.

When raiders returned in greater numbers the next day, Cornelia Screven found a soldier taking the last of her cornmeal from the kitchen. "Please don't take that meal, my children are very hungry, and we have nothing else to eat."

The soldier turned savagely. "Damn you, I don't care if you all starve; get outa my way or I'll push you out the door."

Cornelia's niece, a Miss Maxwell, shouted at the soldier: "Oh, you intolerable brute! If I was a man I'd blow out every particle of your brains. If I had a pistol I'd do it anyhow, woman as I am."

A bright-faced young Pennsylvania soldier known to the women only as Hughes offered them his help and patrolled the hall of the house with a drawn pistol until the raiders had gone. Hughes then entered the room where the weeping women sat: "Ladies, don't cry. I never saw a woman cry in my life, but what I had to cry, too." He wiped tears from his eyes. When the boy left at sunset the women stirred the fireplace ashes and roasted sweet potatoes, the only food left to them.

The small boys of Liberty County had disappeared. Women on plantations were terrified by a rumor flying ahead of the army that the Yankees would kill all male children, and at the first sign of the bluecoats mothers had disguised their young sons in girls' clothing.

In one farmhouse Kilpatrick's raiders admired a small child in a freshly starched dress who slid down the stair rail at breakneck speed. A distraught mother called sharply: "Bessie, my son, come down from there."

The troopers burst into laughter. "I thought it was damn strange," one of them said, "that all the brats in this neighborhood were girls."

An infantry foraging expedition went into Liberty County during the week, a train of one hundred and fifty wagons under guard of the 100th Indiana.

As the column entered a small town in the marsh country, a man on a mule galloped out of a side street and fled ahead of them. Colonel R. M. Johnson shouted, "Halt!" but the rider did not pause.

"Shoot him!" Johnson called.

Sam Blanchard of Company B and one other man raised their muskets and fired. The rider toppled into the roadway, and the mule staggered a few steps and fell. When the soldiers reached the bodies they found that the dead man was quite old—eighty, some civilians said. The troops took up a collection and gave the old man's family money to bury him. Private Theodore Upson grieved for the innocent victim, perhaps in memory of the death of his friend Uncle Aaron Wolford at the little battle of Griswoldville. "It was all we could do," Upson said. "It was one of the accidents of war."

10

"I've got Savannah!"

Within the city, Savannah's defenders thought less of defiance of Sherman and more of escape. General William Hardee had assembled "a mongrel mass" of about 9,000 troops, most of them the Georgia militiamen who had been pushed eastward in Sherman's path. Among them were the old men and boys who had survived the skirmish at Griswoldville.

The fate of the city, it was thought, was in strong hands. The forty-nine-year-old Hardee, at the top of his profession, vigorous and alert, was in appearance every inch the soldier and an inspiration to his troops and the city's civilians. The Confederates could hardly have chosen a more able adversary for Sherman, and now Hardee was defending his birthplace. Neither the public nor the advancing enemy had an inkling of the rebel military scholar's plans for evacuation. An army of slaves still worked on the trenches.

The handsome old city had flourished through three years of war, its prosperity fueled by blockade-runners and the produce of the back country. Its peacetime population of 20,000 was now swollen by Hardee's troops and refugees. The waterfront was piled with cotton, mountains of invaluable bales awaiting shipment to the West Indies and thence to England—an estimated 25,000 to 40,000 bales. Many of the fine old streets were now rutted tracks of sand and oyster shell, since their cobbles had been removed to help build obstructions in the Savannah River. The city's outskirts were scarred by trenches, and its streets were blocked by mounds of earth as Savannah awaited its trial.

Lieutenant General Richard Taylor, who had come here from Macon to inspect the defenses, telegraphed Robert E. Lee that the city could not be held by Hardee's inferior force. Sherman had only to join with Federal warships waiting in the sounds and Savannah would be lost. Taylor urged that Hardee march northward to join Confederate forces in the Carolinas, where they could give Sherman battle in case he turned in that direction.

From his headquarters in Charleston, South Carolina, about a hundred miles to the north, General Beauregard ordered Hardee to build a bridge across the mile-wide Savannah River so that his garrison might escape into South Carolina. The Creole warned Hardee that he was not to risk the troops. The fate of Savannah was secondary to the safety of the army—manpower could not be replaced. A few days later, on December 15, Beauregard sent Hardee a reminder that under no circumstances was he to allow his line of retreat to be cut.

The task of bridging the great river was begun by thousands of laborers, slaves, Federal prisoners, Confederate troops and a few civilians. From both sides of the stream engineers collected boats and rice flats, shallow barges from seventy to eighty-five feet long, ponderous pontoons that were lashed end to end with chains and ropes, floated into place on the tide and held in place by makeshift anchors—wheels stripped from railroad cars. Heavy timbers from Savannah's dismantled city docks were laid across the flats, floored with loose planks and then piled deeply with rice straw, to deaden the sound of the army's passage.

The first section of the bridge spanned the thousand-foot channel between the city and Hutchinson's Island like a shaggy, undulating monster, its timbers lying crazily between floats of all sizes and shapes. Men, mules and wagons crept across the marshy island to dump tons of rice straw, poles and planks until the crude causeway would bear the weight of loaded wagons.

The work went slowly in cold, rainy weather, but it was safely beyond the view of the distant Federals. Beauregard arrived in Savannah for an inspection on the night of December 16, breathing impatience. He erupted in Gallic fury when he found the crossing only one-third complete. His mood was not improved when he discovered that Joe Wheeler's troopers had burned scores of rice flats, supposing that they had been collected by Sherman. The Creole's wrath inspired a miracle: Chief Engineer John G. Clarke and his workmen completed the bridge by dawn of December 19, a second section across the channel from Hutchinson's to Pennyworth Island, and a third span of pontoons to the South Carolina shore. Hardee's line of retreat was open and ready for use. The army would begin to move at dusk the following evening. Hardee ordered a heavy artillery barrage prepared for sundown of December 20, to divert attention from the crossing by the cannonade along the perimeter of the earthworks.

Sherman's deliberate progress through the intricate coastal approaches gave the Confederate defenders a respite. Though the general was not aware of Hardee's completion of the causeway over the Savannah, he realized that a crossing of the river to the north of the city was the Confederates' only hope of escape. Still, he was slow to bar the way. Sherman might have launched an amphibious attack over the difficult terrain—but only at the cost of scattering his troops and delaying their deployment in the siege lines. He was anxious to spare his men an assault—and was also anxious to make contact with other Federal forces along the coast, hoping to enlist their aid in cutting off Hardee's retreat by posting fresh troops on the South Carolina bank of the river.

Sherman's thoughts had turned instead to the southern flank of the city's defenses along the Ogeechee, where his approach to the navy was blocked by Fort McAllister, whose guns pointed downriver into Ossabaw Sound. The commander ordered Oliver Howard to storm the fort on December 13.

The assault force chosen was Sherman's old 2nd Division of the XV Corps, now commanded by General William B. Hazen. These veterans had fought with Sherman at Shiloh and Vicksburg, and his confidence in them was complete.

Sherman and Howard and two signal officers watched from the roof of a rice mill on the north bank of the Ogeechee as Hazen's column moved slowly into position on the opposite side of the river. Hazen formed nine regiments at the edge of an open field some six hundred to eight hundred yards from the fort.

The sun was sinking into the woodlands when a steamer appeared in the river. The red flag of a navy signalman whipped back and forth on the deck.

"My God, Howard, it's a gunboat." Sherman signaled Hazen to attack at once.

The tug signaled: "Can we run up? Is the fort taken?"

"No. Attack underway."

The tug then asked if it could aid the attack, but before Sherman could reply there was a roll of guns from McAllister and Hazen's men fanned into the open. Sherman and Howard turned their glasses across the river.

"There they go, Howard. Not a waver. Grand, grand."

The line charged at a run for two hundred yards, but though the rebels raised a yell at once and several guns opened, few men were hit. The file dropped to the ground in the high grass, and riflemen began to pick off rebel gunners.

Sherman was watching a colorbearer when the line disappeared. He lowered his glasses as if he could not bear to see more, but someone said, "They're up. They're going in!"

Hazen's men threw logs across the ravine, then scrambled across and onto the slope. Explosions ripped Hazen's line and flung a few bodies into the ravine—torpedoes had been buried on the slope—but the blue figures edged upward, into the fort.

"They're on the parapet," Sherman said. "They took it, Howard. I've got Savannah!" He saw the fall of the fort as the key to the capture of the city, since Hardee could no longer prevent an advance on the city by land and water. Now, with the navy's aid, he would soon take the city, by siege or by assault.

Men fought hand-to-hand in the fort for a few moments longer; the Confederates ran into their bomb shelters and fell back from chamber to chamber until they were overcome. There was no formal surrender.

It was five o'clock when a U.S. flag was run up a pole. Hazen's men raced through the work, ignoring ammunition stores, and broke into a well-stocked wine cellar.

Sherman capered atop the mill and shouted, "Hardtack tonight, boys! Hardtack tonight!" He remembered the words of the awestruck old slave on Howell Cobb's plantation who had come to stare at him and called to Howard, "There'll be no sleep for dis nigger dis night."

Sherman scribbled a message to Slocum: "Take a good big drink, a long breath and then yell like the devil. The fort was taken at 4:30 P.M., the assault lasting but fifteen minutes."

Sherman crossed to the south bank of the river on the gunboat after dark, to congratulate Hazen and inspect the fort. He talked with some rebel wounded who lay near the bodies of Confederate artillerymen. He found that Hazen had 135 casualties, 24 of them dead.

Sherman went to sleep in the fort, but was roused by a dispatch-bearer during the night— General John L. Foster was waiting for him downriver. Sherman was rowed to the ship through moonlight in a yawl, in waters that had been sown with rebel torpedoes. Sherman had a low opinion of Foster's abilities, but the newcomer brought good news. He had landed a Federal division on Hilton Head Island on the South Carolina coast, and was ready to help trap Hardee. Admiral John Dahlgren's U.S. fleet lay waiting below Savannah. The war was going well on other fronts: The Confederate John Hood had been defeated by John Schofield in a bloody clash at Franklin, Tennessee, and a second battle was imminent at Nashville, where George Thomas was waiting with his strong, veteran Federal army. Grant still held Lee in his trenches at Richmond.

The day following his interview with Foster, Sherman went out to the fleet and boarded Dahlgren's flagship —almost as if in quest of acclaim. He was greeted as a hero. Hundreds of sailors mounted to the yards of their ships and cheered until the sound was swept with echoes. Officers who gathered to greet Sherman found him in an expansive mood, full of tales of his army's march, praise for the men and scorn for the failing power of the Confederacy.

Lieutenant John Gray of Massachusetts marveled at Sherman's restless energy and his air of serene confidence. The general strode about the cabin with hands jammed in his pockets, came to an abrupt halt, and without pausing in his rapid speech, thrust out an arm and closed his fingers into a fist. "I've got Savannah," he said. "It's in my grip . . . only three miles . . . I'll take my time about it . . . I just wish there were more Rebels in the city."

Sherman excused himself for a few moments and retired to an officer's quarters to write to Grant, Halleck and Stanton. He reported that his army had reached the coast and that he would soon take Savannah.

He wrote Stanton: "The army is in splendid order and equal to anything. The weather has been fine and supplies were abundant. Our march was most agreeable and we were not at all molested by guerrillas . . . We have not lost a wagon on the trip, but have gathered a large supply of negroes, mules, horses, etc., and our teams are in far better condition than when we started. My first duty will be to clear the army of surplus negroes, mules and horses . . . I regard Savannah as already gained."

Sherman soon rejoined the officers in the admiral's quarters, still full of the excitement of his campaign. He had already planned his next move: "I'm going to march to Richmond. I expect to turn north by the end of the month, when the sun does—and when I go through South Carolina it will be one of the most horrible things in the history of the world. The devil himself couldn't restrain my men in that state." The general's face glowed as he described the march through Georgia: "I could look forty miles in each direction and see smoke rolling up like one great bonfire." Officers concluded that Sherman would make little effort to control his troops in South Carolina.

The exultant conqueror was later to protest that much of the depredation along his route was the work of Confederates themselves, but he made no mention of that fact at this moment. Today, in his hour of triumph, he boasted openly of the charred track he had left in his wake, through the heart of Georgia.

Lieutenant Gray was struck by Sherman's belligerent assurance that he could "whip the creation," an air of "almost boastful confidence in himself which in an untried man would be very disgusting, but in him is intensely comic." But the young officer was not sorry to see the general leave the ship: "I never passed a more amusing or instructive day, but at his departure I felt it a relief and experienced almost an exhaustion after the excitement of his vigorous presence."

Sherman returned to his army to find that mail and rations had arrived simultaneously. It was "a frantic sight, men snatching letters, whooping at this first touch with home." Alonzo Brown of the 4th Minnesota said that "when the rations came in sight every soldier who could make a noise jumped and shouted as loud and as long as his strength would let him. Such cheering I never heard." An Illinois soldier remembered: "It was a curious spectacle. The half-starved boys all through the camps reading their letters held in one hand while devouring hard-tack from the other . . . a conflict between appetite and noble sensibilities."

Sherman found Colonel Markland overseeing the distribution of mail. The colonel held out his hand. "I've brought you a message from the President. He asked me to take you by the hand wherever I met you and say 'God bless you and the army.' He has been praying for you."

"I thank the President," Sherman said. "Say my army is all right."

Sherman wrote his wife that night, his first letter to her in a long while; he assumed that she had learned of his progress through newspapers: "I have no doubt you have heard of my safe arrival on the coast . . . We came right along living on turkeys, chickens, pigs, bringing along our wagons loaded as we started with bread, etc. I suppose Jeff Davis will have to feed the people of Georgia instead of collecting provisions of them to feed his armies."

He described the destruction of Georgia railroads, the storming of Fort McAllister, his visit to the fleet and his plans to invade South Carolina: "I never saw a more confident army. The soldiers think I can do anything . . . Await events and trust to fortune. I will turn up where and when you least expect me."

Colonel Orville Babcock, one of Grant's aides, arrived by ship the next day and gave Sherman a message, which he read at once. Sherman's expression did not change, but Captain Dayton saw that he was angry; the general made a nervous involuntary gesture with his left arm, as if pushing away some unpleasant thought.

Sherman wheeled and entered his farmhouse headquarters. "Come here, Dayton!" He banged the door behind them and began cursing, "Won't do it, goddam it! I'll not do anything of the kind!"

Grant had urged him to put his army aboard ships and come to Virginia to aid in the defeat of Lee; he was to fortify and garrison a base on the Georgia coast and come north at once: "Select, yourself, the officer to leave in command, but I want you in person." Grant had stopped short of a peremptory order: "Unless you see objections to this plan, which I cannot see, use every vessel coming to you for purposes of transportation."

Captain Dayton, who had come to know him well, saw that Sherman was almost sick with anxiety and outrage. Grant's proposal would doom his cherished plan of marching through the Carolinas to destroy the last granary of Lee's army—and win fame for Sherman and his army. Grant seemed to be determined to dash all his hopes in the very moment of triumph. But after fuming for an hour that he had been betrayed, Sherman regained control.

He began issuing orders to obey Grant's wishes—he would need at least one hundred ships, which would be weeks in arriving. There should be time to take Savannah—and he did not give up hope that he could still find a way to "punish South Carolina as she deserves."

Sherman wrote to Grant on December 16, assuring him that he would cheerfully obey any orders—but that he believed his original plan of marching through the Carolinas would end the war more quickly than a move by sea to Virginia. He confessed "a personal dislike" for the voyage, and urged that he be allowed to march through the state capitals of Columbia, South Carolina, and Raleigh, North Carolina, and thence into Virginia.

A few days later Sherman wrote to Halleck, pleading for a reversal of Grant's plan, declaring that both Northerners and Southerners "would rejoice to have this army turned loose in South Carolina to devastate that state." He added, "I attach much more importance to these deep incisions into the enemy's country, because this war differs from European wars in this particular: We are not fighting armies, but a hostile people, and must make old and young, rich and poor, feel the hard hand of war . . ."

Sherman then turned to the problem of taking Savannah. He sent Hardee a demand for immediate surrender, offering "the most liberal" terms, which he did not reveal in detail. If Hardee refused, the city would be shelled and stormed, and worse: "I shall then feel justified in resorting to the harshest measures, and shall make little effort to restrain my army—burning to avenge the national wrong which they attach to Savannah and other large cities which have been so prominent in dragging our country into civil war."

Hardee's refusal came promptly. His defense lines were intact, he reminded Sherman, and since Federal ships had not entered the Savannah River (where torpedoes abounded and the city's guns might reach the fleet), his army was in "free and constant communication" with South Carolina. Hardee responded tartly to Sherman's bullying: "I have hitherto conducted . . . military operations . . . in strict accordance with the rules of civilized warfare, and I should deeply regret the adoption of any course by you that may force me to deviate from them in the future."

Sherman then abruptly left his army once more, this time by ship for Hilton Head to persuade the timorous General Foster to block Hardee's escape route into South Carolina. He declined to leave this delicate mission to a subordinate, probably because he felt that he would need all his rank and prestige to win Foster's prompt support. Sherman left behind him orders that Slocum and Howard were to hold their siege lines during his absence of two or three days, but were not to launch an assault on Savannah.

The army had scant hope for Sherman's mission to Foster. Major Connolly said, when he learned that Foster was expected to complete the encirclement of Hardee, "He won't do it . . . Foster's an old granny . . . Those eastern fellows never do anything clever . . . They appear to fail in everything they undertake."

Sherman, in any event, left his army at this moment, expecting to be gone for no more than a day or two. He may have been overconfident, flushed with the unexpectedly easy success of his march to the sea, trusting to luck and his own acuity his hopes of preventing the escape of the Confederate army. Though he realized that Hardee would soon be able to escape over the wide Savannah River, he was unaware that the makeshift bridge had been miraculously completed. Above all, perhaps, he realized that Savannah itself was the true prize, more precious than the capture of the rebel army.

II

"A Christmas gift"

The Confederate army began its escape from the city in the dusk of December 20 amid rolling fog that now and then obscured the moon. From Broad Street, where they had waited for hours, Hardee's troops began to cross the makeshift bridge, tipping gingerly in the uncertain footing of the rice straw. The boats shuddered in the surging tide and planks shifted beneath the men. Behind came the wagons, teamsters cursing and mules braying in terror as heavy loads careened across the swaying pontoons. A few wagons plunged into the dark water, but the army toiled forward, across the three bridges and over undulating causeways to the South Carolina shore. Despite all precautions, sounds of the passage carried to the enemy, even above a rising wind that soon blew a gale. But those of Sherman's troops who heard the rebels were helpless to interfere. Men of the 13th New Jersey, posted on Argyle Island, heard clearly the curses of Confederate teamsters, but could not even report to Federals on the mainland.

Just as the first units of the escaping force moved onto the bridge, Hardee's artillery barrage opened from the trenches of Savannah's landward defenses. The rebel artillery swept the woods and underbrush and marshlands with grapeshot for two hours, firing sporadically so that Sherman's besiegers could not sleep, build fires or launch an attack.

On one sector of the Confederate front, held by old men and boys of the 10th Battalion, North Carolina Reserves, a hat rose over one of the rifle pits and then a stout figure, dimly lighted by nearby campfires—a dummy held up by Lieutenant Charles S. Powell. Half a dozen musket balls ripped the figure and blew moss stuffing from its torn coat; as usual, Federal snipers were alert, "and those western Yankees were good marksmen." Powell was not sorry to learn that they were to abandon the line during the night.

The Georgia militiamen began to retreat from their position not far away. Among them was sixteen-year-old Leroy West Harris, one of the Griswoldville survivors. Harris was barefoot. Patriotic Savannah civilians had sent a wagonload of shoes to the troops—all women's high-heeled shoes. Some of the younger boys now tipped about in the awkward pointed shoes, but not Harris, who had been given a pair "only large enough for my sixteen-year-old toes to stick in."

As the command straggled through Savannah, Harris entered a grocery and braved the suspicious stare of an Irishwoman to gaze into a showcase filled with sweet potatoes. "Oh, if I just had one of them," he said. The woman surrendered: "God bless your heart, you shall have one. You ought to be at home with your mammy." The boy crossed the bridge with the potato cradled inside his shirt.

On one sector where the trenches were only three hundred yards apart, a rebel band struck up "Dixie," and Sherman's men yelled derisively from the darkness: "Played out!"

Federal pickets called to the 5th Georgia Reserves: "Whatcha' doin' there, Johnny? Thought you was getting out tonight?"

"We loves you too good, Yanks. We can't leave you."

"We're gonna blow you away, Johnny."

"Blow up yer ass, Yank. Blow to hell!"

The South Carolina Captain Vincent Martin moved warily along his trench, fearful of turning his back on his company, a collection of captured Union soldiers who had been forced into Confederate service, Irishmen, Germans, Italians and Spaniards, some of whom spoke little or no English. The men avoided Martin's eyes; they looked dangerous, he thought. Yesterday they had joined a plot to kill their officers and desert to the enemy, and seven of their leaders had been shot, a midnight scene Martin would not forget: An inept firing squad of Georgia militia had merely maimed two of the condemned men, and as they raised "such wails and dismal cries as never were heard on the field of battle," the flustered executioners fired at random, tearing wounds in the arms and legs of the victims until the captain halted it and shot the two men in the head. The survivors were still openly defiant; Martin had heard one of them mutter, "Wait 'til Sherman comes, Johnny, we'll get you then."

Martin had been told that the trenches were to be abandoned during the night, but hours passed and the order did not come. His battalion commander, Colonel James B. Brooks, went into Savannah to ask for orders, but was turned away—Hardee and Beauregard were in a council of war, and could not be disturbed. When at last a staff officer told Brooks to join the retreat, it was near three in the morning. An hour later the command was crossing the river. Behind them explosions rocked the navy yard and harbor, where docks and ships were being blown up.

Among the last Confederates to leave the lines were men of the 2nd Georgia Cavalry, a band of cripples, wagon guards and a few of Wheeler's men who had lost their horses. Their captain, a taciturn Tennessean from a scattered infantry regiment, gave them final orders in late afternoon: "The army pulls out at 8 o'clock. March into town when the troops on either side of you fall back. I'll leave a detail to build up the fires."

A. S. McCollum, a seventeen-year-old Georgian, was squatting in the trench a few minutes later when the captain approached. "It's going to be me," McCollum thought. "It's my time to stand guard duty, and the Yanks will catch or shoot the whole detail."

But the captain walked past and halted before McCollum's tent-mate, Sergeant George Cochran. "All right, Cochran, it's your duty. Take five men and keep up the fires. We're pulling out."

"You know it ain't George's turn," McCollum said. "It's mine."

"Cochran stays."

"Damned if I'm going home and have people say I left George to take my medicine. I'll not have it. I'm staying with him."

"Do as you please," the captain said. "But keep those fires up until 11 o'clock. Somebody from the staff will come and get you then."

The five men stirred up the fires, lay flat as they tossed logs into the flames, and rolled across the sand until they were concealed by darkness before rising to their feet. Long after midnight, when no one had come for them, the five men hurried to the rear and joined the column on Broad Street.

The last Confederates were across before dawn. The bridge was cut loose from the Savannah shore by engineers, a few men who crouched aboard the flats until the tide had swung the ungainly structure downstream, and at last scrambled to safety on Hutchinson's Island. Captain Robert Stiles of the engineers noted that it was 5:40 A.M. He saw Yankees running down Broad Street toward the waterfront. Their yells came to him across the river, surprisingly distinct.

The rear guard then cut away the second and third bridges and withdrew across the South Carolina rice fields in the rain. The army was safely across, 9,000 infantry and a few artillerymen whose forty-nine cannon and their caissons, forges and baggage wagons had made the crossing with the loss of a single wagon. Hardee's army was now beyond Sherman's reach.

On the Federal front facing the Savannah defenses, Sherman's troops waited alertly, unaware that their commander was not at hand, but was still far away in the sound on his visit to General Foster.

Private Horatio Chapman of the 20th Connecticut was one of the first of Sherman's troops to realize that the rebels had retreated on December 20. He crouched in a wet trench until the guns in his front had halted, around midnight, then raised his head. At first Chapman saw only the glow of enemy fires, and lay down again. He drowsed and awoke with a start. The lines were silent. A white flag hung on a stick atop the Confederate trenches. He called his lieutenant and they went forward.

Two wounded rebels greeted them. "They're all gone but us," one of them said. "They pulled out in a big hurry."

Chapman and the lieutenant were followed by Captain John Storrs, who rode out to claim the honor of seizing the abandoned line for the regiment but, since he had no flag, was reduced to smearing the barrel of a spiked gun with clay: 20TH CONN. VOLS.

Regiments had entered the rebel lines along the whole front by three in the morning. Sergeant Samuel J. Murphy and Alonzo Kelly of the 2nd Illinois Light Artillery slipped forward to peer through a Confederate embrasure and saw only two Negroes, one sitting on a cracker box and another asleep on the ground.

"Where'd the rebels go?"

"Gone. Left out of here last night—and you better watch out. They put torpedoes all along the railroad."

General Henry Barnum, who reconnoitered along General Geary's front, hesitated before the line of bonfires, but moved ahead when he saw no men about them and sent back word that the rebels had gone. Geary led the 102nd New York toward the city, followed by the whole division.

The Iowa soldier Ben Johnson had drawn three days' rations soon after midnight, but cooked and ate them at once. He was still hungry when he joined the advance on the enemy trenches. When his regiment halted there, Johnson and a companion slipped away in the darkness and entered Savannah on their own. The streets were empty, but the Federals soon found a treasure—and discovered anew the zany inconsistency of the reactions of Confederate civilians to the coming of the Yankee invaders.

At the edge of town the two came upon a grocery store whose rear yard was filled with pens of chickens, turkeys and pigs. A huge Irishwoman confronted Johnson. "Holy saints," she said, "a live Yankee!" She called to her small son: "See this Yankee boy, Mike. Shure and he's as fine a broth of a boy as ever you'll see and won't be stealing from us like them spalpeens of rebels who just went down the street."

Johnson and three Negro drivers began loading grocery carts with flour, sugar, rice, sweet potatoes, chickens, turkeys, pigs, two barrels of whiskey and two demijohns of brandy—and salt and pepper, which the troops had not tasted for weeks. The woman stood by, cursing steadily until the carts were full and the soldiers had driven away.

Johnson was unloading his loot in a cemetery when his regiment appeared, to camp in an adjoining field. "What a commotion there was when I took my loads into the company!" The company used the carts to haul lumber, windows and tin roofing stripped from nearby houses; a small city of shanties sprang up beside the cemetery.

As often happened in such moments, Confederates committed outrages as readily as the most undisciplined of Sherman's troops.

This disposition to looting, though rarely recorded in early American history, was to become a familiar phenomenon in many large cities in twentieth-century America. The young men of the 1860's, who had grown up in an era when strict morality was the rule, had been guided by standards of social acceptance and decorum—but now, freed of restraint and invited to do their worst, many soldiers defied all authority.

Civilian looters were at work in Savannah's streets before the last of Hardee's troops had gone, and were breaking into stores and warehouses as Mayor Richard Arnold and his aldermen rode past them, out the Augusta road to surrender the city. Rebel cavalrymen stole Arnold's horses, and the party walked toward the advancing enemy. Dr. Arnold surrendered to General Geary at four-thirty in the morning of December 21.

A mob of women and children swarmed about warehouses, dragging off sacks and barrels of rice. Sherman's troops applauded women who fought over the rice, cursing, kicking, pulling hair and swinging wildly with their fists—but the soldiers soon joined the pillaging themselves, and carried food, tobacco, wine and whiskey to their camps until midmorning, when Geary posted guards and restored order.

Many miles distant, at Hilton Head, South Carolina, Sherman completed his interview with General Foster, who promised that he would send his division to the South Carolina shore just above Savannah, to block Hardee's escape. Sherman began his return voyage almost at once, on the night of December 20. He was unexpectedly delayed.

Buffeted by high winds, the little steamer *Harvest Moon* ran aground on a mud bank. Sherman set off impatiently in Admiral Dahlgren's barge, was rowed by sailors through the Romney Marshes, and was still there, laboring against tide and wind, on the afternoon of December 21 when he was overtaken by a quartermaster's tug bearing a message from Captain Dayton: The rebels had evacuated Savannah. His troops were already in the city.

Sherman had missed the climactic moment of the march to the sea.

In a cold wind that swept in from the sound, Sherman stood on the roof of the customs house and gazed out over Savannah. The streets he had known as a young officer spread before him, lined with billowing evergreen oaks that gave the city a look of summer. The broad main streets were flanked by miniature parks, where fountains splashed within verdant squares.

Inland, westward of the city, lay the marshes, brown seas rolling to the horizon, cuffed by the wind and threaded by dark waters. The river was dotted with tiny red-and-white flags where the navy had marked enemy torpedoes. The ruined Confederate ram *Savannah,* blown up by its crew, still trailed smoke across the harbor. Northward across the river, behind a network of canals, estuaries and rice fields, lay South Carolina, a painful reminder of Hardee's escape.

It was shortly after nine in the morning of December 22 when the general mounted his perch, after a hurried trip through the marshes and a slow passage through the ranks of the moving army. With his staff he had come, almost unnoticed, down Bull Street to the heart of the conquered city. Though he had been denied a triumphal entry, he was gripped by elation as he stared down upon the goal toward which his army had marched for so long. He also had a sense of unreality: "Like one who had walked a narrow plank, I look back and wonder if I really did it." It seemed ages ago that he had left Atlanta; he could hardly believe that it had been little more than a month since he had ridden out of the burning city.

Sherman was never to confess it, but his exultation must have been tempered by rueful thoughts at this moment—he had allowed Hardee to escape to fight another day, as was the habit of Confederate armies. And the rebels had escaped in his absence; perhaps it would be said that he was overconfident and careless, and that he should not have left the army to subordinates at that moment. There would be no explaining the difficulties of the intricate terrain, nor his helplessness to halt Hardee, so long as the rebels held the Savannah River and the makeshift escape route remained intact.

There was also Grant and his chilling suggestion that Sherman move the army by sea. This superb veteran army, prepared to conquer whatever came into its path, might have seen the last of its service.

Sherman was compulsively eager to get on with the campaign, since he realized that a thrust by the army through the Carolinas was infinitely more important than the dramatic passage through Georgia. He must first garrison the city and then await approval of his Carolinas invasion from Washington. Working furiously at his cigar, he clambered down from the roof and turned impatiently to assume the role of conqueror. He rode to the Pulaski Hotel, where he expected to make headquarters, but he was approached there by Charles Green, a wealthy English cotton broker who offered the use of his home.

"If you don't take it," Green said, "some other general will. I much prefer you."

The house was one of the city's most striking, a formidable blend of Georgian and Victorian Gothic with battlements, a cast-iron porch and stained-glass windows, its rooms filled with Italian sculpture and European canvases. The general was shown to a second-floor suite, a bedroom with a sumptuous bath and dressing room, but was caught up in duties of the occupation before his baggage was unpacked.

One of his first visitors was a U.S. Treasury agent, A. G. Browne, "a shrewd, clever Yankee" who claimed all captured cotton, rice and government buildings. Sherman refused to give them up. The army needed food and supplies, he said, and only the surplus would be turned over to the Treasury. The cotton would be placed under guard.

Browne did not press the general, but he did make a suggestion that was to win Sherman's lifelong gratitude. When Sherman explained that he had not yet reported officially on the fall of Savannah, Browne said quickly, "Have you thought of sending the President the city as a Christmas gift? If you sent it by boat a message would reach Fortress Monroe by Christmas and could be telegraphed from there. I know Lincoln enjoys such pleasantries." Sherman saw the aptness of the proposal and dashed off his message: "I beg to present to you as a Christmas gift the city of Savannah, with one hundred fifty heavy guns and plenty of ammunition, also about 25,000 bales of cotton."

The house of Charles Green was already under siege by Negroes who waited for a glimpse of the commander or a word of reassurance from him. They came trembling with joyous expectation to test the realities of their dreams. Sherman received them in his bedroom, usually ten or twenty at once, rambling in his brusque manner: "Come to see Mr. Sherman, have you? Well, I'm Mr. Sherman—glad to see you." He made few promises and had little to say, but the cordiality of his greeting and his friendly handshake sent them away content.

There was also a procession of white civilians. The wife of the Confederate General Gustavus W. Smith came with a letter from her husband asking protection. General Hardee's brother, a cotton merchant, brought a letter from the general asking help for his family. At her request Sherman visited Mrs. A. P. Stewart, whose husband now commanded the rebel Army of Tennessee; he reassured her that Stewart was still alive, and advised her to go through the lines to her home in Cincinnati to await the end of the war. Another distressed woman came for help and advice, a mother whose six sons were soldiers, three in the Union army, three in the Confederate. Sherman complained to Ellen:

> The women here are . . . disposed to usurp my time more from curiosity than business. They have been told of my burning and killing until they expected the veriest monster, but their eyes were opened when . . . the three chief officers of the Rebel Army fled across the Savannah River, consigning their families to my special care. There are some very elegant people here who I knew in better days and who do not seem ashamed to call on the "Vandal Chief." They regard us just as the Romans did the Goths and the parallel is not unjust. Many of my men with red beards and stalwart frames look like giants.

He also sent Ellen most of his army pay of $550 per month: "I enclose a check for $800. I drew pay for November and December and kept $300 and send you the balance. It is good for you that I keep in the woods where my expenses are small and you get the lion's share of pay . . . "

The general had heard that the state of Ohio was to offer him a home for his family, and he said that though he would accept nothing for himself, he would accept the house, if the state would provide sufficient income to pay the taxes.

12
"An almost criminal dislike of the Negro"

Sherman's telegram reached the President on Christmas Eve. Newspapers throughout the North published it the next morning as the official announcement of the capture of Savannah, and it created a sensation. After almost a month of suspense during which the invading army had been isolated in enemy territory, the Northern people grasped the significance of its passage. The Western army's sweep through Georgia made obvious to everyone the overwhelming power of the Federal armies.

To the administration as well as to the public, this was the most welcome news of the war to date. Secretary of the Treasury Hugh McCulloch said, "Our joy was irrepressible . . . it was an assurance that the days of the Confederacy were numbered. Every member of the Cabinet knew, at last, that the war was won and the Union safe."

The ingratiating telegram itself altered Sherman's public image overnight. A general who offered his triumphs as Christmas gifts was no mere blood-and-thunder soldier, but a man of imagination, one to be remembered.

Lincoln's response signaled a change in Sherman's fortunes. General John Logan, who came to Savannah to take over the XV Corps from Peter Osterhaus, brought the President's reply to Sherman. In the afterglow of reading Lincoln's unstinted praise, Sherman must have taken new hope for his plan of invading the Carolinas: "Many, many thanks for your Christmas gift—the capture of Savannah. When you were about to leave Atlanta for the Atlantic coast, I was anxious, if not fearful; but feeling you were the better judge, and remembering that 'nothing risked nothing gained,' I did not interfere. Now the undertaking being a success, the honor is all yours, for I believe none of us went further than to acquiesce. . . . But what next? I suppose it will be safe if I leave General Grant and yourself to decide."

An admiring Northern public saw in Sherman the war's ultimate hero. Congress passed a joint resolution of praise and gratitude. Sherman smiled as he read Grant's message of congratulations: "I never had a doubt of the result . . . I would not have entrusted the expedition to any other living commander." There was a letter of praise from Professor D. H. Mahan, the eminent authority on military strategy.

Sherman acknowledged to Ellen that he had become world famous: "In the several grand epochs of this war, my name will have a prominent part, and not least among them will be the determination I took at Atlanta to destroy that place, and march on this city . . .

"I have received from high sources highest praise . . . General Grant . . . is almost childlike in his love for me . . . All sorts of people send me presents . . . I receive letters from all the great men, so full of real respect that I cannot disregard them, yet I dread the elevation to which they have got me."

Sherman made detailed reports of the opening phase of his march. He reported to Henry Halleck that his army had swept its path from Atlanta to Savannah of livestock and food, had seized 10,000 horses and mules, and freed slaves beyond counting. Sherman's informal estimate of the damage done to Georgia's military resources was $100 million. The figure seemed fantastic, but the army, in addition, had wrecked more than three hundred miles of railroad in forty counties of central Georgia and burned numberless buildings public and private, though few of the latter were actually homes. "This may seem a hard species of warfare," Sherman wrote, but it brought "the sad realities" home to the rebels.

Sherman's ambivalent feelings about the burning of the countryside and the suffering of Confederate civilians were apparent in his official reports—in striking contrast to the exultant description of his fiery passage he had given naval officers a few days earlier. His true feelings about the horrors of his total warfare were never to be expressed publicly. In his memoirs, published ten years later, the general was to offer the casual confession that his men had been "a little loose in foraging"—but that they had marched to the sea with "as little violence as could be expected."

Sherman's troops shared his pride in their march. One soldier calculated that the army had stolen 100,000 hogs, 20,000 cattle, 15,000 horses and mules, 500,000 bushels of corn and 100,000 bushels of sweet potatoes. Theodore Upson wrote after seeing a Northern paper for the first time in more than a month, "It seems that the good people up there were terribly worried about us. They called us the *Lost Army.* And some thought we would never show up again. I don't think they know what kind of an Army this is that Uncle Billy has. Why, if Grant can keep Lee and his troops busy we can tramp all over this Confederacy . . . "

Troops were turned out in the rain on Christmas Day to hear sergeants read Sherman's order of congratulations, a review ringing with praise of the army's march, "so complete a success . . . that it entitles it to a place in the military history of the world . . . we have at all points assumed the offensive and have completely thwarted the designs of the enemies of our country." In the moment of triumph no one seemed to notice that Sherman relished his own growing prominence in American military annals.

The troops were dismissed to cook their Christmas dinners, which they ate between rainstorms. Fife Major William Humphrey of the 101st Illinois wrote his family: "While you were all eating your good dinner we soldiers would have been glad to have the crumbs that fell from your table. I will tell you what our meals were this day: Breakfast, rice and beef. Dinner, rice. Supper, beef and rice. Rice is our favorite dish now."

Some regiments feasted royally. Indiana troops took wagons to the riverside and returned with several hundred bushels of oysters, which they roasted and served to all comers, a treat for Western farm boys who tasted them for the first time. The headquarters mess of the 16th Illinois Cavalry had a lavish holiday dinner menu: oyster soup, oysters on the half shell, roast goose, fried oysters, roast oysters, rice, raisins, coffee with condensed milk. "A little top-heavy as to oysters," Colonel Charles Kerr said, "but we don't complain."

Sherman himself entertained a dinner party of twenty, including Charles Green, who provided handsome silver and china. Major Nichols had foraged "three or four lovely turkeys," and General Barnum brought in hampers of wine donated by grateful merchants whose stocks he had saved from troops and civilian looters.

Sherman's troops laughed over a story that an Episcopal bishop had asked Sherman's consent to pray for the rebel cause on Christmas. "Hell, yes," Sherman had said. "Jeff Davis and the Confederate government need all the prayer they can get."

The holiday spirit failed to mellow the feeling of loyal Confederates toward the invaders. Townspeople savored the story of a Federal chaplain who offered to assist the Reverend I.S.K. Axson at the Independent Presbyterian Church and was told, "Sir, my people need comfort, and that you cannot give."*

Christmas brought an epidemic of homesickness to the army. General Howard's yearning to see his wife and young children was so strong that he asked Sherman for leave: "Now, let me off. I don't ask but two days at home."

The commander shook his head. "Howard, I'd give a million dollars, if I had it, to be with my children. Would you do more than that?"

Howard threw up his hand. "I'll say no more," he said.

Sherman learned of the death of his six-month-old son Charles, whom he had never seen, from reading a newspaper brought into Savannah. He wrote to Ellen of the baby's death: "All spoke of him as so bright and fair that I had hoped he would be spared us to fill the great void left in our hearts by Willy, but it is otherwise decreed and we must submit."

To his brother John, Sherman wrote of his sorrow over the loss of his two sons, and said plaintively that above all he wanted "to slip out quietly and see more of my family . . . were it not for General Grant's confidence in me, I should insist upon a little rest. As it is I must go on."

The general found some solace in his acquaintances among the people of Savannah. Through an army friend, he met the attractive Gordon family, and won the hearts of two small girls of the household with the aid of the army's musicians.

His troops marched through the city streets almost daily behind

*Dr. Axson was the grandfather of Ellen Louise Axson, who was to become the first wife of President Woodrow Wilson.

blaring regimental bands. Nelly and Daisy Gordon, the small daughters of a Confederate cavalry officer, peered out at the passing troops one day.

"Oh, Mama, is that old Sherman?"

"I'm sure I don't know," Eleanor Gordon said. "I never saw 'old Sherman.' "

When the 2nd Wisconsin's band swept by the house, Daisy said indignantly, "Just hear them playing 'When This Cruel War Is Over' and *they're doing it theirselves all this time!*"

Sherman came to the house soon afterward with letters from Mrs. Gordon's brother, a Federal colonel who was one of the general's old friends. The girls darted behind their mother as Sherman entered the parlor. Eleanor Gordon drew Nelly forth.

"General, here is a little girl who was very anxious to see 'old Sherman' the day of the parade."

Nelly's voice trembled: "I never said 'old Sherman'—it was Daisy!"

"Well, you said it too, Nelly," Daisy snapped. "You did say *'old Sherman'!*"

The general took the girls on his knees and began teasing them: "Why of course you never said 'old Sherman,' because you and I used to play together when I was a little boy, and now we're going to sit right down and talk it over."

The general held the children, laughing and talking with them until their mother sent them to bed, long after their customary hour. Sherman gave Mrs. Gordon news of her family and entertained her with anecdotes of his "narrow escapes" on the march from Atlanta. She never forgot the glimpse of the sensitive nature of the general who was to emerge from the war as the most implacable and vengeful of commanders, an arch vandal who made war on helpless civilians.

Other Federal officers came to the Gordon house, one of them Oliver Howard, who also made friends with Nelly and Daisy.

"Oh, you have only got one arm!" Daisy said.

"Yes, little girl. Aren't you sorry for me?"

"Yes, indeed. What happened to your arm?"

"It was shot off in battle."

"Oh, did the Yankees shoot it off?"

"No, my dear. The Rebels shot it off."

"Did they?" Daisy said. "Well, I shouldn't wonder if my papa did it. He's shot lots of Yankees!"

* * *

These visits of Federal officers did not go unnoticed by one neighbor who passed word through the lines to Mrs. Gordon's rebel husband. Eleanor had a bitter message from her husband, Captain William W. Gordon of Wheeler's command: "The fact of your being in the Federal lines is of course very difficult to bear, but I accept that as the fate of war and will endure it as I would any sacrifice that may be called for. But what really galls me is that you should associate with my enemies upon any terms than those politeness demands from every lady . . ."

Eleanor's friendship with Sherman may have inspired his liberal policy with the city's civilians, whom he offered the choice of remaining "as good citizens" or being taken through the lines to their homes or relatives. Among some two hundred of "the more irreconcilable" who chose to leave, mostly families of Confederate officers, were Mrs. Gordon and her daughters. They went aboard a steamer under flag of truce to Charleston, South Carolina, where a Confederate officer took them in tow and helped them to their destinations.*

There was a good deal of other traffic northward, some of it unofficial.

Captain Charles Belknap, who had brought the two orphaned baby girls he had found over the long route from Sandersville to Savannah, asked city officials to find a home for them, but was turned away: "Nobody had time for 'the little white trash.' " The two little girls were finally taken north by a wounded lieutenant who was going home on a furlough. Belknap wrote many years later: "He took them home to his state, where they reside today in happy homes, beautiful in their motherhood."

Some of the city's high-spirited women were too much for the invaders. One defiant elderly woman once passed General Howard's headquarters and stepped into the sandy street to avoid walking beneath a U.S. flag overhanging the sidewalk. A guard halted her: "Walk under the flag, Madam." When she refused, the woman was taken before Howard.

"Madam, I understand that you refused to pass under my flag."

*After the war the Gordons returned to Savannah, where the captain founded the city's cotton exchange. Daisy, whose given name was Juliette, grew up to marry William Low and became founder of the Girl Scouts of America.

"I did. Am I not at liberty to walk in the sand if I prefer it to the sidewalk?"

Howard's voice rose in uncharacteristic excitement: "Yes, but you intentionally avoided my flag. I'll make you walk under it."

"You cannot make me. You may have me carried under it but then it will be your act, not mine."

"I'll have you sent to prison."

"Send me if you will. I know you have the power. See if you can shake my resolution."

Howard said, "I'll have the flag hung in front of your door, so that you can't go out without walking under it."

"Then I'll stay at home and send the servants. They won't mind."

The frustrated Howard sent her away.

Sherman found that he had not overstated the hatred and scorn he had earned from Southern women. He began to discover in Savannah that the people of the South were to focus their bitterness upon him, and to hold him personally responsible for all the horrors visited upon them in defeat.

Two women from wealthy local families, Nelly Howard and a Miss Moodie, once went to Sherman's headquarters in an effort to recover some captured cotton owned by a relative. They were announced by Charles Green, the general's host.

"There are some ladies in the parlor."

Sherman growled crossly and audibly: "Not to see me, I hope."

Green muttered to Miss Moodie, "You wish to be introduced to General Sherman?"

"Not for the world," she said distinctly. "I have no wish to make his acquaintance; my business is private and entirely with you, Mr. Green, entirely with you."

Green invited the women upstairs to look at a painting. They passed the open doors of handsomely furnished rooms and saw a huge bed.

"Those are General Sherman's apartments."

Miss Moodie wrinkled her nose with disdain.

"Don't you want him to rest comfortably?"

"Indeed not! I wish a thousand papers of pins were stuck in that bed and that he was strapped down to them."

Most soldiers, however, found Savannah's people more friendly than "the ultra bitter sort" they had met in Atlanta and the countryside. Civilians told Major Connolly the city was more peaceful than it had been for three years. Willie Baugh of the 76th Ohio asked one man how he liked the Yankees and was told, "Oh, I'd rather you be here than the rebels."

Many women smiled and waved to admiring soldiers from their balconies. Colonel Oscar Jackson said, "The ladies are the tastiest 'Secesh' I have seen and I rather think would get to like Yankees. The majority do not look a bit mad now."

The army began to enjoy life in the city. Men drew their pay for the first time in months. There was an issue of clothing, mostly shoes; the veterans sensed that long marches lay ahead, and they declined changes of uniform and new blankets as excess baggage. Drills, formations and dress parades were staged to keep men out of trouble. Thousands of men attended "recitation classes" in military education by day and concerts and theatricals at night.

Most of Sherman's troops sought other pleasures. They packed restaurants and hotel lobbies and attended nightly Negro dances. Bordellos were so numerous that Private Samuel Jarrett complained of standing duty every other day "because there are so many whore houses in town which must have a sentinel at each door for to keep them Straight."

One of the general's orders to the troops was a futile ban on gambling, which flourished on every hand. U. H. Parr of the 70th Indiana saw hundreds of men along the slope of a railroad embankment playing poker and chuck-a-luck and rolling dice. Most of the money "was rapidly falling into the hands of the skillful and unscrupulous." Troops flocked to a race track where soldier jockeys raced fine horses captured from Georgia plantations. Betting was heavy and gambling was well organized, but Sherman ended the races after several riots had broken out.

Still, Savannah was no paradise for soldiers. Prices soared. Apples sold for $50 a barrel, butter was $1.50 per pound, condensed milk $1 a can. A shave and hair cut cost 75 cents. A grocer sold a cheese for $300. To the dismay of the troops, Savannah merchants refused to differentiate between worthless Confederate money and U.S. greenbacks.

Extremes of weather made camp life miserable. One night was so cold that water froze in canteens, but men swam in the river the next day and by noon marching troops were grateful for the shade of live oaks in which they escaped the "oppressive heat." The army's blankets and clothing were usually wet from rains, since winds howled at every crack of the hovels. Men of the 50th Illinois slept under shelter tents buttoned together, piled overcoats on top, "then packing down spoon fashion, would lie resting as best they could . . . when some tired one would call out, 'spoon over here, spoon over'; and over the boys would turn to the other side."

The 58th Indiana camped amid slum shanties on a field covered with rice chaff and burning garbage, beside a canal odorous of the city's open sewers. A cold wind filled the air with sand and filth and shook regimental headquarters tents, which were pitched behind a whorehouse. The convenience of the location was lost on Chaplain Hight, who complained, "It is rather a vile place to come a thousand miles to camp."

Sherman found many of Savannah's civilians destitute. Thousands of white refugees had flocked in ahead of the army, worsening shortages of food, fuel and clothing, which were already rationed. The blockade had reduced even wealthy families to a diet of rice and fish. Sherman at first said that since the Confederates had made no effort to care for needy people, he would not undertake to feed them, but he quickly relented. He opened emergency food supplies to the public and turned over to Mayor Arnold more than fifty thousand bushels of captured rice. Within a few weeks shiploads of food and supplies were to arrive, generous donations from the people of New York, Boston and Philadelphia.

There was never a question of burning Savannah and leaving the ruins to Confederates. Its port was an invaluable prize as a naval base and supply center. A Federal garrison here would not only solidify the gains made by Sherman's passage through Georgia—it would close to the enemy one more port to which blockade-runners had been bringing supplies to keep the Confederacy alive.

Sherman began organizing the city for occupation. His choice for military governor of Savannah was General John W. Geary, an experienced administrator who had served as governor of Kansas and mayor of San Francisco. Geary and his provost marshal, Colonel Henry Barnum, had established order at once. Guards were placed over houses occupied by civilians, a curfew was enforced, and soldiers in surrounding camps were allowed to enter Savannah only by pass.

Sherman took pride in the occupation: "The people here seem to be well content . . . Our troops have behaved magnificently; you would think it Sunday, so quiet is everything in the city day and night. . . . No city was ever occupied with less disorder. Women and children . . . walk its streets with as much security as they do in Philadelphia."

The army's peaceful stay in the city owed much to the efforts of Dr. Richard Arnold, the realistic mayor, who had a discomfiting message for Confederate diehards: "Where resistance is hopeless it is criminal to make it."

Official messages still poured into the army's Savannah headquarters, reflecting a mood of buoyant optimism in the North. To Sherman's relief, Grant agreed to his plea that the army be allowed to march through the Carolinas rather than sail to Virginia. Though the nationwide acclaim for Sherman may have prompted Grant's change of heart, he was apparently persuaded by Halleck, who pointed out that it would take two months to assemble shipping and move the army from Savannah to Virginia by sea, and that in any case Sherman should be encouraged to make "another wide swath through the Confederacy." Sherman's emergence as a military hero had rendered it impolitic to halt his spectacular progress in the midst of his march, and Grant realized it as keenly as Halleck himself.

Grant, however, urged Sherman to start northward "without delay" so as to keep the undermanned and discouraged rebels in a state of uncertainty and unable to organize an effective defense in the Carolinas.

Halleck suggested to Sherman that he consider the destruction of Charleston, South Carolina, "and if a little salt should be sown upon the site it may prevent the growth of future crops of nullification and secession." Though Charleston, the cradle of secession, was far from the line of march he had planned, Sherman replied that he would keep the suggestion in mind. He added, "The truth is, the whole army is burning with an insatiable desire to wreak vengeance upon South Carolina. I almost tremble at her fate, but feel that she deserves all that seems in store for her . . ."

Ironically, Sherman's stunning success not only gave him his way in his controversy with Grant, but also tarnished his commander's military reputation. News of the triumphal march through Georgia inspired press criticism of Grant in the North; he was depicted as a dull, unimaginative officer, content to remain idle in Lee's front near Richmond while Sherman's men were slashing their way through the Deep South, capturing the public imagination. There was talk of promoting Sherman to Grant's rank, but Sherman would have none of it. He wrote his brother John, who was now one of the most influential men in the Senate, saying that he would decline a commission that might make him Grant's rival. "I have all the rank I want," he said. He told a friend, only half in jest, "General Grant is a great general. I know him well. He stood by me when I was crazy, and I stood by him when he was drunk; and now, sir, we stand by each other always."

Sherman had probably heard gossip that Grant envied him his new role as a national idol and had sought to keep him as far as possible from Washington. Sherman must have smiled over that charge, recalling Grant's eagerness to have him at his side in Virginia.

It was only now, amid the chorus of acclaim for Sherman, that criticism began to be heard in Washington. His spectacular conquest of Georgia, it was said, was an illusory triumph. In the course of it the general had not only allowed two Confederate armies to escape (Hardee's from Savannah and Hood's from Atlanta), he had shown a lamentable—inexcusable—lack of concern for the plight of slaves. It was charged that he had freed only a fraction of the black hordes he might have brought to Savannah for safe passage to the North, and that he had heartlessly driven thousands of them from his camps.*

Secretary of War Edwin M. Stanton complained to Grant of Sherman's failure to destroy Hardee's army: "It is a sore disappointment that Hardee was able to get off . . . it looks like protracting the war while their armies continue to escape." Sherman confessed his own chagrin over the rebel escape, but insisted that he was blameless.

*This charge had little or no basis in fact. Though some 25,000 blacks joined the army at one time or another in Georgia, most of them turned back to their old homes, weary and disillusioned with the new "freedom." Only 6,800 remained when Sherman reached the coast. Military needs had governed Sherman's policy.

In North Carolina a few weeks later, the *New York Herald* correspondent reported that large numbers of Negroes joined Sherman's army with the aid of their masters on the condition that they would return to work for wages as soon as it was safe for them to do so. In one case, however, white militiamen hanged several Negroes to foil their plan to join Sherman.

"Intervening obstacles" had prevented his complete investment of the city and enabled Hardee to slip away. Content with the almost bloodless capture of Savannah, the general had already begun the task of refitting and supplying his army for the next phase of its thousand-mile march. He hoped to begin the invasion of South Carolina during the first days of January.

In the midst of his preparations to resume the march, Sherman had a sobering letter from Henry Halleck, his first warning of a controversy over his treatment of Negroes that would mar his triumph and influence events beyond the final collapse of the Confederacy. Sherman could not know that Halleck was parroting Stanton, who was deeply disturbed by reports of the general's hostile attitude toward blacks; few Americans beyond the administration's inner circles realized that Washington's Radicals were pressing Stanton to punish Sherman—though it was already clear that Radical leadership had created a gulf between Congress and President Lincoln, who favored a mild form of reconstruction in the South. Edwin Stanton found himself in the midst of this growing controversy.

Halleck minced no words in his letter to Sherman. "Almost everyone" praised the march to the sea as an American military epic, the Chief of Staff wrote, but there were those who were attacking Sherman's reputation: "There is a certain class having now great influence with the President . . . who say that you have manifested an almost criminal dislike of the Negro and that you . . . repulsed him with contempt. They say you might have brought with you to Savannah more than 50,000 . . . but that instead . . . you drove them from your ranks . . ."

Though Halleck did not mention the incident at Ebenezer Creek, where General Davis had abandoned his black camp followers to the enemy, it was the exposure of this affair by James Connolly and others that had inspired protests.

Sherman sent Halleck a denial of the "cock and bull story." He insisted that he had turned back no one from the march—this despite his consistent policy of restricting the numbers of blacks with his marching columns. He explained the fate of the abandoned Negroes at Ebenezer Creek somewhat lamely: "Jeff C. Davis took up his pontoon bridge, not because he wanted to leave them, but because he wanted his bridge. He and Slocum tell me they don't believe Wheeler killed one of them."

The general fumed over the criticism: "Because I had not loaded down my army by the hundreds of thousands of poor Negroes, I was construed by others to be hostile to the black race."

Though Sherman shared certain anti-black prejudices prevalent in his day, even among Northerners, it is evident that he was not at ease in this debate. He realized that General Davis was notorious for his extreme attitude toward Negroes, and must have known from protests of eyewitnesses at Ebenezer Creek that Davis had dealt with the black refugees with undue harshness.

Secretary Stanton, who had been urging Sherman to enlist Negroes as soldiers, found the general stubbornly opposed. Sherman preferred to keep blacks in subordinate positions for some years, he said, "for our prejudices, yours as well as mine, are not yet schooled for absolute equality." If Negroes became soldiers, the general argued, they would demand a voice in government; it was better to use them as laborers, and fill the army's ranks with white men who had stayed at home "for trade and gain." But he ended by writing Stanton, "If, however, the government has determined to push the policy to the end it is both my duty and pleasure to assist."

Almost as if he sought penance, Sherman turned to more immediate problems involving Negroes who had flocked into Savannah on the heels of his troops. He acted to protect the city's black men of military age from recruiting agents of Northern states, who swarmed into the city and herded hundreds of ignorant victims into lockups, to be held until they agreed to enlist in the army—and then to be sold as substitutes for well-to-do draftees in the North. Sherman freed the black victims and threatened the recruiting agents with arrest. He told the Negroes they were no longer slaves, and could not be forced into the army.

Thereafter, blacks besieged Sherman when he appeared on the streets. He wrote of it: "They gather round me in crowds, and I can't find out whether I am Moses or Aaron . . . but surely I am rated as one of the congregation, and it is hard to tell in what sense I am most appreciated . . . in saving him (the Negro) from his master or the new master that threatens him with a new species of slavery. I mean the state recruiting agents."

The blacks also hailed Sherman's troops as saviors. Some soldiers were shocked by the sight of older Negroes falling to their knees, doffing their hats and crying out their gratitude, "crooked-legged, wrinkle-faced, white-haired ragamuffins" who paid homage to the troops all over the city. Lieutenant Colonel Samuel Merrill of the 70th Indiana foresaw a sad day of awakening for these innocents who dreamed of new and untroubled lives of freedom and plenty: "We laugh now at their wild antics and marvelous expectations, but I cannot shut out the thought that the comedy may soon darken into tragedy."

On January 11 Secretary Stanton himself arrived unexpectedly in Savannah. He had come on the advice of Grant, who had failed to persuade Sherman to enlist black regiments and had suggested that Stanton intervene personally to urge Sherman to use blacks for garrison duty, if nothing else, so as to free white troops for combat. Stanton had undertaken the cold sea voyage despite a troublesome illness, taking with him Quartermaster General Montgomery Meigs, Adjutant General B. D. Townsend, and several civilian administrators who were to establish Federal offices in the city.

The ostensible purpose of the visit was to provide a rest for the harried Stanton and to clarify conflicting policies of the Treasury and War departments regarding captured cotton. Gideon Welles, the gossipy secretary of the Navy, theorized that Stanton's true motive was to curry favor with Sherman, now that he had "eclipsed Grant" —but it was, above all else, the Negro problem that had brought Stanton to Savannah.

Stanton greeted Sherman effusively, beaming from a round face half-hidden by a grizzled beard, dark eyes peering over tiny gold-rimmed spectacles. The crafty veteran of Ohio politics who had played a major role in organizing the Northern war effort was a Steubenville doctor's son who had become a bookstore clerk at thirteen, worked his way through Kenyon College, become a wealthy lawyer, and risen to power in the new Republican party.

The fifty-year-old Stanton wheezed asthmatically. He had come, he told Sherman, to recuperate in the salt air and to escape the madhouse that wartime Washington had become. Sherman received him warmly, for it was not long since his brother John Sherman had written, "I live next door to Stanton, and he favors me with the dispatches when they come. By the way, he is your fast friend, and was when you had fewer."

Stanton first dealt with the matter of the captured cotton on the Savannah waterfront, the war's richest haul of its kind, a treasure valued at upwards of $25 million. The secretary dismissed all claims on the cotton except those of the Treasury, and ordered it shipped north to be sold for the government. Sherman would have preferred to have the cotton awarded to the War Department, since his army had taken it, but he was pleased when Stanton rejected rival British claims that the precious cargo had been bought for export and rightfully belonged to its British purchasers. Sherman said, "Our soldiers on every battlefield of the war have been killed by British guns firing British shells, all bought with rebel cotton." His face crimsoned with anger when he spoke of the British subterfuge of shipping arms to the West Indies to be exchanged for cotton: "It would afford me great satisfaction to conduct my army to Nassau and wipe out that nest of pirates. I'd like to take picks and shovels and throw that cursed sand hill into the sea."

Sherman invited Stanton to a review of the cavalry through the streets of Savannah. The general wore a new coat for the occasion, a wonder to his troops—but though he was ablaze with brass buttons, Sherman was otherwise as untidy as ever. The general's gloves were dingy, and he had not given up his "sorry-looking hat" nor his antique sideboard collar, the only one in the army. Chaplain Hight was amused by Sherman's discomfiture as the troopers pranced past in review: "He twitched himself this way and that, tugged at his collar, pulled at his coat and made sundry adjustments . . . but failed to make any improvements in his appearance . . ."

Throughout the review Stanton gazed closely at Sherman's chief officers, as if he suspected all of them as Southern sympathizers and conspirators in a plot to foil the administration's policy of liberality toward the freed blacks. The cavalrymen paraded past the reviewing officers in the sparkling sunlight of a crisp January day, with almost every man turned out in new finery from the stock of recently arrived uniforms.

Kilpatrick, the most resplendent of all, appeared in a new dark-blue coat of rakish cut and sky-blue trousers, new golden gauntlets and sash, all heavily corded with gilt lace. Little Kil, who rode like a boy in the saddle, was the first West Pointer to have been wounded in the war and the first of recent Academy graduates to wear a general's stars. Kilpatrick, who was slightly hunchbacked, had a striking habit of thrusting his head downward, like a restless horse. Little Kil had not committed himself publicly on the Negro problem, nor on other current political issues, and Stanton would have been surprised to learn that the young general nurtured political ambitions—he hoped to become governor of New Jersey and then President.

Sherman's corps commanders also came under Stanton's scrutiny. There was General Alpheus Williams of the XX Corps, his coat buttoned to the chin, fat legs thrust straight out in the stirrups, straining his corduroy trousers, a private's hat perched atop his huge head, looking less a soldier than "a dull old doctor who loves good whiskey with a disposition to the gout." Little was known of Williams' political views.

Stanton saw a familiar figure in handsome red-haired Frank Blair of the XVII Corps, a three-term congressman from Missouri who was still in office. Blair was the son of Francis P. Blair, Sr., who had done much to nominate and elect Lincoln; the Blair family had become a potent political force in Washington, and was often opposed to Stanton on issues of the day. Though he had been educated in the South, Frank Blair's loyalty was unquestioned. He had raised seven Union regiments at his own expense. Sherman was fond of Blair, but did not admire him as a soldier: "He's brave and cool, but loose and scattering."

Stanton was not favorably impressed by Sherman's other corps commanders. Black Jack Logan, another political general, who had replaced Peter Osterhaus, still held office as a congressman from Illinois. A prewar Southern sympathizer, Logan was a fighter after Sherman's heart. As a civilian spectator at the battle of Bull Run, he had seized a soldier's musket to fire at the victorious rebels and was in uniform soon afterward. He had led the Army of Tennessee briefly in the Atlanta campaign, but his distaste for paper work and high command had led to his demotion.

Stanton's gaze rested longest on General Jefferson C. Davis, to whom he imputed the instincts of a slaveholder. In his imagination Stanton saw Davis at the fateful crossing of Ebenezer Creek, heartlessly turning back the blacks who had looked to him for salvation.

Sherman soon discovered that the welfare of the liberated blacks was indeed Stanton's chief concern, and that the army's accomplishment in marching to the sea meant little in Stanton's eyes, since he felt that Sherman and his men had betrayed the true cause of the war, the liberation of slaves. The secretary asked pointedly about General Davis and his attitude toward blacks. Stanton knew the reputation of Davis all too well from the prompting of Radical spokesmen in the past few days. He also probably theorized that Sherman might not have recognized in Davis the animus of white supremacy because of his own outlook.

Sherman defended his general as best he could: "I assured him that General Davis was an excellent soldier, and I did not believe he had any hostility to the Negro." When Stanton produced a newspaper clipping about the incident at Ebenezer Creek, Sherman called in Davis, who maintained that he was innocent of the charge: His pontoons had been in use day and night, Davis said, and were moved rapidly from stream to stream without regard to the safety of those in the rear of his corps. Some Negroes had indeed drowned in panic as they sought to cross the creek. But he did not believe survivors had been butchered by Wheeler's cavalry.

Sherman assumed that Stanton was satisfied with the version of the affair given by Davis in his blunt, forthright fashion, but the secretary persisted in exploring racial problems. He asked Sherman to assemble the city's Negro leaders for a face-to-face conference.

The general called in twenty preachers and lay leaders of Savannah's Negro churches. They met in Sherman's quarters, prepared to tell Stanton what they expected of their new freedom. About half of these former slaves had been freed by Sherman's army.

The group's spokesman was sixty-seven-year-old Garrison Frazier, a Baptist preacher who had bought his freedom from slavery. Frazier was frail, but his voice was firm and his replies prompt and intelligent.

Stanton asked Frazier to interpret the Emancipation Proclamation.

"So far as I understand President Lincoln's Proclamation to the Rebellious States, it is that if they would lay down their arms . . . before the first of January, 1863, all would be well, but if they did not, then all the slaves of the Rebel States would be free henceforth and forever."

"State what you understand by slavery and the freedom that was to be given by the President's proclamation."

"Slavery is receiving by *irresistible power* the work of another man, and not by his *consent.* The freedom as I understand it . . . is taking us from under the yoke of bondage and placing us where we could reap the fruits of our own labor, take care of ourselves . . ."

How could Negroes earn their living?

"The best way we can take care of ourselves is to have land, and turn it and till it by our own labor . . . we want to be placed on land until we are able to buy it and make it our own."

Sherman listened intently, interrupting with an occasional question. Stanton took notes at a table, occasionally putting down his pen to stare in admiration at Frazier, whose replies struck him as "shrewd, wise and comprehensive." The secretary thought the untutored black man could discuss racial problems "as well as any member of the Cabinet."

"In what manner would you rather live—scattered among the whites or in colonies by yourselves?"

"I would prefer to live by ourselves," Frazier said. "There is a prejudice against us in the South that will take years to get over; but I do not know if I can answer for my brethren." He paused to ask each of the others for an opinion. The older men agreed with him; only James Lynch, a twenty-six-year-old free-born preacher from Baltimore, insisted that Negroes and whites should live in the same communities.

"Do you think there is enough intelligence among the slaves of the south to maintain themselves under the Government . . . ?"

"I think there is sufficient intelligence to do so."

After more than an hour of questioning, Stanton asked Sherman to leave the room. The secretary then asked Frazier's opinion of the commander.

"We unanimously feel inexpressible gratitude to him . . . some of us called upon him immediately upon his arrival, and . . . he met us . . . as a friend and a gentleman. We have confidence in General Sherman, and think that what concerns us could not be under better hands . . ."

Young Lynch interrupted to say that he was unwilling to express an opinion of Sherman on so short an acquaintance.

The general returned when the interview was over, and smiled pleasantly until the crowd had gone, but he was inwardly seething over what he felt was a gratuitous insult by Stanton, who had "catechized Negroes concerning the character of a general who had . . . conducted 65,000 men successfully across four hundred miles of hostile territory, and had just brought tens of thousands of freedmen to a place of security."

At Stanton's request Sherman devised a plan to care for the black freedmen of Georgia and South Carolina, and with the secretary's approval ordered it put into effect:

A vast tract of coastal land was confiscated and set aside for Negro homesteaders—all the sea islands south of Charleston, abandoned rice fields on the mainland for thirty miles inland, and all waterfront lands along Florida's St. Johns River. Whites were barred from these areas; each Negro family would be given forty acres, clothing, seed and farm equipment. Sherman's officers began work on the resettlement at once, but the ambitious scheme was to fail during the chaotic period of Reconstruction, subverted by local whites. Negroes of the city were to have a long memory of Sherman and his efforts in their behalf; fifty years afterward they were to date events from "the time Tecumsey was here."

Stanton appeared frequently at Sherman's quarters, where he sat for hours chattering away about his abdominal pains, which he thought were caused by some incurable ailment, and about the bickering among government officials and the threat of inflation which had brought Washington near bankruptcy. He warned Sherman that the war must be ended at once or the government could not survive.

Sherman's junior officers rejoiced when Stanton left the city after four days of hectic activity. "Stanton has been very boorish and bearish, as is his nature," one of them wrote, "and it will be a relief to everyone to have him out of the way." But Sherman felt that he had altered the secretary's views on the enlistment of blacks, and was pleased with the visit. He wrote Ellen: "Mr. Stanton has been here and is cured of that 'Negro nonsense' which arises, not from love of the Negro, but from a desire to avoid service." Though Sherman felt that ex-slaves were not yet qualified for military service, he insisted that he and his men were the best friends of Georgia's liberated blacks: "As regards kindness to the race . . . procuring them food and clothing, and providing them with land . . . I assert that no army ever did more for that race."

Stanton's visit to Savannah did little to allay his doubts of Sherman's trustworthiness on the Negro question. During his voyage back to Washington, the secretary telegraphed Grant and asked for a meeting to discuss "other matters that cannot safely be written" —probably a reference to his suspicions of Sherman. In any case, impressions gathered by Stanton during this visit certainly affected his later tempestuous relationship with the newly famous general.

For his part, Sherman did not trust Stanton. On the day the secretary had interviewed the Negro leaders in Savannah, he wrote

Halleck that though he seemed to be popular with the secretary at the moment, he would not deceive himself; any misstep on the Negro question could "tumble down my fame into infamy."

With Stanton gone, Sherman turned to hurried preparations to move his army out of the city and into South Carolina on its thrust northward. The secretary's visit had delayed the departure for some days, and a devastating flood had kept the army in the city for two weeks longer than planned, an unusually high flood that swept away an army pontoon bridge and drove thousands of soldiers from their tents to higher ground.

Sherman was elated when the army prepared to leave after a full month in Savannah. He was weary of rebel women who begged for protection and Northern speculators who swarmed into the city in search of quick profits. He also felt the call of adventure: "I was quite impatient to get off to myself, for city life had become dull and tame, and we were all anxious to get into the pine woods again."

The troops understood. As Henry Aten of the 85th Illinois said, "They missed the pungent smell of the piney woods . . . the excitement of the march . . . a change of scenery, of duty and diet."

Sherman's first move was to ship Howard's wing to Beaufort, South Carolina, by transports, ready to drive inland in an advance on Columbia. Slocum's wing was to begin to the south of Howard's line, pushing inland on each side of the Savannah River so as to appear to threaten Augusta. The actual goal of the twin drive was Columbia, South Carolina.

Sherman wrote Ellen of his plans to "dive again beneath the surface," make feints at Augusta and Charleston, but march through Columbia, then northward into North Carolina. He warned her to keep secret his plan of campaign: "Don't breathe this, for the walls have ears, and foreknowledge published by some mischevious fool might cost many lives. We have lived long enough for men to thank me for keeping my own counsels, and keeping away from armies those pests of newspaper men . . .

"I will surely be off in the course of this week, and you will hear of me only through Richmond for two months. You have got used to it now and will not be concerned though I think chances of getting killed on this trip are about even."

Sherman sailed from Savannah on January 21 for Beaufort, South Carolina, to join Howard's command on the opening drive into South Carolina. He left the Savannah garrison under command of General Foster and told him that he planned to drive through both Carolinas to meet General J. M. Schofield's corps at Goldsboro, North Carolina. He left Foster with a stern warning: If newspaper reporters discovered this secret plan of campaign, "don't risk them, but imprison them till the time is past." Sherman's relations with the press had not improved since early in the war, when reporters and editorial writers charged that he was insane. He continued to regard reporters as potential spies or, at best, reckless retailers of military secrets to the enemy. Though almost a dozen newspaper and magazine correspondents and artists had made the march to the sea with the army, they had been unable to file their stories until they reached Savannah, and the general thus found them harmless on the route. Sherman now learned that three reporters had been captured by the rebels, and was told— erroneously—that they had been executed. "Good," he snapped. "Now we'll have news from hell before breakfast."

Sherman was brimming with confidence as he opened the second phase of his campaign. He wrote Grant his estimate of the strategy of the Confederate president: "I expect Davis will move heaven and earth to catch me, for success to my column is fatal to his dream of empire." He had learned that he was striking terror into the hearts of Southern civilians and troops as well, and planned to use this terror as a weapon of war: "The soldiers and people of the south entertained an undue fear of our western men, and . . . invented such ghostlike stories of our progress in Georgia that they were scared by their own inventions . . . this was a power, and I intended to utilize it."

The only apprehension Sherman expressed as he made ready to enter South Carolina was that Robert E. Lee might draw away from Grant at Richmond and fall upon his marching army somewhere in the upper Carolinas.

Major Nichols heard the commander tell staff officers one day: "If Lee is a soldier of genius, he'll move his army to Raleigh or Columbia. If he's a man of detail, he'll remain where he is, and his defeat is sure."

In Washington, President Lincoln saw the strategic situation of the unfolding campaign in his own droll way: "Grant has the bear by the tail while Sherman takes off its hide."

13

"No such army since the days of Julius Caesar"

Sherman rode with Oliver Howard's troops as the army advanced into South Carolina. The sweep through the state, he predicted, would be "one of the most horrible things in the history of the world," and added that "the Devil himself couldn't restrain my men." Even so, his staff found the general's attitude toward civilians unpredictable. In personal encounters he was usually warm and sympathetic. The general once scolded a mother for bringing her baby into the cold when she emerged to ask protection for her home and family. He made frequent halts to talk with country people, or to divide his simple lunch with Carolina children who came to his side. Officers noted that the wrinkles disappeared from his face when he talked with children.

Men in ranks talked of the fate in store for South Carolina as if they feared they might otherwise forget their mission. Kilpatrick asked Sherman as they parted at the opening of the South Carolina campaign, "How shall I let you know where I am?" Sherman replied casually, "Oh, just burn a barn or something. Make a smoke like the Indians do." Camp gossips said the cavalrymen had spent five thousand dollars for matches before leaving Savannah. Kilpatrick was said to have declared that future travelers in South Carolina would see only charred chimney stacks in the desolate country and ask the cause: "Some Yankee will answer, 'Kilpatrick's cavalry.' " The army understood that Sherman expected to exact vengeance from the original Secessionists, who, he said, bore a major share of the blame for the war.

The army entered the state on two fronts, marching in the pattern it had used since leaving Atlanta. Howard's wing was now in the northern sector, moving inland from the coastal town of Beaufort. Slocum's command was some fifty miles to the south, slogging through swamps on both sides of the Savannah River. Slocum was to follow the Savannah upstream for some forty miles, then turn northward to parallel Howard's route toward Columbia, the state capital. Once more Sherman had divided his forces to mislead Confederate defenders. His wings still posed threats to Augusta on the south and Charleston on the north—but the army's true course was northwestward, into the Piedmont uplands to Columbia. The general's basic strategy remained unchanged. He would avoid battle wherever possible, and would reveal the actual objectives of his march only at the last practicable moment.

Sherman moved from column to column on each day's march, ceaselessly studying the countryside with his bright, nervous glance, querying couriers and civilians with eager, snappish impatience. He spent the first night of the South Carolina march uncomfortably, on the floor of a deserted farmhouse near the town of Pocataligo, not far from Beaufort. Sherman rose often during the cold night to replenish a fire by smashing a mantel clock and an old bedstead for kindling. It was, he said, "the only act of vandalism that I recall done by myself personally during the war."

The general spent the night of February 1 a few miles farther inland, in the abandoned home of a Mrs. McBride, who had fled to Columbia. On this day he learned that Slocum had crossed the Savannah, and with Kilpatrick leading, was on his way northward. Sherman was now anxious for Howard's men to press forward as rapidly as possible. The outbuildings of the McBride farm were ablaze when Sherman emerged the next morning to resume the march. He saw a soldier put a torch to the large house while he and his staff were mounting their horses, but said nothing. This was unauthorized arson, but as Private Gage of the 12th Indiana noted, "None would attempt to put out the blaze." This was the first recorded incident in Sherman's announced campaign to teach Secessionist leaders of the state the lesson of total war. An Ohio soldier in his ranks wrote his family that South Carolina would pay a terrible price: "We will make her suffer worse than she did at the time of the Revolutionary War. We will let her know that it isn't so sweet to Secede as she thought it would be."

* * *

Though they had been given more than a month's warning by Sherman's passage through Georgia, neither civilians nor military authorities had made serious attempts to prepare for Sherman's coming into South Carolina. Their inertia may have been grounded in the traditional American assumption that the continent was secure from invasion; far into the twentieth century the people of the United States would cling to the illusion that they were safely beyond the reach of any known weapons. South Carolinians, in any event, were almost totally unprepared, and terror swept the state in Sherman's van.

The Confederate General Lafayette McLaws wrote his wife: "There is great alarm all through the country and a strong disposition to give up, among the old residents even, and with the females especially." And Charleston's fire-breathing Secessionist Edmund Rhett declared that the rebel army in Sherman's path was hopelessly demoralized: "The officers are worse than the men. The men desert at every opportunity and run without cause and without any shame."

The state legislature made belated and feeble efforts to stiffen the morale of South Carolinians who sought to flee or to avoid service. A proclamation by Governor Andrew McGrath sought to shame slackers: "Let all who falter now . . . be henceforth marked. If any seek escape from duty or danger at this time let him depart. There is room in the state for but one class of men . . . men who are willing to fight . . ."

The Confederate military command appeared to be equally inept in the emergency. Generals Beauregard, D. H. Hill and Gustavus W. Smith met near Augusta on February 2 to plan a defense of the state. By their optimistic estimate some 33,000 gray-clad troops were ready to meet Sherman. These included Hardee's little band of 9,000, which had moved north from Savannah into the low country near Charleston; there was also General Carter Stevenson's freshly arrived division from the Army of Tennessee, which had streamed eastward after the defeat of Hood at Nashville. The strategists ordered Hardee and Stevenson to hold the line of the swampy tidewater rivers as long as possible, to prevent Sherman's move inland, and then to fall back to protect Charleston. If that city fell, Hardee and Beauregard were to retreat to Columbia.

Beauregard advised President Davis that his forces were too weak to halt Sherman, and begged for reinforcements, but there were few to be had. Robert E. Lee, hard-pressed by Grant before Richmond, could spare no more than a few cavalrymen for the defense of South Carolina. He sent General Wade Hampton to his home state, with a division of riders under General Matthew Butler. South Carolina lay virtually defenseless before the Federal advance.

To add to Confederate frustrations, General Joe Wheeler became involved in one of the endless squabbles of the rebel hierarchy, and was on the point of losing his command. Georgia's Governor Brown complained that Wheeler's men were no more than a band of horse thieves; and a Georgia newspaper said: "General Wheeler . . . has . . . demonstrated to every man in the Confederacy, except the President and General Bragg, that he is not capable of commanding 10,000 Cavalrymen . . ." Beauregard needed little persuasion. He sent Alfred Roman, his inspector general, to investigate. Roman defended Fighting Joe's troopers, but urged that Wheeler be relieved, "not as a rebuke, but for the good of the cause, and for his own reputation . . . Under him, in spite of his . . . soldierly qualities, no true discipline will ever be perfected in his command."

Wheeler defended himself vigorously: "During the last five months my command has been without wagons or cooking utensils. With orders to subsist on the country, its food has been limited to bread baked upon boards and stones and meat broiled upon sticks." His men had not been paid in a year, and unlike Confederate infantry, had no uniforms issued. They had marched an average of sixteen miles a day.

Still, Wheeler said, not a man had deserted in the five-month campaign in Georgia until this investigation, when "I had the mortification to see a body desert who had been informed that they were to be punished without trial for crimes they had never committed."

In the early days of Sherman's march into South Carolina, in any event, Wheeler and his cavalry offered no challenge, but fell back steadily, awaiting opportunities to strike at exposed Federal units. Wheeler did make an effort to save houses in Sherman's path. He sent a note through the lines with the promise that he would burn no more cotton if Sherman would burn no more houses. Sherman replied tartly, "I hope you will burn all the cotton and save us the trouble. We don't want it, and it has been proven a curse to our country. All you don't burn I will . . . Vacant houses being of no use to anybody, I care little about [them], as the owners have thought them of no use to themselves. I don't want them destroyed, but do not take much care to preserve them."

As Sherman's troops advanced through the sparsely settled low country, civilians gave the Federal general good news: Wheeler's troops, only a few miles ahead, were retiring skittishly as the blue infantry appeared; they were at a loss to know where Sherman planned to move. "They brags all the time," a Negro told the general. "They say they're gonna stop you. That you'll never get to Augusta —and they'll fix you if you ever get as far as Branchville."

Sherman anticipated little Confederate resistance in the boggy country behind the coast: "I had a species of contempt for these scattered and inconsiderable forces; knew that they could hardly delay us an hour." Sherman realized that his columns could move swiftly inland toward Columbia, once they emerged from the swamps—but until that day came, he expected nightmare marches: "We must all turn amphibious, for the country is half under water."

General Slocum's advance, far to the south of Sherman, experienced the state's flooded lowlands at their worst. Some divisions struggled all day on marches of two miles, and the drenched and muddy veterans emerged "like hippopotami from the depths of ooze." Rains were almost unceasing.

Some of Slocum's pickets patrolled their campsites in canoes. Men slept standing knee-deep in water. A *New York Herald* reporter who was searching for headquarters after dark was hailed from a tree: "Hello, old fellow. You'd better come up and get yourself a roost." The correspondent found corps commander Alpheus Williams perched in the crotch of a tree, swathed in a blanket, staff officers perched in limbs all about him. Williams was smoking a cigar, "looking as quiet and serene as if he had been in his tent on dry ground."

Even on the highest ground, men waded about their camp in six inches of water. When the corps reached the village of Hardeeville, the troops dismantled every building within sight to make themselves comfortable. The settlement disappeared faster than fire could have consumed it. Sergeant Fleharty watched as the village church was attacked: "First the pulpit and seats were torn out, then the siding and the blinds were ripped off. Many axes were at work. The corner posts were cut, the building tottered, the beautiful spire, up among the green trees, leaned . . . vibrating to and fro. A tree that stood in the way was cut. By the use of long poles the men increased the vibratory motion of the building, and soon, with a screeching groan the spire sunk down . . . and as the structure became a pile of rubbish, some of the most wicked of the raiders yelled out: 'There goes your damned old gospel shop.' "

All other villages in Slocum's path through the swamp country —Purysburg, Robertsville, Lawtonville, McPhersonville—were virtually obliterated, *The Herald*'s man reported: "Houses were burned as they were found. Whenever a view could be had from high ground, black columns of smoke were seen rising here and there within a circuit of twenty or thirty miles."

But it was on the northern flank, where Sherman rode with Oliver Howard's advance, that the army met its first resistance in South Carolina—where William Hardee had industriously entrenched some 10,000 troops along the forbidding Salkehatchie River. The Salkehatchie was the first great barrier in Howard's path, a meandering network of sluggish streams threading boggy woodlands, a watery terrain from three to five miles in width. More than thirty channels wound through these wastes, and the few convenient crossings were commanded by Hardee's waiting cannon.

Howard's vanguard entered the swamp after three days of skirmishing and laying corduroy roads for wagons. When the column entered a marsh known as Whippy Swamp, the divisions of Joe Mower and Giles E. Smith were turned off the causeway into the dark waters and ordered to storm the Confederate position. Sherman was not there to watch the assault through the swamps, but Private F. Y. Headley saw them go:

> At the command, the troops plunge into the timber. So immense are the trees, and so thickly set, that the eye can not reach half pistol range . . . the men force their way through the dense undergrowth, tearing their clothing, and scratching face and limbs . . . Cypress-knees concealed beneath the water wound their feet at almost every step. Now the water grows deeper . . . and the men take off their cartridge-boxes and suspend them from the muzzles of their guns . . . Those who have watches, diaries or money place these within their hats. Now the water reaches to the armpits and occasionally all that can be seen of a short man is his head sticking out of the water.

It was three hours later when these men reached the far shore, after which the rebel garrison fired a final round and fled. A flanking column took the enemy by surprise at Buford's Bridge upstream, charged over an unburned causeway, and the Salkehatchie had been turned. It was the last determined resistance Sherman's main body was to meet in South Carolina.

But though the passage of this barrier was accomplished in two days, Sherman's men had suffered, most of them from blasts of Confederate cannon fire that swept an open area of the swamp. Colonel Jackson saw some of Mower's troops in a field hospital, "men mutilated in every shape conceivable, groaning, begging for assistance and gasping in death." Some did not reach the hospital, since there was no way to carry them from the swamp: "Many have had their heads propped up out of the water where they lay to keep them from drowning."

Oliver Howard praised his troops for the crossings of "the indescribably ugly" Salkehatchie against rebel positions of "incomparable strength." The swift passage of this swamp country, Howard said, had demoralized the rebels and opened up the country for miles in advance.

Sherman's vanguard had performed an astounding feat: Within two days Mower's troops had built bridges a mile and a half long, corduroyed many miles of road, stormed through the swamp and taken breastworks Howard thought "the strongest I ever saw." Sherman was proud of his men: "It is impossible to conceive of a march involving more labor or exposure, yet I cannot recall an instance of bad temper."

William Hardee was incredulous when he was told that the Federal columns had crossed the flooded Salkehatchie, wagons, guns and all: "I wouldn't have believed it if I hadn't seen it happen." The distant rebel General Joseph E. Johnston, who knew the country well, was moved to eloquence when the crossing was described to him: "I made up my mind that there had been no such army since the days of Julius Caesar."

Two days beyond the Salkehatchie lay the less forbidding waters of the Edisto, which Sherman's men crossed after minor skirmishing. There was a four-hour delay at the North Edisto, where a few rebels held up the advance until General Hazen sent a brigade through a swamp to flank the position. Captain Wills watched the attack of the veterans from the road, where he was high and dry: "A large number of foragers waded with them just for devilment. It was from middle to arm-pit deep and I suppose they waded at least a mile. They got 54 prisoners, and the rest threw down guns, knapsacks and everything that impeded their flight. The flanking party did not lose a man. The men of this army surprise me every day with their endurance, spirit and recklessness."

The army moved from the swamps into Orangeburg, a village of about twenty-five hundred people. Sherman, who was one of the first to enter the city, saw that several houses were on fire before any of his skirmishers appeared. A merchant, the general said, had set fire to his own store and several large piles of cotton.

The general visited an orphan asylum in the town, a refugee institution that had moved from Charleston to Orangeburg in hope of keeping its children out of Sherman's path. The general went into the building and looked in at the three hundred children as they ate breakfast of corn meal mush and molasses. Watching soldiers blinked away tears as the children sang their morning songs with the glare of burning buildings lighting the room. Sherman ordered guards posted and left provisions for these children.

A few miles beyond Orangeburg, Sherman's advance came upon Barnwell, a pleasant country town of four hundred inhabitants. Kilpatrick's troopers gave local citizens reason to remember them—and forecast the fate that awaited Columbia. The bluecoat riders were watched from the porch of a large house on Barnwell's main street by Mrs. Sarah Jane Sams and her small children, who were refugees from an adjoining county. Soldiers dismounted and ran to the rear of the house.

The stable burst into flames, and then a nearby barn, an office, store buildings and houses. Soldiers streamed past Mrs. Sams into the house: "Any Rebels here?"

"No. Only women and children."

"How many men were stationed here?"

"A handful. Not enough to face your army."

"You married?"

"I am."

"Where's your husband?"

"In the army, I'm proud to say."

The soldiers left, but others came to question Mrs. Sams, who protested: "We expect civil treatment from gentlemen."

There was a note of the resentment of Southern arrogance toward "Yankee mudsills" in the soldier's taunting reply: "There are no gentlemen in the Yankee army. We're all convicts turned out to end the rebellion."

"Then officers will treat us as ladies."

"You'll find the officers worse than the men," he said.

Other soldiers began to rifle the house, and Mrs. Sams went to headquarters and returned with a guard who forced two soldiers to return loot from the bedrooms. But men overwhelmed the guard, killed animals and pillaged, and at last the house went up in flames.

The women and children found refuge in a neighbor's house, where they kept watch on the last of Kilpatrick's men: "They behaved more like enraged tigers than human beings, running all over the town, kicking down fences, breaking in doors and smashing glasses, also stealing and tearing up clothing."

Kilpatrick, as he had threatened, amused himself during the pillaging of Barnwell by burning the town. His men set a number of houses on fire, and when flames were at their highest, Little Kil and his officers staged a ball in his hotel headquarters. Cavalry officers and black women danced, laughed and sang as the town was destroyed.

Within a few hours Sherman was laughing over a message from Kilpatrick: "We have changed the name of Barnwell to Burnwell."

To at least one astute woman, Sherman's passage through Barnwell signaled the end of Southern dreams of an independent Confederacy. Mrs. Alfred P. Aldrich, the wife of a judge and mother of three Confederate soldiers, was mistress of the nearby plantation Three Oaks. She had prepared for the invaders by hiding her valuables without the knowledge of her slaves, and had sent her three elder daughters to the Ursuline convent in Columbia.

Mrs. Aldrich resolved to put on a brave face for the Federal troops, but when some bummers raced up her lane on February 5, she could think only of atrocity tales from the Georgia plantations, and her resolution failed: "My heart sank within me . . . I felt like falling." The soldiers ran into the house and ate "like hungry wolves": "When one swarm departed, another, more hungry for spoil, would file in. And so we lived for days and nights, with guns and bayonets flashing in our faces and the coarse language of this mass of ruffians sounding in our ears."

Colonel Morton C. Hunter, the brigade commander of the 82nd Indiana, camped in Mrs. Aldrich's yard; his face, she thought, was that of a "fiend." When soldiers set her corncrib on fire, Hunter told her, "Madam, I have very little control over the boys, you must remember we are in South Carolina now; we entered this state with 'gloves off.' " Mrs. Aldrich thought the colonel looked like "a hyena gloating over his victim," but at last he ordered the fire extinguished.

In the quiet after the army had gone, Mrs. Aldrich looked across her yard, with its ruined avenue of great oaks, broken fences and scarred lawns, to the remains of the town of Barnwell, whose courthouse and all other public buildings and stores were gone, and whose blackened chimneys marked the old homesites of the place. She thought of Hunter's forecast of the end of the Confederacy, "and the dread of such a calamity, with all its woe, grew strong as I dwelt upon it, and hung like a pall on my heart."

Rebel resistance was expected on the line of the Charleston and Augusta Railroad a few miles west of Barnwell. Oliver Howard approached the little station of Midway with caution. He halted with his general officers for a roadside conference on a plan of battle and was putting his lead division into line when a forager galloped out from Midway, riding bareback on a white horse. Howard recognized the man as one of his bummers.

"Hurry, General! We've got the railroad."

The vanguard went forward and found that a dozen combative foragers had driven a rebel outpost from the vital rail line and were holding the village against a furious counterattack.

Sherman abandoned his deception once he had reached the high ground west of the swamp country and found that the way to Columbia lay open before him. The two wings of the army now wound toward the northwest, but as a final feint to keep anxious Confederate garrisons in place, Sherman sent Kilpatrick raiding toward Augusta. Rebel scouts detected the move at once.

Joe Wheeler, who had been unable to confront Kilpatrick since early December in the defense of Augusta, now prepared an ambush for the Federal cavalry twenty miles north of Augusta in the little town of Aiken, South Carolina. Wheeler carefully concealed 2,000 troopers along side streets, warned them to remain quiet until the bluecoats had ridden into the trap, and settled to wait. When Kilpatrick appeared a few minutes later at the head of charging men, nervous rebel troopers of an Alabama regiment fired too soon, and a wild cavalry fight swirled through the streets. One of Kilpatrick's veteran sergeants found the melee indistinguishable from other cavalry fights he had known: "A crush of horses, a flashing of sword blades, five or ten minutes of blind confusion, and then those who have not been knocked out of their saddles by their neighbor's horses, and have not cut off their own horses' heads instead of their enemies', find themselves, they know not how, either running away or being run away from."

Several Illinois troopers were shot from the saddle, and many others surrendered. Kilpatrick, who was studying the town through his glasses, was almost captured in this rout. Charging rebels shot down a staff officer and a colorbearer, and were turned back only by a Federal saber charge. Kilpatrick escaped, but lost his hat. His troopers were driven five miles north of Aiken, where they made a stand behind a barricade on the banks of a stream. Kilpatrick withdrew the next day with several wagonloads of wounded. Wheeler claimed to have captured ninety men; Kilpatrick admitted to a loss of thirty-one.

Confederate commanders exchanged congratulatory messages over the salvation of Augusta—but Sherman's infantry was already far to the north, approaching Columbia. The Confederates tended to see the campaign in conventional terms, and failed to appreciate the devastating effects of Sherman's skilled maneuvers. It was to be almost a century before military scholars proclaimed the general as the most original and influential of Civil War field commanders, whose concepts forecast developments in the twentieth century.

A squad of Wheeler's scouts, men of the 3rd Arkansas of Harrison's brigade, were close on the heels of the Federal rear guard when they came upon an old man at a farmhouse, leaning on a gatepost and sobbing.

The old man, a Baptist minister, told the scouts in a choking voice, "My daughter. A bunch of Yankees raped her—they just left here."

The scouts lashed their horses, and several miles down the road overtook a band of bluecoat foragers. They killed all but one of them, a boy who was seriously wounded. The young soldier begged for his life: "Boys, I know why you do this, but I had nothing to do with it." The Arkansans left him at the roadside with the bodies of his companions.

Sherman's advance approached Columbia on February 15, emerging from the barren, sandy uplands into the rich valley of the Congaree not a moment too soon for the weary troops. Charles Brown, a clerk of the 21st Michigan, complained that he had lived for sixty-five days on five days' rations, and was near starvation. "You never heard of a more desolate country. I do not believe you can find food enough in S.C. to keep a dozen chickens over winter."

Even so, Brown was ashamed of the army's progress through this poor country. He wrote his family, "I saw property destroyed until I was perfectly sick of it, and that for me to say in S.C. is considerable."

Brown was one of Sherman's soldiers who deplored the behavior of the army from start to finish, and tried to tell his family back home of the terrors of the march: "I have been thankful ever since I have been in the army that this was South. You never can imagine a pillaged house, never—unless an army passes through your town and if this thing had been North I would bushwhack until every man was either dead or I was. If such scenes should be enacted through Michigan I would never live as long as one of the invading army did. I do not blame the South and shall not if they go to guerrilla warfare."

The first elements of the army arrived before Columbia near dusk on February 15, when a heavy fog concealed the South Carolina capital from the invaders, a few of whom camped along the west bank of the Congaree River and settled to wait for morning. Rebel cannon fire fell among the camps, killing a few men, keeping all troops awake and arousing Sherman's unreasoning wrath. He damned the unseen enemy gunners as cowardly guerrillas and resolved to punish them.

Sherman had his first glimpse of the capital in the bright dawn of February 16: "I could see the unfinished State-House, a handsome granite structure, and the ruins of the railroad depot, which were still smoldering. Occasionally a few citizens or cavalry could be seen running across the streets, and quite a number of Negroes were seemingly busy in carrying off bags of grain or meal."

The defenseless city lay on a rolling plain little more than a mile away; trains were still moving out and rebel horsemen retreated along the broad streets. Through binoculars Federal officers saw handsome houses set in gardens beneath towering trees. Near the center of the city, a rebel flag flew from the incomplete statehouse, a granite building whose walls glittered like alabaster. Soldiers were reminded of towns back home: Captain Wills thought Columbia was much like Peoria from the riverside; Massachusetts soldiers thought of Plymouth and Watertown; and a Pennsylvanian thought of Chambersburg.

The invaders did not realize that the small city was swollen by wartime emergencies. Within two years its population had grown from 8,000 to 20,000 as refugees poured in from surrounding states and, in recent weeks, from the South Carolina low country. Confederate government factories and offices, including the mint, were crowded into the city. Not a house was to be found for rent. Peacetime Columbia had three banks, but now boasted fifteen, for those of Charleston and other lowland towns had moved here in hope that the capital would be spared.

Sherman found one of his batteries firing into the midst of the city, where civilians ran about in terror. The general halted the random fire, but ordered the gunners to drop a few rounds near the depot, to disperse crowds of Negroes who were bearing off food supplies. He also approved the firing of half a dozen rounds at the statehouse; officers and men cheered the bursting of each shell against the granite walls as the artillery crew demonstrated its remarkable accuracy at the distance of more than half a mile.

14
"We'll destroy no private property"

Despite daily warnings of the approach of Sherman's army, life in Columbia had continued much as usual, with a round of parties and bazaars. A symbol of this resolute gaiety in the face of danger was a remarkable, if somewhat dilapidated, carriage that appeared daily on the city's streets, a huge black coach known as "The Beauty Box," gleaming with broad glass windows and silver trim, upholstered in scarlet velvet, drawn by a team of bobtailed bays driven by a lordly black man in livery of scarlet and silver.

This was the carriage of Columbia's reigning belle, nineteen-year-old Marie Boozer, in whose passage most men were apt to forget war and the approaching enemy. Marie was the daughter of Mrs. Amelia Sees Harned Burton Boozer Feaster, a brunette beauty now estranged from her fourth husband. The alluring Philadelphia-born woman was said to harbor Union sympathies.

Amelia, still beautiful at thirty-seven, was said to be so charming that "if she made up her mind to captivate man, woman or child, it was useless to resist—the only safety was in flight." She smoked small Cuban cigars brought through the blockade. Amelia was rumored to have had a succession of lovers and to have visited the Federal prisoners at Camp Sorghum so often that some said she was a Yankee spy. Her estrangement from Feaster was said to date from his enlistment in the Confederate army.

The two women made something of a career of their carriage rides through the city. Mrs. Thomas Taylor, who was not among their admirers, paid tribute to the passage of Marie and Amelia:

"The Boozer coach, with the glass windows folded back on hinges, 'exploited' a rare vision. A mother and daughter—Mrs. Feaster and Marie Boozer—the one rich, dark in coloring and costume, the other (occupying the whole front seat) a girl of golden hair, rose shades, blue orbs, healthy, poised, delicious, pressing into the soft cushions, wrapped in ceil blue and swans-down, leghorn hat, from which plumes fell, curling under the white and pink throat. It was an angel's seeming—and she, beautiful as Venus, the goddess of the chariot."

There was universal agreement that Marie was the most dazzling woman in South Carolina. Old General John S. Preston, who was regarded as an authority, said unabashedly, "Marie Boozer was the most beautiful piece of flesh and blood my eyes ever beheld." Her eyes were said to be her most dazzling feature—large, lustrous and either dark blue or hazel, changing in the light. "Her Roman nose, in exquisite proportion, had that cold, delicate outline and thin nostril that indicate the bird of prey," a sophisticated male observer said. Mrs. James Chesnut, the wife of a Confederate general and a woman who had reigned as a South Carolina belle in her own youth, said of Marie, "The Boozer is a beauty, that none can deny, and they say she is a good girl." But Mrs. Chesnut was uneasy over reports that Marie had been seen walking with Federal officers on parole from the city's prison, and was suspected of hiding one of them in her home: "Why doesn't she marry some decent man, among the shoals who follow her, and be off and out of this tangle while she has a shred of reputation left?"

The daughter of Amelia's second husband, Marie had been adopted and endowed by his successor, and educated by an English governess and at South Carolina College. She was lithe and agile after a childhood spent as a tomboy, was an accomplished rider and rifle shot, and was as friendly, natural and charming as she was beautiful. Gossips did not yet savor tales of her as they did of her mother.

Mrs. Chesnut was of much more serious bent than Amelia and Marie. She saw unmistakable signs of Columbia's approaching doom as reports of Sherman's progress reached the city. Elderly spinsters became flighty: "The fears of old maids increase in proportion to their age and infirmities and hideous ugliness."

Mrs. Chesnut had spent most of the war in Richmond, where her husband served as an aide to President Davis; she knew the shortcomings of Confederate generals, who were "as plenty as blackberries" in Columbia. She despaired as she observed their endless councils of war. "They congregated at our house. They laid their fingers on the maps spread out on the table and pointed out where Sherman was going and where he could be stopped. They argued over their plans eloquently. Every man Jack of them had a safe plan to stop Sherman, if . . ."

The state legislature devoted itself to debating States' rights and condemning the encroachments of the Confederate government.

Mrs. Chesnut realized that Richmond's last-minute moves to shore up Confederate defenses near Columbia were futile, even when Jefferson Davis was forced to surrender command of the armies to Robert E. Lee after clinging to control of them throughout the war. "General Lee is generalissimo of all our forces," Mrs. Chesnut reported. "That comes rather late, when we have no forces." As the Federal columns drew near, Mrs. Chesnut prepared to leave for Lincolnton, North Carolina, in the western foothills, where Sherman was unlikely to march. She filled a box with food, but her husband ordered her to leave it at home; he assured her there would be plenty to eat. North Carolina, he said, was a land of milk and honey. She left in the last train available to civilians: "I took French leave . . . slipped away without a word to anybody." She rode in a car "inches deep in liquid tobacco juice" to the dull little town of Lincolnton, where she found mean accommodations: "Bare floors. For a featherbed, a pine table and two chairs I pay $30 a day. Such sheets!" She mourned the box of food she had left behind.

Nowhere in Columbia did Sherman's approach stir such excitement as in the crude pens where captured Federal soldiers were imprisoned—some of them moved here from Andersonville and other Confederate prisons. Behind the high brick walls of the insane asylum, huddled against the cold in makeshift huts, were almost a thousand of these men.

Among the captives was Adjutant S.H.M. Byers, an infantryman who had spent more than a year in rebel prisons. The inmates were isolated from news of the outside world, and guards tormented them with daily reports that Sherman had been defeated and turned back—but all the while newspapers were being smuggled into the prison. Each morning a Negro brought in loaves of bread to sell to the prisoners, and Byers tore open his loaf every morning to find a copy of the tiny Columbia newspaper folded into a wad no larger than a walnut. The paper's news was distorted by rebel propaganda, but the progress of Sherman's army could not be concealed—it had already swept through Milledgeville and was marching on.

Byers and his friends almost gave up hope, since it seemed that the army would not come near Columbia, but one morning in December, when they read that Sherman had reached the sea, Byers was tremendously excited. In the next two days he composed a poem to celebrate Sherman's feat: "I wondered what so curious a campaign would be called. It was not a series of battles—it was a great *march.* And then the title, almost the words, of the song came to me."

The prison glee club sang the poem, set to the music of "The Red, White and Blue":

Our camp-fires shone bright on the mountain
That frowned on the river below,
As we stood by our guns in the morning,
And eagerly watched for the foe;

When a rider came out of the darkness
That hung over mountain and tree,
And shouted, "Boys, up and be ready!
For Sherman will march to the sea!" . . .

Then sang we a song of our chieftain,
That echoed over river and lea;
And the stars of our banner shone brighter
When Sherman marched down to the sea! . . .

The prisoners cheered the song and author, and Byers was hailed as a hero. The song soon reached New York, smuggled out by a lucky prisoner who had been exchanged, and it became a sensation, sold more than a million copies, and gave Sherman's campaign its popular name.

Byers and the remaining bluecoat prisoners became more hopeful by the day as they read of Sherman's occupation of Savannah and of his thrust into South Carolina. On the day they learned of his approach to Columbia, the prisoners saw their rebel guards making hurried preparations for evacuation. The guards notified prisoners to be ready to move at a moment's notice, and in the next two days more than six hundred officers were shipped out of town in cattle cars, destined for other prisons. Byers and a companion, Lieutenant Devine, were two of a very few who evaded their captors. They spent the night of February 15 cutting through a board in the ceiling of the prison hospital shed, and were crouched in the attic when the last of the other prisoners were led away at dawn. Guards searched the camp for them all day, tearing up huts, digging into old tunnels and stamping through buildings. It was in vain.

Byers and his friend emerged about midnight and made a daring escape from the prison grounds into the city itself. They pulled their old blankets about them, and looking like rebels themselves, joined a group of swearing guards about a campfire. They attracted no attention. The prisoners then approached a sentinel at a gate.

"The captain sent us for water buckets."

"Pass out," the sentinel said.

The two ran into the city streets, where they found a friendly Negro, one Edward Edwards, who hid them in his hut to await the entry of Sherman's troops, which was expected hourly.

In spite of ample warning of Sherman's approach, and the presence of nine generals in Columbia, there was no plan for the city's defense. Confederate resistance was as haphazard here as it had been throughout most of Sherman's march. It was only on the day of the Federal entry that Wade Hampton was promoted to lieutenant general and placed in command of all Confederate cavalry, outranking Wheeler, who was his subordinate. General Beauregard was also at hand, ostensibly in overall command of combined forces—though there was virtually no infantry in the city.

General Hampton responded to his promotion with a defiant gesture. When someone suggested that the city surrender and that a white flag be hung from the city hall, Hampton blustered, "I'll have it torn down." The tall cavalryman vowed that his men would fight for the city from house to house, and urged civilians to burn the place, as the Russians had burned Moscow at the approach of Napoleon.

But the cavalry's defense of the city was a mere charade. Hampton stubbornly refused to allow the mayor, Dr. Thomas J. Goodwyn, to meet the oncoming Federals and surrender the city—but early on February 17, when Federal shells began to fall and a blue column appeared at the riverside, Hampton accepted the inevitable. He rode toward the northern suburbs and safety beyond.

Hampton encountered a band of cavalrymen looting stores and ordered them to move on. The half-drunk troopers, who saw that he was alone, drew their pistols and cursed him. Hampton called to General Chesnut, who was across the street. Chesnut wheeled and galloped headlong at the troopers: "Fall in there! Fall in!" The riders obeyed sullenly and rode off only when Chesnut brought up a squad of infantrymen who had miraculously appeared.

Hampton made no effort to discipline these men. "They didn't know me," he said. "They're too drunk to know anything."

One of Hampton's men who left the city at about this time remembered bitterly that no effort was made to defend the city. E. W. Wells, a South Carolina cavalry private, joined Hampton's rear guard on a hill overlooking the city. The rear guard was no more than a dozen strong, assigned to cover the withdrawal of a wagon train and under orders to defend their wagons with sabers only, since gunfire might provoke the enemy to burn the city.

From his hillside, Wells saw the first of Sherman's troops enter the city across a pontoon bridge far below, "a line of blue pouring steadily like a river." Many witnesses, most of them Federals, were to testify later that Columbia had already begun to burn at this hour, but Wells saw only smoke boiling up from the depot, where military stores were afire. He saw no other smoke or flame. It was late morning when Wells rode out of the city, his horse heavily laden with bottles of madeira stuffed in saddlebags and strapped to the pommel. "I do not suppose any one horse ever carried so many bottles before," Wells said. His last glimpses of Columbians left to face Sherman's men were of an occasional "anxious female face at an upper window" and a few Negroes drinking whiskey before a plundered army commissary.

A few blocks away, near the abandoned prison and the insane asylum, General Beauregard and his staff rode out of the city, "heads bowed as if in great sorrow." Excited women ran after them in the street, shrieking, "What is it, General? Don't leave us! You can't leave us here."

One of the general's aides turned back to explain: "The city's surrendered. The army has gone."

It was a few minutes after eight the morning of February 17 when Mayor Goodwyn and three city aldermen rode toward the river in a carriage, carrying a white flag and a message for Sherman: "The Confederate forces having evacuated Columbia, I deem it my duty . . . to ask for its citizens the treatment accorded by the usages of civilized warfare. I therefore respectfully request that you will send a sufficient guard in advance of the army, to maintain order . . . "

The mayor's carriage met Federal troops just outside the city —an advance unit of the 30th Iowa. Goodwyn asked for their commanding officer, and the carriage was led to Colonel George A. Stone, who accepted the letter for Sherman.

Sherman watched this scene through his glasses from the far bank of Broad River, where he stood with Oliver Howard and several staff officers. "It's no small thing to march into the heart of an enemy's country and take his capital," Sherman said. A boy who overheard him was impressed by the general's tone, which was "without boastfulness, but with deep and evident satisfaction."

The general gnawed on a cigar, "the same cigar he had in Atlanta," a soldier said.

The Federal officers saw Colonel Stone and two or three others climb into the carriage with Goodwyn's party and move back into the city, with files of infantrymen trailing behind.

Sherman was sitting on a log with Howard, watching engineers at work on a pontoon bridge, when Stone's courier arrived with the surrender message. There was also another message from the city, a request for protection of an Ursuline convent in Columbia, a plea from its mother superior, Sister Baptista Lynch. The sister explained that she had once taught Sherman's daughter Minnie in Ohio. Sherman passed the note to his brother-in-law, Colonel Charles Ewing: "See this woman and tell her we'll destroy no private property."

15
"The day of Jubilo has come"

Sherman led his horse across the pontoon bridge and rode into the city with Oliver Howard, Black Jack Logan, Frank Blair and other general officers. It was about two o'clock, February 17. The procession of Federal horsemen moved among roaring throngs. A few people welcomed them by waving handkerchiefs from windows—Northern sympathizers trapped there by war, or turncoats currying favor with the conquerors.

For the rest of his life the general was to be branded by Southerners as a ruthless vandal whose most brutal act was the burning of Columbia, but he apparently did not intend to devastate the city. A few hours earlier he had dictated orders that libraries, asylums and private dwellings be spared, but that most public buildings, including railroad depots, factories and machine shops, should be burned. Ten years later, with the publication of his memoirs, Sherman recalled this bitterly cold, blustery day of his entry into Columbia:

> We found seemingly all its population, white and black, in the streets. A high and boisterous wind was prevailing from the north, and flakes of cotton were flying about in the air and lodging in the limbs of the trees, reminding us of a Northern snow-storm. Near the market-square we found Stone's brigade halted, with arms stacked, and a large detail of his men, along with some citizens, engaged with an old fire-engine, trying to put out the fire in a long pile of burning cotton-bales, which I was told had been fired by the rebel cavalry on withdrawing from the

> city that morning. I know that, to avoid this row of burning cotton bales, I had to ride my horse on the sidewalk.

Oliver Howard, who was at Sherman's side, later recorded the same memory of long rows of burning cotton bales: "Certainly," Howard wrote, "this was done before any of our men reached the city."

Sherman made slow progress through the streets. Blacks pressed about his horse and touched his hand, shouting that he was a savior. Other Negroes were busily ladling out liquor from pails to Sherman's eager troops. Amid the cheers of soldiers and civilians, army bands blared "Yankee Doodle" and "Hail, Columbia."

Among those who cheered the general were men of the 100th Indiana Regiment, who had been in the city for an hour or more and were already becoming drunk. A soldier wearing a top hat and an elegant silk dressing gown staggered toward Sherman, lifted his hat and said solemnly: "I have the honor—hic!—to present you—hic!—with the freedom of the city."

Uncle Billy smiled and an officer hurried the drunk to the rear of the regiment. Sherman pointed out other drunk soldiers, and Oliver Howard ordered in fresh regiments to patrol the city.

Several ragged men pushed through the crowd toward Sherman and said they were Federal soldiers just escaped from the city's prison pen. Among them were Adjutant S.H.M. Byers and his friend Devine. Sherman dismounted and held out his hands to them. Major Nichols of the general's staff saw changes on Sherman's grizzled face: "Not when meeting his dearest friends, not in the . . . moment of victory . . . have I seen his face beam with such exultation and kindly greeting." The general told the escaped prisoners to report to Howard when order was restored so that they could march with the army. Devine handed Sherman a copy of the song Byers had written. The general thrust it into his pocket and rode away.

Major Goodwyn appeared and begged Sherman to save the city from fire. "Not a finger's breadth of your city shall be harmed, Mr. Mayor," the general said. "You can sleep tonight satisfied that your town will be as safe in my hands as in yours."

Sherman asked about the city's fire engines, and when Goodwyn said that they were in good condition, the general said, "I'm pleased to hear it."

The mayor led Sherman and his staff to a large deserted house, the home of Blanton Duncan, a Kentuckian who had been printing Confederate money in the city under contract but had fled.

When he had settled in this headquarters an hour or so later, Sherman went through the dispatches that had come during the day, "overhauled" his pocket, and found Byers' song. He was so taken with it that he read several verses aloud to his staff and sent Major Nichols off to search for the prisoner—but he was not to find the reticent Byers for several days.

Mayor Goodwyn came to Sherman's headquarters with word that one of his old friends from Charleston now lived in the city, and the general went out to visit her, the sister of one of his hunting companions of twenty years before, when Sherman had been stationed at Fort Moultrie. He and Dr. Goodwyn found the woman's house near the depot. Chickens and ducks wandered about the yard and outbuildings, and shrubs were intact; obviously the place had not been raided.

"I'm glad to see you haven't been visited by my soldiers," Sherman said. "They're usually pretty rough on poultry and anything else they can find."

"I owe it all to you."

"Not at all. I didn't know you were here until a few minutes ago."

She showed him a book which he had inscribed to her twenty years before. "Your soldiers came over my fence and chased my ducks and chickens, but I took out this book and showed it to one of them, and he said he knew this was Uncle Billy's handwriting, and so they went away. They even left me a guard."

"Has he treated you well?"

"He's in the next room now, minding my baby. He's a nice boy from Iowa—not five minutes ago he ran off some of your soldiers who came to rob me."

Sherman spent almost an hour in the house, and when he returned to headquarters, sent the woman a supply of rice and ham.

Other Federal regiments moved into the city during the afternoon of February 17, among them diarists who left conflicting accounts of conditions they saw in the streets. Many of these men agreed with Sherman that cotton bales were already blazing in the streets when they entered. The 4th Minnesota's files were forced out of a street onto the sidewalk by the blaze. And the Illinois Lieutenant

Matthew Jamison recorded that he had looked up into the city before his entrance to see "small groups of rebels darting in and out, to and fro, carrying the torch—cotton burning in the streets." The 50th Illinois, one of the first regiments to enter, passed civilians who were trying to put out the flames in "an immense quantity" of burning cotton.

But by the time the 2nd Iowa entered the city, the bales were no longer burning. Private John Bell wrote, "The cotton had been drenched and the street flooded with water and, to all appearances, the fire entirely subdued."

It was only a temporary respite. Flames were soon to reappear, and the worst fears of the city's waiting civilians were to be confirmed. Columbia's apprehensive women, alone as they faced the invaders, saw that their time had come.

Emma LeConte, the daughter of a chemistry professor at South Carolina College, first heard the roar of Sherman's troops about one o'clock in the afternoon, and peering across the city from her home on the campus, saw an American flag flying atop the statehouse. With the fervor of a seventeen-year-old, she wrote in her diary: "Oh, what a horrid sight! What a degradation! After four long bitter years of bloodshed and hatred, now to float there at last. That hateful symbol of despotism!"

Federal guards came to the college soon afterward and built a shed outside the campus walls, where they settled to protect the place. The college was now used as a hospital for the sick and wounded of both armies, and peace was maintained there throughout the day. Still, young Emma could not look at the Federal guards without "loathing and disgust," though she confessed to her diary that she did not now feel the terror of the Yankees which had seized her a few days earlier: "I do not feel half so frightened as I thought I would."

From a mile outside the city, perched on the roof of her Barhamsville Female Academy, Mme. Sophie Sosnowski watched apprehensively as she saw the first smoke and flying sparks rise above Columbia during the afternoon. Madame's pupils, "the loveliest flowers that could adorn a nation," had been sent off to safety by train, and the formidable old woman and her two daughters awaited the invaders, determined to save the buildings of the school.

Within the city itself, the nuns of the Ursuline convent and their sixty girl students watched through shuttered windows as the first Federal soldiers marched past their building. These women waited with a special sense of security, since Mother Superior Baptista Lynch had been a schoolmate of Sherman's sister and had taught his daughter Minnie.

During the morning Sister Baptista sent an aged priest to seek help from Sherman. The priest returned with guards and an assurance from the general that the convent would not be disturbed. The day passed quietly within the massive walls, but in late afternoon a young cavalry officer, Major Thomas Fitzgibbon, called on the mother superior to offer his protection "as an individual."

"Thank you, Major, but I have General Sherman's word that we will be safe."

The major persisted: "This is a doomed city. The whole army knows it. I doubt that a house will be left standing."

When Fitzgibbon had gone, Sister Baptista sent another message to Sherman, reminding him that the nuns and students in the convent were dependent upon his protection.

Once more the general assured her that the convent was safe.

Other Federal officers were becoming more concerned for the fate of the people of the city. A few of Sherman's unruly troops broke into the home of Mrs. Louisa Cheves McCord during the afternoon and littered her yard with debris. In the midst of the turmoil, Mrs. McCord was handed a note by a bluecoat officer: "Ladies, I pity you. Leave this town—go anywhere to be safer than here."

It was a prophetic warning to the women of the city of a fate soon to befall them. But until now, the people of Columbia had been anxiously optimistic. Though some 30,000 of Sherman's troops were in or near the city, unpleasant incidents had been few and there was no threat of a catastrophic fire. Some cotton ignited in the early morning still burned and tossed sparks into the wind; two burning depots still sent smoke plumes skyward; and the inmates of the city's prison, in the spirit of the occasion, had twice tried to set their building on fire.

The city began to burn as dusk approached. Sherman was among the first to realize that the crisis was at hand. Worn by a long day's activities, he had fallen asleep in headquarters during the late afternoon, and awoke to find his room aglow with orange light.

Major Nichols, sent to investigate, learned that a block of buildings was burning and that the blaze was spreading rapidly in the high wind. Sherman sent messengers to Howard and was told that though the army had begun fighting the fire, the flames were already raging out of control.

The general did not leave his headquarters until about eleven that night, but though he walked for several blocks with Colonel Dayton, he saw none of the violence or looting reported by other observers. But the fire had by now become a raging holocaust, and Sherman tried to help his men control some of the flames.

"The whole air was full of sparks and flying masses of cotton, shingles, etc.," he wrote later. "Some were carried four or five blocks and started new fires." As to his troops, he noted only that they "seemed generally under good control, and certainly labored hard to girdle the fire . . ."

The reporter David Conygham, who was in the streets at the same time, wrote of it:

> I trust I shall never witness such a scene again— drunken soldiers rushing from house to house, emptying them of their valuables and firing them; Negroes carrying off piles of booty . . . and exulting like so many demons; officers and men revelling on the wines and liquors until the burning houses buried them in their drunken orgies . . .
>
> A troop of cavalry were left to patrol the streets, but I did not once see them interfering with the groups that rushed about to fire and pillage the houses.
>
> True, Generals Sherman, Howard and others were out giving instructions for putting out a fire in one place, while a hundred fires were lighting all around them. How much better it would [have] been had they brought in a division or a brigade of sober troops and cleared out the town . . .

The novelist William Gilmore Simms, who had fled to the city from the ruins of his home near Orangeburg, was out during the height of the great fire, watching groups of Federal soldiers in the streets,

> drinking, roaring, revelling, while the fiddle and accordion were playing their popular airs . . . Ladies were hustled from their chambers, their ornaments plucked from their persons . . . Men and women bearing off their trunks were seized . . . and in a moment the trunk burst

asunder with the stroke of an axe or gun butt, the contents laid bare, rifled . . . and the residue sacrificed to the fire.

You might see the ruined owner, standing woebegone, aghast, gazing at his tumbling dwelling, his scattered property, with a dumb agony on his face . . . Others you might hear . . . with wild blasphemies assailing the justice of Heaven, or invoking, with lifted and clenched hands, the fiery wrath of the avenger. But the soldiers plundered and drank, the fiery work raged, and the moon sailed over all . . .

There were no reports of raped white women, but black women of the city suffered terribly, Simms claimed: "The poor Negroes were victimized by their assailants, many of them . . . being left in a condition little short of death. Regiments, in successive *relays,* subjected scores of these poor women to the torture of their embraces . . ."

Colonel Dayton of Sherman's staff reported, however, that he shot a man who was trying to rape a white woman in a street, an incident of which no further mention was made.

Years later, looking back to this night of February 17, 1865, Sherman wrote: "Many of the people thought that this fire was deliberately planned and executed. This is not true. It was accidental, and in my judgment began with the cotton which General Hampton's men had set fire to on leaving the city (whether by his orders or not is not material), which fire was partially subdued early in the day by our men; but, when night came, the high wind fanned it again into full blaze, carried it against the frame houses which caught like tinder, and soon spread beyond our control."

Private Bell of the 2nd Iowa, who had noted the sodden bales of cotton in the early afternoon, was marching through the streets about dusk when he saw whiskey being passed by the bucketful to soldiers who would pause to drink; during this time, "a high wind rose . . . and the smoldering fire in the cotton bales was fanned into flames unnoticed in the excitement and by dark the fire had reached the business houses lining the street . . ."

But, as Bell reported, it was the discovery of a local distillery by Federal soldiers that caused bedlam in the city, scattering "ten thousand drunken soldiers" through the streets, men who halted civilians who were fighting the blaze with small fire engines. The drunk soldiers stabbed fire hoses with bayonets and chopped them with axes. Bell remembered it for years: "Hundreds of houses were on fire at once; men swore and women and children screamed and cried with terror; drunken soldiers ran about the streets with blazing torches, the fire engines were manfully worked; soldiers and citizens heartily joined in the effort to subdue the flames as long as there was any hope of success, and long lines of sentries did all in their power to restrain their reckless and desperate comrades."

Officers of high rank were carried away by drink or excitement. The Illinois Lieutenant Matthew Jamison saw General Giles A. Smith sitting on horseback in the middle of a street, surrounded by flames. The general shouted, "Damnation to the Confederacy," raised a flask and drank.

Jamison stopped an old Negro who was passing. "What do you think of the night, sir?"

"I think the day of Jubilo has come," the Negro said.

An elderly white man passed with three pale-faced daughters, fearful that his house would burn. He shrugged off advice that he send a boy to his roof to put out falling sparks, and chattered on, "indifferent and reckless." "I'd sooner lose all I have than have my daughters misused," the old man said.

Jamison heard the band of a regiment from the XX Corps playing in the red light, surrounded by cheering soldiers who taunted nearby civilians. One young soldier shouted to an old man whose store was wrapped in flames: "Did you think of this when you hurrahed for Secession? How do you like it, hey?"

The Reverend Mr. Connor, a Methodist minister whose parsonage was burned, emerged with a sick child wrapped in a blanket. A soldier seized the blanket. "No!" Connor said, "he's sick." The soldier tore off the blanket and threw it into the fire. "Damn you," he said. "If you say one more word I'll throw the child after it."

Men of the 1st Missouri Engineers, whose homes had been burned by Confederate raiders in Rolla, Missouri, long before, carried torches through the streets and tossed them into houses.

Escaped prisoners from Camp Sorghum begged the troops for matches and turpentine. Fourteen-year-old Mike Garber, the son of Sherman's quartermaster, never forgot these men: "Ragged clothes exposed the bare skin in places and rags and skin and the men all over were one hue—a dirty dust color. I had never seen any human beings look so . . . They had hidden in the prison shacks . . . burrowed in the earth and been covered by comrades with dirt." There were few of these survivors: Most of them had been moved away by the rebels—and others had died in their underground warrens when guards burned the shanties of their prison camp.

Colonel M. C. Garber, Sherman's chief quartermaster, who had industriously seized tons of Confederate supplies during the day, lost all in the flames. He, too, ascribed the destruction of the city to heavy drinking among soldiers: "The fire was terrible, the scenes too horrible to describe. Large quantities of whiskey were found, which the men drank to an alarming extent. My estimate is that forty blocks were burned. So much for giving soldiers liquor."

The women of the city confronted the night's terrors with an unexpected courage. Mme. Sosnowski, the mistress of Barhamsville Female Academy, had been assigned a small guard for the night, but except for one young Tennessee soldier, found them worthless. Madame had hidden her valuables and now defended them resolutely. With the aid of the Tennessean she turned several raiding parties from her door, but was then besieged by a drunken band of eighty men fresh from the looting of a neighboring house, where they had found a wine cache, raped several Negro women, and burned the house to the ground.

Mme. Sosnowski, her daughters and the Tennessee soldier barred the doors and finally drove off these intruders, but a few hours later there was a ringing of axes from her stables. Madame charged into the darkness alone and confronted twenty half-drunk soldiers. "When I appeared they looked with astonishment at the coming of a single lady, and really appeared to be ashamed of themselves, as well they might be."

"What are you, thieves or soldiers? To any person of honor you are a disgrace to the military profession."

"Yes, ma'am."

By the time the Tennessee soldier arrived in support, Madame had subdued the marauders and sent them away. She then led her livestock into the house, the cows into the basement dining room, and the horse upstairs and into a dressing room.

Little more than a mile away, Sister Baptista Lynch had been agonizing over the safety of her convent and its young women and girls. When she heard the first reports of spreading fire and violence across the city, the mother superior had written Sherman once more, a reminder of her "personal as well as religious claim" upon his protection through her acquaintance with Minnie and his sister.

Sherman responded once more that the convent was in no danger, and that she and her charges should remain where they were.

It was now too late. The wall of fire advancing through the city raged ever nearer the convent grounds. Father O'Connell, "looking sad and anxious," came in from the streets to whisper with the nuns, who called the girls aside, helped them to tie clothing into small bundles and gave instructions for evacuating their building. The girls listened gravely. The youngest of them was five, and several were under the age of ten.

At nightfall, for the first time flames were visible through the convent windows, and the roar of the doomed city's consuming flames could be heard behind the thick walls. The priests tried to remove the Host from the altar, but were dissuaded by the nuns, who wished to keep it as long as possible. Father O'Connell led a final benediction. The schoolgirls were kneeling, reciting the rosary, when the chapel door was broken in by "the most unearthly battering . . . like the crash of doom. Drunken soldiers piled over each other, rushing for the sacred gold vessels of the altar, not knowing they were safe in the keeping of one blessed of God."

The girls filed past the cursing men into the night: "We marched through the blazing streets with the precision of a military band. It was our safety." Father O'Connell led, followed by Sister Baptista. Sara Aldrich, whose mother had sent her here from Barnwell, thought she would remember the scene for life: "Not a cry, not a moan. The roaring of the fires, the scorching flames on either side . . . did not create the least disorder. That majestic figure of the Mother Superior in the graceful black habit of the Ursuline order . . . The long line of anxious, white young faces of the schoolgirls . . ."

Father O'Connell led them into a nearby church, from which they saw the burning convent roof collapse into a fiery grid of timbers. The sturdy building endured until long after nearby structures had burned to the ground, but at three in the morning its cross plunged earthward in a cascade of flames and embers.

Laughing soldiers taunted the nuns and blew cigar smoke in their faces. "Oh, holy! Yes, holy! We're just as holy as you are! . . . Now, what do you think of God? Ain't Sherman greater?"

* * *

Mrs. St. Julien Ravenel, the wife of the director of the local army medical laboratory, had stayed behind with her six children and her elderly mother when her husband fled with his staff and supplies into North Carolina. She had been warned of the terrible punishment in store for Columbia, but refused to leave her home. Like many another victim of Sherman's bummers, she never forgot nor forgave the plundering of her home during the Federal occupation—but she found the invaders the most gentlemanly brigands imaginable, even in their most terrifying actions.

At dusk, when the first soldiers pounded on her door, Mrs. Ravenel was assailed by crowds of "drunken, dancing, shouting, cursing wretches," all carrying torches. It was a procession that ended only with the dawn: "A roaring stream of drunkards passed through the house, plundering and raging, and yet in a way curiously civil and refraining from *personal insult.*" The soldiers found little of Harriott Ravenel's treasure, for she wore dozens of gold double eagle coins in a belt about her waist, and had buried almost five hundred silver dollars in her garden. And though they swore incessantly at every breath, the soldiers addressed Mrs. Ravenel as "lady," even while they were rending apart everything they could not carry away. When Mrs. Ravenel stood quietly beside them as they fought over a trunk, the men turned away as if in shame.

Mrs. Ravenel's mother, Mrs. Rutledge, sat through the night in a rocking chair, sewing without betraying the slightest sign of fear. "Old lady, why don't you look scared?" one soldier asked. "Because I'm not." He nodded approvingly and returned the scissors he had snatched from her.

"I'm sorry for the women and children," one soldier said. "But South Carolina's got to suffer. Got to be *destroyed.*"

Some of the men tried to burn the Ravenel house by tossing burning books on the porch or torches into closets, but did not persist when the women and children scurried to beat out the flames—"dreadfully fatiguing work," Mrs. Ravenel said.

Mrs. Ravenel sent to General Frank Blair's nearby headquarters to ask for a guard, but the servant returned with the message that General Blair "was very sorry, but was too sleepy to do anything."

The Reverend P. J. Shand, the rector of Trinity Episcopal Church, driven from his home by the flames, carried out a trunk filled with the communion silver of the church. He and a servant were carrying the trunk and Mrs. Shand was with them when five soldiers surrounded them.

"Put it down. Whatcha got in there?"

"My church silver."

"Give us the key."

When Shand said he had no key, four of the soldiers banged at the chest and the other drew a pistol, grabbed the minister by the collar and demanded his watch.

"I have no watch."

After being thoroughly searched, Shand was left in the street by the five, who disappeared with the trunk.

Young Emma LeConte and her mother were frightened by swarms of drunk soldiers staggering about the South Carolina College campus, cursing and singing such ribald songs that "we were forced to go indoors." The women barricaded themselves in the cellar of their home and tried to sleep, but at four in the morning, when the roar of flames awakened them, they went up to the front door and saw the statehouse wrapped in fire. The burning city had a terrible beauty for Emma:

> Imagine night turning into noonday, only with a blazing, scorching glare that was horrible—a copper-colored sky across which swept columns of black rolling smoke glittering with sparks and flying embers . . . Everywhere the palpitating blaze walling the streets as far as the eye could reach—filling the air with its terrible roar . . . every instant came the crashing of timbers and the thunder of falling buildings. A quivering molten ocean seemed to fill the air and sky. The Library building opposite us seemed framed by the gushing flames and smoke, while through the windows gleamed the liquid fire.

Several college buildings burst into flames, and Emma saw scores of dark figures fighting the flames: "All the physicians and nurses were on the roof trying to save the buildings, and the poor wounded inmates, left to themselves, such as could, crawled out . . ." Many wounded Confederate soldiers died in the blaze that consumed their emergency hospital.

The storm of sparks began to subside near dawn of February 18, and bugles called through Columbia's streets. Soldiers disappeared and flames receded. By seven o'clock the last fire had flickered out. Emma noted: "The sun rose at last, dim and red through the thick, murky atmosphere. It set last night on a beautiful town full of women and children—it shone dully down this morning on smoking ruins and abject misery."

Mme. Sophie Sosnowski, no longer confident that she could save the Barhamsville Female Academy from roaming bands of troops, walked into the city alone on the morning of February 18, seeking more guards. She made her way to Sherman's headquarters, where scores of the city's civilians had taken their troubles during the day and night.

Madame, the widow of a Polish army officer, noted with disdain the shambling, informal air of Sherman's troops, so unlike the highly trained soldiers she had known in Europe. She found the general himself equally informal, for she was shown into his room without delay, as if he welcomed all comers. The Polish woman asked him for a guard, and then proceeded to lecture the general:

"I am surprised and indignant that your army should behave so toward a conquered people who have surrendered their city and do not resist. I have always told people we had nothing to fear, except the accidents of war—but I do not consider the deliberate burning of a city an accident."

Sherman glared at her.

"I have told my friends private property and females would be protected when you came. But no, instead of this you have waged warfare that is a disgrace to our history."

"What do you mean by that, Madam?" Sherman said angrily.

"I meant exactly what I have said."

Sherman burst forth "in strong terms of the responsibility of Columbia, of South Carolina, of the sufferings by Secession; indeed, as he only advocated one side of the question, he spoke well." The general ended with a threat: "You have suffered much already, but if I have to come back again . . ."

He refused Mme. Sosnowski's repeated requests for guards: "There will be no need. I expect to leave tomorrow, and must have all troops at their posts."

"Then I will detain you no longer, Sir."

Sherman escorted her to the door and she returned to the school, where she was fortunate enough to find a band of Irish soldiers who protected the academy from drunken bluecoats the rest of the night.

Another high-spirited Columbia woman who invaded Sherman's headquarters browbeat the general into assigning her a guard.

Mrs. Campbell Bryce, who was resolved to save her family property from the marauders, found the general busily writing at his desk. She waited as his pen scratched on. He was, Mrs. Bryce noted, "decidedly untidy" in his soiled, rumpled shirt: "He was quite pale, his hair light and stood up from his brow, his eyes blue and penetrating, and a large, firm mouth. Altogether his appearance was to me rather that of a pedagogue than a great general."

Sherman turned to face her. "What can I do for you?"

"I want a guard."

"What are you afraid of?"

"Of your soldiers."

"Oh, you needn't be. The poor fellows are hungry, and want a chicken. Give them a chicken."

Mrs. Bryce then ripped off a sheet of his paper and pushed it toward the general. "Would you please give me an order for a guard?"

"Oh, yes. But you won't need one."

Mrs. Bryce stood until he had written an order, and then went home with her guard. Her house was not seriously molested thereafter.

Other women were less fortunate in the assignment of guards. Mrs. Agnes Law, a seventy-two-year-old widow who was in ill health, was allowed four guards for the tall brick house in which she had lived most of her life. Mrs. Law, her sister and a niece with a young baby were the only occupants of the place. The four Federal soldiers, Mrs. Law was relieved to note, were "well-behaved and sober." She served them supper and faced the evening with growing confidence that they would protect her.

Fires broke out in the neighborhood in late afternoon, and Mrs. Law wanted to move her furniture from the house. The guards protested. "Your place is in no danger," they said. "Leave everything just where it is."

But the guards then took lighted candles and went up to the second floor. Mrs. Law's sister, who followed them, clattered back down in excitement: "They're setting the curtains on fire!" The women could already hear the crackling of flames overhead. Mrs. Law hurried her sister, niece and the baby from the house to find a place of safety.

The guards came downstairs, their manner abruptly changed: "Old woman, if you don't want to burn up with your house you'd better get out."

Mrs. Law went onto her porch to look for help in descending the steps and passing through the streets, but she saw only a mob of soldiers and was forced to go alone, moving slowly for fear of falling, though trembling in terror of the walls of flames between which she passed. She reached the home of a friend, where she spent the night without harm under the guard of a sympathetic officer.

Despite her survival of the ordeal, Mrs. Law, a devout Presbyterian, was unforgiving toward the invaders: "I cannot live long. I shall meet General Sherman and his soldiers at the bar of God, and I give this testimony in full view of that dread tribunal."

Harriott Ravenel was one of the few women in Columbia whose house escaped the flames, a miracle accomplished by a young Irish soldier who had come in off the streets, drawn by the sweet Irish accent of Mrs. Ravenel's maid. The boy soldier had pretended to be a guard, though his musket lacked a bayonet, and he had driven away bands of men who threatened to burn the house.

Late in the night of the fire the Irish boy went to Mrs. Ravenel: "I'm going to keep safe everything you own—but there is one thing I would like to have. Will you give it to me?"

"Anything! Anything I own is yours. Please take what you wish. We owe everything to you."

The soldier ran up the stairs and reappeared a few minutes later wearing a purple velvet cloak and doublet and white satin hose—an old fancy dress costume that Dr. Ravenel had once worn to a ball, dressed as Sir Walter Raleigh.

Soon afterward, at the roll of reveille drums, the men in the Ravenel house hurried away, the Irish Walter Raleigh last of all, waving farewell and vanishing with a swirl of the purple velvet cloak.

16
"For the first time I am ashamed"

It was almost dawn of February 18 when the Ursuline nuns led their schoolgirls into the church where they had taken refuge after the burning of their convent. The sisters calmed those who sobbed and watched over them until they fell asleep on the cushioned pews. Here, the girls were told, they would surely be safe.

But it was only a few moments later when the doors burst open and several soldiers rushed in shouting, "All out! We're blowing up the church!"

The small girls fled in terror through the doorway, scampering across the graves of the churchyard, floundering against tombstones, to hide in the hedges. Officers soon arrived and drove off the drunk soldiers, but the children refused to reenter the church. They huddled on the wall and about the doorway until sunrise. They were there, grouped about the mother superior, when Sherman arrived to visit the woman of whom he had heard so much in the past two days.

Sister Baptista's face betrayed her exhaustion, but she stood erect and proudly. Sara Aldrich, the refugee from Barnwell, thought the mother superior had the air of "an injured empress dethroned."

The general took Sister Baptista's hand and spoke brightly, affecting nonchalance: "Oh, there are times when one must practice patience and Christian endurance."

She spoke to him calmly: "You have prepared for us one of these moments, General."

"I'm very sorry your convent is burned. The fire got beyond

control, from buildings I had to burn . . . If the people had not left liquor for my men . . ."

Sherman's manner was haughty, but Sara Aldrich saw that he was "not so calm." He snatched his cigar from his mouth, replaced it hastily, and chewed it in a fury.

The mother superior swept a hand toward the convent and the ruined city beyond. "General, this is how you kept your promise to me, a cloistered nun."

"Take any of the houses left standing in the city," he said. "Use the one you wish as a convent."

"General Sherman, I do not think the houses left are yours to give, but when I make arrangements, I will thank you to move us and provide food."

Sherman left her, a defeated man in the eyes of young Sara Aldrich. Later in the day Sister Baptista wrote to the general once more, asking the use of the John S. Preston house for her charges. In response, Sherman sent Colonel Charles Ewing of his staff to negotiate with the mother superior. Ewing glowered at the nun, slapped his boot with a whip, and sought to intimidate her: "Don't you know that house is General Logan's headquarters?"

"Yes, but General Sherman promised me any house I wished, and this one suits me better than any other."

"Well, I've come to move you, but that house, I know, has been ordered burned tomorrow morning when the army leaves—but if you'll take it for a convent I'll ask the general to countermand the order."

When the nuns arrived at the Preston house with their white-clad girl charges, General Logan was preparing to ignite barrels of pitch in the cellar. Logan swore fearfully when he was handed Sherman's order, but removed his barrels and left the house. The stately home was little worse for wear—though Sherman's soldiers had mutilated some fine paintings and statuary, adding mustaches to portraits and clothing to nude figures.

A shift in the wind about three in the afternoon of February 18 halted the march of the flames through the city and spared sections whose doom had appeared imminent. Two hours later, according to the reporter David Conyngham, sober troops ordered into the city had brought rioters under control.

Conyngham walked the streets of Columbia in the first light of day. It was "a city of ruins . . . The noble-looking trees that shaded the streets, the flower gardens that graced them, were blasted and withered by fire. The streets were full of rubbish, broken furniture and groups of crouching, desponding, weeping, helpless women and children."

The reporter saw a richly dressed woman with three handsome children clinging to her. They sat upon a mattress, with fine paintings and a few pieces of sculpture strewn about them, the only survivors of their home. Elsewhere, "old and young moved about seemingly without a purpose. Some mournfully contemplated the piles of rubbish, the only remains of their late happy homesteads . . . Some had piles of bedding and furniture which they had saved from the wreck . . . Children were crying with fright and hunger; mothers were weeping; strong men, who could not help either them or themselves, sat bowed down with their heads buried between their hands."

Some of Sherman's men surveyed the ruins with a sense of shame. Captain George Pepper, who also entered the city early, met crowds of soldiers who repelled him, "yelling, singing, waving gold watches, handsful of gold, jewelry and rebel shinplansters in the air, boasting of having burned the town." In the crowded yard of the asylum, where the city's homeless were clustered, Pepper heard a group of soldiers about a piano, singing "John Brown's Body."

Private Joe Saunier of the 4th Ohio went back into the burned district with companions: "Never in all our lives have we seen such destruction and such desolation. The people were in the parks and the woods and the fields without shelter . . . without homes or property."

At four o'clock, when a brigade of the 2nd Division of the XV Corps was called out to suppress a riot among the looters, two soldiers were killed. During the night 30 had been wounded and 370 arrested. The Minnesota soldier Alonzo Brown, who saw many of these looters arrested, said indignantly, "Some of them should be shot. For the first time I am ashamed of the 15th Corps."

David Conyngham was already concerned with fixing the guilt for the burning of the city: "Who is to blame . . . is a subject that will be long disputed. I know the Negroes and escaped prisoners were infuriated, and easily incited the inebriated soldiers to join them in their work of vandalism." He felt that Governor Magrath and General Hampton were partly to blame, since they had rejected the pleas of Mayor Goodwyn and General Beauregard to destroy the city's liquor supplies and surrender the city to Sherman when he was still far away from its gates. On the other hand, Conyngham thought, Sherman should have brought the rioters under control by ordering in enough troops to clear the streets.

Sherman himself, though he said he deplored the destruction of the city, probably felt at this time as he did years later when he said, "Though I never ordered it and never wished it, I have never shed many tears over the event, because I believe it hastened what we all fought for, the end of the war." On another occasion he said, "If I had made up my mind to burn Columbia I would have burnt it with no more feeling than I would a common prairie village; but I did not do it . . . God Almighty started wind sufficient to carry that cotton wherever He would, and in some way that burning cotton was the origin of the fire."*

There was no doubt in the minds of Columbia's victims that Sherman bore the blame for the city's destruction— or that he was guilty of inhuman, uncivilized warfare. Emma LeConte, for one, regarded every man in blue as a fiend. She tried to avoid seeing the guards who swarmed about the college, since it was to her "a contamination even to look at these devils." When she heard an exaggerated report of the deaths of Federal soldiers in an explosion at a railroad depot, she exulted: "How I rejoice to think of any of them being killed. Dr. Bell says about 200 of them were burnt up Friday night— drunk perhaps—if only the whole army could have been roasted alive!" (Major Nichols reported "several" Federal dead and twenty wounded in the depot explosion, which led Sherman to remark that he valued the life of a single soldier more highly than he did the city of Columbia.)

Emma LeConte, for all her feeling of revulsion toward Sherman's men, already realized that the city would be worse off when they had gone, with the "whole country laid waste and the railroads

*The controversy over the origins of the fire raged for years and prompted several investigations. A postwar commission composed of an Englishman, an American and an Italian investigated British claims for cotton losses in Columbia and concluded that neither Federal nor Confederate officers could be charged with blame.

cut off in every direction. Starvation seems to stare us in the face! . . . Oh, the sorrow and misery of this unhappy town!"

Emma could not bring herself to visit the burned district at once. "Sometimes I try to picture it to myself as it now is, but I cannot. I always see the leafy streets and lovely gardens—the familiar houses. I cannot imagine the ruins and ashes to save my life. How I *hate* the people who have done this!"

When she finally went into the town, she found the desolation even worse than she had expected, with the entire heart of the city in ashes. "As far as the eye can reach, nothing is to be seen but heaps of rubbish, tall dreary chimneys and shattered brick walls . . ."

On Main Street, everything familiar was gone. "The wind moans among the bleak chimneys and whistles through the gaping windows . . . the market is a ruined shell . . . its spire fallen in and with it the old town clock whose familiar stroke we miss so much . . . the old bell—'Secessia'—that had rung out every state as it seceded, lying half-buried in the earth . . ."

Officially, it was reported that almost three-quarters of the city was destroyed—more than 366 acres—with 1,386 houses, stores and other buildings burned to the ground.

Young Emma LeConte was one who refused to give up hope. "So far as I can see, the people are undemoralized and more determined than ever. The Yankee officers . . . paid tribute to the women of the State of saying they were the most firm, obstinate and ultra-rebel set of women they had encountered—if the men only prove equally so!"

Not all of Columbia's women had been hostile to the invaders; no fewer than fifty families were preparing to go north with Sherman's army, among them Mrs. Amelia Feaster and her daughter, Marie Boozer. Mrs. Feaster had lost her fine house on Washington Street in the flames, but she and Marie had been seen with the bluecoats all about town.

Later, when one South Carolina woman heard a rumor that Marie had married a Federal officer from Philadelphia, she said, "No doubt, and by this time she has married one from Boston, and from New York indiscriminately. Will she marry the whole Yankee army?"

The morning after the fire, in the words of Mrs. Harriott Ravenel, Sherman's men vanished from the streets "like ghosts at cocks-

Sherman in Atlanta. ABOVE: On the city's fortified line, astride Sam, whose "horribly fast" walk was the dismay of the general's staff. BELOW: The John Neal House, Sherman's Atlanta headquarters, then a six-year-old showplace with towering Corinthian columns and a stained-glass cupola. The house later served as a school and college, and was razed in 1930 to make way for Atlanta's city hall.

ARCHIVES OF ATLANTA HISTORICAL SOCIETY

ALL PHOTOS ON THESE TWO PAGES COURTESY LIBRARY OF CONGRESS

Sherman's Favorites. ABOVE: Generals Henry W. Slocum *(left)* and Oliver O. Howard, wing commanders during the march, both heros of the fighting against the army of Robert E. Lee. LEFT: General Jefferson C. Davis, whose abandonment of black refugees at a stream crossing in Georgia outraged many of his officers, incurred the wrath of Secretary of War Edwin M. Stanton, and involved Sherman in bitter controversy.

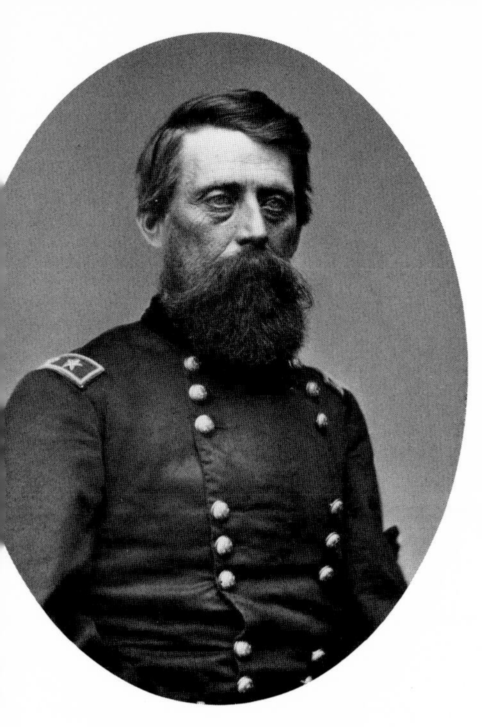

The Mavericks. ABOVE: Generals and Corps Commanders Francis P. Blair *(left)*, regarded by Sherman as a "noble and intelligent soldier," but "erratic and unstable" in politics—which he practiced throughout the war—and John "Blackjack" Logan, an ardent fighter given to exceeding his authority. RIGHT: General Joseph Mower, the aggressive division commander whose bold assault (in violation of orders) might have destroyed the Confederate army at the battle of Bentonville but for Sherman's recall of the assault waves.

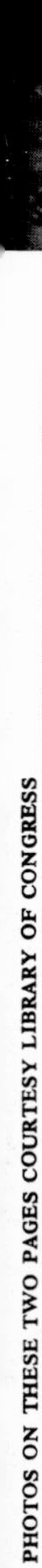

The High Command. This triumvirate, virtually all-powerful in the final days of the war, shaped Sherman's military career. ABOVE: Chief of Staff Henry W. Halleck *(left),* who commanded Sherman's generals to disregard his orders, and Secretary of War Edwin M. Stanton *(right),* who clashed with Sherman over treatment of freed slaves—and charged the general with insubordination and treason because of generous peace terms he extended to defeated Confederates. LEFT: U. S. Grant, who gave his reluctant consent to the epic march, and ended by defying Stanton's order to remove Sherman from command.

The Last Adversaries. ABOVE: Generals William Hardee *(left)* and Joseph E. Johnston led rebel armies opposing Sherman's advance—Hardee through Georgia and South Carolina, and Johnston in the final days in North Carolina. The veteran Johnston, dean of Confederate generals, protested that he was returned to command to serve as scapegoat. BELOW: The rebel cavalry leaders Wade Hampton *(left)* and Joe Wheeler, whose troops fought fiercely, if ineffectually, against Sherman's overwhelming forces.

SOUTH CAROLINIANA LIBRARY

LIBRARY OF CONGRESS

Love in the Ruins. ABOVE: Marie Boozer *(left)*, reputedly the most beautiful woman in South Carolina, went north with the Federal army after the burning of Columbia as temporary mistress to General Hugh Judson Kilpatrick *(right)*, chief of Sherman's cavalry and a celebrated Don Juan. "Little Kil," Sherman said, "was a hell of a damned fool," but an ideal cavalry chief. BELOW: Columbia's ruins after the fire, viewed from atop the statehouse. Eighty-four of the city's 124 blocks were gutted by the flames.

SOUTH CAROLINIANA LIBRARY

STATE DEPARTMENT OF ARCHIVES AND HISTORY, RALEIGH, N.C.

Surrender and Celebration. ABOVE: The crude farmhouse of Daniel Bennett, near Durham, North Carolina, was the scene of Johnston's surrender to Sherman. The reconstructed house stands at left. BELOW: Henry Slocum's staff climbs the hill on Pennsylvania Avenue toward the White House during the victory parade of May 24, 1865. From this point Sherman violated his own orders to look back and see his troops marching in perfect order, and saw in their precision the fulfillment of his mission on the thousand-mile march. Later he said, "I believe it was the happiest and most satisfactory moment of my life."

LIBRARY OF CONGRESS

LIBRARY OF CONGRESS

Sherman in Triumph. Resplendent in the unaccustomed finery of a new uniform, the general posed for Mathew Brady in Washington, May 1865, his face so wrinkled that his wife thought he looked to be more than sixty. A Federal officer said of Sherman's appearance about this time: "All his features express determination, particularly the mouth, which is wide and straight with lips shut tightly together . . . a very remarkable-looking man such as could not be grown out of America—the concentrated quintessence of Yankdom . . . he believes in hard war."

crowing," and she lost little time in trying to find a way to feed her family, which had left to it only the house, the gold coins in Harriott's heavy money belt—and the hundreds of silver dollars buried in the garden.

Mrs. Ravenel recovered the silver with some difficulty, since moles, working heroically during the burning of the city, had somehow torn the cloth covering and dragged away many of the heavy coins, some for as far as thirty feet along their runs. After several hours of digging, Harriott found all but five or six of her dollars, and added this treasure to the little hoard with which she was to build a new life.

Mrs. Louisa McCord, whose home stood in a district spared by the fire, appeared at Federal headquarters the day after the conflagration to beg for help for a less fortunate neighbor. She found Sherman and Oliver Howard sitting together, and handed her message to Howard, who read it rapidly and sought to reassure her that the worst was over for the city's people. He also exaggerated Federal casualties during the destruction of Columbia:

"You may rest satisfied, Mrs. McCord, that there will be nothing of the kind happening tonight. The truth is, last night our men got beyond our control; many of them were shot, many of them were killed; there will be no repetition of these things tonight. I assure you there will be nothing of the kind. Tonight will be perfectly quiet."

Sherman looked on during this exchange and said nothing. He now seemed determined to shift responsibility to Howard, who, as wing commander, was technically in command of the city's occupation.

When Mayor Goodwyn went to Sherman to plead for help, he, too, was directed to Howard. Goodwyn threw himself upon Sherman's mercy: "How can I feed these homeless and destitute people? There's nothing left."

"Go to Howard," Sherman said brusquely. "His troops hold the city. He'll treat you better than your own generals did."

Sherman's bluff manner may have concealed a sense of guilt for the city's destruction; it was unlike him to have a subordinate shoulder blame.

When a church delegation appeared to ask protection for their remaining buildings, Sherman barked in the same quick way: "Howard runs the religion of this army. See him."

Howard dealt gently but firmly with Goodwyn. He offered to

leave half of his cattle herd and half the rations in his wagons for use of the people of the city.

The mayor still complained petulantly. "All that will soon be gone," he said. "What will I do then?"

"Organize your people," Howard said. "Send them into the country where our foragers did not reach, and requisition supplies from the farms. Keep careful records. Issue certificates to the farmers for later redemption." The mayor put Howard's suggestion into effect, and was able to sustain the city for several months.

Howard, like Sherman, sympathized with Columbia's stricken civilians, but did not mourn the fate of the city. He was, he said, reminded of an old politician who when asked if he had attended burial services for one of his bitter enemies, said, "No, I didn't patronize the funeral, but I approve of it."

Howard also tried to control the lawlessness of his troops by calling in additional regiments to stand guard in the city, and denounced the "organized banditti" in ranks who were robbing Columbia's people of watches, jewelry and money. There were still reports that soldiers on the streets would ask civilians for the time of day, and when the unsuspecting victims looked at their watches, would snatch the timepieces and walk away, threatening any who protested with violence.

Despite his talk of a virtual crime wave in the city, Oliver Howard apparently caught only one thief in Columbia, in a case whose circumstances defied belief. A Dr. Greene went to headquarters with a complaint: "General, would you allow your men to take a man's watch?"

"No. You know I wouldn't."

"But a soldier took mine."

"Please describe him, doctor."

"Oh, I can't do that. They're all alike."

But then, by Howard's account, Greene's twelve-year-old daughter spoke up to say that she could identify the man, and described him so effectively that Howard's provost marshal found him, incredibly enough, and had him return Dr. Greene's watch; then, as Howard said with satisfaction, "I ordered the man drummed out of the army."

The irony of this punishment for the minor offense amid the ruins of the burned city evidently escaped Old Prayer Book, who took comfort in the fact that in this instance, at least, he had observed the civilities expected of an officer and a gentleman.

As his hour of departure neared, Howard was saddened by his last look at the city. "I had never expected to leave such a wild desert . . . covered with blackened debris, smoldering embers and lone chimneys."

The passage of Sherman's troops from the city on February 20 was watched with varying emotions by the women left behind. Many of those on the streets hissed and booed the bluecoats, some spat on the soldiers, and "not a few of the women undertook to lay violent hands" upon them.

A young woman whose modesty led her to write as "E.L.L." watched anxiously from her bedroom window as the interminable Federal column moved past her house, men and wagons laden with food and stolen goods, drawn by fat Carolina horses.

"The trains were so long in passing," she wrote, "that the ear grew weary of the grating of the wheels . . . At last they were gone! Then came the overwhelming sense of our destitution. The great stillness after the storm of destruction was oppressive, stifling! What next?"

As night fell, the wakeful E.L.L. heard an occasional footfall in the street and was comforted—Columbia's old men had organized patrols to protect the remaining houses against stragglers and prowlers.

Lily Logan, one of the white refugees who had come from Charleston, was one of the most optimistic women left behind in Columbia. She watched Sherman's troops move out, undismayed even by the "odious notes of 'Yankee Doodle' " and the sight of almost every Columbia horse, carriage, cow and mule disappearing to the north. Lily wrote to her brother, Thomas, a young general serving with Wade Hampton's legion, now on his way into North Carolina, where the small Confederate forces hoped to make a stand: "I am sure we will be victorious soon, and are ready to bear even more for our glorious cause. May God strengthen you all, my brave brother, and hasten to bring the bright days coming . . . Keep up your spirits, and let us whip Sherman soon."

As the last of Sherman's column left Columbia after three days in the city, a housewife saw one of her former slaves in the caravan of camp followers, an elderly black woman who sat in a stolen carriage drawn by stolen horses, wearing a huge hat of prewar fashion and fanning herself with a palmetto fan, despite the day's chilly temperature.

The distraught mistress ran into the street and called to her departing servant: "Aunt Sallie! Where are you going?"

The old woman gave her a regal glance: "Law, honey! I'se gwine back inter the Union!"

17
"Death to all foragers"

The army trailed northward from Columbia with a few disorganized rebel bands falling back before it. Even now there were no signs of serious resistance to Sherman's advance. Slocum's wing, which had bypassed Columbia, now rejoined Howard's column, and the troops turned again to the destruction of railroads in the region with the aim of completing the isolation of the South Carolina capital. In the prosperous farm country between Columbia and the North Carolina border lay scattered villages and small towns—Ridgeway, Winnsboro, Chester, Cheraw, Lancaster, Camden.

Sherman planned to pass through these towns, feigning an advance on Charlotte, North Carolina, while his true course was to the northeast, through the North Carolina towns of Fayetteville and Goldsboro, and thence to the state capital, Raleigh.

Even now, with the end apparently in sight, the war remained to be won. Robert E. Lee's besieged army had beaten off every attempt of Grant's superior forces in the trenches about Richmond—and the Confederate capital seemed to lead a charmed life. Elsewhere on the fighting fronts there was little action.

The blue columns were joined by fresh thousands of civilians as the troops left the ruined capital, most of them blacks in search of freedom—in this case apparently unmolested by Sherman's officers. At least eight hundred of the newcomers were whites—escaped prisoners, loyal Unionists, or natives who had befriended the Yankee invaders and feared the vengeance of neighbors. Most of these people walked in the wake of the troops, bearing packs on their backs. A few were more fortunate.

Near the head of the caravan of civilians were Marie Boozer and her mother, who rode in a handsome black carriage of the Elmore family, which Marie had "exchanged" for her own less roadworthy vehicle. Under an escort of cavalry, the young beauty passed through the countryside like an Oriental queen receiving homage from adoring subjects. As a South Carolina newspaper later reported: "Officers before the carriage, officers behind and at each window, were in one continual struggle to be near her, to catch the sound of her voice or even a fleeting smile." Her baggage followed in an army wagon, which was also under guard. Marie had now become the special charge of General Judson Kilpatrick, who seemed to hang about the blond beauty by night and day, fending off rival officers and overwhelming Marie with attentions. The girl's mother looked on with indulgent smiles.

In marching the first few miles north of Columbia, Sherman's men felt that civilian morale in the region was breaking. Tablecloths hung from farmhouse windows, crudely lettered: HAVE MERCY ON ME! The few white men to be seen were abject and fearful. In this region even Negroes hid from the passing troops.

In at least one instance, however, farm women found a way to frustrate Sherman's raiders. When foragers descended upon a plantation house almost within sight of Columbia, three frail, black-clad sisters emerged and stood motionlessly on their porch until the soldiers began their mischief. While chickens squawked and hogs squealed in terror, the ghostly sisters marched on the porch, singing a hymn, then dropped to their knees and sobbed out prayers, assuring the Lord that they were ready to die.

This was too much for these foragers, who rode away. "This strange incantation," the reporter David Conyngham wrote, "had a stronger superstitious influence on the bummers than a squad of Hampton's cavalry."

The rape of another South Carolina white woman when the army was only two days out of Columbia set off a savage exchange of executions and retaliations between Federals and Confederates.

The rebel General James Chesnut, who had halted at a farmhouse in search of fodder for his horse, found that the owner, identified by Chesnut only as a "Mr. M.," had fled from home. The farmer's wife found some forage for the general's mount.

Chesnut admired her daughter, a beautiful girl in her teens. "You should send her away," he told Mrs. M. "You're in the track of the armies, and the stragglers will do anything."

The girl insisted upon remaining with her mother. A squad of Wheeler's men overtook Chesnut in camp that night and brought news of the "M.'s."

The Confederates had reached the house in the afternoon to find it a shambles. The girl was dead. Her mother was raving insanely—seven Federal soldiers had come, bound her hand and foot, and one after another, had raped her daughter.

As they had in the previous case of the unknown girl raped by Federal soldiers near Aiken, Wheeler's troopers took immediate and impulsive revenge. Galloping along a country road in the tracks of the bluecoat raiders, the rebel troopers overtook the supposed rapists, killed them at once, cut their throats and left the bodies at the roadside bearing a sign: THESE ARE THE SEVEN.

This incident opened a new phase of grim retribution between the armies. Almost daily, other Federal soldiers were found at the roadside, within plain view of the blue columns, lying with slashed throats. General Slocum reported finding twenty-one bodies of his slain soldiers tumbled into a ravine.

On February 22, eighteen of Kilpatrick's men were killed in this way, and some of the bodies bore crudely lettered messages: DEATH TO ALL FORAGERS. In an effort to halt the murders, Sherman ordered his commanders to kill a Confederate prisoner for each such Federal corpse they found, and the impulse to revenge became official army policy.

Sherman realized that his bummers and foragers had prompted the executions by the Confederates, and told his generals: "If our foragers commit excesses, punish them yourself, but never let an enemy judge between our men and the law."

Kilpatrick sent a message to Wheeler describing the murder of his eighteen soldiers, all of whom, he said, had been slain after their surrender: "Unless some satisfactory explanation is made to me before sundown, February 23, I will cause 18 of your men, now my prisoners, to be shot at that hour, and if this cowardly act is repeated . . . I will not only retaliate . . . but there shall not be a house left within reach of my scouting parties on my line of march . . . I know of no other way to intimidate cowards."

Wheeler replied immediately, expressing his shock at the charges. He promised to investigate and to see that "justice is done," but warned Kilpatrick that innocent men must not be killed: "I have no desire to make counter threats, but should you cause eighteen of my men to be shot . . . I shall regard them as so many murders committed by you and act accordingly . . ."

Kilpatrick agreed to take no further action at that time, but ended the exchange with a threat that any further murders would be avenged.

Soon after he left Columbia, Sherman thought of the escaped prisoner Adjutant Byers, who had written the inspiring song about the army's march. The commander called Byers to headquarters, but found him reluctant to appear in his prison rags. Only when a staff officer was sent for him did Byers appear at headquarters, where Sherman welcomed him and congratulated him on his song: "Our boys will all sing it—and I want you on my staff, Byers. I'll get you a horse and everything you need." He led the adjutant into his dining tent, where staff officers greeted him curiously, "doubtless wondering what General Sherman had picked up," as Byers said.

Sherman put the young officer at ease by seating him at his side and devoting his full attention to him during dinner. Byers lost himself in telling stories of prison life in the South and of his escape. Sherman talked at length of the problems concerning prisoners, revealing a streak of cruelty unsuspected by his staff. "Prisoners would be better off if they were killed on the battlefield," Sherman said. "I'm almost satisfied that it would be just as well to kill all prisoners. They would be spared these atrocities. And the more awful you can make war, the sooner it will be over . . . war is hell, at the best."

Byers was shocked—"I thought him heartless"—but after hearing a long monologue by the general, became convinced that Sherman never gave a harsh order without suffering "heart-pain," and that the general's first thoughts were always of the welfare of his men.

Sherman had Byers dressed in the surplus clothing of his staff officers, promoted him to major, and had him ride with the headquarters party thereafter.

The XIV and XX Corps hurried along parallel roads toward Winnsboro, a pleasant village of 2,500 some forty miles north of

Columbia. The Reverend W. W. Lord, rector of Christ Episcopal Church, and a four-hundred-pound vestryman who was the local doctor rode from Winnsboro to the Federal camp and begged for the town's protection. They were too late. Bummers entered the place in advance of the main columns and began their familiar rites. Mr. Lord's son recalled, "Like truants out of school these overgrown 'Boys in Blue' played snowball along the fire-lit streets with precious flour; made bonfires of hams and sides of bacon; set boxes and barrels of crackers afloat on streams of molasses and vinegar; fed horses from hats full of sugar." The foragers, it was said, destroyed enough food for Winnsboro's annual supply.

Much of the town, at least thirty houses, went up in flames. The Episcopal Church was burned to the ground after soldiers had removed the organ so that they could play "the devil's tunes" on it. Calling upon the dead to witness the fun, the pranksters dug a coffin from the graveyard, split it with an axe and stood it on end so that its recently dead occupant could take in the ceremony.

Rivalry between the XX and XIV Corps came into the open in Winnsboro when General John W. Geary, leading the XX Corps, arrested a number of looters in the village. The indignant XIV Corps troops avenged themselves on civilians. The Illinois Private John Batchelor of the XIV Corps wrote indignantly: "Here we meet the 20th Corps. They steal everything they can see, even to a silver bugle from the bugler."

Sherman was still unable to impose a workable policy on plundering by his troops. He denounced the constant pillaging by the 8th Missouri Regiment and threatened to send the unit to the rear of the army, but was deterred by memories of its bravery in battle. He said at last, vacillating once more, "I would have pardoned them for anything short of treason." By now, he said, he had concluded that his wide-ranging foragers saved many lives for the army and kept the enemy in a state of terror and uncertainty.

Ten years later, offering his rationale for failing to control his predatory troops, Sherman wrote: "Fighting is the least and easiest part of war, but no General ever was or will be successful who quarrels with his men, who takes the part of citizens against the petty irregularities or who punishes them unduly for gathering fire-wood, using wells and springs of water and even taking sheep, chickens and food when their regular supplies are insufficient."

In Winnsboro, at any rate, Sherman made one of his sporadic efforts to control the army's excesses. The army's trains were thoroughly searched for the first time since leaving Columbia. In the baggage wagons of one division of the XV Corps alone, five tons of tobacco, table silver, utensils, civilian clothing and household goods were "piled in one grand heap" and burned.

A golden figure of Christ, stolen from a Columbia church, was found in a headquarters wagon of the same corps. Captain Wills wrote: "They are too wicked to tell. This army has done some awful stealing. Inspectors pounce down upon the trains every day or two now, and search them. Everything imaginable is found."

This unusual exercise of discipline may have lightened Winnsboro's ordeal. In the home of the Reverand Josiah Obear, who conducted a boarding school for girls, women and children were spared harm because of a sick boy. One of the inmates was Mrs. W. Perroneau Finley of Aiken, whose young son Leighton had broken out in a scarlet rash as the Federal troops entered Winnsboro. There was no time to find a doctor or to diagnose young Finley's disease. Since Mrs. Finley was afraid to be left alone in her room with the child, she persuaded about twenty other refugees to crowd in with her. They were waiting there when the door burst open to reveal three or four Federal soldiers. One of the intruders glimpsed the Finley boy and retreated. "Back!" he said. "Go back! Disease in here." Guards were posted to prevent soldiers from exposure, and the household escaped harm thereafter.

Emboldened women in the house began taunting soldiers who were ransacking nearby houses. One of these was young Lilla Carroll, who had come from Columbia with her mother and sisters. Lilla walked Obear's porch, singing loudly, "Oh, yes, I am a Southern girl —I glory in the name." She glared defiantly at Federal soldiers in the street and went back into the house. A stone was flung through a window, showering glass over Leighton Finley's sickbed, but though much of the town was burned, the Obear home escaped. The worst was over. The Federal troops had left Winnsboro by sundown.

Sherman changed his course as the columns left this town, now moving toward the northeast, in the direction of Cheraw. Beyond lay his actual goal—though he still made feints toward Charlotte with his cavalry, hoping to prevent the concentration of Confederate forces in upper South Carolina.

The army left civil unrest in its wake as it moved from Winnsboro. In her plantation house just outside the town, Mrs. Nancy Furman awaited the arrival of the enemy. Her brother-in-law had been a signer of the Ordinance of Secession, and Mrs. Furman had reason to expect the worst. But she and several other women in the house fared no worse than others on the army's route. Soldiers hurried in and out, stealing clothing, silver and small objects, opening drawers and closets, smashing furniture, but causing no physical harm to the women.

To Mrs. Furman's consternation, one of Sherman's officers took a pretty mulatto girl of the neighborhood as his bride: "One of the Yankee officers was married to her by a Roman Catholic priest and then demanded from Mrs. Yarborough her best bed to sleep on."

The black-white marriage seems to have been an omen of racial disturbance in the region.

When the Federal horde had passed on, Mrs. Furman said, there was "a good deal of insubordination" among the freed slaves who were left behind. Negroes took over several farms in the community from whites and divided the land among themselves in a bold first step to taking possession of the property of their former masters — one of the first recorded instances of these black innocents attempting to improve their lot as freedmen. As was usually the case, there was no recorded evidence of the details of this venture by slaves. The name of their leader is unknown, and only Mrs. Furman seems to have recorded the incident, which came to a swift, bloody conclusion.

Confederate soldiers from the Army of Tennessee who were passing nearby put down the "uprising": "A company from Chisholm's cavalry, of Cheatham's Division, stopped on this side [of] the river and restored order in a good degree," Mrs. Furman wrote. As to the fate of the black leaders, she noted only, "Several have been shot and a great many severely whipped."

About this time Sherman had news of major developments in his theater. The rebels had evacuated both Charleston and Wilmington, and the Confederacy was now without a major port. More important to the invading army, General Joseph E. Johnston had been recalled to command and ordered to halt Sherman's advance. Sherman realized that the Confederates were now desperate, since relations between President Davis and Johnston were strained; the move could have been made only as a last resort. But Sherman needed no reminder of Johnston's competence. The army was soon to be tested—somewhere in North Carolina, Sherman judged. He estimated that the Confederates could summon at least 40,000 troops to meet him, including the remnants of the Army of Tennessee, now gathering in his front after trickling across the mountains from Tennessee and their disastrous campaign under John Hood. Though he expected now that he must fight a final battle, Sherman was confident of victory. He issued a general order, predicting to his troops that the campaign would end within six weeks.

Some of Sherman's troops got a further indoctrination in race relations under the slave system in the town of Lancaster, a few miles to the north. Soldiers burst into the home of Mrs. Virginia Green and ransacked it, leaving to her and her two young sons only a chunk of smoked hog jowl that had fallen into a trough of corrosive lye soap. For almost two weeks the Greens ate only what their faithful carriage driver and his wife, Mary, smuggled to them. Mary was frequently cursed by soldiers: "If you carry another morsel to that white woman and her children we'll kill you."

One of the household servants was "Mammy" Pickett, a stately mulatto mistaken for Mrs. Green's mother by the soldiers. Mammy was frequently ordered to give up her money and her watch.

"I'm a servant," she explained to one soldier.

"What! You a slave? Anybody who has you for a slave ought to be killed!"

The angry man turned on Mrs. Green: "Ain't that right, Lady?"

"There she is, ask her for yourself."

Mammy Pickett replied, as she did each time with an imperturbable dignity, "No, sir. I'm treated as one of the family. Just as my mistress lives, I live."

The relationship, a not uncommon one between white slaveowners and house servants, was incomprehensible to the intruders.

In Lancaster some of Sherman's troops came upon another sick boy, this one an eighteen-year-old cadet from The Citadel, a refugee fleeing with his family. Seriously ill with pneumonia, the anonymous boy, together with his family, was surprised by bummers before the main body of the army reached the town. The boy's mother was kneeling at her morning prayers when the first bluecoat entered and seized her arms from behind. "Get up, old woman, praying will do you no good now, for Sherman's bummers are upon you." Soldiers snatched her gold spectacles, emptied her pockets and ransacked the room. Her daughters carried the old woman upstairs, where the three of them huddled with the small children. Soldiers tramped up the steps and banged on the door. A six-year-old girl lay in bed with her favorite doll and a cake of fragrant soap that she had treasured during her journey, and just before the soldiers entered she darted under the bed to hide.

Soldiers ransacked the room. The child's mother described the next moments: "At length one of the men approached the bed, and finding it warm, in dreadful language accused us of harboring a wounded Rebel, and swore he would have his heart's blood! He stooped to look under the bed, and seeing the little white figure crouching in a distant corner, caught her by one rosy little foot and dragged her forth. The child was too terror-stricken to cry, but clasped the little doll and her soap fast to the throbbing little heart. The man wrenched both from her and thrust the little one away with such violence that she fell against the bed."

When they had stripped this room, the troopers turned to that of the sick cadet. The mother stood in the door, barring the way until an officer came. "He's very ill," she said. "I'll hand you anything in the room except his bed. In the name of humanity don't take his last chance of life."

"I can promise you nothing," the officer said. "Our men are under no restraint in South Carolina. I'll try to get them to enter one at a time, but that room must be searched."

A day or so later General Smith Atkins took the house as headquarters and sent a surgeon to visit the sick boy. The doctor questioned the mother about his illness.

"Has he ever served in the regular army?"

"He's eighteen years old, a State Cadet, and has never served in any other way."

"He's quite feeble," the doctor said. "He needs a stimulant. Why haven't you been caring for him?"

"Because your men have taken everything from us."

The doctor promised to send food and medicine and said, "The General wishes to speak to one of the ladies of the house."

The sick boy's aunt went downstairs, where she was treated rudely by General Atkins and other officers of Kilpatrick's cavalry command. Several officers sat about the fireplace with their boots off. They did not speak.

"Who wishes to speak with me?" the young woman asked.

"I do," Atkins said. "Take a seat."

The general questioned her about Hampton's cavalry and about the location of roads, bridges and railroads. The woman could tell him little, since she was a stranger to the region. Atkins thought her replies were evasive. "You know less than any woman I ever saw, but none of this will save you. Our forces are throughout your state. We'll soon see the proud women of Carolina like those of Georgia, with tears in their eyes, begging crusts of bread from our men for their famishing children." The woman never forgot the expression on Atkins' face when he described the abject miseries of helpless women in Georgia. "Oh, it was glorious to see such a sight," Atkins said.

The passage of Marie Boozer was also noted in Lancaster. The home of Daniel Brown, a wounded Confederate cavalryman who fled at the coming of the invaders, was used as headquarters by General Kilpatrick. The house was rifled by foragers first, but after Kilpatrick arrived, quiet returned. Guards surrounded the house. Mrs. Brown was allowed to remain on the first floor, but the general and his staff took the upper floor. Mrs. Brown and her daughters noted that the officers were not alone in their private quarters: "General Kilpatrick occupied a front room in the second story; a *woman,* handsome and tall, who wore fine clothes, occupied the room opposite his; and his officers the other two."

One of the Brown daughters retained a vivid memory of Kilpatrick: "A very insignificant-looking man. He was small, with ugly reddish-looking hair . . . and a most irritable disposition . . . He always paid court to the woman who came with him . . . she took her meals with him."

The Brown family did not suffer now. There was always the reassuring tread of a guard in the hallway. Officers played with the baby and reminisced about their own children back home. Every evening Kilpatrick and some of his officers went into the sitting room and remained with the Brown family until bedtime. The officers smoked good cigars and idly questioned Mrs. Brown about life in the South. Sometimes musicians came to entertain them. Only once did the *woman* come into the sitting room.

The family was not allowed to leave its first-floor quarters, but was treated courteously—and once Mrs. Brown was permitted to lead some servants into the yard, and as Major Estes watched, hams, silver, and china were dug up and carried into the house. The angry soldiers were forbidden to interfere.

Mrs. Brown was outraged by Kilpatrick's farewell after a week in the house. The general escorted the *woman* into the yard, handed her into the Browns' fine carriage and was driven off with her. In the front seat, piled so high that the driver was almost hidden, were Mrs. Brown's finest white blankets.

Almost on the heels of the general's carriage escort, Wheeler's gray riders raced into Lancaster, driving the Federal cavalry rear guard before them, scattering the bluecoats before they could burn the town. Only the jail and courthouse were set on fire.

18

"Rebels have no rights"

Sherman's right wing—now nearing the North Carolina border—swept through the handsome old village of Camden on February 21, a cold, rainy day. Colonel Robert N. Adams led the advance into town after scattering a few of Wheeler's cavalrymen who had fired from a hill known as Kirkwood, the site of a celebrated battle of the Revolution.

Rebel resistance was so weak that more than a dozen gray troopers were captured by a rush of Federal pickets, and Sherman's men felt that the enemy had lost their taste for battle. Theodore Upson said: "I think the Johnnys are getting rattled; they are afraid of our repeating rifles. They say we are not fair, that we have guns that we load up on Sunday and shoot all the rest of the week. This I know, I feel a good deal more confidence in myself with a 16 shooter in my hands, than I used to with a single shot rifle."

Other bluecoats thought the rebel troopers were carrying out a new strategy revealed in a dispatch allegedly captured about this time, a distressed plea from Hampton to Butler: "Do not attempt to delay Sherman's march. For God's sake let him get out of the country as soon as possible."

Women and Negroes emerged from several of Camden's large houses, invited officers to dine and fed the soldiers at the roadside, with "lavish offers of good things to eat and drink." Hospitality did not deter Colonel Adams from carrying out his orders. He burned two railroad depots, a bridge, two thousand bales of cotton, a large flour mill stocked with grain, and warehouses filled with hams, bacon and other stores. Adams and his command passed on after two hours, but the town suffered in his wake.

Dr. E. P. Burton of the 7th Illinois noted that "the soldiers went in to plunder," gutted the town's stores, got drunk on wine and left a number of stragglers behind.

The troops found large stocks of whiskey and wine, some of the wine corks sealed with the date of 1832. The weary men, soaked to the skin, enjoyed "a copious application of the captured juice of the grape, which counteracted fatigue, drove away trouble, and cheerfulness reigned throughout the camp."

Most of the town's old men, who had fled to the woods, were tracked down by bummers and herded in with wagonloads of food, silver and fine furniture.

The heroine of Camden's townsfolk was Miss Sally Chesnut, a spinster who lived with her ninety-three-year-old father in a stately plantation house known as Mulberry, just outside the town. When a Federal officer entered and sat before the fire while the Chesnuts were at breakfast, Sally said, "Rebels have no rights, but I suppose you have come to rob us. Please do so and go. Your presence agitates my blind old father."

The enraged officer rose and shouted, "What do you take me for? A thief?" He stormed out empty-handed.

Other bluecoats came, but the self-possessed Miss Sally was not molested, and the bummers took only two bottles of champagne, a gold-headed cane, two horses and a carriage. Only one of the many Chesnut slaves deserted to join the Federal raiders, "a fly-brush boy called Battis whose occupation in life was to stand behind the table and with his peacock feathers brush the flies."

The master of the Mulberry plantation, old man Chesnut, though blind and deaf at ninety-three, strode boldly at every step, striking about with his walking stick and trusting to his huge black slave Scipio to shield him from harm. The raiders also found Scipio a worthy adversary. When soldiers urged him to follow the army, Scipio said, "Master can't do without me. There's nobody to look out for him. I'll never leave."

"If you want to stay so bad, he must have been good to you."

Scipio made no response; as he told Miss Sally, "It makes 'em mad if you praise your master."

Mary Boykin Chesnut, the old man's daughter-in-law, saw in

Chesnut the passing of the plantation South, a fate she did not wholly mourn:

"Partly patriarch, partly grand seigneur, this old man is of a species that we will see no more; the last of the lordly planters who ruled this Southern world. His manners are unequalled still, but underneath this smooth exterior lies the grip of a tyrant whose will has never been crossed. . . . He came of a race that would brook no interference with their own sweet will by man, woman or devil . . ."

The old man's son, General James Chesnut, noted that many Southerners were exultant at the downfall of landowners like his father. He heard one man say, "They will have no Negroes now to lord it over. They can swell and peacock about and tyrannize now only over a small parcel of women and children, those who are their very own family."

Camden's richest treasures remained undiscovered until, two or three days later, foraging parties of two Illinois regiments struck gold in nearby woodlands. Privates Jesse McQuade and Charles Hartsell, of the 102nd Illinois, who were leading a band of raiders far from the main column, found three covered wagons in hiding and stumbled into a party of civilian guards who were escorting the deposits of a Camden bank. The raiders found in the wagons $2,500 in gold and silver bullion, $700 in specie and $35,000 in Confederate bonds, all of which was taken to corps headquarters by the commanders of the foraging party.

A second bank was captured in its flight toward Cheraw by bummers of the 34th Illinois. Two bankers in disguise were found hiding in the woods, "seedy-looking individuals wearing butternut clothes and shocking bad hats," a Mr. McDowell and a Mr. Anderson, president and cashier of the Bank of Camden. Beneath a wagonload of broken-down office furniture, the bummers found an antiquated safe containing $800 in gold and silver coins and $1.5 million in Confederate bonds and currency—but a few of the more enterprising raiders who went through the wagons more thoroughly found more gold, $400 in coins, which they divided among themselves.

Continual rains flooded the rivers in the army's northward path to Cheraw, South Carolina. One of Sherman's columns was held up for four days at Lynch's Creek, a small stream then swollen to a width of three-fourths of a mile. Several bridges were laid in succession, but the surging current dashed driftwood against the pontoons and smashed them; poles laid on the muddy bottom of the approaches to the stream floated away; parties of Confederate cavalry attacked on both banks, and in the confusion of driving off the enemy, horses and mules floundered and wagons were lost.

Charles Herbert of the 50th Illinois went into the crossing with the column, holding his rifle and cartridge box high over his head, wading for three hundred yards about waist-deep over the treacherous footing of the submerged poles, breaking a thin skin of ice at each step. Then, after plunging down a muddy slope to the main channel, "the men would hesitate and draw a long breath . . . as they viewed that wide expanse of cold water, of unknown depth, covered with a coating of ice. But the men behind were crowding and there was no turning back, so in they go, down into the water, deeper and deeper, until it was up to the necks of the shortest men . . ."

Spectators in the rear ranks were treated to a ludicrous scene as skirmishers, already stripped to wade the stream, were hurried aside to meet Confederate attackers and fought naked, chasing the rebels over muddy fields, clad only in boots and hats and carrying only rifles and cartridge boxes. This process was repeated day after day as fresh divisions came up and were halted at the crossing of Lynch's Creek.

Sherman watched the crossing efforts for two days, then ordered General Jefferson C. Davis to speed his march by killing his horses and cattle and burning his wagon train if he had not crossed by March 1. The tail of the corps passed the raging stream at last, and the army moved on, its animal herds intact.

The column struggled seventy-nine miles in the next four days, and laid twenty-five miles of corduroy road by piling the trunks of saplings in the watery roadway. Farms were stripped clean for forty miles in either direction, and food became scarce once more. It was the first time the troops had suffered from hunger since their passage of the Georgia swamps in front of Savannah.

Tempers were short, and men in ranks often failed to cheer at the sight of Sherman riding by in the rain. Captain Charles Wills wrote, "Sherman has been heard to say this army can live on fresh meat alone for 30 days. I'd like to see it tried on him." Soldiers slaughtered all the native cattle to be found, but the animals were tiny and sickly. Chaplain Hight complained, "They are the most miserable stock I have ever seen. The largest are but little larger than dogs, and all are mere shadows."

Private Sam Paulding of New York's Dutchess County Regiment remembered the nights in this country as worse than the days, since there was no way to sleep on the cold, sodden ground: "We thought ourselves in luck when we could recline against a big tree and thus pass the night . . . I sometimes wonder that any of us lived through it."

The army's bummers, ranging far afield in this sandy country, had unusual adventures. One party found two of Kilpatrick's riders and five Confederate lieutenants fraternizing in a drunken bout of revelry, and took them into camp.

Ben Johnson, the accomplished forager from Iowa, demonstrated the ability of his kind to circumvent the most zealous of Sherman's disciplinarians. Johnson found a rich plantation far from the army's line of march, occupied by only four white women and their slaves, and robbed it of its delicacies despite the best efforts of a young Federal officer who caught him at his pillaging and tried to put him under arrest.

Ben arrived in advance and entered the Negro quarters, where an old black woman gave him milk and corn bread and rubbed her hands in glee as he ate. "Glory, glory," she said. "All gwine to be free. Captin Sherman's comin' with his treadin' company."

Ben showed a plug of tobacco to a Negro man, who said plaintively, "That's the first piece of flat tobacco I've seen since befo' the war."

"Now where are all the chickens?"

"Lord, the folks at the house would kill me if I was to tell."

"How will they know? I'll never tell. And you'll get half this plug."

The old man succumbed. "They're upstairs in the big room with the turkeys, hams and taters."

Ben went into the big house, walked upstairs past the women "amid their curses and scorn," and emerged laden with live poultry. As Johnson left the house two young Federal riders entered the yard, a newly commissioned lieutenant with an officious orderly at his heels. Johnson scornfully appraised the newcomer as "the nephew of some Congressman."

The women ran from the house to greet their unexpected deliverer. "Oh, General, this brute has been robbing us of everything we have to eat." The lieutenant, Johnson said, "began to swell up like a little toad," and commanded his orderly to arrest Ben.

The orderly moved forward, but Ben halted him with a quiet threat: "If you want to see your mother again, don't come a step closer."

Johnson scolded the women: "You're as big fools as he is—General, my foot! He's a hanger-on at some headquarters and ain't fit for the uniform."

He swung his musket toward the lieutenant. "Don't get near me," he said. "I'm going back to the road where the column is."

"I'm going right with you."

"If you do, you'd better not get too close."

The three Federals then rode off to rejoin the army, the lieutenant calling out from a safe distance, "You're under arrest!" and Ben Johnson retorting, "All right, General. Why don't you come arrest me and take my gun?"

When they reached the column, Ben saw that he was in luck—his own regiment had halted nearby, and when he told his story to friends, the regiment rushed for the lieutenant, who raced along the column in full flight. The Iowans called derisively after him, cawing like crows. Other regiments took up the sport, and the raucous cawing followed the galloping boy lieutenant and his orderly until they were out of sight.

One of Marie Boozer's former friends glimpsed the turncoat beauty near the village of Liberty Hill during the last days of February. Mrs. Mary Eleanor Poppenheim, a refugee from a low-country plantation, stood with a woman companion at the roadside while one of Sherman's long columns passed, waiting for the chance to ask some general for protection. The two women waited a long time, gazing at passing Federal troops and the civilians who had fled from Columbia. Mrs. Poppenheim recognized several of these people, and was then startled to see a beautiful, familiar face—it was Marie Boozer, riding in a carriage with her mother, in animated conversation with a laughing officer who rode at her side. Mrs. Poppenheim felt a wave of nausea. "Let's go back," she said. "I can't wait here, general or no general."

The women turned back toward the house to which they had fled. Mrs. Poppenheim moved awkwardly, for she had sewn more than a hundred thousand dollars in Confederate bills inside the lining of her dress. They reached the house safely, but found there a party of Federals who had plundered the house and discovered Mrs. Poppenheim's husband, a wounded Confederate cavalry officer.

One Federal captain eyed Chris Poppenheim's gray vest and brass buttons. "You're a Rebel officer," he said. When a soldier found an old sword in the attic, the bluecoats said it was Poppenheim's.

Chris was led toward the door. "Mary," he said, "this man thinks I'm a captain in the Rebel army, and wants to take me prisoner to camp."

"Oh, he's not!" Mary said. "I swear he's not. We've just been married a few weeks and we're on our way to my father's plantation."

When she saw a look of disbelief on the captain's face, Mary made a final effort to save her husband: "I gave him the Masonic sign of distress (which my brother gave me before going to war); he looked down, shut his mouth tight, then said, 'Go on.' We lost no time in going."

Both wings of the army passed through the sleepy tree-shaded village of Cheraw, on the Pee Dee River within a few miles of the North Carolina border—and found it an astonishing storehouse of treasure. Its warehouses, stables and sheds were bursting with valuables that had been shipped from Charleston for safety. The furniture, books, paintings and statuary accumulated by Charleston's wealthy families for generations were assembled here, and Sherman's bummers, who were first into the town, lost no time in falling upon the tempting loot.

Colonel Oscar Jackson, who had seen the army in its most lawless moods, said, "Such stealing was astonishing even in our army. It beats Columbia in many respects."

Among the choice stores were cases of fine liquor, brandy and wine that had been shipped through the blockade. Jackson recorded their fate in his diary: "Our division occupies the town and there is scarce a squad of soldiers but can treat you this evening to a bottle of fine wine and brandy. I went out among the boys and like to have got intoxicated. A gay time this."

The best of the captured wine found its way to Sherman's headquarters. His staff officers picked over the eight wagonloads of imported vintages, and the officers at headquarters were soon "pretty nearly drunk." Howard, Kilpatrick, Logan, Hazen and many division commanders were on hand, but Sherman evidently did not take part. Officers sang while Black Jack Logan played a violin. Logan called on Major Byers for a rendition of his poem, which drew a thunderous applause. The officers then sang the song itself. The noisy celebration lasted for hours. It was only later that Sherman expressed his disapproval.

A staff officer who had become drunk began an apology at dinner that night, but Sherman cut him off: "Never mind explaining," he said without looking up from his food. "Just see that the like of that doesn't happen again." The commander's mood improved during the evening. He visited with a local family, the Woodwards, whose home was being used as a regimental headquarters for the night, and spent an hour or so conversing easily with them. Edwin Lybarger, an officer of the 43rd Ohio who was present, noted that Sherman laughed and talked with the Southerners in a normal way, but that he revealed in every word "his implacable hatred of the rebel cause."

Woodward asked the general, "Where do you plan to go next?"

Sherman smiled at his innocence. "I have about 60,000 men out there," he said, "and I intend to go pretty much where I please."

The day in Cheraw had been notable for its noise. Scores of Confederate cannon had been captured, including one bearing a brass plate: FIRST GUN FIRED ON FORT SUMTER—the cannon that had opened the Civil War. Sherman's gunners had fired twenty-three of these old guns in salute to President Lincoln, who was inaugurated for his second term in Washington during the day; some of the aged barrels had burst, but did not dampen the army's enthusiasm.

There were also a number of accidental explosions. Theodore Upson, the Indiana veteran, was on hand when an estimated three tons of gunpowder exploded: "When we made a fire to cook our coffee there was a little flash of powder ran along the ground and one yelled, 'Look out for the magazine!' We did look out and ran for the river. The powder flashes ran in every direction . . . Then there was a tremendous explosion . . . The dirt and stones flew in every direction . . . We made some pretty quick moves."

Hundreds of soldiers were knocked to the earth, six soldiers and several civilians were killed, and three houses were demolished as shot and shell rained over the city. A Confederate magazine had been destroyed.

John Arbuckle, a diarist of the 4th Iowa, recorded Sherman's reaction: "Gen. Sherman was thoroughly aroused and was on the point of ordering the city reduced to ashes, and the Mayor and other city officials placed before a firing squad before it was found they weren't to blame."

Sherman's grim standing order that his officers take revenge for Confederate atrocities was carried out in a macabre scene in Cheraw, to the indignation of some of his troops. In camp near the town the 30th Illinois found the body of one of its men, bearing the telltale rebel warning: DEATH TO FORAGERS. The victim was a private of Company H of this regiment, by name Woodrough, a soldier who had been none too popular with his mates.

Major William Rhoads, the regimental commander, at first refused to execute a Confederate prisoner in retaliation for the murder of Woodrough, and did not issue the order until Sherman threatened him with a court-martial.

Guards were sent to the prison corral, and the captive rebels were forced to draw lots. A soldier passed among them holding aloft a hat with several slips of paper, one of which bore a black mark. A gray-haired old man named Small drew the black-marked slip.

Chaplain Cole of the 31st Illinois prayed with the victim and led him into a ravine where he was to be shot. The regiment formed a hollow square above.

"Do you have anything to say?"

The old man's voice was flat and unhurried: "I was forced into the army. Never was in a battle. Never wished the Yankees any harm."

After a pause he said, "I have nine children, all girls. I'm a Methodist preacher back home." Chaplain Cole could bear no more. He hurried to his tent and remained there. Private G. B. McDonald saw that several Federal soldiers were blinking tears from their eyes as the firing squad shuffled into place. The old man was blindfolded and placed against a tree.

"Don't tie me," he said. "Just let me stand here." Major Rhoads nodded and the old man leaned on the tree, hands at his sides. A soldier placed a handkerchief in one of Small's hands. "Drop it when you're ready," he said. The major turned to the firing squad. "Be sure to take good aim," he said. "Don't wound him."

The Wisconsin soldier Hosea Rood watched sadly: "When all was ready, there was a few seconds of death-like stillness and suspense, every eye being riveted on the handkerchief in the old man's hand; it fluttered to the ground." The volley rolled and Small's body stiffened, quivered and fell to the ground. "As the smoke floated away among the tall pines our boys looked with sadness upon the bleeding corpse of a brave old man who had met death unflinchingly and heroically for the crime of another man . . . If the old man had bounded away into the forest we'd never have run a step to catch him."

Still, as Private McDonald conceded, Sherman's harsh revenge was effective. The rebels no longer left murdered foragers at the roadside. Oliver Howard reported, "I do not remember an instance after that in my command of brutal slaying."

The army left Cheraw on a pontoon bridge across the Pee Dee, leaving most of the town in flames. But at least a few marauders who were caught at their work in the village were punished. One soldier was posted on the pontoon bridge as the column marched out, guarded by two sentries and wearing a barrel with its ends knocked out, which bore the sign, I AM A THIEF. The whole corps passed within a few feet of this prisoner and an occasional soldier made a joke, but most passed as if they did not see him.

In Sherman's ranks Lieutenant Charles S. Brown bid the state a somber farewell as he crossed the border into North Carolina: "South Carolina may have been the cause of the whole thing, but she has had an awful punishment."

Not many miles distant, retreating with General Hardee's little Confederate force through the North Carolina pinewoods, General James Chesnut wrote his wife: "We have been driven like a wild herd from our country, not so much from a want of spirit in the people or the soldiers, as from want of energy and competence in our commanders. Hampton and Butler are the only ones who have done anything."

19
"Kilpatrick's shirt-tail skedaddle"

Sherman's army crossed into North Carolina through a somber forest of pines whose tops towered a hundred feet above the roadway. From an occasional clearing a few natives stared at the stream of men, horses, wagons and cannon. Lieutenant Matthew Jamison wrote of women on porches who "looked at us floundering knee-deep in mud and torrents of rain. We glanced ruefully at them out of the shadow of our lowering, drenched hat brims."

Sherman said of this passage, "It was the damndest marching I ever saw."

There was now less pillaging and almost no burning of houses, since Sherman had made it clear that North Carolinians, never fanatical Secessionists, bore little responsibility for starting the war. Though the southern region of the state was predominantly rural, there were a few scattered small towns, the largest of which was Fayetteville, an inland port on the navigable Cape Fear River. Fayetteville's importance to Sherman lay in its Confederate arsenal, which he intended to destroy.

A spirit of optimism was growing in Sherman's ranks. The troops sensed that the Confederacy was on the verge of collapse, though they seemed oblivious to the prospect that they might yet be tested in a full-scale battle—which, in fact, lay a scant two weeks away.

As they entered North Carolina's longleaf-pine country, soldiers seemed to understand the general's strategy for the first time, to realize that he had led them through three states without fighting a pitched battle. They were now convinced that their march from Atlanta was bringing the war to an end. The great march, they saw at last, had been a decisive and unique campaign.

The sandy country was a center of the tar, pitch and turpentine industry. Resin pits burned in the woods and smoke towered high into the air, until the tops of the pines were lost in a gray cloud. Colonel W. D. Hamilton of the cavalry wrote, "It was like a fire in a cathedral."

One soldier saw the enormous smoke cloud "as big as a mountain. It was awful. It rose four miles toward heaven, leaping and roaring like a bursting volcano." When a cavalry column splashed through a creek in the burning woods, men discovered the incredible heat of the flames: "The water was so infernally hot that it took the hair off the horses' legs as they went through it on the double-quick."

Major Byers, the headquarters newcomer who knew little of Sherman's relations with his troops, noted without comment that men cheered thunderously at every glimpse of the general, but older staff officers were astounded by these spontaneous roars of applause. Overnight, it seemed, Sherman had become a hero to his cynical veterans, who had grasped the significance of their long march from Atlanta.

Sherman responded warmly to the adulation of his troops. He no longer passed them by with a casual wave of his cigar, but halted and talked with soldiers who crowded about him, speaking in his quick, erratic way, gruffly candid, as if discussing the campaign with equals.

The army cherished the thought that he knew every man in his ranks. Byers said wonderingly, "He seemed to know the names of hundreds."

Sherman's habits were otherwise unchanged. His clothing was always unkempt and dirty. He prowled the camps restlessly at night, and usually lay abed no more than two hours. "He seemed to sleep no more than a bird," one soldier said.

The troops watched the general more closely than ever, as if he had become their special charge; they seized upon anecdotes that seeped down from the staff, and recounted and expanded them endlessly:

Sherman lost his way one night as he prowled through the camp searching for the headquarters of the 1st Division. He thumped on the wall of an officer's tent, and a sleepy quartermaster called crossly, "Who's that?"

"Could you tell me where General Jackson's quarters are?"

"How the hell do I know?"

"Aren't you a quartermaster in his division?"

"That's no reason I'd fish up his quarters for every jackleg that comes huntin' 'em."

The general halted a clerk who was entering the tent. "Soldier, I'm General Sherman. I want to go to General Jackson's. Will you please show me the way?"

The quartermaster popped out of his tent, babbling apologies. "General Sherman, I'll go with you."

"No, no," Uncle Billy said. "You're too busy. I won't take your time. This man will come with me."

Sherman and the XV Corps staff spent an uncomfortable night in a country Presbyterian church called Bethel. The troops huddled about campfires in "a terrible storm of rain." Inside the church, officers made a bed of carpet for Sherman on a platform before the altar, but the general refused: "No. That's for some of you younger fellows. I'm used to hard sleeping." He stretched out on a pew.

The general's pride in his army was evident in his first letters from North Carolina. He wrote Grant of passing over roads that would have halted "almost any other body of men I ever heard of." He told Stanton, "There is now no place in the Confederacy safe against the army of the West." He felt that the long marches and camp life in winter had made the army as hardy as the hordes of Genghis Khan. "I have not heard a man cough or sneeze in three months," he said. He had seen wounds which would have sent men to a hospital for months in 1861 now shrugged off as "mere scratches."

Confederates were also taking note of Sherman's growing reputation. The *Richmond Sentinel* said: "The Yankees certainly think he is the first of their commanders, even the fires of Lieutenant-General Grant have paled before the splendor of Sherman's achievements. . . . Sherman is their hero . . . the idol of the hour . . . the populace babble of him."

The Richmond correspondent of the London *Times* reported that Sherman's strategy would probably force Lee to evacuate Richmond. This reporter found Sherman an enigma: "During this war I have seen no man who seemed to me to possess so much of the temper of Cromwell as Sherman. . . . Vain, eager, enthusiastic, fanatical, at times gloomy and reticent, at others impulsive and talkative, by some regarded as half-mad when the fit is on him, General Sherman possesses a character which, unless I am mistaken, is of the stuff of which great and mysterious actors in history are often made."

Sherman's resolve to treat civilians more leniently when the columns left South Carolina was reflected in his order to Kilpatrick: "Deal as moderately, and fairly by North Carolinians as possible, and fan the flame of discord already subsisting between them and their proud cousins of South Carolina. There never was much love between them . . . " But though few houses were burned in North Carolina, the plundering continued to terrorize the women who lived in the army's path.

Young Nellie Worth lived on a farm called Glen Burnie, a few miles southwest of Fayetteville. Early in the morning of March 9 she was astounded to see about a hundred and fifty bluecoats on horseback. In less than ten minutes the house was stripped of all valuables, and when they found no watches, the soldiers turned on Nellie, who did not know where her father had hidden them.

"Where's the watches?" one said.

"I won't tell you."

The soldier put his pistol to her head, but she said nothing. "I was as firm as a rock and though I was completely in his power, I defied him to touch me." The soldier gave up.

"You're the damndest rebel I ever saw," he said.

An officer appeared at last, a Lieutenant Bracht, who posted a guard when Mrs. Worth appealed for help. It was too late for the family's food, silver, blankets and clothing, but Bracht saved the house. "I did not think there was a gentleman in the whole Yankie army, but now I know there is one if no more." Bracht also saved the family's watches, for when soldiers were about to find them, Mrs. Worth took them to the lieutenant, who kept them as long as he stayed.

The village of Wadesboro, not far from the Worth home, was pillaged by a band of Kilpatrick's raiders, who swept through the town systematically, taking everything of value from the houses. North Carolina's Episcopal bishop, Thomas Atkinson, was robbed at gunpoint of his watch, jewelry, clothing and horse. A wealthy old farmer, James C. Bennett, who had been robbed by soldiers a day or so earlier, was shot to death in his doorway when he told Kilpatrick's raiders he had no money or watch to surrender.

In the town of Lumberton a few miles away, Washington S. Chaffin, a Methodist minister, was making his diary entry for March 9: "The Yankees are said to be in two different places near here. I am incredulous . . . " He was interrupted by shouts: "The Yankees are coming!" Chaffin saw the street filled with bluecoats, two of whom fired at one of his neighbors as he fled. A cavalryman burst in, robbed Chaffin of his wife's watch and took his fine mare, Kate, from the stable. Smoke drifted over the town as troopers burned the depot and boxcars and a railroad bridge over the Lumber River. The troops had hardly left town when the methodical minister returned to his diary, little concerned for his "greatly excited" wife, but distraught over the loss of Kate, who had been his favorite for "five years, 11 months, 17 days—she had never been sick—I traveled with her on horseback, etc., 17,102 miles."

Sherman was aware that such depredations were creating havoc in Confederate armies, and did little to halt them. The march, he thought, was bringing the war to an end: "The simple fact that a man's home has been visited by an enemy makes a soldier in Lee's or Johnston's army very, very anxious to get home to look after his family and property."

Confederate commanders knew this all too well. North Carolina soldiers deserted from the Richmond trenches so rapidly that Robert E. Lee urged Governor Zebulon Vance to bolster public morale in the state: "Desertions are becoming very frequent . . . occasioned by letters written to the soldiers by their friends at home."

A group of soldiers wrote Vance from Virginia: "It is not in the power of the Yankee Armies to cause us to wish ourselves at home. We can face them, and can hear their shot and shell without being moved; but, Sir, we cannot hear the cries of our little ones and stand."

Kilpatrick, leading the army northward, had crossed the rampaging Pee Dee River on the Carolinas border with difficulty and only after engineers had labored several days to span the stream with pontoons and wagon beds. Once in North Carolina, Little Kil's troopers began to clash with Hardee's rear guard. It was a forecast of severe cavalry fighting to come, and an incident in which Kilpatrick was to narrowly escape disaster.

In the pelting rainstorms lashing the back country, friends and foes became scattered and confused; there was no longer a Federal front, for wide-ranging Confederate troopers were everywhere. Kilpatrick, marching toward the city of Fayetteville, learned from prisoners that General Wade Hampton was in his rear with a strong rebel cavalry force. In an effort to trap the Confederates, Kilpatrick divided his command into three brigades and spread his ranks across the country to cover all nearby roads. He hoped to bring Hampton to battle before the Confederates could reach Fayetteville itself. This was unpleasant duty, for Kilpatrick was forced to leave his carriage and Marie Boozer for a few hours.

One man who would never forget this day was H. Clay Reynolds, a rebel cavalryman who had been captured the previous night and was now tethered to the rear of Kilpatrick's Victoria, forced to hobble along in misery at the pace set by the carriage horses. Reynolds had been relieved of his magnificent Russian leather jackboots and given a pair of rough brogans. By the end of the day his feet were covered with blisters and his toenails were worn to the quick.

Reynolds was incensed by Kilpatrick's display of luxury. A French chef presided over the cavalryman's mess, and his wagons were filled with fine foods this country could not afford—wine, brandy, herbs, spices, bags of coffee beans and precious loaf sugar. Little Kil's star was rising; he was soon to become a major general, a stepping stone to a postwar career in diplomacy.

Almost equally galling to Reynolds was the spectacle he was forced to watch in the Victoria. When he returned from his cross-country rides, Kilpatrick lay in the carriage with his boots thrust over the side, his head in Marie's lap. Reynolds was tormented by the scent of her perfume and the sounds of their laughter and whispered intimacies.

Kilpatrick went into camp that night at the edge of a swamp near an isolated settlement known variously as Longstreet Church,

Monroe's Crossroads, and Solomon's Grove. Little Kil and Marie settled in a small house in the center of the camp, which they shared with staff officers. Kilpatrick left his charming companion for an hour or so to prowl anxiously about the countryside, inspecting the terrain and planning his interception of Hampton's cavalry. During Kilpatrick's brief absence, Lieutenant Clay Reynolds took advantage of the foggy darkness to make his escape.

Wade Hampton, who had followed Kilpatrick's force closely, learned that the Federal cavalry brigades were separated, and planned an attack on Kilpatrick's campsite. Confederate officers who reconnoitered the camp found no pickets in one sector and rode quietly to the campfires without alarming the sleeping Federals. When he learned that the camp was open to attack from the west, and that determined riders might also force a way through protective swamps on other flanks, Hampton ordered an attack at dawn. General Butler would lead a column from the west, and Wheeler would attempt to cross the swamp and fall upon the Federal rear.

The chill dawn of March 9 came slowly. A fog bank covered the Federal camp, where grotesque figures stirred as sentries changed posts and cooks kindled fires. Before the headquarters house where Kilpatrick and Marie Boozer slept, a Federal bugler raised his horn to sound reveille, but at that instant, a few yards away, Wheeler's bugler, Pelote, sounded the charge. The bluecoat's horn never reached his lips. Over the bugle call rose a quavering rebel yell.

Kilpatrick leaped from his bed and ran outside in his nightshirt, leaving the terrified Marie behind. A Confederate squadron dashed into camp. "It was the most formidable cavalry charge I ever saw," Kilpatrick said. "My God," he thought, "four years of hard fighting and a Major General's commission gone up in four minutes."

Several horsemen wearing Federal uniforms rode up to him. "Where's General Kilpatrick's quarters?" one of them asked.

Kilpatrick quickly detected their disguise and pointed. "Down the road about half a mile," he said. The duped Confederates spurred away, and Kilpatrick escaped capture.

The Confederate Lieutenant Wells caught a glimpse of Kilpatrick as he bolted toward the swamp, "a sorry-looking figure in shirt and drawers. The fugitive made no fight, but cutting loose and springing astride a horse . . . sped for safety through the fog and powder-smoke . . ."

The rebel prisoners held in the camp were crazed by the sound of Pelote's bugle: "Whoooooeeee! Hit's Wheeler, Yanks! You'd better git!" These men overran their guards and dashed into the path of the horsemen, waving their arms and yelping with joy. Two who reached up to embrace the necks of the leading horses were cut down before they could be recognized. One rider found that he had killed a lifelong friend.

Captain Sam Pegues of the 3rd Alabama, one of the first men to reach Kilpatrick's quarters, was startled to see "a beautiful young Irishwoman, in scanty nightdress," who leaned from a window and called to him for help.

"Get back," Pegues said. "Our people won't hurt you."

Marie Boozer disappeared for a moment, but when bullets rattled on the house, she emerged "in wild alarm" and ran toward her Victoria as if she intended to drive away, but then realized that she had no horses.

Wells took her from the porch amid heavy fire and hurried her into a ditch, where the girl crouched during the fight—though she raised her head now and then to watch, proof positive, Wells thought, "that female curiosity is stronger even than love of life."

Private Posey Hamilton, one of Wheeler's boy troopers from Alabama, was near Kilpatrick's quarters when Butler's riders swept by: "The Yankee camp looked like a cyclone had struck it all at once. Their blankets were flying in the air and the men were running about in every direction in their night clothes . . . If this was not a stampede on foot, then I never saw one."

The gray riders raced through the camp, then wheeled and rode twice more over the blanket-wrapped Federals, who raised muffled shouts of surrender. When they saw so few rebels, the bluecoats scrambled out with their carbines and began firing. Butler's squadrons were separated as they rode upon the Federal artillery in the center of the camp, and some troopers dismounted and tried to hitch horses to the cannon. Other Confederates, so Kilpatrick said, turned aside to plunder and lost interest in the battle. Wheeler's men, blocked by a deep morass at the edge of the swamp, were slow in advancing, and most of them were unable to get out of the swamp.

The skirmish across the high ground of the camp roared on in growing confusion. Gun smoke thickened the fog and obscured the struggling men and horses. By now the rapid fire of Kilpatrick's Spencer carbines had driven the Confederates across the camp in retreat, and though they swarmed back and the skirmish crackled for about two hours, the rebels were overcome. At eight o'clock, when a bluecoat infantry brigade came to Kilpatrick's rescue, the Confederates withdrew.

Little Kil had escaped, but the diversion had left open the road to Fayetteville, and Hampton hurried his command into the city, leaving the Federal cavalry behind.

Wheeler reported that he had taken more than 350 prisoners and had freed 175 Confederates. (Marie Boozer was not among them.) Kilpatrick said that only 103 of his men were captured; he reported 19 Federal dead and about 75 wounded.

Confederate losses were especially severe among officers. Generals Humes, Hannon and Hagan had been shot, and Hagan's brigade lost every field officer. Sergeant Sam Cothran and sixty other South Carolina troopers had died within a few minutes at the edge of the swamp, blocked by the impassable bog and helpless before the repeating weapons. Several of the dead rebels were boy troopers of the cadet company from The Citadel in Charleston, South Carolina.

Kilpatrick's humiliation in the dawn attack was a delight to Sherman's infantrymen. Captain Wills of Illinois wrote: "Hear that Hampton whipped Kilpatrick splendidly. Don't think that is any credit to him." And Alonzo Brown of the 4th Minnesota said, "Little Kil was caught napping that time, and the boys think it a good joke." The skirmish was afterward known to the bluecoat infantry as "Kilpatrick's shirt-tail skedaddle."

There were also envious infantrymen who were mystified by Little Kil's attraction for beautiful women. Lieutenant Matthew Jamison studied him closely without discovering charms that might have lured Marie Boozer to his bed: " . . . wiry, thin light hair, almost bald, sloping forehead, heavy and full at the brows, large Roman nose, thin lips well compressed." Jamison was offended by Kilpatrick's personal entourage, "his orderlies and two wench cooks; his nephew 'Billy' . . . this boy don't know his place; insults everybody on the staff."

The Ohio Private Albion Tourgee, who was to become a well-known novelist, a carpetbagger judge and author of the Constitution of North Carolina, also took note of Little Kil's charms: "Had a good chance to study Kilpatrick's angular features. Don't much like them."

20
"I can whip Joe Johnston"

In the central North Carolina back country a few miles to the north of Sherman's position, Confederates were already gathering in strength to challenge the Federal invaders. His recall to command had reached Joe Johnston in Lincolnton, North Carolina, far to the west of Sherman's track. Mrs. James Chesnut, the fugitive from South Carolina, saw Johnston that day, when, still humiliated from his loss of command at Atlanta, he resumed his task though the cause seemed to be lost. Still, Johnston devoted himself to explaining "all of Lee's and Stonewall Jackson's mistakes" to Mrs. Chesnut. The fussy, erect little general was angered by his orders. He felt that Jefferson Davis would sacrifice "wife, children, country and God to satisfy his hate for Joe Johnston."

"They're only calling me back so that I will be the one to surrender," Johnston said. Mrs. Chesnut understood his apprehension: "He might well be in a rage, this on-and-offing is enough to bewilder the coolest head." But she had little confidence in Johnston: "He always gives me the feeling that all of his sympathies are on the other side."

While Joe Johnston was traveling toward his new command, Sherman's columns were closing upon Fayetteville. Confederate cavalry clattered into the town on March 10, another day of chill rain, and Sherman was not far behind. Townspeople, alarmed by the Federal approach, welcomed the gray-clad horsemen almost hysterically, as if this insignificant force could resist the invaders and protect the city and its arsenal. Wade Hampton and his officers were invited to spend the night in private homes. Pickets were posted, somewhat carelessly, and Butler's troopers camped on the bank of the Cape Fear River, overlooking a bridge that entered the city from the south. The Federals were not long in making an appearance.

In the half-light of dawn on March 11, Captain William Duncan and sixty-seven bluecoat riders from Howard's headquarters scouted toward the city, found the bridge lightly guarded, brushed aside the few rebel pickets and rode recklessly into Fayetteville. This little band was seen at once by Hugh Scott, a Confederate cavalry scout, who burst in upon Wade Hampton while the general was at breakfast: "General, there's a hundred Yankees outside! Give me four or five men and I'll run 'em out of town." Hampton and the young scout, reinforced by staff officers and a few South Carolina troopers —seven men in all— charged noisily toward Duncan's party with drawn sabers, firing pistols and gobbling the rebel yell. The startled bluecoats fled, milled in confusion at a street corner a hundred yards distant, and were routed. Twelve Federals were killed. The intrepid Captain Duncan and ten others were captured. The only Confederate casualty was a handsome mare, killed by a pistol shot.

This brief melee provided the merest of respites, for a Federal infantry column entered the town and Mayor Archibald McLean rode out to make a formal surrender. The Federal advance rode past the bodies of Duncan's casualties sprawled in the street; a U.S. flag soon flew over the market house in the center of the town. Sherman's troops thus began a five-day occupation of the town, an occupation that was to reflect Sherman's mild policy toward North Carolina. Fayetteville's sufferings under the invaders, though they were to live long in local legend, paled in comparison with those of South Carolinians.

One of those who would not forget the coming of the invaders was little Sally Hawthorne, who, with her sister and the young son of the family cook, sent the last of the Confederate cavalrymen on their way with sandwiches. Sally recalled it years later: "A wide street filled with Confederate soldiers on horseback, riding pellmell up the street, on the sidewalk, anywhere, so as to be going uptown. As they passed near enough to reach the sandwiches they would bend for the package, and then go on at breakneck speed." Sally and her sister and the tiny black boy held the basket as high as they could reach until the sandwiches were gone.

A man yelled from a nearby house, "Go home! The Yankees are here!" Sally had hardly reached home when Federal officers rode up and demanded her father's keys to vacant houses in the neighborhood for the use of General Howard's staff.

"They are not my houses," Mr. Hawthorne said. "They belong to my brother. I don't know that I have the right to turn them over to you."

The officers laughed. "The keys, if you please."

The bluecoats settled in the houses, barns and stables. Several of Howard's officers made quarters in Sally's house and forbade the family to leave without permission.

The alarm found Mrs. James Kyle in one of the city's hospitals, nursing Confederate wounded from the skirmish in Kilpatrick's camp. A Confederate officer called through the door, "Ladies, if you have a home and children you'd better go to them. Sherman's coming into town."

Mrs. Kyle was helped across the crowded street by an officer who was captured by the Yankees a moment later. She hurried toward her home, but was halted in her tracks by a shocking spectacle: "I saw a Yankee soldier make a man take off his clothing in the street. When I reached my room at home I sank into a chair and felt that I must give up." She revived when a servant thrust her infant son in her arms. At a glimpse of the helpless child, she thought resolutely, "I must be brave."

Sherman himself reached Fayetteville in midmorning and made temporary headquarters in the old U.S. Arsenal, a group of stuccoed brick buildings, seized by the Confederates in 1861, that had produced arms and ammunition throughout the war. Sherman ordered Colonel Orlando Poe of the engineers to prepare the arsenal for demolition a few days later. "I hope the people at Washington will have the good sense never to trust North Carolina with an arsenal again," he said. The general soon rode off on an inspection of the town, leaving Major Byers in charge.

Byers was confronted by Edward Monagan, a well-dressed civilian who complained that his house was looted by soldiers.

"General Sherman is an old and dear friend of mine," Monagan said. "We were at West Point together." Monagan waited for the general's return, telling Byers of escapades he had shared with Sherman as a cadet.

"I know he'll be pleased to see me," he said. "You just watch Sherman's face when we meet."

Byers was so impressed that he hurried a guard to the Monagan home.

Sherman appeared soon afterward, and as he dismounted Monagan went toward him with open arms. Byers saw that "for a moment there was a ray of pleasure illuminating Sherman's face," but it disappeared.

"We were friends, weren't we?" Sherman said.

"Oh, yes."

"You shared my friendship and my bread too, didn't you?"

"That I did."

Sherman's face became grim, almost stricken.

"You have betrayed it all. Betrayed me, your friend, betrayed the country that educated you for its defense. And here you are—a traitor—asking me to be your friend once more, to protect your property. To risk the lives of brave men who were fired on from houses here today."

The general paused. "Turn your back to me forever. I won't punish you. Only go your way. There is room in this world even for traitors."

Monagan left hurriedly, and Sherman sat on the arsenal steps to eat lunch with his staff. Byers saw that the general could hardly eat: "The corners of his mouth twitched . . . the hand that held the bread trembled and for a moment tears were in his eyes."

General Howard came up a few minutes later to report that his troops were still under fire from rebel sharpshooters who hid in houses. He thought the snipers were Texans.

"Then shoot some Texas prisoners," Sherman said.

"We've got no Texans."

"Then shoot others, any prisoners. I will not have my men murdered." He turned abruptly into the arsenal. Howard rode away. Byers never learned whether rebel prisoners in Fayetteville were executed in retaliation.

On Sunday, March 12, whooping Federal troops welcomed the army tug *Davidson* to Fayetteville after she had chugged up the Cape Fear River from Wilmington, opening a supply line from the sea. Sherman expressed the joy of his men, who were so eager for news that they had been paying five to ten dollars for the privilege of reading an old issue of *The New York Times:* "The effect was electric, and no one can realize the feeling unless, like us, he had been for months cut off from all communications with friends."

Sherman spent several hours at a desk in the town hotel during the afternoon. He wrote ten dispatches and then wrote Ellen for the first time in almost two months. The general told his wife that the army's sweep through the Carolinas was more important than the march to the sea: "South Carolina has had her visit from the West that will cure her of pride and boasting."

He predicted that the Confederate army would make a stand near Raleigh, but he was confident of the outcome: "I can whip Joe Johnston unless his men fight better than they have since I left Savannah." He shrugged off Confederate threats: "The same brags and boasts are kept up, but when I reach the path where the lion crouched I find him slinking away."

The *Davidson* was off at six that afternoon with her decks piled high with sacks of mail. Since no telegraph lines were at hand, the steamer also carried Major Byers, who was sent by Sherman with a confidential message for Grant—news that the army was nearing its goal in fighting trim, with morale high and in no danger from the enemy.

Also aboard the small ship were Theo Davis, the *Harper's Weekly* artist who had been traveling with the army from Atlanta, and the alluring Marie Boozer, who was now leaving Judson Kilpatrick forever. As she left the army, Marie was on the threshold of a bizarre and romantic career—she was to marry a wealthy Northerner, and after a sensational divorce case would become the wife of a French count and reign as a queen of international society. (The tragic end of her life is obscure: One legend has it that she became the mistress of a Japanese prime minister, who had her beheaded; another holds that she was a concubine of a Chinese war lord, who had her ankle tendons severed to prevent her escape, and fattened her into a three-hundred-pound beauty.)

The *Davidson* returned to Fayetteville two days later, laden with coffee, sugar and oats, but without the uniforms Sherman had hoped to issue to his troops.

One day during the brief occupation of the town, young Sally Hawthorne watched Federal soldiers slaughter all the family livestock except the milk cow. Young officers sat on the back porch, making sport of killing poultry, calling on servants to release chickens, ducks or turkeys, and shooting the birds as they ran to forage on the fresh grass.

When Mr. Hawthorne was told by an officer that his textile mills were to be blown up, he persuaded Mayor McLean and the town board to accompany him to Sherman's headquarters to protest that these mills offered the only employment to men and women of the farm region. Sherman heard them out and said, "Gentlemen, niggers and cotton caused this war, and I wish them both in hell. On Wednesday these mills will be blown up. Good morning."

Hawthorne went to the homes of his mill hands with a Federal guard at his side, telling them to take all the cotton and cloth they wished, since the buildings were to be destroyed. For the rest of the day Sally's father watched as mill hands bore away his stock, and the next day the mills went up "with a terrible noise and dense smoke that surrounded us for hours."

Colonel Poe and his engineers battered the arsenal buildings into piles of rubble, and then burned and blew up the ruins. Tremors shook houses throughout the city, and several nearby homes caught fire from the intense heat. Even so, the Confederates had managed to salvage something from the wreckage, for much of the arsenal's machinery had been shipped out before Sherman's arrival to be hidden in a coal mine in a nearby county; ordnance stores had been carried to Greensboro by wagon.

Federal troops burned a few other buildings, including the local bank and the plant of the *Fayetteville Observer,* whose editor, E. J. Hale, a prewar Whig and opponent of Secession, had become an ardent supporter of the rebel cause. Sherman's officers whipped up such feeling against Hale that "even a chicken coop was unsafe if it had his name on it."

The town was defenseless, but some of its pious women battled the invaders with prayer and scripture. Federal officers who took over an old woman's house for a dinner party invited her to eat with them.

"General," she said, "aren't you going to ask a blessing?"

"Well, madam, I don't know how. Will you do it for me?"

As the hostess remembered it: "So I asked a blessing and prayed a short prayer. I asked the Lord to turn their hearts away from their wickedness and make them go back to their homes and stop fighting us, and everything I was afraid to tell the Yankees, I told the Lord, and they couldn't say a word!"

The invaders found Fayetteville more rebellious than they had expected—"offensively rebellious," said Major Nichols of headquarters staff.

In the country near Fayetteville, civilian victims complained that they were terrorized, in much the same pattern visited upon plantations in the army's path from Atlanta onward. One anonymous woman of the neighborhood reported the murder of two men, one a wounded Confederate soldier, and said that three men and a woman were hung up by soldiers "in order to make them tell where their valuables were concealed." A few others were stripped naked and whipped for the same purpose.

Mrs. Jane Evans Elliot, the wife of a Confederate officer, whose plantation was called Ellerslie, told a typical tale of the foragers who beset her: "They pillaged and plundered the whole day and quartered themselves upon us that night . . . took all our blankets and the Colonel's clothes, all our silver . . . all our luxuries, leaving nothing but a little meat and corn . . . Oh, it was terrible beyond description . . . one night they strung fire all around us."

Mrs. Elliot turned to her diary when the ordeal ended: "I have been trying to teach my dear children to improve the day as well as I could, but my mind wanders and is so confused that I find it hard to fix my thoughts on any thing."

All of Sherman's army was across the Cape Fear River and on the move by March 15, after an unexpected delay to await supplies and to destroy the massive masonry arsenal buildings and the textile mills. The general sent most of his civilian hangers-on to Wilmington, on the coast, via the Cape Fear, in order to eliminate "useless mouths" and speed his movements. A bewildered crowd, largely of blacks, was herded on small river steamers, bound toward an unknown fate in a city where they were not expected. Other thousands of those who had followed the army walked or rode overland toward the coast.

Departing Federal troops also sent loads of stolen furniture and other valuables homeward by steamer. Mrs. Kyle, the volunteer nurse of Fayetteville, was gratified to hear later that the ship bearing this loot to New York burned on its voyage, "and we had the comfort of knowing that none of our handsome furniture and household treasures reached their destination."

One of the army's final acts in Fayetteville was to destroy some of its worthless horses and mules. A thousand of these animals, jaded after months of service, were herded into a field beside the Cape Fear, where they plunged about in terror for hours as soldiers shot them. Bodies were left where they fell; hundreds floated down the river. Soldiers crowded another herd into a corral near the center of town, shot all the animals and left the hundreds of carcasses to the townspeople. "They were burned," Alice Campbell wrote, "and you may try to imagine the odor, if you can."

One of the last Federal officers to leave Fayetteville was a Michigan captain, Dextor Horton, who had found the local people friendly and kind. Horton had slept in a clean, comfortable feather bed in a private home. He was aroused by a courier at one in the morning as his regiment moved out, and got an affectionate farewell from his hostesses. "They really felt bad to see me go," he remembered. "The old lady shed tears and said, 'Let us part as friends,' and hoped I would reach my family in safety."

Horton and his companions of the army's rear guard crossed the river in utter darkness, stumbled down a bank to a pontoon bridge and clambered up a rutted cliff of mud. At two o'clock Horton lay on the sodden ground for a brief sleep: "Quite a change from sleeping undressed in a feather bed."

Horton rode in the army's wake in the early morning, shivering with cold and wondering, like most of his companions, what fate lay ahead. He scrawled in his diary that night: "When will Crazy Billy give us a base to clothe us and give us rest?"

21
"He shall have no rest"

The long blue columns snaked out of Fayetteville over miserable roads, threading toward the northeast. Once more, in the hope of avoiding or postponing battle and dispersing Confederate forces, Sherman separated his wings to obscure his destination. Slocum's wing feinted in the direction of Raleigh and Howard's moved toward Goldsboro, the actual goal, where Sherman was to meet General John Schofield and his 30,000 fresh troops, now marching up from the coast.

Sherman rode confidently near the head of a column. His troops were ready to fight. Divisions in the advance of each corps were stripped for action, their heavy equipment following in the wagon trains. He ordered the columns to remain close together: "I will see that this army marches to Goldsboro in compact form." The commander seemed to be aware, at least, that the threat of a Confederate attack had finally become a reality.

Sherman wrote John Terry, one of Schofield's corps commanders: "We must not lose time for Joe Johnston to concentrate at Goldsboro. We cannot prevent his concentrating at Raleigh, but he shall have no rest."

General Johnston had arrived in Sherman's path on March 15 to take command of his gathering forces. Major Bromfield Ridley of General A. P. Stewart's staff, who guided him to headquarters, found the old Confederate chief "surprisingly social," and of rare modesty: "He endeavors to conceal his greatness rather than to impress you with it." Johnston said he was happy to rejoin his old command as it faced its greatest test, but he added somberly, "I'm afraid it's too late to make it the same army."

Johnston soon found himself in conflict with bureaucrats of the expiring Confederate government. Quartermasters in North Carolina were under orders to send food and supplies only to Lee's army in Virginia; there were none for Johnston's troops. When he ordered coffee, sugar, tea and brandy from a navy storehouse in Charlotte, Johnston was refused; the Confederate navy had ceased to exist, but there was no precedent for the transfer, and officials would not budge. When he requested money for the troops, many of whom had not been paid in two years, Johnston was stunned by a telegram from John Breckinridge, the new secretary of war—the Confederate treasury was empty.

Johnston must also preside over a bewildering array of general officers, many of them thin-skinned and sensitive, disposed to fight to the last for every prerogative of rank—two full generals, three lieutenant generals, fourteen major generals and brigadiers almost too numerous to count. These commanders all but outnumbered the troops now gathering near the little east Carolina town of Smithfield: Braxton Bragg's 5,000, who had been driven from Wilmington; Hardee's worn corps from Savannah, now reduced to 10,000 by loss of its South Carolina brigade, which had been called home by Governor McGrath; Hampton's 6,000 cavalry; and all that was left of the Army of Tennessee.

The veteran rebel army from the West was now dribbling in after a heroic hegira. P.G.T. Beauregard, sent to Tupelo, Mississippi, to inspect its remnants, had said, "If not, in the strict sense of the word a mob, it was no longer an army." The Creole found that almost 18,000 men were on the muster rolls, but deserters streamed away nightly, 3,500 were furloughed home, 4,000 were marched off to defend Mobile, and the rest—three skeleton corps—were herded eastward to confront Sherman.

The veterans who had survived John Hood's bloody battles at Franklin and Nashville could still muster a song. Their favorite was a wry jingle set to the tune of "The Yellow Rose of Texas":

So now I'm marching southward;
My heart is full of woe.
I'm going back to Georgia
To see my uncle Joe.

You may talk about your Beauregard
And sing of Ginral Lee
But the gallant Hood of Texas
Sure played hell in Tennessee.

For more than six weeks this ghost of an army had made its way eastward and then northward—on foot, by steamboat and rail, through Mississippi, Alabama, Georgia and the Carolinas.

The ever present Mrs. James Chesnut had watched General Stephen D. Lee's corps of this army march through Chester, South Carolina, amazed to hear them singing: "There they go, the gay and gallant few, doomed, the last flowers of southern pride, to be killed, or worse, to a prison. They continue to prance by, light and jaunty . . . with as airy a tread as if they believed the world was all on their side, and that there were no Yankee bullets for the unwary. What will Johnston do with them now?"

In the end, Johnston reported, only 5,000 troops from the Army of Tennessee reached him, some of those too late to be thrown into battle against Sherman. With the belated addition of these veterans of three years of war, Johnston prepared to fling the last Confederate resources of manpower into combat.

Sherman met serious rebel resistance for the first time since Atlanta in the afternoon of March 15. Judson Kilpatrick, skirmishing with Wheeler's troopers along the road to Raleigh, ran into Confederate infantry some six miles south of the village of Averasboro on the Cape Fear River. Within a few minutes fighting raged through the swampy woodland, and Kilpatrick's men hurriedly threw up crude breastworks. They were soon heavily engaged with General William B. Taliaferro's division.

The Confederates blocked the road to Raleigh by fortifying a narrow peninsula between the Cape Fear and Black rivers, which was flanked by difficult swamps. Sherman must move them or abandon his feint against Raleigh—but the spirited fighting that ensued soon became a more serious matter than the mere testing of a strategic refinement. In fact, Sherman's advance had collided with General Hardee's rear guard, and Hardee, who had planned to rest for the day, determined to fight in order to develop Sherman's strength and intentions on that front. The Federal troops, in any case, were to be tested for the first time since the battle of Atlanta.

The Confederates were not content to wait for the enemy, but launched numerous charges and were beaten back only after hours of desperate fighting. Kilpatrick's men, on the point of losing their barricades, were reinforced by Colonel William Hawley's brigade of the XX Corps as darkness fell. By three in the morning of March 16, the Federal newcomers, "encased in an armor of mud," were struggling through swamps toward an invisible enemy. Soon after daylight the rebels came howling toward Hawley's line in a charge that shook the command and threatened its flanks. Slocum sent more infantrymen forward, this time the division of General Alpheus Williams, which relieved Hawley's worn men. The stubborn fight dragged through the day.

The Confederate front line finally sagged and broke, and its men then fled rearward "like so many frightened birds," under a Federal charge, leaving behind cannon, knapsacks, guns, horses, their dead and wounded, and a few men who waved handkerchiefs overhead, "begging for mercy." These rebels were artillerymen from Charleston, thrown into their first battle, men whose experience had been limited to firing coastal guns, including those of the captured Fort Sumter. Most of their expert gunners and virtually all the horses were dead, and the heavy guns could not be moved rearward over the boggy ground. This inexperienced command had almost literally been shot to pieces.

Rebel artillery, as if to atone for the setback, began firing rapidly from the rear, under cover of a second line of low breastworks. The Illinois soldier William Grunert joined an attack on this line with his regiments, but quickly flopped to the ground with his companions and hugged the wet earth. The 129th Illinois had already lost twenty men. "Never before had we been exposed to such a fire of shells and grape," Grunert said.

Federal casualties mounted during the afternoon fighting. After dark, a few men of Grunert's regiment left their supper fires and floundered into the dark swamps to rescue rebels who called for help from pools of quicksand. Sergeant Henry Morhaus lay awake in the camp of the 123rd New York: "Now and then the Rebel cannon would belch forth . . . but with no serious results . . . Above all could be heard the wild wind singing among the pine tops, while now and then the rain would sweep down in passionate, fitful showers upon the unprotected heads of the soldiers."

Among the rebels captured by Sherman's men during this day were survivors of the artillery corps from Charleston. Ben Johnson, the accomplished Federal forager from Indiana who helped take prisoners in, was astonished to see one of the rebel enlisted men pounding one of his own officers in the face with his fists. Johnson could halt the irate Confederate only by pricking him with a bayonet point.

"That's my captain," the rebel said hotly. "He's abused me shamefully, and I've done told him I'd lick him once I got the chance. Now we're both prisoners and I'm as big a man as he is. I'm gonna give him what he's got coming."

Johnson was forced to interfere several times to prevent the angry gunner from striking the battered and demoralized captain.

Sherman's extraordinary behavior during the engagement at Averasboro was a mystery to his staff. The general spent the day of March 16 in the rear, listening to the crackling of fire from the front. To the disgust of Henry Hitchcock, Sherman kept his staff "lying around in the woods" during the fighting, out of sight of the action. Only twice did gunfire approach them—a stray grapeshot that fell in the mud nearby and a bullet that sang through the treetops. A later dramatic newspaper account of "Tecumseh directing the battle under a warm fire," Hitchcock said, was "more poetry than truth." Neither Hitchcock nor more veteran officers, who had frequently seen Sherman expose himself under fire, could imagine why he remained in the rear at Averasboro.

During this brisk fighting, Sherman encountered a striking prisoner, the commander of the heavy artillerymen from Charleston—an encounter which added to Hitchcock's irritation with the general.

Captain Theo Northrop, the chief of Kilpatrick's scouts, accompanied by three of his men, had blundered into Confederate lines by mistake and captured a handsome young rebel colonel who wore a fashionably cut uniform trimmed with gold braid—and the most splendid jackboots in the rebel army.

The young Confederate was confused by the approach of the strange Federals, and seemed to think they were his own men up to some mischief. "Do you realize who you're talking to, sir?" was his response to a demand for surrender.

"I don't give a damn," Northrop said. "I'm taking you back."

The colonel still imagined that he dealt with Confederates. "You'll watch your language when you speak to me, Officer. General Hampton will hear of this."

Not until a pistol was thrust to his head did the rebel colonel realize that these were Federals and give his consent to ride with them into their lines. The haughty colonel was Alfred Rhett, until recently the commander of Fort Sumter's rebel garrison, the son of the Confederate Congressman Barnwell Rhett, a Charleston editor who had been a candidate for president of the Confederacy.

Colonel Rhett was soon scolding Kilpatrick: "I was taken by my own fool mistake, but you damned Yankees won't have it your way for long. We've got 50,000 fresh men waiting for you in South Carolina."

"Yes," Kilpatrick said, "and we'll have to hunt every swamp to find the damned cowards."

The two exchanged insults until Kilpatrick sent the Carolinian rearward to Sherman, who had by now sought shelter from the rain under an old shed. Sherman grinned over Rhett's indignant explanation of his capture, fell to talking with him of mutual friends in Charleston, and invited him to have supper at headquarters. Rhett accepted as a matter of course. Major Hitchcock was offended by the casual intimacy the Confederate assumed with Sherman, and by Sherman's treatment of Rhett as an honored guest.

Rhett denounced Confederate President Jefferson Davis as "a fool" for allowing the army to march through Georgia without a battle. He told Sherman, "We'd have whipped you if it had cost us 30,000 or 40,000 men."

"But you can't afford to lose 30,000," Sherman said.

"Oh, men! We have men aplenty. I could take a cavalry regiment and raise a hundred thousand troops in a month!"

"Men rounded up like cattle would never fight."

Rhett persisted: "Conscripts are just as good as any other soldiers. *Discipline's* the thing. It's all discipline. Why, I myself have shot twelve men in the last six weeks. Not long ago I took a pack of dogs into the swamps and caught twenty-eight men in three days."

Hitchcock was repelled by Rhett's manner. The rebel, he said, was "a devil in human shape," a symbol of the arrogant Southern ruling class that had plunged the nation into war: "This class must be *blotted out.*"

But Sherman, who admired aristocratic Southerners—evidently even South Carolinians—found Rhett entertaining. He ordered a horse for the prisoner and told officers to see that the colonel was treated with respect. Rhett was led away to Kilpatrick's prison pen for the night, complaining to everyone about him, "making himself offensive by his ill-concealed bitterness and contempt for the Yankees"—as if in demonstration of an epigram coined by one of his female relatives: "The world, you know, is composed of men, women and Rhetts."

Colonel Rhett got no such considerate treatment from Kilpatrick. Guards yanked the shining Russian boots from his legs and tossed him a pair of rough brogans. Kilpatrick grinned. "They'll feel better on the march tomorrow, Colonel. You won't ride horseback. This is one time you'll be riding shank's mare." Kilpatrick's officers gambled for Rhett's boots, but lost interest when they saw that they were too small for any of them to wear, and returned the costly boots to the colonel.

As March 16 drew to a close, whispered orders were passed along the Confederate line; the troops built fires as if they were settling for the night, then crawled rearward on all fours. Hardee withdrew his small corps, leaving behind only the inevitable troopers of Wheeler as rear guard. The savage little engagement of Averasboro had come to an end.

Slocum and Kilpatrick reported 682 casualties for the day. Hardee's losses were slightly fewer. Joseph Johnston, when he was told of Federal losses, commented that Sherman's men had been demoralized by months of looting Southern plantations, had lost their taste for fighting, and were no longer the crack troops of the Atlanta campaign. Major Nichols of Sherman's staff saw a different reason for the army's inability to drive off the rebels: Confederate skirmishers at Averasboro had "shown more pluck than we have seen in them since Atlanta."

Sergeant Morhaus reported that his division alone had captured 217 prisoners and buried 108 Confederate corpses. "And yet," the sergeant said, "Averasboro is not put down in history as a battle, but simply a skirmish. We will say, however, it was a very lively skirmish." Men of New York's Dutchess County Regiment, who had fought for ten hours without relief during March 15–16, remembered this as the most severe action of the war. Still, a much more formidable challenge lay ahead. Joe Johnston was still gathering his forces, hoping to trap an unwary Federal column.

Casualties from Averasboro overflowed houses and barns in the neighborhood. Fifty wounded Confederates were taken to the home of Farquhar Smith, where Slocum made headquarters, and many of the victims were held down, screaming in pain, while Federal surgeons amputated wounded arms and legs. Seventeen-year-old Janie Smith wrote, "The scene beggars description. The blood lay in puddles in the grove." The wounded cursed and moaned, one of them a boy whose chest had been torn by a shell. He called incessantly, "Mama . . . Jesus . . . Mama. Jesus have mercy on me. I don't think I've been a very bad boy." The voice faded, the eyes closed, and the boy died.

Sherman went visiting the emergency hospitals, stepping over piles of severed arms and legs to enter, and in one blood-spattered room he met a rebel captain, one McBeth, who recalled that Sherman had visited his family in Charleston years before. Sherman asked to be remembered to the McBeth family, and helped the boy to send a letter to his mother. He then ordered Federal surgeons to remain at the place until they had performed all necessary operations on Confederate wounded.

Such kindnesses failed to impress Janie Smith, who complained that the Yankees "left no living thing but people and one old hen, who played sick, thus saving her neck, but losing her biddies." The girl wrote to a friend: "If I ever see a Yankee woman I intend to whip her and take the clothes off her very back . . . When our army invades the North, I want them to carry the torch in one hand and the sword in the other. I want desolation carried to the heart of their country; the widows and orphans left naked and starving, just as ours were left."

Federal casualties also suffered. There were no ambulances with Slocum's wing, and as the army moved eastward from Averasboro, the wounded were jolted over wretched roads in springless flatbed wagons. Burial parties trailed the caravan, inspecting the wagons at each halt to remove those who had died. Graves were dug hurriedly at the roadside and marked with names and regiments, in cases where those were known.

Colonel Fahnestock, who commanded the wagon guard, rode all day with a chorus of groans and wails ringing in his ears. He halted several times to see Private Henry Nourse of his regiment, who was in agony from the amputation of a leg. "It's my toes, Colonel. Oh, God, my toes! I could stand it except for my toes."

22
"They don't drive worth a damn"

The rumble of Slocum's fight at Averasboro carried to Oliver Howard's columns throughout March 16, but the right wing did not pause in its northeastward course toward Goldsboro. The gap between the wings of Sherman's army began to widen hour by hour. Slocum's wing was now in danger of being isolated. Excited Confederate scouts took news of this development to Joe Johnston, who had planned for such a moment. Johnston studied his maps and prepared to attack Slocum again before Sherman could come to his aid with Howard's forces.

Howard's pace slowed the next day, his column moving only six miles—but Slocum's men, who might have moved closer, were delayed by swampy terrain, and thus the gap between the wings remained. Sherman spent the night with Slocum in the lowlands and rode with him the next day, evidently oblivious to the fact that the left wing of the army had begun to present a tempting target to Johnston.

Slocum's men were now stretched out on a single road, under clouds of sooty smoke from burning turpentine stills. General Jefferson C. Davis' XIV Corps was in the lead, and his advance, the division of General James D. Morgan, was skirmishing constantly with Wheeler's cavalry, which fell back stubbornly from one pine grove to another, as if they were covering an infantry movement. In the Federal rear on this road, the XX Corps fell behind, floundering in the rutted road, laying corduroy and repairing bridges, which broke repeatedly under heavy loads. The wagon trains were now stretched out for many miles.

Major Charles Belknap, who was out with Federal foragers during the morning, was told by a civilian that the Confederates had gathered at Bentonville to make a stand. Belknap sent a report to Sherman, who shrugged it off.

General J. J. Carlin, who halted for lunch at a farmhouse, met an anxious planter who had seen Confederate infantry nearby and feared that a battle was to be fought on his land. Carlin passed a warning to General Davis, who reported it to Sherman. The commander shook his head. "No, Jeff. There's nothing there but Dibrell's cavalry. Brush 'em out of the way. Good morning. I'll meet you tomorrow at Cox's Bridge." Sherman was convinced that Johnston would not risk a stand in the neighborhood with the Neuse River in his rear. The commander seemed to have become overconfident after marching hundreds of miles through enemy country, challenged only by civilians.

Slocum's column halted late in the day near the village of Bentonville, and went into camp. On its roads to the east, Howard's wing was six to twelve miles distant. For all his resolve to keep the moving army concentrated, Sherman had allowed it to straggle apart.

Before sunrise on March 18, Joseph Johnston learned that Goldsboro was Sherman's actual objective, and that the Federal right wing, under Howard, was far from the left. If the Confederates could concentrate promptly in Slocum's path, they might destroy his exposed wing before Sherman could come to the rescue. Johnston realized that his small war-weary force could not challenge the entire Federal army, but a lone column was a temptation he could not resist.

Without hesitation, Johnston prepared to carry out his audacious battle plan, hoping for a decisive victory. He approved, sight unseen, a spot two miles south of Bentonville chosen by Wade Hampton as an ideal site to assemble the troops for a surprise confrontation. He then called together his three corps.

By marching all day, the troops of Generals Braxton Bragg and A. P. Stewart arrived soon after nightfall in Bentonville, a remote village some twenty miles west of Goldsboro. Hardee found the march from the vicinity of Averasboro too long for the weary men of his small corps, and camped on the road six miles from Bentonville.

* * *

The dawn of Sunday, March 19, was bright and clear. The sun rose on a countryside already touched with green. Apples and peaches bloomed in abandoned orchards, and the swamps were filled with bird songs. Sherman, "supposing that all danger was over," left Slocum's column early in the morning and rode across country to join Howard's right wing. He was accompanied by only a few staff officers and orderlies.

General Carlin, whose division was to lead Slocum's wing on the day's march, rose before his usual hour and put on a new uniform so that he could be properly identified in case of his capture or death. Positive that the day would bring battle, Carlin sent wagons and mules to the rear and marched forward at seven. Rebel skirmishers halted his troops at the edge of their camp, and the bluecoat veterans sent back an ominous report: "They don't drive worth a damn."

Slocum rode forth with Carlin to peer at the enemy position, but the wing commander, like Sherman, was still convinced that the path was blocked by nothing more than rebel cavalry. Slocum called up an infantry brigade on either side of the road and pushed it forward to the edge of a field. The brigade was driven back by musketry and cannon fire. It was the first roar of full-scale battle the army had heard since the bloody struggle for Atlanta. By now Sherman was far away on his way to Howard, beyond the sound of Slocum's guns.

The rebel advance had come up at dawn and settled in a drab landscape about the fields of an old plantation known as the Cole place, surrounded by a dense growth of young blackjack oaks, whose tangled thickets enclosed a single narrow road. Last summer's leaves still clung to bristly trees, a rustling leathery cover that shut off the view in every direction. Putting troops into position here, as Johnston said, "consumed a weary time."

General Robert F. Hoke's North Carolina division lay in the center, across the road and along the edge of the open field, with its left concealed in almost impenetrable oak scrub. General A. P. Stewart's Army of Tennessee, which had been so long in coming from the Western theater, took the right flank. Hardee's troops were approaching when Federal infantry pushed through the crackling scrub and fell upon Hoke's line. Abruptly a little battle raged with such fury that the nervous Braxton Bragg, whose sector came under attack, called for reinforcements, moments before the enemy was repulsed.

The Federal troops fell back to their line in some disorder, but since Hardee was not yet in position, Johnston could not press a counterattack. His battle plan was abandoned in the first moments.

As the first Federal battle line fell back, it was joined by three men who had run out from the rebel front, refugees who were soon telling Slocum their story—they were Federal soldiers who had been captured and joined the Confederate army to escape prison, hoping for an opportunity to desert. One of them, a soldier from Syracuse, New York, said that Johnston was lying in wait with his whole army, poised to overwhelm the XIV Corps. Slocum dismissed the report as the unreliable tale of a double agent until Major W. G. Tracy of his staff hailed the soldier as an old friend and vouched for his reliability.

Convinced at last, Slocum called on Sherman for help: Howard's wing must hurry to the support of the vulnerable column. Joe Foraker, Slocum's youngest staff officer, galloped off with this message, riding toward the right wing at full speed, staying well clear of rebel patrols. Slocum then pushed the rest of the XIV Corps into position, called up the XX Corps from his rear, and ordered the leading troops to dig in and fight for their lives. The exposed divisions raised sheltering lines of breastworks. The most formidable work of logs rose before General Morgan's 2nd Division of the XIV Corps, whose front was in a swampy pine woodland. Sergeant F. M. McAdams of the 113th Ohio, who led his men in the frantic work on this sector, was grateful for the delay in the rebel attack: "The enemy seemed to wait on our movements, as if unwilling to meet us until we were ready to meet him. At the end of forty minutes we were nearly ready. . . . All at once our skirmish line came bounding over our works, telling us to be ready, for they were coming close in their rear."

It was three-fifteen before Johnston sent forward his ragged lines, the last hope of the Confederacy. The men moved with assurance, led by veterans of the Army of Tennessee, who hurried out as if resolved to redeem their reputation. The files crossed the open field behind mounted officers, one of them the crippled General W. B. Bate of Tennessee, who rode with crutches strapped to his saddle. The troops moved "with colors flying and line of battle in such perfect order . . . it looked like a picture," but men who watched from the rear saw how thin the ranks were. Only handsful of men clustered about each flag. Regiments were now reduced to the size their companies had once been.

As the rebels came under fire they shrilled their battle cry and trotted forward. It was a charge, Johnston said, whose success was never in doubt. It poured over the first line of Federal works and drove the bluecoats to the shelter of the XX Corps lines in the rear. The Federal Lieutenant Charles Brown confessed that he and his men led the way in this panic of retreat with "some of the best running ever did." Most of Carlin's line was swept backward.

By now Carlin's whole division had been routed, and the general himself, conspicuous in his new uniform, ran for safety toward the rear, hid in some bushes with some of his men for a few minutes, trying to alarm Confederates by making noises, gave it up and dashed rearward once more. He found artillery horses tied to a tree, but could not free them, and walked the rest of the way to safety.

The start of the rout was seen by Alexander McClurg of General Jeff C. Davis' staff, a veteran who had been a prewar book dealer in Chicago: "The attack came upon us like a whirlwind . . . Almost immediately I met masses of men slowly and doggedly falling back along the road . . . retreating, and evidently with good cause . . . but they were not demoralized. Minie balls were whizzing in every direction."

McClurg passed two guns of a retreating Indiana artillery battery whose lieutenant bawled, "For God's sake, don't go down there! I'm the last man of the command. Everything in front of you is gone."

McClurg was incredulous until he saw the long line of advancing rebels "stretching across the fields to the left as far as the eye could reach, advancing rapidly, and firing as they came . . . the onward sweep of the rebel lines was like the waves of the ocean, resistless . . . "

The entire Federal line was giving way, so far as McClurg could see, except for General Morgan's division on the far right. Field hospitals were ordered abandoned, and men were posted to stay with the wounded in captivity; they were saved only by the arrival of the XX Corps troops from the rear.

The rebels chased the blue line until officers ordered a halt. When a captain called for volunteers to go farther, young Sergeant Walter Clark of a Georgia regiment stepped forth, "not caring to let the boys know how scared I am." They charged on over ground littered with debris of the Federal flight, a lady's garter, a preserve dish, leather-bound books.

A solid shot struck the colorbearer of the 1st Georgia, who was "knocked six or eight feet and disemboweled." Litter bearers hurried off with a wounded boy who whimpered loudly, "My haversack! Get my haversack!" An Oglethorpe private rose from the cover of his log to snatch up the haversack and toss it on the stretcher.

When the gray line had driven all before it for almost a mile, Hardee halted it to re-form the ragged files.

Savage fighting now erupted in Hardee's rear, where Morgan's Federal division had been bypassed. Some of these bluecoats attacked the flank of advancing Confederates, who turned upon them and opened a battle that veterans found hotter than the battle of Gettysburg: "The raging leaden hailstorm of grape and canister literally barked the trees, cutting off the limbs as if cut by hand."

At four-thirty Braxton Bragg's troops moved up belatedly and charged the log barricades in Morgan's front. In charge and countercharge, with both armies suffering heavy casualties, Bragg and Morgan fought for the ground which held the key to the battle. The Federal General Jefferson C. Davis, watching anxiously, told a staff officer, "If Morgan's troops can stand this, all is right; if not the day is lost. There is no reserve—not a regiment to move—they must fight it out."

Sergeant McAdams of the 113th Ohio had never seen such fighting. His regiment knelt in two lines, the rear men loading and passing muskets to the men in front. His rear man, Mike Huddleston, shouted into the sergeant's ear, "My God, Mac, the guns are too hot. We've got to rest." But firing continued until there was a lull. McAdams was sent forward to gather ammunition from the dead and wounded.

"I came upon a rebel who was fatally wounded. He cried out, 'Is there no help for a widow's son?' I told him he was beyond help, and that I had no time to give to his wants, but that, as he had no further use for the cartridges in his box nor for the Yankee knapsack on his back, I would relieve him of both." The sergeant gave way before a rebel charge, and the fighting became even fiercer. Rebels burst into the rear of Morgan's line, but McAdams and his companions merely leaped the barricade and fought from the other side.

Colonel McClurg, who had seen Sherman's army on many

fields, said, "Seldom have I seen such continuous and remorseless roll of musketry. It seemed more than men could bear . . . Soldiers in the command who have passed through scores of battles . . . never saw anything like the fighting at Bentonville."

The confused struggle went on until after nightfall, when men of McLaws' Confederate division reinforced General Bate on Johnston's flank, too late to drive the enemy from the field. The exposed rebel advance then fell back to its original position.

The cries of the rebel wounded around the camp of the 113th Ohio kept Sergeant McAdams awake most of the night. His captain sent him out to help one man who whimpered and called for help so pitiably that he aroused the whole regiment, but pickets refused to let him pass their line. The Ohioans fell asleep at last, so weary that they forgot they had not eaten supper.

It was dark before Sherman learned that Johnston's entire army had fallen upon Slocum's wing at Bentonville. The general was asleep in Howard's tent at a place called Falling Creek Church when Joe Foraker found him and delivered Slocum's message. Sherman leaped from his cot and rushed to a campfire, where he stood barefoot, in long drawers and a red undershirt, his hair standing out wildly, hands clasped behind him, calling out orders in a staccato voice that filled the campsite with officers and couriers "hurrying to and fro and mounting in hot haste." The right wing was off on a night march that was to test its most durable veterans. Bentonville was only twelve or fifteen miles away, but the deep roads crossed many streams and threaded past extensive swamps.

Sherman ordered Hazen's division of the XV Corps, which was nearest the battlefield, to retrace its march and join Slocum. The rest of the corps, under Logan, was sent from its advanced position near Cox's Bridge over the Neuse River on a route that would put Logan in Johnston's rear. Black Jack's lead brigade drove rebels from the bridge, forced them to burn it, laid pontoons in the glare of flames and was off at a trot, pushing Confederate pickets ahead of it. The XVII Corps followed Logan toward Bentonville.

The first of the right-wing troops reached Slocum soon after dawn. By noon all of the XV Corps was in line, and the XVII Corps arrived during the afternoon. Slocum was safe. The Confederates now faced a force twice their strength—yet Sherman was content to wait. The morning passed while his troops filed into position, bolstering the lines and flanks. Sherman wrote Slocum: "Johnston hoped to overcome your wing before I could come to your relief. Having failed in that I cannot see why he remains . . . I would rather avoid a general battle but if he insists on it, we must accommodate him." He felt that Johnston would retreat during the night; Schofield would reach Goldsboro the next day with some 30,000 fresh Federal troops, making the Confederate position hopeless.

Skirmishing crackled through the afternoon at Bentonville as Howard sent waves of men against the front held by Hoke's North Carolinians. Some of the hottest of this fighting was against the child soldiers of Hoke's command, Junior Reserves led by seventeen-year-old Major Walter Clark, who, as Hoke said, "repulsed every charge that was made upon them." These boys, none of them over eighteen, held their flimsy breastworks under pressure that drove back veteran troops to the right and left of them. Young Clark, who was to become chief justice of the North Carolina Supreme Court, said the skirmishing was "a regular Indian fight . . . behind trees."

Sherman listened to the rattle of fire from a grove of large trees far to the rear, following the course of the fight from the volume of musketry and the faint shouts of clashing lines. He asked a passing officer for a light, took his cigar to revive his own stub, then absently tossed the officer's cigar to the ground and paced away, his head cocked, listening to the guns, oblivious to all else. The officer glared angrily, then laughed and recovered his cigar.

Rain continued to fall the next day, March 21. Heavy skirmishing began in the early morning and rattled through the swamps and woodlands all day. The bluecoats lay behind their breastworks for hours, showing no disposition to attack. Once more, Sherman waited far in the rear.

In the end it was the combative Major General Joe Mower, a Sherman favorite, who seized the initiative and broke the stalemate. Mower, a prewar merchant without formal military training, fought as fiercely as he had in the Salkehatchie swamps. Mower's patience snapped at four in the afternoon, and without warning, and without orders, he plunged his 1st Division of the XVII Corps into a woods road on the right flank, resolved to cross Mill Creek and flank the rebels. Mower went on foot at the head of his troops as they floundered through a swamp, broke through a line of dismounted cavalry on the Confederate flank, and hurried onward, brushing aside one gray line after another, scattering hurriedly assembled units before they could combine to meet Mower's rush. Mower was within sight of the Mill Creek bridge, which was Johnston's only escape route, when he was halted by a combined force of rebel infantry and cavalry. Mower called for reinforcements.

By now Hardee, Hampton and Wheeler had led troops into position across Mower's front. A brigade of Alabama cavalry struck the Federal flank, and another thin file of horsemen moved into the open from the rebel lines, all that remained of the hard-riding 8th Texas, now commanded by Captain Doc Matthews, "a mere boy."

Wheeler's troopers galloped against Mower's heavy lines, reckless riders who held reins in their teeth and fired big navy pistols with both hands. Some bluecoats fell back before the noisy stampede. Hardee's sixteen-year-old son Willie rode in this attack as a volunteer; only a few hours earlier his father had reluctantly given him permission to join the Texans, kissed him goodbye and sent him into the battle. Willie was mortally wounded as the horsemen drove upon the enemy line, and was mourned in both armies; many Federal officers had known him well, particularly Oliver Howard, who had been his Sunday school teacher at West Point.

Howard had sent Frank Blair to support Mower, but an order came from Sherman before his troops could move: Mower was to return to his place in the line at once, before he was cut off. The rest of the army was to cover his withdrawal by heavy firing. Mower returned, the break in Johnston's lines was not exploited, and the rebels continued to send their wounded across the bridge.

Sherman's opportunity to win a smashing victory was gone, and he realized it quickly: "I think I made a mistake there," he wrote later, "and should have rapidly followed Mower's lead with the whole of the right wing, which would have brought on a general battle." With greatly superior numbers, he realized, he could have destroyed Johnston's army in the one pitched battle of his march, but that was not his major concern; as ever, Sherman's focus was upon winning the war rather than on single victories, and he clung to his strategy of avoiding battle if possible.

Oliver Howard had not forgotten the roaring afternoon in the rain at Bentonville when he wrote of Sherman years afterward: "Strategy was his strongest point. Take him in battle and he did not seem to me to be the equal of Thomas or Grant." In short, Howard felt that Sherman's gift was as a planner of campaigns, and that he had no special talent for handling troops in detailed tactical movements on the battlefield. A later biographer was to surmise that Sherman lacked "moral courage to order his whole army into an engagement"—though there was plentiful evidence that Sherman never lacked for moral courage in any undertaking. It is possible that the strain of his long campaign dulled his fighting instincts at Averasboro and Bentonville.

The Confederates retreated during the night, as Sherman expected, covering their long trains of wounded and shielding the rear with swarms of cavalrymen. Sherman made no move to follow. The severe little battle had cost both armies heavily. Casualties, reported inaccurately as usual, were 1,500 Federal and 2,600 Confederate, 673 of the latter captured—though Oliver Howard reported that his wing alone took 1,300 prisoners.

Someone asked Sherman what he thought Johnston would do next. "Joe Johnston and I aren't on speaking terms," he told his laughing staff. He wrote of Bentonville to his wife with an obvious sense of pride, as if he had not yet perceived the dimensions of his lost opportunity: "They abandoned all their cities to get enough men to whip me but did not succeed . . . Johnston attempted to prevent my making a junction with Schofield but he failed and I drove him off the field with my own army without the help of a man from Schofield . . . I will now conduct with great care another move . . . " The irony of this declaration seems to have escaped the general.

The army moved from Bentonville on March 22, a clear, mild, but windy day. The veterans passed two divisions of General Alfred Terry's command just moving up from the coast, one white and one black. The white newcomers complained that they had been "cut off without mail for seven days." Sherman's men moaned in derision: "Too bad—aw, what a shame! Suppose you'd been with us. We got our last mail January 12—seventy days ago."

Well-dressed Negro troops watched the veterans of the long march shamble by: "Ain't that a hard-looking set, man?"

23
"Splendid legs! Splendid legs!"

Sherman's forces joined Schofield's Army of the Ohio, which had come eastward in a rapid transfer from the battlegrounds of Tennessee. The combined army was now some 90,000 strong. The small town of Goldsboro had hardly settled under Schofield's occupation when the approach of Sherman's men was heralded by columns of smoke from burning farmhouses along the Neuse River.

Sherman and Schofield and other officers gathered in the Goldsboro town square, where they watched the veteran troops come in from Bentonville. Only when they saw Sherman surrounded by a dozen generals did the troops realize that they must pass in review before they went into camp. Between the enemy and wicked little sandstorms they had suffered the night before, the men had lost three nights' sleep, were battle-worn, irritable, and in no mood for a parade. Captain Rhoderick Rockwood of the 18th Missouri betrayed his resentment in his diary: "The authoritys think all men are fools. But all men know that *they* are fools."

It was an absurd caricature of an army, with hardly a complete uniform in its ranks. Half the men were barefoot or wore wrappings of old blankets or quilts. Socks had disappeared months before. There was a sprinkling of rebel uniforms, and thousands were in civilian clothes—battered silk top hats, cutaway coats and tight-legged breeches of the Revolutionary era. Some wore women's bonnets. Trousers were tattered; many wore only breechclouts. Sleeves had been torn from coats to make patches for trousers, crudely stitched with white cotton twine. Faces were still smudged from pine smoke and gunpowder. Lank hair protruded from ruined hats; many of the hatless wore handkerchiefs around their heads. Hundreds were without shirts, bare to the waist. The 81st Ohio came by with all of its shoeless and hatless men merged into one company, men who seemed to march more proudly than all the rest. Some men of the 75th Indiana wore a boot on one foot and a shoe on the other; many of the trousers had one blue leg and one gray.

Schofield's troops lined the roadside, laughing at men in the shambling files. Sherman's men shrilled catcalls at the scrubbed and freshly shaven spectators: "Oh, you white gloves!" "Bandbox soldiers!" A voice roared from the passing ranks: "Sonny boys, you get your butter ration every day?" "Yeah—but we trade it off for soap!" The column and the onlookers roared with laughter. The files passed on, making awkward attempts to close ranks that had been loosely formed on so many marches that the men seemed to have forgotten proper drill. "They are the motliest troops that ever marched through the country," a newspaper correspondent said.

Even Sherman was taken aback by the state of the army; it had never been so ragged. He told Schofield, "They don't march very well but they fight." Reviewing officers admired the bare legs swinging past, scratched and dirty but with knotted, muscular calves, like the legs of ballet dancers. "Look at those poor bare-legged fellows," Frank Blair said.

"Splendid legs! Splendid legs!" Uncle Billy said. "I'd give both of mine for any one of 'em."

One captain carried a basket on his shoulder. "There," the general said. "That's the way my officers live. They don't look well on review, but that's the way they have to get along."

It was the way he liked to see the army, "dirty, ragged and saucy . . . all in fine health and condition . . . and I will challenge the world to exhibit a finer looking set of men, brawny, strong, swarthy . . . " He longed to march it through the streets of New York, "just as it appears today, with its wagons, pack mules, cattle, niggers and bummers."

But the general seemed to realize suddenly that his review was a failure, and led the generals from the square after two or three brigades had passed. The troops filed silently to their campsites at the edge of town.

Sherman had found one of Grant's staff officers waiting for him in Goldsboro with a report on the siege of Richmond and Petersburg, where Lee's demoralized army was beginning to melt away through desertion. Grant had moved to cut Lee's last railroad supply line and raid up the valley of the Appomattox. If Lee left his trenches, Grant would follow.

Sherman felt a need to talk with Grant. Soon, he wrote, he might "run up to see you for a day or two before diving again into the bowels of the country." Two days later, with a couple of staff officers, he was on his way, jouncing by locomotive to the coast, where he told a *New York Herald* reporter, "I'm going up to see Grant for five minutes and have it all chalked out for me and then come back and pitch in." He sailed north up the coast on the little captured steamer *Russia.*

After a brief rough voyage, Sherman found Grant at City Point on the James River, overlooking a harbor filled with barges, tugs, warships, troopships and cargo steamers. He was surprised to learn that President Lincoln was also there, having come down by boat from Washington to confer with Grant on the final movements of the war.

Grant and Sherman talked for an hour, then went aboard the little paddle-wheeler *River Queen* to see Lincoln.

Sherman was shocked to see how four years of war had aged the President—he was almost like a cadaver, the general thought: "His arms and legs seemed to hang almost lifeless, and his face was care-worn and haggard." But Lincoln was transformed the moment he began to speak. The long face brightened, "his tall form . . . unfolded, and he was the very impersonation of good-humor and fellowship."

The President fretted over the safety of the army in Goldsboro during Sherman's absence. Sherman assured him that Schofield was capable, but Lincoln was not convinced. "Suppose Johnston escapes south again by railroad, and you'll have to chase him over the same ground all over again."

"He can't do it," Sherman said. "I have him where he can't move . . . I've destroyed the railroads, so that they can't be used for a long time."

Grant broke his silence: "What's to keep them from laying the rails again?"

"My bummers heat every rail and twist 'em until they're as crooked as a ram's horn. They'll never be used again." He spoke with growing confidence, as if there had been no flaw in his campaign against Johnston. He was positive that the issue was settled. "I can dictate my own terms," he told Lincoln. "Johnston will have to yield."

Lincoln seemed to fear that Sherman's terms might be too harsh. "The surrender of Johnston's army must be obtained on any terms," he said.

Grant and Sherman saw the President again the next day, this time accompanied by an observant reporter, Charles Coffin of the *Boston Journal,* who found Sherman the most striking of the trio: "Tall, commanding forehead, almost as loosely built as the President. His sandy whiskers were closely cropped. His coat was shabby with constant wear. His trousers were tucked into his military boots. His felt hat was splashed with mud."

Grant used a map to explain his planned moves against Lee, an assault that should force the rebels from the trenches. "Things are coming to a crisis," Grant said. "My only worry is that Lee will not wait long enough."

"My army is strong enough to fight Johnston and Lee combined," Sherman said. "If Lee stays here another two weeks, I can march up to Burkeville, and we'll starve him out, or make him come out and fight."

One of the armies, the generals said, must fight a final bloody battle. "My God, my God," Lincoln said. "There's been enough bloodshed. Can't we avoid another battle?"

"We can't control that," Sherman said. "It's in the hands of the enemy. Lee and Davis will be forced to fight, and I expect it will fall on me, probably near Raleigh."

Lincoln paused during the long, somewhat rambling talk and said abruptly, "Sherman, do you know why I took a shine to you and Grant?"

"I don't know, Mr. Lincoln, you've been extremely kind to me, far more than my deserts."

"Well," Lincoln said, "you never found fault with me."

Sherman had a clear memory of his final instructions from Lincoln. "All I want of you is to defeat the rebel armies and get the Confederate soldiers back on the farm," Lincoln said. He added his hope that Jefferson Davis would escape, but said he could not say so publicly. This reminded him of a story, he said:

A man who had taken a pledge to drink no more liquor was invited by a friend to take a drink, and refused. His friend served him lemonade instead, and as he mixed the drink, pointed to a brandy bottle. "It would be more palatable if I poured in a little brandy."

"All right," the teetotaler said. "If you can do it unbeknown to me, I won't object."

Lincoln smiled as he shook Sherman's hand to say goodbye. "I'll feel better when you're back at Goldsboro."

Sherman was never to see him again. He carried a memory of these hours with Lincoln for many years: "Of all the men I ever met he seemed to possess more of the elements of greatness, combined with goodness, than any other."

Sherman halted in New Bern, North Carolina, on his way back to the army, and had breakfast with his postal officer, Colonel A. H. Markland. He told Markland that he intended to offer generous terms to Joe Johnston.

"What will be done with Davis and his Cabinet?"

"Mr. Lincoln said, we will leave that door open; let them go! We don't want to be bothered with them in getting the government to running smoothly."

On the last of March, a cold, wet, windy day in Goldsboro, the army prepared for an execution. A private of the 12th New York Cavalry, who was to be remembered as "a brute named Bryant," had been convicted of raping a sixty-five-year-old Goldsboro woman, a spinster who was said to be descended from the Washington family. Bryant had narrowly escaped capture after the rape of a young girl in nearby Kinston a few days earlier. By one o'clock troops had formed a hollow square in a clearing.

Billy Bircher, the Minnesota drummer boy, watched from his place near the open grave, hearing only the mourning of the spring wind in the pines, until a band approached, playing "The Dead March."

A firing squad followed the band, trailed by four men bearing a new pine coffin and then the prisoner, surrounded by guards. Next came a dozen or more prisoners sentenced to witness the execution. The procession halted before the sandy pit, and a chaplain knelt to pray with the doomed man. The sun came out, gleaming weakly in a dark sky.

Bryant's eyes were bandaged and he drew himself erect, folded his arms across his chest and waited. A bugle sounded and the commander of the firing squad barked his commands.

The command to fire was drowned by the crash of a volley; the squad and its victim were briefly obscured by smoke. Two or three surgeons examined the corpse and the bands struck up a lively march. Bircher found the "harsh contrast" almost unendurable. The men passed the grave, glancing down at Bryant's body. Bircher saw "many a rough fellow" trying to conceal his tears, pretending to tug at his hat to screen his eyes from the weak sun, furtively wiping weathered cheeks.

At least one rapist escaped with his life, a soldier of the 48th Illinois who was belatedly tried by a court-martial and found guilty of raping a woman in Georgia. His head was shaved, a burly sergeant blacked his eyes, and his forehead was painted in red ink with the letters D R, to brand him as both deserter and rapist. As the prisoner was drummed out of his brigade, his colonel followed, bellowing after him, "You dirty hog, you!" Ten men with bayonets drove the unarmed culprit into enemy country, leaving him to make his way home as best he could.

Sherman returned from Virginia on March 31, back with his troops before the enemy or "newspaper spies" had missed him. He found the troops still in need of supplies, clothing—and money. Most of the men grumbled, but there were no serious complaints. Private Charles Brown of the 21st Michigan, who had not been paid in seven months, said, "I don't care. I can forage enough to eat and steal enough to wear."

Even the general was hard up. He had drawn no pay since January 1, and though he needed a new pair of boots, could not buy them. Ellen had sent big boots from Cincinnati, which he'd worn through the swamp country, but they were too hot for the spring weather. Sherman had been trying to send Ellen some money, since he knew she was "short," but the paymasters could not catch up with the army. On April 9 he sent her two hundred dollars he had borrowed from a quartermaster.

Sherman continued to brood over his stature as a soldier. This had become a refrain in his letters to Ellen, to whom he insisted that his march had ended the rebellion: "I almost fear the consequences of the reputation this will give me among military men. . . . I continue to receive the highest compliments from all quarters and have been singularly fortunate in escaping the envy and jealousy of rivals." Lincoln, he said, had been "lavish in his good wishes."

He suffered an occasional attack of modesty. "But enough of this vanity," he told Ellen. "My wants are few and easily gained, but if this fame which fills the world contributes to your happiness and pleasure, enjoy it as much as possible."

But Sherman realized that an important final step lay ahead, that he must end his brilliant campaign by making an acceptable peace. He foresaw that negotiations with the Confederates would be delicate. He wrote his brother-in-law, Tom Ewing: "You need not fear my committing a political mistake, for I am fully conscious that I would imperil all by any concessions in that direction. I have and shall continue to repel all advances made me of such a kind."

Paymasters arrived at last, and the camp erupted in celebration. New uniforms and rations were distributed. Most of the men burned or buried their odorous rags and turned to sweeping and cleaning, cooking, frying, baking and feasting. Sherman reorganized the army for the final days of campaigning. Slocum's left wing became the Army of Georgia. Sherman's favorite, Joe Mower, took over the XX Corps, and the popular Mexican War veteran Alpheus Williams was sent back to his old division. Many officers criticized the demotion of Williams, but Sherman was adamant; he wanted the aggressive Mower in command in case of a final battle.

The army moved out of Goldsboro on April 10 in high spirits, "straight against Joe Johnston wherever he may be," as Sherman said. "Poor North Carolina will have a hard time, for we sweep the country like a swarm of locusts."

The first day of the march toward Raleigh bore the promise of summer. Trees were leafing out and the roadsides bloomed with dogwood. Sherman watched the troops, in fresh uniforms, "as proud as young chicken cocks, with their clean faces and bright blue clothes . . . new clothing, with soap and water, has made a wonderful change in our appearance." The army was slowed the next day, April 11, as the advance skirmished lightly with Confederates. Several houses burned along the roads, set afire by the retreating Johnnies or by Negroes who had taken revenge on their masters.

There were a few rounds of rebel cannon fire, but to some soldiers the reports had an unreal sound, as if the enemy were firing blanks—the war was over and everything had changed. Several men were killed or wounded, two of them—William Toohey of the 103rd

New York and Absalom Waddle of the 33rd Indiana—said to have been the last battle casualties of the campaign.

The XX Corps was in Smithfield by two o'clock. Many regiments camped within twelve miles of Raleigh in the late afternoon.

It was during a halt on this march that the troops had momentous news from Virginia and learned that their war was over, or almost so. General J. D. Cox and his staff were near Smithfield when a staff officer galloped toward them, gesturing excitedly. Men broke into cheers as he passed, and began "cutting strange antics." Cox heard the shouting as he came nearer: "Lee's surrendered!" Men flung their hats at the rider, and one screamed after him: "You're the sonofabitch we've been looking for all these four years!" An officer leaped into the air, cracked his heels together and turned a somersault in the roadway.

Almost simultaneously word reached the 123rd New York, whose men cheered themselves hoarse. Sergeant Henry Morhaus thought they might not survive the excitement: "Hats, caps, cracker boxes, knapsacks were flung high in the air, and small colored boys were tossed high in blankets." Some men broke the muskets against trees, and General W. B. Hazen was so excited that he "tore up his hat and threw it to the four winds." The roar of the army echoed through the countryside, frightening civilians.

The 83rd Indiana had just drawn a ration of fresh beef, and after the Hoosiers had flung "thousands of hats fifty feet into the air" in their excitement, they celebrated in a bizarre fashion, tying chunks of meat to the tops of saplings and letting them fly into the air to hang there for crows.

Bands played "Marching through Georgia" and "John Brown's Body." John Boyle of the 11th Pennsylvania noted that "the colored people on the plantations joined in the contagious enthusiasm, and even the southern dogs barked for joy."

General Cox passed a house where a woman stood with several small children, waiting by her gate. Tears rolled down her cheeks when she understood the meaning of the wild shouts. She clasped two of her children and said quietly, "Daddy's coming home now."

The troops were halted to have Sherman's order of the day read to them: "All glory be to God! All honor to our brave comrades toward whom we have been marching! A little more toil; a few more days of labor, and the great race is won . . . "

Men of the 102nd Illinois who passed the general soon afterward in the town of Smithfield thought he would never be recognized as the author of these ringing phrases. Uncle Billy paced restlessly on the sidewalk, hands clasped behind, deep in thought, puffing vigorously at a cigar. Except for his uniform he might have been an anxious local farmer fretting over the passage of the troops.

It was late afternoon before the good news reached the 100th Indiana. Sergeant Theodore Upson was posting guards for the night's camp when General Woods called to him, "Dismiss the guard, Sergeant, and come into my tent."

Upson stared in disbelief. "Why, General? What's the matter?"

"Don't you know Lee has surrendered? No man shall stand guard at my quarters tonight. Bring all the detail here."

Upson's men were ushered into the general's tent two at a time to drink with officers from a bowl of strong punch. A tin cup passed swiftly among the crowd. General Woods made a speech: "Boys, Lee's given up, Richmond is ours, the war's over, and we're going to celebrate as we never have before." Upson's guards joined with enthusiasm, but the boy sergeant restrained himself: "I was pretty careful. I never had drank liquor, and I didn't know what it would do to me."

A regimental band began to play, but its men drank so much punch that they were finally playing "two or three tunes at once."

Upson's commander, Colonel Johnson, under the inspiration of the punch, seized Upson by an arm and presented him to General Woods as the finest sergeant in the army. Woods shook the boy's hand.

"Sergeant, I'm promoting you right now. Consider yourself a Lieutenant."

When Colonel Johnson continued his praise of Upson, Woods said, "By God, Sergeant, I'm promoting you to Captain."

Upson thought he might have risen to the rank of Colonel if Woods had not been dejected by the collapse of the band, which fell asleep.

Theodore was demoted in the aftermath of this celebration: "A day or two later the General addressed me as Sergeant the same as ever. But one thing is sure. Lee has surrendered and Richmond is ours."

24
"Who's doing this surrendering, anyhow?"

An opéra bouffe was in the making on April 12 in the city of Raleigh, where North Carolina's perplexed leaders debated how—and whether—they should surrender to the approaching Sherman. At three in the morning Governor Zebulon Vance was at his desk in the otherwise deserted capitol, dashing off dispatches. For a week or more Vance had been harrying his staff as it directed rail shipment of supplies to westward stations beyond Sherman's reach, mountains of food and clothing that Vance had withheld from the stricken Confederacy despite the pleas of Jefferson Davis; the governor placed the needs of his state above the cause itself.

Dim lamps on the desk revealed a coarsely handsome, barrel-chested, six-foot mountaineer with a leonine head, flowing locks and intense blue eyes. He had been a remarkable war governor. Even now it was a point of pride with Vance that he had been a Union man until the moment that war became inevitable. As he told the story, the governor had been pleading, with upraised hand, the Union cause before constituents when he had word that Lincoln had called for volunteers to suppress the rebellion: "When my hand came down from that impassioned gesticulation," Vance said, "it fell slowly and sadly by the side of a Secessionist."

Vance had openly scorned "the little men" who directed the Confederacy, but under his leadership North Carolina had fought the war with a fierce and uniquely independent spirit, as if she were fighting alone. Vance had raised almost 200,000 troops, more than any other rebel governor—and 41,000 of these had been killed. Vance had resourcefully clothed his troops from state-owned textile mills and armed them with British weapons smuggled in by the state's own blockade-runners. But now, as panic spread among Raleigh's civilians and there were frequent reports of Sherman's steady approach to the city, the governor realized that the end was at hand. He did not seem to rue the day: "The great popular heart is not now and never has been in this war," he said. "It was a revolution of the politicians, not the people." Even so, the proud, strong-willed Vance did not propose to capitulate in the name of North Carolina, so long as the Confederacy had a spark of life remaining.

It was three days since Lee had surrendered to Grant at Appomattox, but the news had not reached Raleigh—the rudimentary telegraph system had been disrupted, and ranking Confederates who had learned of the event kept the secret; Joseph E. Johnston, for example, had heard the news the day before, but told no one. Rumors were reaching nearby Confederate camps, but parolees from the Virginia army were denounced as liars and traitors, and some were imprisoned until their stories could be verified. Vance knew nothing of this as he worked before dawn of April 12; he imagined that it was he who must conduct unprecedented high-level negotiations with the enemy.

The governor was interrupted by a delegation of two former governors, both also staunch Union men of prewar days—William A. Graham, who had also been a senator, secretary of the Navy, and candidate for Vice-President; and David L. Swain, who was now serving as president of the University of North Carolina. The old men urged Vance to call the legislature into emergency session so that North Carolina could sue for peace and invite other rebel states to join her. If Sherman arrived before that could be done, Vance should ask for an armistice until the assembly had acted. The trio conferred through an early breakfast, and Vance agreed to their proposal for a truce—but only after he had talked with General Joseph Johnston, who had arrived in the city. The general advised Vance to remain in Raleigh and to attempt to negotiate, provided Sherman treated him "with respect."

Vance, Graham and Swain composed a letter to Sherman, which Vance signed, a request for a personal interview to discuss "a suspension of hostilities" and "the final termination of the war." Vance appointed Graham and Swain commissioners to deliver his message to Sherman, and then sought a safe-conduct pass for them from Johnston. There was a delay. Johnston had been summoned west to the town of Greensboro, where President Davis, paused in flight, was trying to deal with the collapse of his government. General Hardee finally issued the pass, and the old men set forth to find Sherman, who was advancing along the railroad from Smithfield to Raleigh.

The aging peacemakers, apparitions from the past in old-fashioned long-tailed coats and beaver hats, drew attention as they strode through Raleigh streets with three state officials at their heels. Word of their mission had leaked out in some way, for several Confederate officers growled after them as they passed that "such cowardly traitors ought to be hanged." The procession reached the railroad station about ten-thirty that morning and boarded its "train"—a rickety car drawn by a wood-burning locomotive of uncertain age—which was in charge of Conductor Dallas Ward, a nineteen-year-old lately promoted from the rank of newsboy. The purpose of the excursion was a mystery to Ward until he was ordered to fly a scrap of dirty white cloth atop his engine, when he realized that surrender was at hand.

Ward was apprehensive, and the peace party did little to allay his fears: "Only a few words were spoken, and they were almost in whispers." The engine heaved asthmatically and the train moved out of Raleigh, past groups of staring Confederate soldiers; Ward expected them to open fire on the car at any moment.

The peacemakers were buffeted by a series of unanticipated adventures. First, the imperious General Wade Hampton halted the train, examined their papers and denounced the mission, but ended by rushing a courier ahead to Sherman, asking him to receive Graham and Swain. The train crept forward once more, but was halted within less than two miles by a rider from Hampton: Hardee had withdrawn his safe-conduct pass, and the train must return to Raleigh. Graham and Swain protested that Hampton must deliver this order in person, and within a few moments the cavalryman rode up to explain that he had already notified Sherman that the conference had been cancelled—and that he had also arranged safe passage for them back to Raleigh by writing to General Kilpatrick, whose troops had by this time seized the railroad near the city.

The engineer reversed the train and backed it in the direction of Raleigh, but as they passed through a cut, Federal soldiers boarded the car. "They piled down on us like wild Indians," Ward remembered. Graham and Swain were ordered out and led to Kilpatrick's quarters, and most of the other men of the party were systematically robbed by the Federals, who took $2,200 in Confederate currency and a watch from Ward's pockets.

Little Kil greeted Graham and Swain in an ebullient mood. He read to them a dispatch—their first news of Lee's surrender—and lectured them while the old men stared in shocked silence, stunned by the almost incredible report. "The war is virtually over now," Kilpatrick said, "and any man who sheds blood will be a murderer." He had a band play "Dixie" for the old men, then sent them toward Sherman once more, a few miles to the southeast at Gulley's Station.

The train now moved even more sedately, for thirty or forty Federal soldiers rode atop the coach. Along the route, other bluecoats were cheering—for Lee's surrender or for the train itself, which they supposed had come to offer the surrender of Johnston's army.

Sherman greeted the old men at the track, and assured them that he would do all in his power to arrange peace terms with North Carolina. He echoed Kilpatrick's sentiments: The fighting was over, so far as he was concerned.

It was now late afternoon, and Sherman invited the peace party to stay overnight—though Vance had expected their return no later than four o'clock. The general talked with Graham and Swain for hours during and after supper, his speech as rapid, darting, disconnected and vivid as ever. He said he wanted to make "an amicable and generous" settlement with North Carolina, and that he hoped Vance and other officials would remain in Raleigh and keep the government in operation. He wrote a response to Vance's letter, enclosing a copy of an order he issued to Federal troops, who were to "respect and protect" Vance and other officials of the state and city. The rather perfunctory letter ended: "I doubt if hostilities can be suspended between the army of the Confederate Government and the one I command, but I will aid you all in my power to contribute to the end you aim to reach, the termination of the existing war."

Sherman's manner became abrupt when someone mentioned the burning of Columbia. The subject had obviously become a tender one: "I've been grossly misrepresented in regard to Columbia," he said. "I changed my headquarters eight times during that night, and with every general officer under my command, strained every nerve to stop the fire. I declare in the presence of my God that Hampton burned Columbia, and that he alone is responsible for it."

Later in the evening Sherman reminisced about his career as an educator, and told Swain that he had captured several of his former students from Chapel Hill during the war, soldiers so young that they should not have left the campus. The conversation prompted a reunion between Swain and the Missourian general, Frank Blair, commander of Sherman's XVII Corps, who had attended the University of North Carolina almost twenty years earlier.

Graham slept in Sherman's tent with the general, and staff officers shared quarters with others of the party. Henry Hitchcock, whose mother had been one of Swain's schoolmates, gave up his tent for the old man.

During the afternoon of April 12, Governor Vance had waited anxiously in Raleigh, since he and other state officials were in danger of capture in the absence of word from Sherman. Late in the day he had a report from General Wheeler that the commissioners had been captured, and Vance then decided to flee. He first wrote Sherman, saying that Raleigh's mayor, William H. Harrison, was authorized to surrender the city; he asked that Sherman spare public buildings, including the capitol and the state museum. Late in the night, accompanied by two volunteer aides, Vance rode westward on horseback to a Confederate camp eight miles outside the city. The governor complained bitterly of fainthearted friends: "Many of my staff officers basely deserted me at the last . . . I rode out of Raleigh at midnight without a single officer of my staff with me! Not one. I shall hit the deserters some day, hard."

In Sherman's camp, the peace commissioners rose before dawn and were escorted to their train by the general, who sent them off with hearty handshakes. "I wish you a safe trip back to Raleigh," Sherman said. "I'll be there in a few hours." Graham and Swain and their entourage rode toward the capital, expecting to meet Vance and then return to Sherman to confer over terms before Federal troops entered the city. Five miles outside Raleigh the train was halted by Kilpatrick, who told the commissioners they could proceed under their flag of truce, but he sent them off with a warning: "If I meet any resistance in Raleigh I'll give you hell." Kilpatrick's manner, as usual, was "a happy compound of braggart and brute," and his profanity was incessant: "It is 'By God' and 'God-damn' all the time" with Kilpatrick, a Confederate officer noted.

When they were within a mile of the city, Graham and Swain

saw smoke towering above the depot, which had been plundered and burned by Wheeler's departing troopers. The pillage caused no surprise in the capital. Vance had paid wry tribute to the gray riders: "If God Almighty had yet in store another plague worse than all the others, I am sure that it must have been a regiment of half-armed, half-disciplined Confederate cavalry." The train halted, and the peace party began walking through the almost deserted streets, whose silence was broken only by the smashing of store windows on Fayetteville Street, a block or so away. Confederate cavalrymen were busy at their looting. Rain was now falling in torrents.

Raleigh's second peace mission, whose purpose was to save the city itself from ruin, had gone out to meet Kilpatrick sometime before. Little Kil halted it a mile outside town—a carriage bearing Mayor Harrison, two city councilmen and Dr. Richard Haywood, who had been taken along because he had been General Blair's classmate at Chapel Hill. One of the councilmen, Kenneth Rayner, asked Kilpatrick to spare property and lives, and the Federal agreed after "some blustering." The carriage turned back, and the blue column soon entered Raleigh. Its leading squadron met unexpected resistance.

A dozen of Wheeler's stragglers were still dragging plunder from stores along Fayetteville Street despite the pleas of Governor Swain. "I've just come from Sherman," the old man said. "If there's no plundering and we don't resist him, he'll spare the city. Please go with your command. Stop this at once."

"Damn Sherman and the town, too," one soldier said. "We don't care a damn for either one."

All but one of the stragglers mounted hurriedly and galloped away when the head of Kilpatrick's cavalry came into view. The lone defender was a rebel officer known to onlookers only as Lieutenant Walsh of Texas, who sat his horse calmly until the Federal horsemen were within a hundred yards, then shouted, "God damn you!", scattered the leading files with five harmless shots from a revolver, and wheeled away, chased by half a dozen troopers. The Texan's black horse fell at a corner, and though Walsh remounted he was soon overtaken and brought back to Capitol Square. Kilpatrick ordered Walsh executed at once, denied his request for five minutes to write a letter to his wife, and had him hanged in the rear yard of a nearby house. The body was buried beneath the hanging tree.

Kilpatrick paused in the city to watch his men chop down a flagpole and raise a U.S. flag over the cupola of the capitol, and then pushed westward, skirmishing with Wheeler's rear guard.

Sherman entered Raleigh at seventy-thirty and took over the governor's mansion as headquarters. He telegraphed Grant of his arrival and then issued his troops orders against pillage in unusually stern terms. He also urged them to show kindness to North Carolinians, especially to the poor. Even now the army did not take him seriously. Albion W. Tourgee of the 105th Ohio felt that Sherman was to blame for all atrocities committed by his bummers: "By seeming to forbid, and failing to prevent, he left the blame to fall upon the men . . . As a consequence the opprobrium falls upon the soldiers, instead of resting where it ought, upon the General."

General Frank Blair found his old college friend, Dr. Richard Haywood, in a handsome Georgian brick house near the capitol, and made headquarters there as a protection to the Haywood family. The doctor told Blair that the family's silver service was buried in the garden, and that a pair of massive brass andirons were in the well.

"Get them out," Blair said. "Those are the first places bummers will look." His advice saved both andirons and the silver for future generations—though the towering coffee pot suffered a dent from a servant's hoe when it was recovered from the garden. Sherman visited the Haywood house a day or so later and drank with Blair and Haywood, toasting the end of the war.

Some seventy-five miles to the west of Raleigh, in the overgrown village of Greensboro, the remnants of the Confederate government had halted in their flight southward. On April 11 a decrepit train came down from Virginia bearing President Davis and five members of his cabinet, the last load of fleeing rebel officialdom, part of a striking wave that had rolled from Richmond ahead of Grant's advancing troops. Young John Wise, an eighteen-year-old Virginia soldier, had watched it pass, "a government on wheels . . . the marvelous and incongruous debris of the wreck of the Confederate capital . . . In one car was a cage with an African parrot, and a box of tame squirrels, and a hunchback."

A few days earlier another train had reached Greensboro under guard of Confederate sailors, a treasure train carrying a hoard of half a million dollars in U.S. double eagle gold pieces, Mexican silver dollars, gold ingots and nuggets, silver bricks, silver and copper coins of all kinds and sizes—the combined wealth of the Confederate treasury and Richmond's private banks. This train had moved on south, leaving behind in Greensboro two boxes of gold coins, almost seventy-five thousand dollars to be divided between Davis and his cabinet and Johnston's army.

The Confederate president and his party found Greensboro, a small town of 2,000 and a rural county seat, now overrun by soldiers of Johnston's army. The town saw in the great men of the Confederacy travel-worn figures in top hats and Prince Alberts: Secretary of State Judah P. Benjamin; Stephen Mallory of the Navy; Postmaster General John Reagan; Attorney General George Davis; Secretary of Treasury George Trenholm.

The visitors also found the town inhospitable. Greensboro had resisted Secession, and only a year before, in the midst of war, prominent citizens had staged a Union meeting, hoping to lead North Carolina out of the Confederacy. Only by browbeating a reluctant landlord did officers find lodging for President Davis, a second-floor bedroom of a modest house near the railroad. The cabinet settled in cold discomfort in a leaky passenger car at the depot, where they ate frugal meals from tin plates with the use of pocket knives.

The one cabinet member to escape the track barracks was Treasurer Trenholm, who was borne off by John Motley Morehead, the town's richest man. Davis' secretary suspected that the hospitality of the host in the elegant townhouse was related to Morehead's enormous investment in Confederate bonds and currency, which he hoped to exchange for gold: "Mr. Trenholm was ill . . . at the house of his warm-hearted host, and the symptoms were said to be greatly aggravated, if not caused, by importunities with regard to that gold."

Jefferson Davis had summoned Joseph Johnston to Greensboro on April 12, and the general entered the president's headquarters, taking with him the fox-faced Creole Beauregard. It was a conference chilled by the war-long hostility between Johnston and the president. Without pausing to ask advice or information, Davis launched a monologue: "Within two or three weeks we will have a large army in the field." The president, lost in a dream world, talked of conscripting more old men and boys and forcing deserters back into ranks, as if he had taken no note of mounting Confederate catastrophes. The generals sat in silence until they were dismissed.

John C. Breckinridge, the new secretary of war, reached Greensboro with official word of Lee's surrender at Appomattox, and the next day met with Davis and several cabinet members, a "funereal session," as John Reagan recalled it. Davis doggedly repeated his theory of eventual victory: "Our last disasters are terrible, but I do not think we should regard them as fatal. I think we can whip the enemy yet, if our people will turn out."

The president then asked Johnston's opinion, and the general advised Davis to sue for peace, since the Confederacy lacked money, credit, troops and ammunition. "It would be the greatest of human crimes" to continue the war, he said. The president could not conceal his irritation. He nervously folded and unfolded a newspaper until the general had finished speaking.

In the end, after a long, aimless discussion, Johnston said, "It is traditional for field commanders to open negotiations. Why not let me approach Sherman?" Davis acquiesced and dictated a brief message, which he ordered Johnston to forward to Sherman. The president then prepared to continue his flight to the south.

Johnston's message reached Sherman late on April 14, asking for a truce "to permit the civil authorities to enter into the needful arrangements to terminate the existing war."

Sherman replied immediately, saying that he could offer the terms of Appomattox. Pending a settlement, the armies should hold their positions. The general telegraphed this dispatch to Kilpatrick to be rushed through the lines, but the cavalryman was in no hurry. He argued that Johnston would use trickery to escape. "I have no confidence in the word of a rebel, no matter what his position. He is but a traitor at best."

Kilpatrick rode off to Durham's Station, a few miles away, leaving the message to be delivered by his staff officers, who delayed it for hours.

By the morning of April 16, when Johnston received Sherman's reply, Jefferson Davis had fled southward. The rebel general, left on his own, proposed to Sherman a meeting between the lines for the next day. The delighted Sherman telegraphed Stanton that he thought the rebels would surrender, and sent copies of the correspondence with Johnston. He added, "I will accept the same terms as General Grant gave General Lee, and be careful not to complicate any points of civil policy."

On April 17, as Sherman and other officers boarded a train for the front, a telegrapher brought a freshly decoded message from Stanton, which Sherman read with a sense of shock: "President Lincoln was murdered about 10 o'clock last night in his private box at Ford's Theatre in this city, by an assassin who shot him through the head with a pistol ball . . . "

Andrew Johnson was already serving as President. Secretary of State Seward had also been attacked by a conspirator—stabbed, though not fatally. The message ended with a warning: "I find evidence that an assassin is also on your track, and I beseech you to be more heedful than Mr. Lincoln of such knowledge."

Sherman thrust the paper into his pocket and turned to the telegrapher: "Has anybody else seen this?"

"No."

"Then don't tell anyone—by word or look, until I return. I'll be back this afternoon."

The little train puffed toward Durham's Station, some twenty-five miles away, while staff officers chattered about the coming truce and the solemn commander sat, alone with his secret.

Kilpatrick and a cavalry escort met the general at Durham's Station and rode with him toward Hillsboro. Within four or five miles they met a group of Confederate officers, and Sherman greeted Johnston, whom he had never met in all their years of army service. In contrast to the disheveled Sherman, the Southerner was immaculate in a handsome gray uniform, his silver beard and mustache neatly groomed, a frail and soldierly little man with a prominent forehead, a Roman nose and wide mouth—a gamecock who looked as if he would peck, one soldier thought. Colonel Joe Waring of Hampton's staff appraised the conquerors coldly: "Sherman is hard-featured and ill-favored. What shall I say of Kilpatrick? His looks and his deeds favor each other."

Johnston's staff officers guided the party to a tiny farmhouse nearby, the home of Daniel Bennett. Mrs. Bennett met the generals at the door, agreed to give them use of her house, and took her four children to an adjoining cabin. Sherman and Johnston entered a room about eighteen feet square, simply furnished but clean, its pine floor scrubbed as white as a bone.

Sherman handed Johnston Stanton's telegram announcing the death of Lincoln. Sweat beaded the Confederate's face as he read. "It's a disgrace to the age," he said. "The greatest possible calamity to the south. I hope you don't charge this to the Confederate government."

"I know that you or General Lee would have no part in it—but I can't say as much for Jeff Davis . . . and men of that stripe." Sherman then said his own troops knew nothing of the murder and that he feared they might react violently to the news. "I'm afraid some foolish man or woman in Raleigh might say or do something to madden our men and that the town would fare worse than Columbia did."

The generals agreed that continuing the war would be "murder" and began a general discussion of peace terms. Sherman said he wanted to spare the Southern people further suffering, and offered the terms Grant had given Lee. Johnston reminded him that his message of April 14 had merely requested a truce so that civilian authorities could negotiate.

Sherman shook his head. "The United States does not recognize the Confederate States, and I can't submit an agreement from civil authorities."

Johnston retorted quickly: "My situation is not at all what Lee's was," he said. "I'm four miles in advance of you, and I'm not surrounded." The Confederate then proposed that they overlook minor differences and make a permanent peace—he would surrender all remaining Confederate armies in the territory south to the Rio Grande. Though Sherman questioned Johnston's authority to make such a sweeping settlement, he was excited by the prospect. He seemed to forget his instructions. His eyes sparkled; Johnston noted his "heightened color" as he spoke of restoring peace and unity to the country. Lincoln and Congress had agreed that restoring the Union was the object of the war, Sherman said—his recent conference with Lincoln had convinced him of that.

The generals seemed to be near an understanding until Johnston asked amnesty for Jefferson Davis, his cabinet and ranking officers. The two were still haggling over this question when Johnston left the cabin briefly to send a message to Confederate Secretary of War John Breckinridge, asking him to join the negotiations the next day.

Officers of both armies lounged outside the cabin in the sunshine, reminiscing of the war. Wade Hampton stretched his great body on a bench, his face "bold beyond arrogance," Major Nichols thought. Hampton made no effort to conceal his hostility. "If I were in command," he said, "no surrender would ever be written. You'll never see me give up. I'll go to Mexico and fight with Maximilian."

Major Hitchcock, who was offended by the South Carolinian's "vulgar insolence," described Hampton as "a man of polished manners, scarcely veiling the arrogance and utter selfishness which marks his class, and which I hate with a perfect hatred."

Bystanders grinned as Kilpatrick and Hampton bickered over skirmishes of the campaign. Kil's voice rose when he spoke of the dawn attack on his quarters near Fayetteville, when he had fled in his underwear: "If we'd known you were coming that morning we'd have taken care of you once and for all."

Rebel cavalrymen were also short-tempered. When a Federal soldier offered to hold Munce Buford's mount, the young courier said, "No damn Yankee's going to hold my horse! I never saw one of you sonsofbitches who wasn't a horse thief." And when one of Sherman's officers tempted Wade Manning with a steaming cup of coffee, the South Carolinian snapped, "Not until I see you drink from it first."

Sherman returned to Raleigh in the early morning, strengthened his provost guard, cleared the streets, and herded troops into their camps. Only then was the news of Lincoln's death announced to the army. Most soldiers took the news calmly—some too calmly. Private Charles Cornell of the 11th Iowa was heard to say, "Old Abe should have been shot three years ago"—and was arrested and placed under guard. A civilian who expressed "satisfaction" at news of Lincoln's murder was shot to death by a Federal soldier.

Other troops were in a dangerous mood. When soldiers of Ben Johnson's Iowa regiment began to call for revenge, someone snatched a torch from a campfire, shouted, "Let's burn the goddam town!" and scores of men were soon hurrying toward Raleigh, carrying torches. Other troops of the XV Corps joined them, forming a mob that "grew wilder" as it went.

Black Jack Logan met these men as they entered the city, sitting upon his horse in the road. "Use your common sense, men. The people in Raleigh had no part in the killing. Don't do something you'll be sorry for. Go back to camp."

A few men hurried past him in the road, but Logan waved his sword and shouted, "Go back! You must go back to camp!"

The leaders hesitated, and after milling about for a few minutes the mob turned back to camp.

It was a long night for Raleigh's civilians, most of whom sat up until dawn, expecting trouble. Even Sherman's guards who patrolled the streets threatened to burn the city.

Sherman and Johnston resumed their conference at the Bennett cabin the next day. The Confederate began by assuring Sherman that he had authority to surrender all Southern armies, but asked that in return Sherman grant "political rights" to rebel soldiers.

Sherman replied that Lincoln had long since offered to restore rights of citizenship to surrendering Confederates below the rank of colonel. "And Grant at Appomattox extended this to all officers, including General Lee."

Johnston was not satisfied. "I have John Breckinridge with me," he said. "He's a better lawyer than either of us. I'd like to call him in."

Sherman objected that Breckinridge was a cabinet officer, and that the settlement must be purely military.

"Oh, he's a major general, too. He wouldn't come as Secretary of War."

Sherman agreed that Breckinridge might join them, and the hulking Kentuckian appeared, an imposing figure, dignified and urbane, reputed to be "the handsomest man in the south." Breckinridge had been a prewar congressman, Vice-President under Buchanan, and a reluctant candidate against Lincoln in 1860. Breckinridge was "heavy and dull" today, Johnston thought, probably for lack of his daily whiskey ration. The Kentuckian began talking of the rights of Confederate soldiers, but Sherman interrupted to call for his saddlebags. Officers who waited outside interpreted this as a sign of an agreement, but Sherman pulled out a bottle and treated the Confederates.

Breckinridge's eyes glowed with a "beatific light." The thirsty Kentuckian tossed his tobacco quid into the fire, rinsed his mouth with a dipperful of water, and downed "a tremendous drink," took a fresh chew of tobacco, stroked his mustache, and launched into a discourse on military and international law so eloquent that Sherman broke in: "Gentlemen, who's doing this surrendering, anyhow? If this goes on, you'll have me sending an apology to Jeff Davis."

A courier arrived with a draft of an agreement written by John

Reagan in Hillsboro, a few miles away. Johnston and Breckinridge read together and passed it to Sherman. He cast it aside. "It's too verbose," he said. "Too general. Let me try."

Sherman sat at one of Bennett's crude tables and wrote rapidly, composing, as he later explained, "some general propositions, meaning much or meaning little, according to the construction of the parties—what I would call 'glittering generalities'—and sent them to Washington . . . That would enable the new President to give me a clew to his policy . . . and to define to me what I might promise, simply to cover the pride of the Southern men . . . "

Sherman paused once during this writing, took a drink from his saddlebag, replaced the bottle and turned back to the table, heedless of the woebegone gaze of Breckinridge. Sherman handed the draft to Johnston:

The armies were to remain in position under a truce that could be suspended after a forty-eight-hour notice. Meanwhile, President Johnson and his Cabinet would consider the terms Sherman had offered: The rebel armies would disband and deposit their arms in state arsenals; the troops would agree to keep the peace and obey Federal laws, but some of them were to keep their arms for use against guerrillas.

Upon taking oaths, state officers would be recognized and local governments would continue to function. Federal courts would be reestablished.

Southerners were guaranteed "their political rights and franchises, as well as their rights of person and property."

Once Confederate armies disbanded, there would be a general amnesty.

Sherman handed his draft across the table. "That's the best I can do," he said.

Johnston and Breckinridge saw at once that Sherman's hastily written terms were quite as generous as those Reagan had written; Sherman was, once more, a victim of his impulsive, mercurial nature. He had made no mention of the issue of slavery. Sherman had kept his promise to embrace the Southern people in brotherhood when they laid down arms—and out of political naïveté or lack of experience, he had included important civil issues. In effect, Sherman's proposal guaranteed the right of property in slaves, made possible the payment of the Confederate war debt, and in recognizing rebel governments, placed Union authority in border states in jeopardy. They were terms Lincoln could not have approved. Johnston and Sherman signed the agreement and went out into the spring dusk.

Johnston gravely tipped his hat to Sherman and his officers, but Breckinridge strode off without a farewell.

As they mounted their horses Johnston asked, "How does Sherman strike you?"

"Oh, he's bright enough and a man of force, but"—the Kentuckian raised his voice—"Sherman is a hog. Yes, sir, a *hog*. Did you see him take that drink by himself?"

"He was thinking of something else," Johnston said, "probably of your own masterful arguments."

"Ah! No Kentucky gentleman would ever have taken that bottle away. He knew how much we needed it. Needed it badly."

Years later, when a Confederate officer told him this story, Sherman laughed. "I don't remember it, but if Joe Johnston told it, then it was true. Those fellows hustled me so, I was sorry for the drink I did give them." This was the only hint Sherman ever gave of his awareness that the canny Southerners had bested him at the peace table.

Sherman's generals were almost unanimous in their praise of the surrender document. Logan and Blair urged him to sign the agreement unconditionally, without so much as submitting it to Washington for approval. There was, apparently, only one outspoken dissenter, Slocum's chief of staff, the little Missouri General Carl Schurz, a German immigrant who had become a liberal Republican leader. Sherman's reckless overstepping of his military authority was denounced by Schurz, especially his generous treatment of rebel officers and recognition of state governments. "They'll never approve in Washington," Schurz told his friends. This criticism did not reach Sherman, but he realized that his drafted terms had imperfections. In dispatches to Halleck and Grant enclosing the surrender terms, he explained, after a fashion, his failure to include so much as a mention of slavery:

"Both Generals Johnston and Breckinridge admitted that slavery was dead, and I could not insist on embracing it in such a paper, because it can be made with the States in detail. I know that all the men of substance [in the] South sincerely want peace, and I do not believe they will resort to war again during this century."

He urged both Halleck and Grant to help persuade President Johnson to sign the agreement: "Influence him not to vary the terms at all, for I have considered everything." And he wrote to Ellen of his pride in the settlement: "I can hardly realize it, but I can see no slip."

Early the next morning he sent Major Hitchcock to Washington with the agreement, asking him to bring back a reply as quickly as possible. "You must deliver it only to Halleck or Grant— or Stanton. Don't give the greedy newspaper writers a whiff of it."

Sherman announced to his troops that "the agreement, when formally ratified, will make peace from the Potomac to the Rio Grande . . . The General hopes and believes that in a very few days it will be his good fortune to conduct you to your homes."

The general was oblivious to the fact that he had dispatched a bombshell to Washington, where Stanton and the Radicals—"the grannies of New England," for whom Sherman had only contempt—were conspiring to destroy the influence of the temperate Lincoln. Sherman's manner was that of a proud, confident soldier who had done his duty well and was awaiting the applause of his countrymen.

25
"Sherman has fatally blundered"

Thousands of troops from both armies swarmed about the tiny railroad village of Durham's Station, mingling so freely that, as the Ohio Private Ben Sweet noted, "You could not tell which army you was in." These men found unexpected delights—a warehouse full of shredded bright leaf tobacco, a light, sweet smoke developed by North Carolina growers some years earlier and still unknown to most of the country. Soldiers bought or stole the entire stock of the manufacturer, J. R. Green, and rolled their own cigarettes; Green was soon to be swamped by orders from many parts of the country, all demanding more of his "Best Flavored Spanish Smoking Tobacco." To foil imitators, Green adopted a Durham bull as his trademark, a symbol destined to serve for fifty years as the world's best-known tobacco brand.

Federal troops in Raleigh found a recruit in a bizarre incident at the state insane asylum during the days of waiting. Samuel Toombs of the 13th New Jersey met a persuasive inmate who shouted through the bars, "Get me out of here! I'm as sane as any of you—the damned rebels are holding me illegally."

Soldiers gathered to hear the story of this patient, one Lavender, a New Yorker whose family had moved to North Carolina. His family had urged him to join the rebel army, but Lavender had refused:

"My father threatened everything, but I'd sooner suffer hell's fire than fight against my country! So they threw me in this hole. You don't know what torture's like till you're in with these crazy men. Please, please, get me out of here!"

Lavender was released after an examination by army doctors. He found some friends in a New York regiment and left Raleigh with the army a few days later.

In the countryside near Raleigh the occupation continued. Retreating Confederate cavalry passed through the college town of Chapel Hill on April 14. General Joe Wheeler's wounded, casualties of a skirmish the previous day, came on wagons, and for about two days rebels held the place to protect their passage. Wheeler abandoned the village on Sunday, April 17.

Chapel Hill's villagers waved farewells to the gray riders and sat on their porches to await the coming of the enemy. Silver had been buried in springs and streams, as it had in scores of towns; other treasures were hidden in fence corners, woodlands and cellars. There was little food to be concealed. Smokehouses were almost empty. Wardrobes were scanty and simple after four years of war, largely reduced to homespun and jeans. The town's chief anxiety was for the safety of the university buildings, especially the library.

General Smith Atkins of Kilpatrick's command entered the town the next morning at the head of 4,000 cavalrymen, and Chapel Hill became the last town to suffer occupation by Sherman's invaders during their hostile sweep through the South. Their first act was to raise U.S. flags on the university buildings, one of them an enormous banner that dwarfed its staff.

A local observer, Mrs. Cornelia Phillips Spencer, noted that perfect order prevailed, and that the most grievous offense to the town's civilians was the flying of the American flag. Mrs. Spencer was surprised by her own reaction: "Never before had we realized how entirely our hearts had been turned away from what was once our whole country, till we felt the bitterness aroused by the sight of that flag shaking out its red and white folds over us."

Guards were placed at the houses almost at once, and Chapel Hill lived for three weeks under an orderly occupation. Life went on much as usual and families were not molested, but buildings of the university became stables and barracks for the Federals. Horses were stabled in alcoves of the library, and townspeople saw mounts looking out the windows of the venerable Old West building. Damage by the invaders was slight, however, estimated by President Swain at a hundred dollars. The village swarmed with freed Negroes, but Mrs. Spencer noted that they "behaved much better, on the whole than Northern letter-writers represent them to have done." She had high praise for the blacks: "I do not know a race more studiously misrepresented than they have been . . . They behaved well during the war: if they had not, it could not have lasted eighteen months." The high-minded Mrs. Spencer quite unconsciously expressed the prevailing bias that the most laudable blacks were those who knew their place and were content to keep it.

People of the town bore the new conditions stoically, and most of them, as Mrs. Spencer noted, tried "to wear a look of proud composure." This effort broke down on the day that the first group of dusty, ragged strangers in gray walked slowly into town. Townspeople stared and someone shouted, "Lee's men!" Women burst into sobs at the sight of the defeated soldiers: "They were here," Mrs. Spencer wrote, "the heroes of the army of Virginia, walking home, each with his pass in his pocket, and nothing else." Women ran into the streets to embrace these men who had walked home from Appomattox, crying over them, inviting strangers in to dine, and seeking to console them in defeat, "just as if it had turned out differently."

Mrs. Spencer watched the returning soldiers sadly. "Day after day we saw them, sometimes in twos and threes, sometimes in little companies, making the best of their way toward their distant homes, penniless and dependent on wayside charity for their food, plodding along, while the blue jackets pranced gayly past on the best blood of Southern stables."

The bearing of these men gave villagers new hope. "They were not unduly cast down nor had any appearance of the humiliation that was burning in our souls. They were serious, calm and self-possessed. They said they were satisfied that all had been done that could be done, and they seemed to be sustained by the sense of duty done and well done . . . It was a fair fight, they said, but the south had been starved out."

Within a few days after Federal troops arrived, the town began to observe a striking courtship—General Smith Atkins was a frequent caller at the home of President Swain to see his blond daughter, Eleanor. Villagers were outraged by the romance. One diarist wrote: "Who can sympathize with or even pity a young lady who willingly throws herself into the arms of a Yankee General, while his sword is yet reeking with the blood of its victims, her own relations or at least her own countrymen." But nothing deterred Ellie and Atkins. Their engagement was announced.

Mrs. Spencer reported the town's reception of the news: "Very few attended the party . . . invitations were torn to pieces and spit upon. The whole state was in an uproar. That a high official of the state . . . should have countenanced a marriage between his daughter and . . . an avowed enemy, was considered an affront to the whole commonwealth.

"Governor Swain lost much of the esteem and honor in which he had been held, and when he was killed not long afterwards by a runaway horse that had been given to him by General W. T. Sherman, there were some who said: 'Served him right' . . . "

Mrs. Spencer could not bring herself to like Atkins, who was not well educated, she said—and even more deplorably, "talked through his nose."

On April 23, after three days of waiting for word of Washington's reception of his terms of truce with Johnston, Sherman read disturbing news in New York newspapers: In the wake of violent public reaction to Lincoln's murder, there was a cry for harsh treatment of the South. An order by Lincoln permitting the Virginia legislature to assemble had been rescinded.

Sherman telegraphed a warning to Joseph Johnston: "I fear much the assassination of the President will give such a bias to the popular mind, which in connection with the desire of our politicians, may thwart our purpose of recognizing 'existing local governments' . . ."

His truce agreement seemed to be in jeopardy.

Henry Hitchcock had reached Washington with Sherman's message on April 21, the day Lincoln's funeral train left the city on its long journey to Illinois.

Edwin Stanton, who had assumed charge of the government largely by browbeating Cabinet members, called an emergency meeting of the Cabinet to consider the terms Sherman had offered to Johnston. Stanton also summoned General Grant to the session. The anti-Sherman bias of the secretary of war became evident from the start. When Grant had read Sherman's memorandum and the peace terms proposed, Stanton burst out in excited condemnation of Sherman: The war had been fought in vain, Stanton said. The South would keep its slaves under the proposed terms, local governments would remain intact, and rebel leaders would escape scot-free. The distraught secretary of war spoke as if Sherman had signed a binding, final treaty rather than submitted a proposal for consideration in Washington. There were echoes of Ebenezer Creek, and of the Sherman-Stanton controversy in Savannah, in the secretary's denunciation of Sherman. But it was President Johnson who took action, directing Stanton to advise Sherman of the Cabinet's disapproval and ordering a resumption of hostilities after giving the Confederates a forty-eight-hour notice.

The impassive Grant sat silently during the attack upon his friend, saying nothing even when Stanton directed him to advise Sherman that the peace terms were unacceptable—but Grant was resolved to handle the matter in his own way.

Stanton dismissed the Cabinet and held a private talk with Grant. The commanding general was to take a ship for North Carolina during the night, in complete secrecy. Sherman was not to be trusted with advance knowledge that his treaty had been rejected. Stanton ordered Grant to relieve Sherman and to take over his command. Not even Cabinet officers were to be told of this mission or its purpose.

While Grant was at sea the vindictive Stanton had an inflammatory telegram from Henry Halleck, the Chief of Staff, who had been sent to Richmond to impose a harsh truce on Virginia; the pliant Halleck had replaced General Godfrey Weitzel, who had re-called the Virginia legislature into session for the purpose of reestablishing state government. Halleck, with the relish of a practiced gossip, had heard fanciful tales from Richmond's bankers: Jefferson Davis and some of his cabinet, fleeing southward with millions of dollars in gold, hoped to bribe their way to freedom in case they were caught —perhaps to bribe Sherman himself.

Halleck, acting on secret orders from Grant (perhaps at the direction of Stanton), had ordered General George Meade to lead the Army of the Potomac into North Carolina to cut off Johnston's retreat, just as if no negotiations had taken place. Not content with that, Halleck had also sent orders to Sherman's corps commanders, directing them to disregard all orders from Sherman.

Shortly afterward, Stanton also learned that Sherman had summoned to Raleigh General George Stoneman, whose cavalrymen had been raiding through the western North Carolina mountains. This transfer, which would throw the troopers across the escape route being followed by the fugitive Confederate president, was misinterpreted by Stanton. In his agitation, Stanton confused the locations of two North Carolina towns—Salisbury and Statesville—and erroneously concluded that Sherman's orders would permit Davis to escape. Stanton told newspaper reporters of his conclusion, and inferred that Sherman's aim was deliberate. This was the nigh-hysterical Stanton of the spring of 1862, when he had become terrified by news of the Confederate ironclad *Merrimac* and proclaimed that she would descend upon Washington and obliterate the seat of government.

The next day Stanton issued a public denunciation of Sherman, a devious blend of half-truths in which he accused the general of willful disobedience of Lincoln's orders and hinted that Sherman was susceptible to bribery by the fleeing Jeff Davis.

Not merely did Stanton charge Sherman with de facto recognition of rebel governments and with placing in Confederate hands arms that might be used to continue the war; he charged that the general had relieved rebel leaders "from all pains and penalties for their crimes," and had sought to perpetuate slavery. Sherman's terms, Stanton said, went far beyond even those liberal ones proposed by Lincoln.

Stanton did not lack for courage in his vendetta against Sherman, whose enormous popularity he recognized; he certainly saw that the Copperhead faction of the Democratic party cherished the general as a possible presidential candidate. In any case, the secretary had done everything possible to present Sherman in the most unfavorable light as he laid his case before the public.

The charges against Sherman appeared in newspapers that bore black borders of mourning for Lincoln, and set off a furor of protest by politicians and newspapers. The *New York Herald* said: "Sherman's splendid military career is ended, he will retire under a cloud . . . Was he caught napping or was he too eager for the laurels of the peacemaker? . . . Sherman has fatally blundered, for, with a few unlucky strokes of his pen, he has blurred all the triumphs of his sword."

Other newspapers insinuated that Sherman might have been involved in the plot to murder Lincoln. The usually friendly *Chicago Tribune,* though it stopped short of charging him with treason, said that Sherman's signing of the surrender agreement could be explained only by his "stark insanity."

Attorney General James Speed, under Stanton's influence, told the Cabinet a day or so later that Sherman undoubtedly planned to seize the government and install himself as a dictator. "Suppose he should arrest Grant?" Speed asked. This specter had almost certainly been raised by Stanton, who had heard that Sherman's officers, waiting in Raleigh, had met to form The Society of the Army of the Tennessee, a social organization that planned postwar reunions. Speed's question, at any rate, echoed uneasily in Washington offices while Grant steamed southward, bound for Sherman's headquarters in Raleigh.

Of all this furor, public and private, Sherman yet knew nothing; the slow pace of communications served to sustain him in his mood of euphoria.

26

"Washington is as corrupt as hell"

Ulysses Grant arrived in Raleigh near dawn of April 24 after a rough voyage from Washington, and rode through deserted streets to Sherman's quarters in the governor's mansion. The astonished Sherman was still in his night clothes when the commander made his unexpected appearance.

Grant's coming also surprised Sherman's field officers, but Henry Slocum, for one, felt a sense of relief, for though he admired Sherman as a general, he deplored his political naïveté. "All is well," Slocum wrote. "Grant is here. He has come to save his friend Sherman from himself." It was an accurate appraisal.

Grant's manner was gentle and understanding throughout. He told Sherman that the settlement with Johnston had been disapproved, and that he was to reopen negotiations, offering the Confederate only the terms of the Appomattox agreement with Lee. Though he had gleaned intimations of the problem through newspapers, Sherman did not dream of the extent of Stanton's machinations, and felt no sense of alarm. Grant gave him no details of the frantic Cabinet meeting, and no hint of charges that he had permitted Jeff Davis to escape nor of the fears of some that he was plotting to seize power in Washington with his army of veterans at his back. As a matter of course he told Sherman nothing of the secret orders he had passed to Halleck. And, since he had no intention of obeying Stanton's order to remove Sherman from command, he made no mention of that. It was a tour de force in duplicity uncharacteristic of Grant, but he achieved it with an aplomb that completely deceived his old friend.

Sherman moved to repair the damage at once. He notified Johnston that he could offer only the terms of Appomattox, warned him that their truce must end after forty-eight hours, and ordered his army to prepare to move against the rebels once more.

The troops, already aware that something had gone wrong, grumbled at prospects of another battle. Their complaints, Harvey Reid of Wisconsin said, were "not loud but deep." Men of the 102nd Illinois cursed President Johnson, and the regiment was aroused by a rumor that Sherman had resigned: "The men could not tolerate the thought," Sergeant Fleharty said. "They wanted no other leader."

Grant sent Stanton a reassuring telegram, making it clear that Sherman had acted promptly to make amends. His complete message read:

> I reached here this morning and delivered to General Sherman the reply to his negotiations with Johnston. He was not surprised but rather expected the rejection. Word was immediately sent to Johnston terminating the truce and [relaying the] information that civil matters could not be entertained in any convention between army commanders. General Sherman has been guided in his negotiations with Johnston entirely by what he thought was precedent authorized by the President. He had before him the terms given by me to Lee's army and the call of the rebel legislature of Virginia as authorized by General Weitzel as he supposed with the sanction of the President and myself. At the time of the agreement General Sherman did not know of the withdrawal of authority of the meeting of the legislature. The moment he learned through the papers that authority for the meeting had been withdrawn he communicated the fact to Johnston as having bearing on the negotiations.

Stanton's reply of the next day was an uncompromising rejection of Grant's explanation and defense of Sherman. He responded coldly:

> Your dispatch received. The arrangement between Sherman and Johnston meets with universal disapprobation. No one of any class or shade of opinion approves it. I have not known as much surprise and discontent at anything that has happened during the war . . . the hope of the country is that you repair the misfortune . . .

Stanton then carefully excised those portions of Grant's message which clarified Sherman's motives, and released the emasculated text to the press:

> A dispatch has been received by this Department from General Grant dated Raleigh, 9 A.M., April 24th. He says, "I reached here this morning and delivered to General Sherman the reply to his negotiation with Johnston. Word was immediately sent to Johnston terminating the truce and information that civil matters could not be entertained in any convention between army commanders."

The full copy of Grant's telegram, which made plain Sherman's reasoning and subsequent cooperation, was so well hidden in Stanton's files that it was not to be found until years later, after Stanton's death.

In his ignorance of this exchange, and of Stanton's handling of the matter, Sherman telegraphed the secretary a candid, almost humble, apology:

> I admit my folly in embracing in a military convention any civil matters but unfortunately such is the nature of our situation that they seem inextricably united, and I understood from you at Savannah that the financial state of the country demanded military success and would warrant a little bending to policy . . .
>
> I still believe that the General Government of the United States has made a mistake but that is none of my business.

Sherman and Johnston met in the Bennett house once more, on April 26, and this time Sherman was accompanied by Howard, Schofield and Blair. Sherman had invited Grant, who refused lest he give the impression of superseding his friend and branding him as an unreliable negotiator. Sherman and Johnston went into the cabin alone, but after an hour or more Schofield was called in. "We can't agree," Sherman said glumly.

Johnston said he could not accept the terms of Appomattox and loose his hungry men upon civilians. He said that Lee's disbanded veterans, without food since their surrender, were wandering through the countryside, robbing farms in their homeward path.

But now Sherman was adamant. Washington, he said, would disapprove any terms except those Grant had given Lee.

Schofield said he could cope with predatory Confederate veterans: "I'll be in command here, and I'll handle any problems that arise." He offered to write terms of surrender. "I think Schofield can fix it," Johnston said. While the two commanders paced slowly across the room, Schofield wrote his proposal and passed it to the Confederate. "I believe this is the best we can do," Johnston said. He handed the sheet to Sherman, who agreed to the terms at once, and when copies had been made, Johnston and Schofield signed their names.

The brief agreement provided that Johnston's army was to disband and leave its arms in Greensboro; that the men would take an oath that they would no longer resist the government, and in return would be allowed to go to their homes in peace.

Sherman and Schofield then made a generous verbal agreement with Johnston, allowing the Confederates to keep their own horses and mules and promising to supply others that were needed. As a defense against guerrillas and bushwhackers, each rebel unit could keep one-seventh of its arms until it reached its state capital. The Federals would also supply 250,000 rations to Johnston's troops.

Sherman returned to Raleigh at dusk and pushed his way through a crowd of officers on the porch of the governor's mansion, anxious to confer with Grant. Through a window Hitchcock saw the peacemakers at work, "Grant and Sherman sitting at the center table, both busy writing, or stopping now and then to talk earnestly with the other general officers in the room . . . " The mansion was crowded with officers most of the night, and a regimental band serenaded endlessly from the lawn.

Grant approved the revised terms and said casually that he could have wished for only one revision—a reversal of the signatures of the two commanding generals so that Johnston's would not have appeared first when published.

Grant was anxious to return to Washington, but the troops had one brief glimpse of him when he joined Sherman to review the XVII Corps, which streamed past the capitol grounds between crowds of other troops and Confederate civilians. Sergeant Fleharty of Illinois saw Sherman at once and then stared in disbelief: "But who was that with him . . . short, heavy-set, iron-featured; looking travel-worn, yet having the bearing of the quiet great man. It was Grant . . . the glorious old 17th Corps marched proudly. It was a pleasure to them to dip their tattered flags to the chief whom they had known at Vicksburg."

Grant left for Washington, leaving Sherman in command and without an inkling that Stanton had ordered his removal. Sherman called in his generals to issue final orders. His army would march northward at once, leaving Schofield's troops in Raleigh to occupy North Carolina.

Sherman himself prepared for a hurried inspection trip to Savannah, planning to return by coastal steamer and rejoin his army in Richmond. He was completing these plans when copies of Northern papers of April 24 reached Raleigh. All of them bore Stanton's accusations, which virtually charged Sherman with treason. The general was livid with rage.

Carl Schurz saw him pacing the floor of headquarters before several officers "like a caged lion, talking to the whole room with a furious invective which made us all stare. He lashed Stanton as a mean, scheming, vindictive politician who made it his business to rob military men of their credit earned by exposing their lives . . . He berated people who blamed him for what he had done as a mass of fools, not worth fighting for . . . He railed at the Press which had become the engine of vilification."

Sherman wrote to Grant in a fury, denying the implications of Stanton's charges and accusing the secretary of deliberately loosing "the dogs of the press" upon him, of violating military secrecy—and of sheer absurdity in the insinuation that he had permitted Davis to escape. "Even now," Sherman said angrily, "I don't know that Mr. Stanton wants Davis caught."

As to a charge of insubordination made by *The New York Times,* "I have never in my life questioned or disobeyed an order, though many and many a time I have risked my life, health and reputation in obeying orders or even hints to execute plans and purposes not to my liking. . . .

"It is true that non-combatants, men who sleep in comfort and security while we watch on the distant lines, are better able to judge than we poor soldiers, who rarely see a newspaper, hardly can hear from our families, or stop long enough to draw our pay . . . "

Sherman demanded that Grant have his letter published as a reply to Stanton.

Above all, Sherman sought revenge: "To say that I was merely angry . . . would hardly express the state of my feelings. I was outraged beyond measure, and was resolved to resent the insult, cost what it might."

In that mood he was off to Savannah, leaving his corps commanders to lead the march northward toward Washington, where the army was to appear in a final review.

The last blaze set off by his troops in North Carolina was in defense of Sherman. When Henry Slocum saw soldiers crowded about a burning cart on a Raleigh street and sent a staff officer to investigate, he received a defiant message: "Tell General Slocum the cart is loaded with New York papers full of the vilest abuse of General Sherman. We haven't followed him for a thousand miles and through all his battles to have these slanders peddled to his own men." Slocum did not interfere.

In Savannah, as if to atone for the desolation left in the wake of his army, Sherman dispensed food and other supplies so lavishly that his garrison troops almost ran out of rations. Wilson, his cavalry commander in Georgia, began by issuing 250 bushels of corn daily to civilians—and he was soon to pass out 45,000 pounds of meal and 10,000 pounds of flour to Atlanta families in a single week. Georgia's leaders were so touched that three judges from Thomas County wrote: "The generous spirit evinced by the order of General Sherman . . . has had a happy effect upon the whole people of our state, and will convince them that you and your colaborers have a humane and Christian feeling for them, which will be properly appreciated."

After a few days in Savannah, Sherman sailed back up the coast. In harbor at Morehead City, North Carolina, where his steamer took refuge from a storm, the general met Chief Justice Salmon P. Chase of the Supreme Court, who had come south to investigate the problems of Negro voting. Sherman showed Chase a blistering attack on Stanton which he had written and planned to publish "to counteract the effect of the insult so unjustly inflicted on me by the Secretary of War." Though sympathetic to any disparagement of Stanton, the devious Chase was alarmed by Sherman's violent mood, sought to soothe him, and sent several messages to Washington in hope of ending the controversy.

Sherman wrote Ellen after his talks with Chase, a brusque declaration notable for its impersonal reference to himself: "A breach must be made between Grant and Sherman, or certain cliques in Washington, who have a nice thing, are gone up . . . Washington is as corrupt as hell, made so by the looseness and extravagance of war. I will avoid it as a pest house . . . "

* * *

The army began its march northward from Raleigh on April 30. Tents disappeared from the fields about the capital as if by magic, and troops fell into ranks, shouting in cadence as they passed through city streets between files of Schofield's men.

The head of the column had gone only a few miles when it began to meet ragged, hungry veterans of Lee's army. The Federals invited the rebels to eat and sleep with them and sat up until almost dawn, talking of the war. Yankee coffee and rations mellowed the half-starved rebels. "We all have been fools to fight you," one of them said. The rebels seemed to feel only relief that the war was over, and to feel such affection for their bluecoat enemies that the morning's parting was "like leave-taking of old friends."

Spontaneous bursts of cheering swept the blue ranks on the second day out as the column passed a modest farmhouse. Sam Neil of the 31st Ohio heard the roaring of the troops far ahead of his regiment, and at last saw the cause of it: An American flag flew from a pole at the roadside, and beneath it a heavily bearded old man with flowing hair, hat in hand, bowed to the marching soldiers.

The old man explained to the soldiers: "When they fired on Fort Sumter I vowed I'd never shave nor cut my hair 'til this flag waved again over the whole country."

Each regiment gave him a cheer, and men in ranks who turned back for a last glimpse of the old Tarheel saw him still gravely bowing his shaggy head at the roadside.

In this region near the Carolina-Virginia line, the army was greeted by thousands of Negroes who stared in wonder at the first Federal troops they had ever seen. An Ohio soldier paused to talk with an old man and his wife who were at work in a field: "Do you get pay for your work?"

The bewildered Negroes refused to believe that they were no longer slaves. Private Sam Neil explained the Emancipation Proclamation and the defeat of Confederate armies in vain. The old black man argued stubbornly, "Lincoln might of freed us, but we're still in slavery." The old couple turned back to their labor in the field as their liberators marched from sight.

27

"They march like the lords of the world"

Some of the army's last casualties died of hard marching in the move northward from Raleigh toward the Virginia line. One day the 27th Ohio was hurried through a driving rain to make the day's goal though men could hardly keep their feet on the slippery clay road. Private Ben Sweet wrote, "I don't remember of ever being in a harder rain . . . We did not stop until four in the morning and from there on to Richmond we travelled like we were in a race."

Gossips said Sherman's commanders had laid bets as to whose corps would reach Richmond first, and that the infantry was to be sacrificed. Private Alonzo Brown of the 12th Wisconsin wrote home of the race into Petersburg, won by his XVII Corps: "The 15th Corps tried to run past us but could not . . . They stripped one division of all except their guns and equipment and marched all day and part of the night. Then our general sent in some of his staff ahead and got our badge in first. The 15th Corps lost quite a number of men by marching so fast."

The army was put to the test on May 9, a day of unseasonable heat when some units were driven thirty-two miles, their longest march of the war. Scores fell by the roadside, and even some officers dismounted and finished the march in ambulance wagons. When the 2nd Iowa went into camp along the Boydton Plank Road in southern Virginia that night, only six of forty-two men in one company were in ranks—the others were scattered for miles in the rear, felled by sunstroke. Some of these men died. Private John Bell saw tough veterans of many campaigns "drop to the ground with foaming lips and staring eyes and writhe in the dust with agony . . . murdered by the heartless indifference of corps and division commanders."

To add to the army's discomfiture, rebel barnyards and chicken roosts in this region were protected by guards who took their duties seriously, and there was little foraging. Discharged rebel soldiers appeared more frequently, and the army greeted them like old friends, reserving its catcalls and profane jibes for the occasional bluecoat cavalryman of the Army of the Potomac who passed along the route; there was no love lost between Sherman's men and the Easterners who had fought under Grant.

The Westerners could hardly be restrained when they reached Richmond and found themselves barred from the Confederate capital by General Halleck's garrison troops. Men of the XV Corps stoned some of Halleck's outposts, and veterans relished a report that Black Jack Logan had sat his horse nearby, laughing at the discomfiture of the Easterners. A squad from the 85th Indiana took matters into its own hands: It tossed a provost guard into the James River and went into the city looking for trouble.

A few troops of the XVII Corps were challenged at a bridge by a dozen of Halleck's guards who had fallen into line across the road with rifles at the ready. "This caused the boys from the western army to smile, such a smile as could be heard quite a distance," the Illinois Private Charles Herbert said. An officer who rode up, told Sherman's men to disperse, and ordered the guards to fire if necessary was knocked from his saddle by a brick, and the troops rushed over the bridge, joined by hundreds of others. They found their way blocked by a gun crew with a loaded cannon, and fell back sullenly.

When Sherman arrived by boat from Savannah to rejoin the army outside Richmond, he was besieged by officers and men who pleaded for permission to storm their way into the city. A day later, when Halleck ordered the XIV Corps to enter the city and pass in review before him, Sherman refused, scolding his estranged friend for the "deadly malignity" he had shown in the affair of the truce with Johnston. Sherman said he would march through Richmond only when Grant ordered it, and he warned Halleck to remain out of sight when the army of the West was passing. "If loss of life or violence result," Sherman wrote bitterly, "you must attribute it to the true cause—a public insult to a brother officer."

Sherman wrote Ellen:

> Tomorrow I march through Richmond with colors flying and drums beating, as a matter of right and not by Halleck's favor, and no notice will be taken of him personally or officially. I dare him to oppose my march. He will think twice before he again undertakes to stand between me and my subordinates . . .
>
> Stanton wants to kill me because I do not favor the scheme of declaring the Negroes of the south, now free, to be loyal voters, whereby politicians may manufacture just so much more pliable electioneering material. The Negroes don't want to vote. They want to work and enjoy property, and they are no friends of the Negro who seek to complicate him with new prejudices.

The army passed through the city on May 11, jeered by Eastern soldiers who lined the streets: "Sherman's greasers!" "Slouch hats!" "You never had to handle Bobby Lee!" The tanned veterans of the long march hooted insults at the white-collared Easterners in return: "All quiet on the Potomac! Advanced one mile yesterday and retreated two today!" A soldier of the 15th Iowa shrieked, "Bob, ain't that my dog over there? My dog wore a collar!" As they passed Halleck's headquarters, where a haughty guard stood at attention in a faultless uniform, a ragged Westerner left the ranks, inspected the bandbox soldier scornfully and squirted a stream of tobacco juice over the sentry's freshly shined boots.

The army rested around Richmond for another day, complaining of sutlers' prices, inspecting Libby and Belle Isle, the Confederate prisons where many of them had been kept. Curious soldiers loitered before Robert E. Lee's tall brick house on Franklin Street, hoping for a glimpse of the celebrated general, just back from Appomattox, but "the fallen chief kept close, and could not be seen." They wandered through the charred blocks of the city, which had burned in April and clambered over earthworks surrounding Richmond and Petersburg, which they scorned as less forbidding than those of Atlanta. "We could have walked right over them," Ben Johnson of the 15th Iowa said.

Unknown to the army, its vanguard had already reached Washington—two bummers who crossed the Potomac far ahead of the army, ragged and heavily armed young men mounted on fine horses. The country around the capital swarmed with thieves and highwaymen from Union and Confederate armies, and security was tight.

A guard halted the two at the bridge into the city:

"Who're you?"

"We're the advance of Sherman's army, on the way to Washington."

They were led to headquarters in the city, where a skeptical general questioned them: "Why are you here when your army is still in Richmond?"

"Well, general, we've always made it our business to keep to the front, all the way."

The two were taken to the guardhouse, howling in protest, to be released only when the main army reached the city.

Sherman's troops marched northward from Richmond on four parallel roads and at a less hectic pace so that men could see the celebrated Virginia battlefields. The general switched from corps to corps so that he could inspect many fields. Near Fredericksburg the right wing halted, and the troops walked over the torn fields of the Wilderness. Some of Sherman's regiments had fought here in the bloodbaths of 1863 and 1864, but the veterans did not recognize the nightmare landscape. They probed the thickets, where whitened skeletons of Union soldiers lay in windrows, and tree trunks were pocked with musket balls and torn by cannon fire.

At Chancellorsville soldiers retraced the route over which they had retreated before Lee's Army of Northern Virginia in the last of its great victories. One man found a skull which he thought he recognized as his brother's.

At Chancellorsville a *New York Tribune* reporter found a tree stump still red with blood of the wounded—and still more bones: "Within a circle of 150 yards, where an unsuccessful assault was made upon the enemy's works, I counted fifty skulls polished by time, reflecting grimly the rays of the sun."

The army moved on. The next day some regiments made a detour eight miles or more to Mount Vernon, marched slowly around Washington's mansion and saluted as they passed his tomb. That night they settled in camps around Alexandria on filthy, littered fields that had served the Eastern armies for four years.

It was all over. The ruins of Atlanta were now six months and a thousand miles away, almost lost in memory down the track of devastation winding through the heart of Georgia and the Carolinas. It was incredibly long ago that Sherman's men had marched into a still grimly defiant South, cheered on by a newly confident Lincoln in the flush of an election victory they had won for him. The larking farm boys to whom the march had been an endless Halloween did not yet think of the campaign as a wound that had hastened the end of the Confederacy.

No one would count the charred chimneys that marked their route—"Sherman's sentinels" of the burnt country; the toll of ruin, perhaps as much as one billion dollars, would never be totted up. In its passage the army had left the wreckage of the plantation society. For the first time in American history a vast region had been scorched and plundered, and war had been taken to women and children.

The army had sacked and burned one state capital and taken two others, seized and reclaimed a great seaport, taken a fort by storm, fought one pitched battle, overwhelmed the enemy in two lively skirmishes that passed as minor battles, and endured months of constant bushwhacking. The pioneer corps—labor battalions, many of whom were Negroes—had laid more than four hundred miles of corduroy roads in the swampy country, and engineers had strung countless miles of pontoon bridges.

By official count the army had lost almost 5,000 men—nearly 600 dead, 2,700 wounded and 1,600 missing (though Confederates set the toll much higher; Hampton said he had wounded 3,000 to 4,000 bluecoats in the Carolinas alone).

Sherman wrote a friend during the week:

> I confess, without shame, I am sick and tired of fighting—its glory is all moonshine; even success the most brilliant is over dead and mangled bodies, with the anguish and lamentations of distant families, appealing to me for sons, husbands and fathers . . . And, so far as I know, all the fighting men of our army want peace; and it is only those who have never heard a shot, never heard the shrieks and groans of the wounded and lacerated (friend or foe), that cry aloud for more blood, more vengeance, more desolation. I *know* the rebels are whipped to death, and I declare before God, as a man and a soldier, I will not strike a foe who stands unarmed and submissive before me, but would rather say—"Go, and sin no more."

Sherman was ordered to prepare his troops for a grand review, their final duty of the war. The general reported to Grant:

> I will be all ready by Wednesday, though in the rough. Troops have not been paid for eight or ten months, and clothing may be bad, but a better set of arms or legs cannot be displayed on this continent. Send me all orders and letters that you may have for me, and let some newspaper know that the vandal Sherman is encamped near the Canal bridge . . . where his friends, if any, can find him. Though in disgrace, he is untamed and unconquered.

By now, in fact, the Eastern press was troubled with second thoughts on the Sherman affair. Horace Greeley of the *New York Tribune* declared that Sherman's truce terms may have been unwise, but they were not treasonable; he branded as "flapdaddle" Stanton's charge that Sherman had conspired to help Jefferson Davis escape. There was also support for Sherman within the Cabinet. Secretary of the Navy Gideon Welles said, "We were all imposed upon by Stanton for a purpose. He and the Radicals were opposed to the mild policy of President Lincoln on which Sherman acted, and which Stanton opposed and was determined to defeat."

Sherman had written Ellen that she should not travel to Washington for the review, since he was living in "a common tent, and overwhelmed with papers and business," but now he changed his mind and wired her in Lancaster, asking her to hurry to Washington so that she could see his army parade down Pennsylvania Avenue in its final appearance.

The general wrote Oliver Howard, who had been assigned to head the Freedman's Bureau and oversee the transition of four million blacks from slavery to freedom, to say that the task could not have been placed in "more charitable and more conscientious hands," but added: "I hardly know whether to congratulate you or not . . . So far as man can do, I believe you will, but I fear you have Hercules' task . . . though in the kindness of your heart you would alleviate all the ills of humanity, it is not in your power . . . to fulfill one-tenth of the part of the expectations of those who framed the bureau . . . It is simply impracticable . . ."

Sherman realized that political leaders would frustrate Howard's efforts and that Southerners would resist racial equality to the end. The general also felt that most former slaves were poorly prepared for new lives.

Grant called Uncle Billy into the city for a long talk and tried in vain to persuade him to make peace with Stanton. When he emerged, Sherman was summoned to the home of Andrew Johnson, in a house at Fifteenth and H streets. The President rose from his chair, and with both hands outstretched to greet him, said, "General Sherman, I am *very glad* to see you—*very glad*—and *I mean what I say.*" The President assured him that he had not known of Stanton's attack until it appeared in the newspapers. Johnson was friendly and appeared to understand Sherman's purpose in the original peace terms extended to Joe Johnston.

His staff saw little of Sherman in these days, but in their brief meetings Hitchcock saw that the general was in high spirits. "Stanton's already backing down," Sherman said. "He's sent half a dozen people to me to try and make it up —but I'll have nothing to do with him until he makes public apology."

The general's brother John tried to make peace. Stanton, he said, was frightened and embittered by the Lincoln assassination plot. Sherman was not appeased. He scoffed at the cordons of guards around homes of Cabinet members and said there was no reason for such "a sense of insecurity."

The troops spent their time sprucing up for the parade, mending clothes, currying animals and cleaning weapons. There was an issue of new uniforms on May 22, but the supply was soon exhausted. Bliss Morse of the 105th Illinois got only a pair of pants and socks, and joined thousands of others along the banks of the Potomac to wash his worn uniform. Some, like Alonzo Brown of the 4th Minnesota, resented the least addition of new finery: "We wanted to go on the review in our old clothes." Many officers—those who still had money —bought new outfits in Washington stores.

The penniless were angry and resentful. Alonzo Brown complained to his family:

> No pay since Aug. 31, 1864 . . . somebody is to blame for this great crime . . . many families are suffering at home for want of money due the men in the field . . . our men are still trying to live on the same short rations of crackers and fresh beef. The Army of the Potomac is fat and hearty and have drawn pay up to January 1 and I think March 1. Do you wonder that men are indignant? Shame on a government that uses the best army it ever had in such a damnable manner.

On the day that some of his troops drew their fresh clothing, Sherman was summoned to appear before the Senate's Committee on the Conduct of the War, whose chairman was the grim Radical leader from Ohio, Benjamin Wade. This committee, dominated by Radicals, hoped to establish through Sherman's testimony that his first lenient agreement with Joseph Johnston had been dictated by Lincoln—and thus demonstrate that the murdered President had been incompetent to direct Reconstruction. Sherman's manner was one of cold defiance. He recounted his negotiations with Johnston under Wade's questioning, and managed to denounce Halleck and brand Stanton as "a two-faced scoundrel." He avoided all mention of Lincoln until, as he was explaining that he had invited Zebulon Vance to continue as governor of North Carolina, he said, "I did so because President Lincoln had encouraged me to a similar course with the Governor of Georgia when I was at Atlanta . . . Had President Lincoln lived, I know he would have sustained me."

Wade was not content, but forced Sherman to recall his meeting with Lincoln aboard the *River Queen* shortly before Johnston surrendered. Wade then asked: "In those conferences, was any mention made with you and General Grant . . . in regard to the manner of arranging business with the Confederacy in regard to the terms of peace?"

Sherman said promptly—and evasively—that there had been "nothing definite. It was simply a matter of general conversation, nothing specific and definite." (Only the day before, Sherman had written his friend General Stewart Van Vliet that he had "strictly, literally" followed Lincoln's policy in dealing with Johnston.)

The committee excused the difficult general, whose testimony was published the next day. His friend Colonel Markland, the army postmaster, who felt that Sherman was assuming a sacrificial burden in order to protect the reputation of Lincoln, begged the general to allow him to give the truth to newspapers. Sherman asked him to remain silent. (Since Grant was almost mute, there was an impression that the dead President had imposed secrecy of his peacemaking plans on the generals. But though Sherman's true motives were to remain a riddle, it was clear that he had not, as he thought, followed Lincoln's policies in dealing with defeated Southerners. The President's views were much more astute and pragmatic than those of the general.)

Sherman turned gratefully to the final reviews of the two conquering Federal armies. The Easterners of the Army of the Potomac paraded on May 23, a hot, windless day filled with the roaring of crowds. The city was still draped in mourning for Lincoln, and the dead President's widow left the city that day. Sherman's soldiers, who were forced to wait another day before they could parade, noted mournfully that the capital's grog shops were closed.

Sherman sat with other dignitaries in the reviewing stand before the White House as General George Meade's infantry streamed past for six hours, its men faultlessly dressed, even to white gloves. Sherman's critical eye detected ragged footsteps, and he diagnosed the trouble as the "pampered and well-fed bands taught to play the very latest operas." Uncle Billy cringed inwardly when the Eastern soldiers came abreast of the reviewing platform and "turned their eyes around like country gawks to look at the big people on the stand." He resolved that his troops would commit no such unsoldierly breaches tomorrow.

Sherman turned to the grizzled George Meade: "I'm afraid my poor tatterdemalion corps will make a poor appearance tomorrow when contrasted with yours."

Meade's air was condescending. "The people in Washington are so fond of the army that they will make allowances," he said. "You needn't be afraid."

Sherman gave him a grim, wrinkled smile.

General Augur, commander of the District of Columbia, came up to offer his two magnificent concert bands for the appearance of the Western army the next day. Sherman declined, and said he would rely on his campaign-worn regimental bands.

Before leaving the White House grounds, he sent word to his officers: "Be careful about your intervals tomorrow. Don't let your men look back over their shoulders. I'll give you plenty of time to go to the Capitol and see everything afterward, but let them keep their eyes fifteen feet to the front and march by in the old customary way."

It was almost as if the conquest of Washington's throngs had become as vital as victory in the field.

Sherman's bummers were confident that they would outshine the Easterners, for whom they had a good-humored contempt. Private Alonzo Brown explained to his family in Wisconsin: "The Potomac Army has no doubt had some hard fighting, but it has been on a different scale than ours and most of it was done in the newspapers."

In the late afternoon of May 23 three corps of Sherman's army marched from their Virginia camps across the Potomac bridges and bivouacked in the streets around the Capitol to be fresh for the review the next morning. Thousands of men wore new uniforms, but many were still in rags and some were still barefoot. General Hazen tried valiantly to force men of the XV Corps to trim their hair, but they still wore lank, dirty locks over their shoulders. There were not enough uniforms to go around in the 50th Illinois, where some wore new hats and shoes with tattered coats and pants. The regiment was disgusted with the "half and half" uniforms, and longed for its "old ragged greasy clothing." Still, there were many who had no new issue. Charles Herbert saw many of "Sherman's wolves" barefoot, "with ragged pants tied around the legs, or pinned together with sticks; hair sticking through their hats; all looking lean and hungry."

A Washington official pressed Sherman for a roster of his troops, to be distributed among the crowds of spectators, but Uncle Billy scoffed, "There's no damned printing press with this army."

By five o'clock the morning of May 24, Sherman's sergeants were barking roll calls, and the column soon moved into position to begin the march. The *New York World* reporter wrote: "Directly all sorts of colors, over a wild monotony of columns, began to sway to and fro, up and down, and like the uncoiling of a tremendous python, the Army of Sherman winds into Washington."

The morning was bright and the air cooler than on the previous day, but streets were dustier despite water wagons that trundled past. By eight o'clock the head of the column had formed ranks behind the Capitol. These men were astonished to see Sherman there in a new uniform, almost unrecognizable, "dressed up after dingy carelessness for years." A young woman slipped a wreath over the neck of the general's horse, and the mount was soon draped with flowers and greens. A woman tried to give Uncle Billy another wreath, but his horse shied and Sherman waved her to the one-armed Howard, who was barely able to manage the reins of his restless gray stallion.

A signal gun fired at nine o'clock, and the 9th Illinois Mounted Infantry led the way out into Pennsylvania Avenue, followed by Sherman and Howard and their staffs. Sherman's face broke into "a grim smile" as the army went forward to face the enormous crowd.

The head of the column rounded the Capitol, and farm boys in ranks stared nervously down across a sea of spectators that wound out of sight up the distant hill toward the White House. Banners hung overhead: THE PUBLIC SCHOOLS OF WASHINGTON WELCOME THE HEROES OF THE REPUBLIC. HONOR TO THE BRAVE!

Regiments cheered as they marched beneath the streamers. At intervals thereafter, spontaneous bursts of wild cheering rose from the ranks as excited marchers realized that this was the climax of the long miles, the chicken stealing, the looting of plantations, the rowdy camaraderie of camp, the skirmishes and battles.

Alonzo Brown of the 4th Minnesota recalled the moment: "The band at once struck up a beautiful march, the column moved . . . like one footfall—Rap! rap! rap! down Pennsylvania Avenue. The pavements are lined with spectators; boys as thick as locusts; windows crowded with ladies; roofs of the houses are jammed full of people. Everybody is looking on with astonishment and awe as the Army of the Tennessee, formed into a monster column, closed in mass, full company front, moved down the avenue. The earth shakes under our feet . . . The air is bristling with bayonets . . . "

Pioneers passed, carrying picks and axes over their shoulders; there were two pontoons, one of them stripped to its skeleton to reveal its construction. The regimental flags were in tatters, some of them mere shreds of fluttering color. The flag of one Illinois regiment was "hardly enough to wad a gun." Many of the regiments were small, fewer than three hundred men.

The 7th Iowa was far behind the leaders as it wheeled onto Pennsylvania Avenue. Samuel Mahon, riding near the head of his men, looked ahead: "For a mile you could see it . . . a moving wall of bright blue tipped with glittering steel, every man keeping step, the whole looking like one connected body." Now and then, as the ragged flag of the 7th went by, someone shouted, "What regiment is that?" The endless refrain followed the hurrying column down the street as each unit passed: "What regiment?" Women shouted and waved, and Mahon was tantalized because he could not turn his head, even when a girl sent him a wreath of flowers to hang across his horse's neck. "I only hope she was young and good looking," he said.

When the 50th Illinois heard the cry, "What regiment," a deep voice called, "Same old regiment! New clothes!" The nearby crowd broke into cheers. Some men of this regiment were unseen by spectators, men so nearly naked that they were kept in camp, ordered to hide in wagons to escape public notice.

Sobbing women lifted babies above the crowd to see the troops. In the ranks of the 19th Illinois, Private J. W. Anderson heard people praying. Bands played the national anthem or "The Battle Hymn of the Republic," and the crowd sang with them. Hands reached from the throng, stuffed flowers into musket barrels, and tossed them about the necks of men and horses until some regimental bands looked like "moving flower gardens." The street was soon covered with flowers.

The farm boys were not prepared for such a vast throng. Harvey M. Trimble of the 93rd Illinois described it:

> Both sides of the broad and beautiful Pennsylvania Avenue, from one end to the other, were literally packed with men and women from the building lines to the two sides of the moving column. All the porches and balconies, and all the doors and windows, were filled . . . The tops of houses and business buildings . . . were covered with multitudes of people. And, for blocks upon blocks, away from the line of march, there were still additional multitudes upon multitudes. And all these people had flags and banners of all sizes, and wreaths and bouquets and flowers, of all colors . . . and parasols and handkerchiefs, in red, white and blue, and all manner of devices, and all of them were happy and enthusiastic and exultant.

It was as if the nation had gathered in the capital's streets to celebrate the triumphant close of the war which had so nearly wrecked the Union.

Spectators and marchers alike sensed that these men were unlike the Easterners who had passed the day before. *The New York Times* reporter described them as "tall, erect, broadshouldered men, the peasantry of the west, the best material on earth for armies. The brigades move by with an elastic swinging step."

Frank Malcom of the 7th Iowa wrote: "The difference in the two armies is this: They have remained in camp and lived well; we have marched, fought & gone hungry and ended the war."

Samuel Mahon, who had seen the Easterners march the previous day, now swelled with pride in Sherman's army: "The discipline was better, the marching better . . . our men larger, tougher and sinewy . . . then we marched with heads straight to the front. . . . we were there to be seen and not to see."

Even the Eastern regiments of the XX Corps—New Yorkers, Pennsylvanians, New Jerseyans, Connecticut and Massachusetts men—seemed to have taken on the look of their comrades: "They walked like westerners."

There was an odd cadence of sound as marching units swept through the crowds; bursts of cheering ceased abruptly when spectators caught sight of the rear of each brigade, where ambulances jolted along with stretchers lashed to their sides, the canvas darkly splotched with old bloodstains. The hush was then broken by roars of delighted laughter as the mess attendants came into view, cooks and foragers with their families—towering Negro men astride miniature white mules, their feet almost dragging the ground, small black boys perched like acrobats on the pack saddles amid pots and baskets strapped to mules. A menagerie of raccoons, geese, turkeys and roosters rode with them, the cocks alternately crowing and staring at the throng with bright eyes. A few goats rode amid the litter in precarious balance, bleating at the crowd.

Two oxen shambled by, "Chattanooga" and "Chickamauga," their horns tied with scarlet ribbon, soldiers' pets rescued from army butchers long ago in Tennessee, pampered along the thousand-mile route as if they had been kittens.

Then came Kilpatrick's cavalry, mounted on the finest horses from Georgia and the Carolinas, every mane smartly clipped to the crest, saddles and bridles polished by long service. Sunlight glanced from the nicked and stained blades of sabers carried on the shoulders of the troopers. The men rode stirrup to stirrup, their files as precise as those of the infantry, staring sternly forward through storms of cheering, ignoring the tossing of flowers. Only Conyngham noted lapses of discipline: Now and then the veteran looters glanced longingly at the windows of jewelry stores as they passed.

The column marched beneath other banners: HAIL TO THE WESTERN HEROES. THE ONLY DEBT THE NATION CAN NEVER PAY IS GRATITUDE TO ITS DEFENDERS.

Marchers caught sight of names that stirred memories of strangely distant places, as if from a campaign trail on another planet, fought by some other army in another age: DONELSON, SHILOH, VICKSBURG, CHATTANOOGA, ATLANTA, SAVANNAH, BENTONVILLE.

The troops did not cheer as they glimpsed these banners.

* * *

As the column neared the Treasury building, Conyngham noted with surprise that Sherman was actually handsome, a slight, erect figure on his gleaming bay, quite at ease in his new uniform. Uncle Billy's nervous gestures had disappeared, and he no longer wore the grimace of the clenched smile. He rode calmly at the slow pace, smiling occasionally and nodding into the sea of faces, his ears ringing with the endless din of cheers. The reporter hardly recognized in him "the fierce leader of the march."

Sherman had disciplined himself to keep his eyes front, but the temptation to turn his head grew with each swelling of cheers and laughter in the rear. In rare intervals when he could hear the footfall of the column, their boots seemed to be striking the earth as one, but he was consumed with curiosity to know whether his men were marching well. As he rode up the gentle slope beyond the Treasury building, Uncle Billy could bear it no longer. He disregarded his order and wheeled to look back at his troops. His eyes were suddenly wet. He saw that they were marching as they had never marched before: "The sight was simply magnificent. The column was compact, and the glittering muskets looked like a solid mass of steel, moving with the regularity of a pendulum."

He was to remember this sight as "the happiest and most satisfactory moment of my life."

The column came within sight of the reviewing stand. Sherman looked up to a window to see the mutilated face of Secretary of State W. H. Seward, weird and forbidding, clamped with steel and rubber bands and swathed in bandages, the result of an assassination attempt and injuries in a runaway carriage. Sherman waved his hat and Seward slowly lifted a pale hand.

As he approached the reviewing stand, Sherman adjusted the unfamiliar stiff-brimmed hat on his head and saluted with his sword.

Theodore Upson of the 100th Indiana, who was just behind Sherman, wrote: "President Johnson, General Grant, foreign officers and nearly all the great men of the nation and many from other nations, they all rose to their feet and with bared heads cheered and cheered."

Upson glanced down the line of his platoon and saw that every man had eyes front, all were in perfect step, "and on the faces of the men was what one might call a *glory look* . . . My, but I was proud of our boys."

The nearby *New York World* reporter noted: "The acclamation given Sherman was without precedent . . . greater than the day before . . . the whole assemblage raised and waved and shouted as if he had been the personal friend of each and every one of them . . . Sherman was the idol of the day."

His wife and young son Tom, who had arrived in Washington at the last moment, caught their first glimpse of him in eighteen months: the general seemed quite thin to Ellen, and his beard was grizzled. The crowds cheered Howard, Logan, Hazen, Jeff Davis, and Mother Bickerdyke, a formidable Illinois widow who had nursed troops through the campaign as far as Atlanta, organizing hospitals, civilian knitters and bandage-rollers back home, defying Sherman when officers complained of her interference, until he had surrendered: "She outranks me. I can't do a thing." Mother Bickerdyke was a symbol of the army's triumph now, a homely but regal figure in her sunbonnet and calico dress, riding sidesaddle among her adopted sons.

Abruptly a deeper roar engulfed the square. Officers bellowed an order to their men, and the troops, "without turning their heads, their eyes still front, relax their imperturbable faces and break into wild yells, tearing off their hats with free hands and waving them in the air—their eyes still front." It was a cheer for Grant and President Johnson, but also for Sherman and the Western army—its survivors and those it had left behind. It was a moment of deep emotion for the men. A private of the 12th Wisconsin said, "We couldn't look at the reviewing stand. If Lincoln had been there I'm afraid our line would have broken up."

The column seemed to move more swiftly now. General Carl Schurz was thrilled by the sight of the veterans marching at their stride—they were "nothing but bone and muscle and skin under their tattered battle-flags."

The German ambassador sat beside Bishop Edward R. Ames, an old frontier evangelist. When the XV Corps was passing, the German said, "An army like that could whip all Europe." When the XX Corps had gone by, he said, "An army like that could whip the world." And when the XIV Corps came past, he said, "An army like that could whip the devil."

Sherman's old friend Tom Corwin, who had been governor of Ohio, senator and secretary of the Treasury, was deeply moved as he watched the thousands of tall figures swing by. "They march like the lords of the world," he said.

The general left the column for the reviewing stand, where he kissed his wife and son and greeted Ellen's father, Senator Thomas Ewing. He then shook hands with President Johnson and Grant. Next in line stood Edwin Stanton, his round, whiskered face, never very expressive, now immobile and watchful. Sherman stiffened at the sight of Stanton.

The secretary held out his hand, but the general looked coldly past him, waiting for a long moment to make clear the pointed insult, and then moved on. A murmuring undertone passed through the crowd nearby. E. J. Copp, a War Department telegrapher who sat a few feet away, had a clear view of Uncle Billy's face as he spurned the secretary's handshake: "Sherman's face was scarlet and his red hair seemed to stand on end." Noah Brooks, a reporter who observed the scene through binoculars, pondered whether Sherman's flush denoted anger or triumphal revenge.

The gentle Ellen Sherman, mortified by her husband's public insult to the secretary of war, sent Mrs. Stanton a bouquet the following day as "a mute appeal for forgiveness"—and called on the Stantons a few nights later in a further attempt to make peace between the two stubborn and rather vain men. Stanton assured Ellen that he bore the general no ill will, but Sherman nursed his resentment for years.

Sherman turned to review his troops, a post he kept for hours, smiling to officers he recognized, pointing out regiments to those on the stand, now and then saluting. His troops were, he said, "in my judgment the most magnificent army in existence."

Many states had flown their streamers near the stand, and the regiments sent up roars of greeting as each of them caught sight of its home banner. The men could see little else. Samuel Toombs of the 13th New Jersey had the odd sensation that he was being swept through a sea of faces that were afloat in flags, ribbons and evergreens, all drifting past on the periphery of his vision.

Sherman was touched by the crowd's reaction: "Many good people . . . had looked upon our Western army as a sort of mob; but the world then saw, and recognized . . . that it was an army . . . well organized, well commanded and disciplined; and there was no wonder that it had swept through the south like a tornado.

"For six and a half hours that strong tread of the Army of the West resounded along Pennsylvania Avenue. Not a soul of that vast crowd of spectators left his place . . . "

As each regiment passed the White House grounds, the men resumed the long, easy route step they knew so well—but for most of them there was no halt for rest here. The column wound back across the river into Virginia before ranks were broken.

Until now the troops were so excited by their reception that they had not felt thirst or the heat of the sun, but by noon they had begun to sweat. By the time the 129th Illinois came within sight of the White House, the crowds had become unmanageable and pushed out into the street. For a quarter of a mile they had to force their way through, barely able to maintain their company fronts. When they passed the White House, some of these troops were so worn that they fell out of ranks and flopped on the grass, where women and children passed them milk and water.

Only at four-thirty, when the last of the pack mules and their Negro riders had gone from sight, did Sherman attempt to leave the stand. He was almost engulfed by the throng. Telegrapher Copp watched from the platform as people threw bouquets upon him, put wreaths over his head and shook his hand furiously. "At first he was affable, then he grew less cordial as the crowds crushed in. He pushed down the steps, step by step, and refused proffered hands, finally exclaiming, 'Damn you, get out of the way, damn you!' "

Sherman left the army after the parade and took Ellen and Tom to a house provided for them in the city. The next night, when he had gone to the Metropolitan Hotel with other generals and politicians for an impromptu celebration, he was cornered by admirers. A large crowd led by a band first besieged Sherman's house and then marched to the hotel and clamored until the general appeared. He spoke in nervous bursts: "I'm sorry I wasn't at home when you called tonight . . . I am here a stranger in a strange house . . . but I thank you for your kindness to me and the army I command."

He was interrupted by cheers.

"There are too many noisy omnibuses and streetcars in this town for me."

Laughter.

"We like the pine woods better, for there we can be heard, and felt, too."

Cheers drowned his voice: "Hurrah for Sherman! He's the boy for the rebels!"

"There are no rebels now. They have gone up."

Laughter.

"I have not and will not make a speech, but you must regard my further silence for what I mean. . . . For when I speak, I speak to the point, and when I act, I act to the point. If a man minds his own business I let him alone, but if he crosses my path, he must get out of the way. I want peace and freedom for every man to go where he pleases . . . "

A voice called from the crowd to ask about gossip that the army would march to Mexico to drive out Emperor Maximilian: "How about going to Mexico, General?"

"You can go there and you can go to hell if you want to!"

He was cheered loudly, the band played a march, and Sherman disappeared.

Howard and Slocum were called out and said a few words, but the rapidly growing crowd shouted for Sherman once more. He reappeared, grinning broadly through the short beard, his red hair abristle in all directions.

"I don't intend to make a speech," he said, "but merely to say that I'm a thousand times grateful to you—I repeat it from my heart —grateful for the magnificent reception you gave us yesterday."

He would say no more, but waved and retreated into the hotel.

A few days later Sherman wrote an affectionate farewell and had it distributed to his troops. It was almost as if he already felt nostalgia for the days of the long march:

> The time has come for us to part. Our work is done, and armed enemies no longer defy us. Some of you will go to your homes, and others will be retained in military service. . . .
>
> How far the operations of this army contributed to the final overthrow of the Confederacy . . . must be judged by others, not by us; but you have done all that men could do . . . and we have a right to join in the universal joy that fills our land because the war is over. . . .
>
> Your general now bids you farewell, with the full belief that, as

> in war you have been good soldiers, so in peace you will make good citizens; and if, unfortunately, new war should arise in our country, "Sherman's army" will be the first to buckle on its old armor and come forth to defend and maintain the government of our inheritance.

In the twenty-six years of life remaining to him, Sherman served his country as chief of the army, as the most popular toastmaster of his day, and as a perennial presidential possibility.

He rose to the rank of full general in the wake of Grant, but out of distaste for the social life of Washington officialdom, he peremptorily moved army headquarters to St. Louis, where he lived for several years before his retirement.

Both Democrats and Republicans sought to send him to the White House in successive presidential seasons, but he resisted with a ferocity unequaled in the country's political history.

His most famous utterance on the subject was, "I will not accept if nominated and will not serve if elected." That was not enough, for he was wooed by both parties until near the end. He scorned them variously: "I would account myself a fool, a madman, an ass, to embark anew, at sixty-five years of age, in a career that may, at any moment, become tempest-tossed by the perfidy, the defalcation, the dishonesty or neglect of any one of a hundred thousand subordinates utterly unknown to the President of the United States."

"No, I wouldn't take it if elected . . . It would kill any man of sensibility in a year."

"It's simply absurd. I wouldn't think of it for the fortieth part of a second. I lead a peaceful life here and if I ran for President I'd wake up some morning and find all over the papers that I'd poisoned my grandmother. Now you know I never saw my mother's mother, but the newspapers would say I killed her, and *prove* it."

He also protested that if he were elected, Ellen would keep the White House filled with priests and arouse the anger of the electorate.

It was as an after-dinner speaker that the nation came to know him best, and his later career became, in the words of a biographer, "one long chicken dinner." He was the rival, if not the superior, of such celebrated contemporaries as Mark Twain and Chauncey M. Depew, who became his intimate friends.

Depew, who thought Sherman "the readiest and most original" of speakers, regarded him as almost superhuman: "I don't believe that he ever made the slightest preparation, but he absorbed, apparently while thinking and while carrying on a miscellaneous conversation with those about him, the spirit of the occasion, and his speech, when finished, seemed to be as much of a surprise to himself as it was to his audience . . . Once I was with him from ten o'clock in the morning until six in the afternoon and he talked without cessation for the whole period . . . I only regretted that the day was limited."

Though he was badgered with invitations to speak from all parts of the country—at the rate of almost one hundred per month—Sherman complained bitterly of his lot, and accepted many of them. Clubs and committees, he growled, would be the death of him. Yet he reveled in his role as a kind of walking oracle of patriotism and law and order, feigning resistance all the while.

He once replied to an invitation from a county fair in Illinois: "I have a family of six children and seven grandchildren. Now the question is, Shall I abandon them, take to the road and consume all my time? Were you to see my mail for any three days in succession you would exclaim, 'For God's sake allow an old soldier a little rest.' " He also despised the handshaking that accompanied his appearances, and said he had lost a fingernail and almost lost a finger among the after-dinner mobs. At a veterans' reunion in Milwaukee he faced a crowd with his hands jammed in his pockets and shouted, "Get out! This is no place to shake hands. Come down to the hotel. I'll hire a man to shake hands for me."

Old soldiers and their welfare became his chief concern outside his large and "expensive" family. The doorbell of his home rang frequently each day to announce the coming of some veteran, usually one in search of a handout. Sherman said he gave about a third of his meager income to needy veterans. He marched in numberless parades, always in the plain blouse of a private adorned with his four silver stars. It was to a veterans' group, in 1880, that he made his celebrated and casual remark, "War is hell," and he continually reminded his audiences that it was little else. "I think we understand what military fame is," he once said. "To be killed on the field of battle and have our names spelled wrong in the newspapers." Again, he said: "War is usually made by civilians bold and defiant in the beginning but when the storm comes they generally go below." He also said, somewhat disparagingly, "What is strategy? Common sense applied to the art of war. You've got to do something. You can't go around asking corporals and sergeants. You must make it out in your own mind."

The only office he ever sought was that of president of the Society of the Army of the Tennessee, which he held from 1869 until his death. And he continued to relive the Civil War: "Now the truth is we fought the holiest fight ever fought on God's earth." And though he opposed the Fourteenth Amendment, which assured Negro voting rights, and had numerous Southern friends, he despised the Confederacy to the day of his death: "How any Southern gentleman can still boast of 'the lost cause' or speak of it in language other than that of shame and sorrow passes my understanding," he said.

Ironically enough, the South respected and admired Sherman because of his resistance to Negro voting rights and a harsh Reconstruction—but he lost this friendship with the publication of his *Memoirs* in 1875. His two-volume work was a model of its kind, candid, bluff and unadorned, assessing the roles of individuals and governments alike without sentiment. The book raised howls from wounded contemporaries, including Jefferson Davis and a number of Federal generals. Southerners, outraged by his realistic account of his predatory march and his curt dismissal of the Confederacy as a kind of idiotic and criminal conspiracy, made Sherman their *bête noire.* But the Northern public, which learned for the first time of his rational and highly perceptive prewar statements, took Sherman to its heart—and there was an immediate revival of the presidential boom, which became more insistent than ever.

The *Memoirs* were challenged as inaccurate and self-serving by an army staff officer, but Sherman dismissed this as the work of disgruntled contemporaries at headquarters, and the complaints drew little attention.

After retirement from the army, Sherman found St. Louis "too slow," and he moved to New York, where he blossomed as a first-nighter, a founder of The Players Club and an habitué of the Union League Club. He was lionized by the city's theatrical set and by business and society leaders. For the last three or four years of his life he lived in a large house at 74 West Seventy-first Street, where he occasionally entertained—but frequently became a hermit. He developed a habit of slipping away to read in his basement office, chiefly the novels of Dickens and the poetry of Robert Burns.

The general's appearance became amazingly more youthful during the seventies and eighties. Wrinkles disappeared from his face, and he was as spry and active as ever. He became a phenomenal attraction to women. His old songwriter, S.H.M. Byers, who had become consul in Switzerland, saw the old man on a European tour in 1871 and reported: "I never saw a man so run after by women in my life. When he was leaving a train at Bern a whole crowd of women, old and young, pretty and ugly, children and all, kissed him."

Orators at meetings of veterans often hailed him as "that great American soldier who whipped every foeman who stood before him and kissed every girl that he met." Cadet Charles King, who met Sherman when the general was on a visit to West Point, remarked, "What an eye he had for pretty girls!" Thomas Bryan of Chicago, attending a White House reception in the early seventies, noted that Sherman "amused himself and everybody else by his frolicsome snatching of kisses from young women, whose ringing laugh attested their willing tribute to his age and distinction . . . If all the fair of our land had but one pair of lips and Sherman were anywhere within reach, terrific would be the concussion."

But as the years passed, much of Sherman's time was spent at funerals of old friends—Grant, Logan, Kilpatrick, Thomas, Blair, Sheridan, Burnside and Hancock. Sherman said that he and Stanton became friendly before the secretary's death—though there is little evidence of that elsewhere—and he sent the widow a generous note when his old adversary died.

At last, when he was sixty-nine, he told Ellen that he would attend no more funerals of generals. "I'll attend my own funeral, but must be excused from others." A few weeks later Ellen herself was dead, and Sherman was left broken in spirit and health, weakened by his lifelong ailment, asthma.

In February 1891, Sherman caught a severe cold while attending a theater party and a wedding, and within a few days he was dead of some respiratory condition diagnosed as asthma. His funeral services, which he had hoped would be simple, were attended by a crush of mourners. Some 30,000 veterans and active-duty soldiers marched in his procession, and President Harrison, ex-Presidents Hayes and Cleveland, and many Cabinet officers appeared.

Sherman's old opponent Joseph E. Johnston, who was among the crowd, stood bareheaded as an honorary pallbearer despite the urging of a friend that he wear his hat. The eighty-two-year-old

Johnston replied, "If I were in his place, and he were standing here in mine, he would not put on his hat." The old Confederate was dead of pneumonia ten days later.

Sherman was buried in St. Louis beneath a stone of his design, which was covered with the corps insignia of his old marching army.

Among the eulogies raised to the departed general, the terse words of his friend Whitelaw Reid seemed to summarize most perceptively the mercurial Sherman: "He never acknowledged an error and never repeated it."

Bibliography

This account of Sherman's march is based upon eyewitness accounts too numerous to detail here. No previous attempt has been made to present the march in the words of these hundreds of witnesses and participants. Most of those previously unused by historians are in Midwestern historical societies, and though individually of minor importance, contribute to an understanding of this climactic episode of the war.

In lieu of footnotes, this unconventional bibliography offers a guide to the accounts of participants, both Federal and Confederate, arranged alphabetically. Except as otherwise indicated, accounts by Southern women appear in the following: Mrs. Alfred P. Aldrich, *Our Women in the War* (Charleston, S.C.: 1885); Lucy L. Anderson, *North Carolina Women of the Confederacy* (Fayetteville, N.C.: 1926); U. R. Brooks, *Stories of the Confederacy* (Columbia, S.C.: 1912); F. B. Simkins and J. W. Patton, *The Women of the Confederacy* (Richmond: 1936); Mrs. Thomas Taylor et al., *South Carolina Women in the Confederacy* (Columbia, S.C.: 1903); *War Days in Fayetteville, N.C.* (Fayetteville: 1910). These sources are hereafter referred to as *Aldrich, Anderson, Brooks Stories, Simkins, Taylor* and *War Days.* A valuable modern compendium of these accounts is Katharine M. Jones, *When Sherman Came* (Indianapolis: 1964).

Participants and Eyewitnesses

CONFEDERATE

Aldrich, Mrs. Alfred P. *Our Women in the War.* Charleston, S.C., 1885.

Anderson, Mrs. John H. *Confederate Veteran,* Vols. 32 (1924), 35 (1927), 36 (1928).

Anderson, Mrs. Kirby-Smith. *Reminiscences of Confederate Soldiers,* Vol. XII. Georgia Department of Archives and History, Atlanta.

Anderson, Lucy London. *North Carolina Women of the Confederacy.* Fayetteville, N.C., 1926.

Andrews, Eliza F. *The Wartime Journal of a Georgia Girl,* ed. Spencer E. King, Jr. Macon, 1960.

Andrews, M.P. *The Women of the South in War Times.* Baltimore, 1923.

Andrews, R.Q. *Reminiscences of Confederate Soldiers,* Vol. XI. Georgia Department of Archives and History, Atlanta.

Anonymous girl in Winnsboro, S.C. *Taylor.*

Anonymous mother to daughter "Gracia." Manuscript Division, South Caroliniana Collection, University of South Carolina Library, Columbia.

Anonymous refugee in Lancaster, S.C. *Aldrich.*

Anonymous woman's account, Fayetteville, N.C. Copied in Emma Mordecai, Diary. Southern Historical Collection, University of North Carolina Library, Chapel Hill.

Barnett, Mary A. *Confederate Veteran,* Vol. 7 (1899).

Baugh, Willie G. *Correspondence.* Emory University Library, Atlanta.

Bennett, A.O. *Reminiscences of Confederate Soldiers,* Vol. VII. Georgia Department of Archives and History, Atlanta.

Blackburn, J.K.P. "Reminiscences of the Terry Rangers," *Southwestern Historical Society Quarterly,* Vol. 22 (1918).

Bonner, James C., ed. *The Journal of a Milledgeville Girl.* Athens, Ga., 1964.

Boyd, David F. Memoirs (manuscript). Walter L. Fleming, Nashville.

Brooks, James H. *Confederate Bible Records,* Vol. IX. Georgia Department of Archives and History, Atlanta.

Brooks, U.R., ed. *Stories of the Confederacy.* Columbia, S.C., 1912.

Brown, Mrs. Daniel. *Taylor.*

Bryce, Mrs. Campbell. "Personal Experiences . . . " *South Carolina Pamphlets,* Vols. 1–17. Philadelphia, 1894.

Buford, M.M. *Confederate Veteran,* Vol. 28 (1920).

Burge, Dolly S.L. "Diary . . . ," ed. James I. Robertson, Jr. *Georgia Historical Quarterly,* XLV (December 1961).

Butler, General Matthew C. *Confederate Veteran,* Vol. 13 (1900).

Campbell, Alice. *War Days.*

Canning, Nora. *Aldrich.*

Carroll, James P. "Report of Committee Appointed . . . in Relation to the Destruction of Columbia, S.C. . . . " *Southern Historical Society Papers,* Vol. 8 (1880).

Carroll, Lilla. *Brooks Stories.*

Carter, "Uncle George." *Reminiscences of Confederate Soldiers,* Vol. XII. Georgia Department of Archives and History, Atlanta.

Cay, Raymond. *Reminiscences of Confederate Soldiers,* Vol. XI. Georgia Department of Archives and History, Atlanta.

Chaffin, Reverend W.S. Diary. Duke University Library, Durham, N.C.
Chapman, R.D. *Confederate Veteran,* Vol. 38 (1930).
Chesnut, Mary Boykin. *A Diary from Dixie.* Boston, 1949.
Clark, Walter, ed. *Histories of the Several Regiments . . . from North Carolina . . . ,* 5 vols. Raleigh, 1901.
———. *Papers, 1783–1920.* Manuscript Division, North Carolina Department of Archives and History.
Clark, Walter Augustus. *Under the Stars and Bars . . .* Augusta, Ga., 1900.
Cody, E.L. *Reminiscences of Confederate Soldiers,* Vol. XI. Georgia Department of Archives and History, Atlanta.
Cole, Mrs. B.T. *Reminiscences of Confederate Soldiers,* Vol. XII. Georgia Department of Archives and History, Atlanta.
Collier, Elizabeth. Diary. Southern Historical Collection, University of North Carolina Library, Chapel Hill.
Cook, Anna Maria Green. Diary. Special Collection, University of Georgia Library, Athens.
Cooper, Miss A.C. *Aldrich.*
Cornwell, Mrs. Louise C.R. "Diary." *Diaries of Soldiers and Civilians,* Vol. 13. Georgia Department of Archives and History, Atlanta.
Davis, Jefferson. *Rise and Fall of the Confederate Government,* Vol. 2. New York, 1881.
Dodge, David (pseud.). "Home Scenes at the Fall of the Confederacy." *Atlantic Monthly,* LXIX (May 1892).
"E.L.L." *Aldrich.*
Eckles, J.J. *War Record.* Georgia Department of Archives and History, Atlanta.
Elliott, Mrs. Jane Evans. *Diary,* compiled by Mrs. Jennie E. McNeill. Raleigh, N.C., 1908.
Elmore, Captain A.R. "Testimony about Burning of Columbia." *Confederate Veteran,* Vol. 20 (1912).
Furman, Nancy A. Letter to Jane C. Furman, March 8, 1865. Furman Papers. Furman University Library, Greenville, S.C.
Gardner, Captain G.B. Letter to his wife. Georgia Department of Archives and History, Atlanta.
Gillis, Dan. *Confederate Veteran,* Vol. 18 (1910).
Glassell, Mrs. Janie A. *Confederate Veteran,* Vol. 36 (1928).
Gordon, Eleanor K. *Reminiscences of Sherman's Visit to Savannah.* Georgia Historical Society, Savannah.
Gott, Julia F. Letter to Annie Gott, February 27, 1865. South Caroliniana Collection, University of South Carolina Library, Columbia.
Green, Virginia. *Taylor.*
Hamilton, Posey. *Confederate Veteran,* Vols. 29, 30 (1922).
Hampton, General Wade. "Letter on Burning of Columbia." *Southern Historical Society Papers,* Vol. 7 (1879).

Haney family. *Reminiscences of Confederate Soldiers,* Vol. IX. Georgia Department of Archives and History, Atlanta.

Hargis, O.P. "Reminiscences." Southern Historical Collection, University of North Carolina Library, Chapel Hill.

Harmon, George D. "The Military Experiences of James A. Pfeiffer." *North Carolina Historical Review,* Vol. 32 (1955).

Harper, Major G.W.F. *Confederate Veteran,* Vol. 18 (1910).

Harris, Leroy W. *Reminiscences of Confederate Soldiers,* Vol. IX. Georgia Department of Archives and History, Atlanta.

Hawthorne, Sally. "Reminiscences" (typed copy). North Carolina Department of Archives and History, Raleigh.

Haywood, Richard B. In M. De L. Haywood, *Builders of the Old North State.* Raleigh, N.C., 1968.

Herriott, Robert. *Confederate Veteran,* Vol. 30 (1922).

High, Emma. *Reminiscences of Confederate Soldiers,* Vol. IX. Georgia Department of Archives and History, Atlanta.

Howard, Nelly. In Frances T. Howard, *In and Out of the Lines.* New York, 1905.

Inzer, Lieutenant Colonel John W. *Confederate Veteran,* Vol. 32 (1924).

Jackson, A.J. *Diary* (microfilm). Georgia Department of Archives and History, Atlanta.

Johnston, Joseph E. *Narrative of Military Operations.* New York, 1872.

Jones, Joseph A. *Confederate Veteran,* Vol. 19 (1911).

Kelly, Rufus. Account of in T.D. Tinsley, *Reminiscences of Confederate Soldiers,* Vol. XIII. Georgia Department of Archives and History, Atlanta.

Kyle, Mrs. James. *Aldrich.*

"L.F.J." *Aldrich.*

Law, Agnes. *Southern Historical Society Papers,* Vol. 12 (May 1884).

Lawrence, R. de T. *Confederate Veteran,* Vol. 29 (1921).

LeConte, Emma. *When the World Ended.* New York, 1957.

LeConte, Joseph. *'Ware Sherman.* Berkeley, Calif., 1937.

Lee, Julia. Correspondence. Mrs. J. Hardy Lee Papers, Southern Historical Collection, University of North Carolina Library, Chapel Hill.

Leverette, Mary. Letter to Caroline, March 18, 1865. South Caroliniana Collection, University of South Carolina Library, Columbia.

Logan, Lily. Letter to General T.M. Logan, March 2, 1865. In *My Confederate Girlhood . . . ,* ed. Lily Logan Merrill. Richmond, Va., 1932.

Lovett, Howard M. *Confederate Veteran,* Vol. 26 (1918).

Lynch, Baptista. *Aldrich.*

MacLean, Mrs. Clara P. *Southern Historical Society Papers,* Vol. 13 (1885).

Mallard, Mary Jones, and M.S. Jones. *Yankees A' Coming,* ed. Haskell Monroe. Tuscaloosa, Ala., 1959.

Manley, Emma. *Reminiscences of Confederate Soldiers,* Vol. XIII. Georgia Department of Archives and History, Atlanta.

McCollum, A.S. *Reminiscences of Confederate Soldiers.* Georgia Department of Archives and History, Atlanta.

McCord, Mrs. Louisa Cheves. *Southern Historical Society Papers,* Vol. 8 (1880).

Mills, Rachel Chamblee. Diary. Georgia Department of Archives and History, Atlanta.

Mitchell, Ella. *History Washington County, Georgia.* Atlanta, 1924.

Mordecai, Mrs. Ellen. Letter to Emma Mordecai. Southern Historical Collection, University of North Carolina Library, Chapel Hill.

Morgan, D.B. *Confederate Veteran,* Vol. 32 (1904).

Morgan, James R. *Reminiscences of Confederate Soldiers,* Georgia Department of Archives and History, Atlanta.

O'Bear, Katherine T. *Through the Years in Winnsboro.* Columbia, S.C., 1940.

Olmsted, Charles H. "Memoirs," ed. Lilla Mills Hawes. *Collections of the Georgia Historical Society,* Vol. 14 (1964), Savannah.

Poppenheim, Mary Eleanor. *Taylor.*

Powell, Charles S. "Recollections." *Military Collector and Historian,* Vol. 10 (Summer 1958).

Quillen, Martha A. Letter to Cousin Sallie. Davis-Quillen Papers. Atlanta Historical Society.

Ravenel, Harriott. *Taylor.*

Ravenel, Samuel W. *Confederate Veteran,* Vol. 29 (1921).

Reagan, John H. *Memoirs.* New York, 1906.

Reynolds, H. Clay. *See* DuBose; *Confederate Veteran,* Vol. 20 (1912).

Richardson, Sara Aldrich. *Taylor.*

Riley, Mrs. Pauline B. "Reminiscences." *The Southern Magazine,* Vol. 2, No. 10.

Rowe, Mary. *Confederate Veteran,* Vol. 60 (1932).

Salley, Marian. *Confederate Veteran,* Vol. 32 (1924).

Sams, Sarah Jane. Letter to husband, Robert R. Sams, February 8–13, 1865. Courtesy Therese Sams Colquhoun, Beaufort, S.C.

Sanders, Robert W. *Confederate Veteran,* Vols. 34 (1926), 37 (1929).

Scott, Hugh. *Brooks; Butler.*

Screven, Cornelia. *Aldrich.*

Simkins, Francis, and James W. Patton. *Women of the Confederacy,* Richmond, 1936.

Simms, William G. *The Sack and Destruction of the City of Columbia . . .*

Smith, Jennie Pye. *Reminiscences of Confederate Soldiers,* Vol. III. Georgia Department of Archives and History, Atlanta.

Smith, Mason, ed. *Mason Smith Family Letters.* Columbia, S.C., 1950.

Sosnowski, Mme. Sophie. "Burning of Columbia." *Georgia Historical Quarterly,* Vol. 8, No. 3 (September 1924).

———. *Taylor.*

Spencer, Cornelia P. *The Last 90 Days of the War in North Carolina.* New York, 1866.

Stiles, Captain Robert. Diary. Southern Historical Collection, University of North Carolina Library, Chapel Hill.

Swain, D.L. Papers. Southern Historical Collection, University of North Carolina Library, Chapel Hill.

Tarver, Mrs. Fanny H. *Reminiscences of Confederate Soldiers.* Georgia Department of Archives and History, Atlanta.

Taylor, Richard. *Destruction and Reconstruction.* New York, 1879.

Taylor, Mrs. Thomas, et al. *South Carolina Women in the Confederacy.* Columbia, S.C., 1903.

Thomas, Mrs. Ella Gertrude Clanton. Diary and letter. Duke University Library, Durham, N.C.

Tomb, Captain James H. *Confederate Veteran,* Vol. 32 (1924).

Townsend, Harry C. *Diary.* Richmond, 1907.

Travis, Allie. *Aldrich.*

Trezevant, Daniel H. *The Burning of Columbia*... Columbia, S.C., 1866.

Vance, Zebulon B. Papers. North Carolina Department of Archives and History.

War Days in Fayetteville, N.C. The J.E.B. Stuart Chapter, UDC, Fayetteville, 1910.

Ward, Dallas T. *The Last Flag of Truce.* Franklinton, N.C., 1915.

Waring, Joseph F. Diary. Southern Historical Collection, University of North Carolina Library, Chapel Hill.

Warren, Edward A. *A Doctor's Experiences.* Baltimore, 1885.

Wells, E.L. "A Morning Call on Kilpatrick." *Southern Historical Society Papers,* Vol. 12 (1884).

———. "Who Burnt Columbia?" *Southern Historical Society Papers,* Vol. 10 (1882).

White, Mrs. Thomas. "Reminiscences of Benjamin Jordan." *Reminiscences of Confederate Soldiers,* Vol. IX. Georgia Department of Archives and History, Atlanta.

Wise, John S. *The End of an Era.* New York, 1899.

Worth, Josephine B. "Sherman's Raid." *War Days.*

Worth, Nellie. Correspondence, March 21, 1865. North Carolina Collection, University of North Carolina Library, Chapel Hill.

Participants and Eyewitnesses

FEDERAL

Arbuckle, John C. *Civil War Experiences*... Columbus, Ohio, 1930.

Aten, Henry J. *History of the 85th Illinois Regiment.* Hiawatha, Kans., 1901.

Atkins, Smith D. *History of the 92nd Illinois Volunteers.* Freeport, Ill., 1875.

Ayers, James T. "Diary," *Occasional Publication No. 50, Illinois State Historical Society,* Vol. XXV.

Baker, Francis R. Journal. Illinois State Library, Springfield.

Barber, Lucius. *Army Memoirs.* Chicago, 1890.

Batchelor, John. Diary (manuscript). Illinois State Historical Library, Springfield.

Belknap, Charles Eugene. "Recollections of a Bummer," *The War of the Sixties,* ed. Edward R. Hutchins. New York, 1912.

———. "Bentonville: What a Bummer Knows about It." *Military Order Loyal Legion U.S.,* Washington, D.C., Commandery, 1893 (hereafter *MOLLUS*).

Belknap, W.W. *History of the 15th Regiment Iowa Volunteers.* Keokuk, Iowa, 1887.

Bell, John T. *Tramps and Triumphs of the 2nd Iowa Infantry.* Omaha, 1886.

Bennett, L.G., and W.M. Haigh. *History of the 36th Regiment Illinois Volunteers.* Aurora, 1876.

Benton, Charles Edward. *As Seen from the Ranks.* New York, 1902.

Bircher, William A. *Drummer Boy's Diary.* St. Paul, 1889.

Bishop, Judson W. *The Story of a Regiment.* St. Paul, 1890.

Blake, Ephraim. *A Succinct History of the 28th Iowa Volunteer Infantry.* Belle Plain, Iowa, 1896.

Boies, Andrew J. *The Record of the 33rd Massachusetts Infantry.* Fitchburg, Mass., 1880.

Boyle, John. *Soldiers True.* New York, 1903.

Bradley, George S. *The Star Corps or Notes of an Army Chaplain.* Milwaukee, 1865.

Brant, Jefferson E. *History of the 85th Indiana Volunteer Infantry.* Bloomington, 1902.

Branum, John M. *Letters of Lieutenant J.M. Branum.* New Castle, Pa., 1897.

Brown, Alonzo. *History of the 4th Regiment, Minnesota Volunteers.* St. Paul, 1892.

Brown, Charles S. Correspondence. Duke University Library, Durham, N.C.

Brown, Thaddeus C.S., Samuel J. Murphy, and William G. Putney. *Behind the Guns: History of Battery I, 2nd Regiment, Illinois Light Artillery.* Southern Illinois University Press, Carbondale, 1965.

Bryant, Edwin E. *History of the 3rd Regiment Wisconsin Volunteers.* Madison, 1911.
Burton, Dr. E.P. Diary (typescript). Historical Records Survey, Des Moines, 1939.
Byers, S.H.M. *What I Saw in Dixie.* Dansville, New York, 1868.
———. *With Fire and Sword.* New York, 1911.
Calkins, William W. *The History of the 104th Regiment, Illinois Volunteer Infantry.* Chicago, 1895.
Canfield, Silas S. *History of the 21st Regiment.* Toledo, 1893.
Carpenter, Frank B. *Six Months in the White House.* New York, 1920.
Chamberlin, William H. *History of the 81st Ohio.* Cincinnati, 1865.
Chapman, Horatio Dana. *Civil War Diary . . . of a 49'er.* Hartford, 1929.
Chase, John A. *History of the 14th Ohio.* Toledo, 1881.
Cody, A.D. Diary (manuscript). Minnesota Historical Society.
Coffin, Charles C. *The Boys of '61.* Boston, 1896.
Connelly, Thomas W. *History of the 70th Ohio.* Cincinnati, 1902.
Connolly, James A. *Three Years in the Army of the Cumberland,* ed. Paul Angle. Bloomington, Ind., 1959.
Conyngham, David P. *Sherman's March through the South . . .* New York, 1865.
Copp, Elbridge J. *Reminiscences.* Nashua, N.H., 1911.
Courtwright, Cornelius C. Diary (manuscript). Chicago Historical Society.
Cox, Jacob D. *The March to the Sea.* New York, 1900.
Crooker, Lucien B. *The Story of the 55th Regiment.* Clinton, Mass., 1887.
Davidson, Henry M. *Fourteen Months in Southern Prisons.* Milwaukee, 1865.
Downing, Alex G. *Diary,* ed. Olynthus B. Clark. Des Moines, 1916.
Eaton, Clement, ed. "Diary of an Officer in Sherman's Army" (Captain Dextor Horton). *Journal of Southern History,* Vol. 9 (May 1943).
Fahnestock, Colonel Allen L. Diary (manuscript). Peoria Public Library.
Fleharty, Stephen F. *Our Regiment: A History of the 102nd Illinois Infantry Volunteers . . .* Chicago, 1865.
Floyd, David B. *History of the 75th Indiana Regiment.* Philadelphia, 1893.
Foote, Corydon E. *With Sherman to the Sea.* New York, 1960.
Gage, Moses D. *From Vicksburg to Raleigh.* Chicago, 1865.
Garber, Michael C. "Reminiscences of the Burning of Columbia." *Indiana Magazine of History,* Vol. XI (December 1915).
Glazier, Willard. *The Capture, the Prison Pen, the Escape.* New York, 1868.
Grigsby, Melvin. *The Smoked Yank.* Sioux Falls, S.D. 1888.
Grunert, William. *The 129th Illinois Infantry.* Winchester, Ill., 1866.
Hamilton, William D. "In at the Death." *MOLLUS,* Ohio Commandery, VI. Cincinnati, 1908.
———. *Recollections of a Cavalryman . . .* Columbia, S.C., 1915.
Hazen, W.B. *A Narrative of Military Service.* Boston, 1885.
Headley, F.Y. *Marching through Georgia.* Chicago, 1890.

Hedley, Fenwick W. *Marching through Georgia.* Chicago, 1890.
Heer, George W. *Episodes of the Civil War.* San Francisco, 1890.
Hight, John J. *History of 58th Regiment Indiana Volunteer Infantry,* compiled by Gilbert Stormont. Princeton, Ind., 1905.
Hinkley, Julian W. *A Narrative of Service with the 3rd Wisconsin.* Madison, 1912.
Hitchcock, Henry. *Marching with Sherman,* ed. M.A. deWolfe Howe. New Haven, 1927.
Horton, Captain Dextor, *see* Eaton.
Howard, Frances Thomas. *In and Out of the Lines.* New York, 1905.
Howard, O.O. *Autobiography.* New York, 1907.
Humphrey, William. Diary and letter. Chicago Public Library.
Humphreys, Charles A. *Field, Camp, Hospital and Prison.* Boston, 1918.
Hunter, Alfred G. *History of the 82nd Indiana Volunteer Infantry.* Indianapolis, 1893.
Hurst, Samuel H. *Journal—History of the 73rd Ohio.* Chilicothe, 1866.
Jackson, O.L. *The Colonel's Diary*... Sherron, Ohio, 1922.
Jamison, Matthew. *Recollections of Pioneer and Army Life.* Kansas City, Mo., 1911.
Johnson, William B. *Union to the Hub and Twice around the Tire.* Balboa, Calif., 1950.
Johnson, William C. *The March to the Sea.* Department of Ohio GAR War Papers, 1891.
Kerr, Charles D. "From Atlanta to Raleigh." *MOLLUS,* Minnesota Commandery, 1st Series. St. Paul.
Kinnear, John R. *History of the 86th Regiment Illinois Volunteers.* Chicago, 1866.
Lamb, Alfred. *My March with Sherman to the Sea.* NP, Paddock Publications, 1961.
Logan, John A. *The Volunteer Soldier.* Chicago, 1887.
Lucas, Daniel R. *History of 99th Indiana Infantry.* Lafayette, Ind., 1865.
Lybarger, Edwin L. *Leaves from My Diary.* Coshocton, Ohio, 1910.
Macy, Jesse. *An Autobiography,* ed. K. Macy Noyes. Springfield Ill., 1933.
Mahon, Samuel. "Civil War Letters." *Iowa Journal of History,* Vol. LI (1953).
Malcolm, Frank. "Such Is War." *Iowa Journal of History,* Vol. LVIII (1960).
Markland, A.H. Address to Society of Army of the Tennessee, reunion of 1885.
McAdams, Francis M. *Every Day Soldier Life, Or a History of the 113th Ohio.* Columbus, 1884.
McArthur, Henry Clay. *The Capture and Destruction of Columbia.* Washington, D.C., 1911.
McBride, John R. *History of the 33rd Indiana Volunteer Infantry.* Indianapolis, 1900.

McCain, Warren. *A Soldier's Diary.* Indianapolis, 1885.
McDonald, Granville B. *A History of the 30th Illinois Volunteers.* Sparta, Ill., 1916.
McKeever, Elliot B. *He Rode with Sherman.* Aberdeen, S.D., 1947.
McNeil, Samuel A. *Personal Recollections of Service in the Army of the Cumberland.* Richwood, Ohio, 1910.
Merrill, Samuel. *History of the 70th Indiana Regiment.* Indianapolis, 1900.
———. "Letters from a Civil War Officer." *Mississippi Valley Historical Review,* Vol. XIV (1928).
Morhaus, Henry C. *Reminiscences of 123rd Regiment, New York Volunteers.* Greenwich, N.Y., 1879.
Morse, Bliss. *Civil War Diary.* Pittsburg, Kans., 1964.
Morse, Charles F. *Letters Written during the Civil War.* Boston, 1898.
Nichols, George W. *The Story of the Great March . . .* New York, 1865.
Nourse, Henry S. "The Burning of Columbia, S.C." *Papers, Military Historical Society of Massachusetts,* Vol. IX.
Orendorff, H.H., et al., eds. *Reminiscences of the Civil War from Diaries of Members of the 103rd Illinois Volunteer Infantry.* Chicago, 1905.
Osborn, Hartwell. *Trials and Triumphs—The Record of the 55th Ohio.* Chicago, 1904.
Owens, Ira S. *Green County Soldiers in the Late War.* Dayton, 1884.
Payne, Edwin W. *History of the 34th Regiment, Illinois Volunteer Infantry.* Clinton, Iowa, 1902.
Peddycord, William F. *History of 74th Indiana.* Warsaw, Ind., 1913.
Pendergast, Harrison. Diary. H. Pendergast Papers, Minnesota Historical Society.
Pepper, George W. *Personal Recollections of Sherman's Campaigns.* Zanesville, Ohio, 1866.
Perry, Sergeant Elias. Diary. Western Historical Manuscript Collection, University of Missouri Library, Columbia.
Pike, James. *The Scout and Ranger.* Cincinnati, 1865.
Porter, Anthony Toomer. *The History of a Work of Faith and Love in Charleston, S.C. . . .* New York, 1881.
Porter, David D. *Incidents and Anecdotes of the Civil War.* New York, 1885.
Potter, John. *Reminiscences of the Civil War.* Oskaloosa, Iowa.
Putney, Frank H. "Incidents of Sherman's March." *MOLLUS,* Wisconsin Commandery, Vol. III., 1900.
Reid, Harvey. *The View from Headquarters—Civil War Letters of Harvey Reid,* ed. Frank L. Byrne. Madison, Wis., 1965.
Remington, Cyrus K. *A Record of Battery I 1st New York Light Artillery.* Buffalo, 1891.
Rice, Franklin G. *Diary of 19th Michigan Volunteer Infantry.* Big Rapids, not dated.

Rockwood, Captain Rhoderick R. Diary. State Historical Society of Missouri.

Rood, Hosea M. *Company E Twelfth Wisconsin Regiment.* Milwaukee, 1893.

Ross, Sergeant Levi. Diary. Illinois State Historical Library, Springfield.

Rushing, James F. *Men and Things I Saw.* Cincinnati, 1899.

Saunier, Joseph A. *A History of the 47th Ohio.* Hillsboro, 1903.

Schofield, John M. *Forty Six Years in the Army.* New York, 1897.

Schurz, Carl. *Reminiscences*... New York, 1908.

Sharland, George. *Knapsack Notes of General Sherman's Grand Campaign.* Springfield, Ill., 1865.

Sherlock, Eli J. *Memorabilia of Marches and Battles.* Kansas City, Mo., 1896.

Sherman, W.T. *Home Letters of General Sherman,* ed. M.A. deWolfe Howe. New York, 1909.

———. *Memoirs*... 2 vols. New York, 1875.

Sherman, W.T., and John Sherman. *The Sherman Letters.* New York, 1894.

Smith, Charles H. *The History of Fuller's Ohio Brigade.* Cleveland, 1909.

Stewart, Nixon B. *Dan McCook's Regiment, 52nd Ohio Volunteer Infantry.*

Storrs, John W. *The 20th Connecticut Regiment.* Ansonia, Conn., 1886.

Sweet, Private Benjamin F. "War Record" (journal). Western Historical Manuscripts Collection, University of Missouri Library, Columbia.

Toombs, Samuel. *History of the 13th New Jersey.* Orange, 1878.

Tourgee, Albion W. *The Story of a Thousand.* Buffalo, 1896.

Trego, Lieutenant Alfred H. Diary (manuscript). Chicago Historical Society.

Trimble, Harvey M. *History of 93rd Regiment, Illinois Volunteer Infantry.*

Upson, Theodore F. *With Sherman to the Sea*... Bloomington, Ind., 1958.

Welles, Gideon. *Diary,* 3 vols. Boston, 1911.

Wills, Charles Wright. *Army Life of an Illinois Soldier.* Washington, D.C., 1906.

———. "Diary," *see* Orendorff.

Wilson, Captain Ephraim. *Memoirs of the War.* Cleveland, 1893.

Biographies

Dawson, George F. *Life and Services of General John A. Logan.* Chicago, 1887.

Dodson, William C. *Campaigns of Wheeler and His Cavalry* . . . Atlanta, 1899.

Dowd, Clement. *Life of Zebulon B. Vance.* Charlotte, N.C., 1897.

DuBose, John W. *General Joseph Wheeler and the Army of Tennessee.* New York, 1912.

Dyer, John P. *"Fightin' Joe" Wheeler.* Baton Rouge, La., 1941.

Fielder, Herbert.... *Life and Times of Joseph E. Brown.* Springfield, 188?.

Gorham, G.C. *Life of Edwin M. Stanton.* Boston, 1899.
Hughes, Nathanael C., Jr. *General William J. Hardee.* Baton Rouge, La., 1965.
Moore, James. *Kilpatrick and Our Cavalry.* New York, 1865.
O'Connor, Richard. *Hood, Cavalier General.* New York, 1949.
"One Who Knows" (pseud.). *A Checkered Life: Being a Brief History of the Countess Pourtales, Formerly Miss Marie Boozer.* Columbia, S.C., 1878.
Seitz, Don C. *Braxton Bragg . . .* Columbia, S.C., 1924.
Slocum, Charles E. *Life and Services of Major-General Henry Warner Slocum . . .* Toledo, 1913.
Thomas, Benjamin P. *Stanton: The Life and Times of Lincoln's Secretary of War.* New York, 1962.
Wellman, Manly W. *Giant in Gray: A Biography of Wade Hampton . . .* New York, 1949.
Wells, Edward L. *Hampton and His Cavalry in '64.* Richmond, 1899.

WILLIAM T. SHERMAN

The most important collections of Sherman papers are in the Library of Congress Manuscript Division (especially the forty-four volumes of "Letter Books"); the University of Notre Dame; the Ohio Historical Society; the Huntington Library; the Wisconsin Historical Society; and the libraries of the following universities: Michigan, Yale, Duke and Louisiana.

The Official Records of the War of the Rebellion (Washington, D.C.: 1898–1901) are essential to an understanding of the great march. Volume XLIV, Series 1, deals with the Georgia phase, and Volume XLVII with the Carolinas phase. These works should be supplemented by the *Report of the Joint Committee on the Conduct of the War* (Washington, D.C.: 1865) and its two-volume *Supplement* (Washington, D.C.: 1866). Of equal importance is *General Sherman's Official Accounts of his Great March through Georgia and the Carolinas* (New York: 1865).

Biographies

The most able, if somewhat adulatory, of these is Lloyd Lewis' *Sherman: Fighting Prophet* (New York: 1932). Others:

Bowman, Samuel M., and R. B. Irwin. *Sherman and His Campaigns.* New York, 1865.
Burne, Alfred H. *Lee, Grant and Sherman.* New York, 1939.
Force, Manning F. *General Sherman.* New York, 1899.

Headley, Joel T. *Grant and Sherman.* New York, 1865.
Liddell Hart, Basil H. *Sherman: The Genius of the Civil War.* London, 1930.
———. *Sherman: Soldier, Realist, American.* New York, 1929.
Macartney, Clarence E. *Grant and His Generals.* New York, 1953.

Special Studies of Sherman

Boyd, David F. *General W.T. Sherman As a College President.* Baton Rouge, La., 1910.
Boynton, Henry V.N. *Sherman's Historical Raid.* Cincinnati, 1875.
Cook, Harvey T. *Sherman's March through South Carolina . . .* Greenville, 1938.
Moulton, Charles W. *The Review of General Sherman's Memoirs in the Light of Its Own Evidence.* Cincinnati, 1875. (A response to Boynton's scathing review of Sherman's *Memoirs.)*
Who Burnt Columbia? Part 1, Official Depositions of William T. Sherman, General of the Army of the United States . . . Before the Mixed Commission on British and American Claims. Charleston, S.C., 1873.
Williams, John B. "General William T. Sherman and Total War." *Journal of Southern History,* Vol. 14 (1948).

Other Sources

Andrews, J. Cutler. *The North Reports the Civil War.* Pittsburgh, 1955.
Barrett, John G. *Sherman's March through the Carolinas.* Chapel Hill, N.C., 1956.
Bartlett, John R. *The Literature of the Rebellion.* Boston, 1866.
Battles and Leaders of the Civil War, Vol. 4. New York, 1888.
Bibliography of State Participation in the Civil War, 1861–65. Washington, D.C., 1913.
Bonner, James C. "Sherman at Milledgeville." *Journal of Southern History,* August 1956.
Brooks, U.R. *Butler and His Cavalry.* Columbia, S.C., 1909.
The Confederate Records of the State of Georgia (Candler), Vols. 2 and 3.
Coulter, Eliis M. *Travels in the Confederate States.* Norman, Okla., 1948.
Dornbusch, Charles E., ed. *The Military Bibliography of the Civil War,* 2 vols. New York, 1913, 1961, 1967.
Dyer, Frederick H. *A Compendium of the War of the Rebellion.* New York, 1959.
Garrett, Franklin M. *Atlanta and Environs.* Athens, Ga., 1969.
Gibbes, James G. *Who Burned Columbia?* Newberry, S.C., 1902.
Gibson, John M. *Those 163 Days.* New York, 1961.
Hartridge, Walter C. *The Green-Meldrin House.* Savannah, 1943.
Hesseltine, W.W. *Civil War Prisons.* Columbus, Ohio, 1930.

Hicken, Victor. *Illinois in the War.* Urbana, 1966.
Hinman, Wilbur E. *The Story of the Sherman Brigade.* Alliance, Ohio, 1897.
History of the Confederate Veterans Association of Fulton County, Georgia. Atlanta, 1890.
Hoehling, A.A. *Last Train from Atlanta.* New York, 1958.
Hoole, William S. *Alabama Tories.* Tuscaloosa, 1960.
Horn, Stanley F. *The Army of Tennessee.* Indianapolis, 1941.
Ingersoll, Luston D. *Iowa and the Rebellion.* Philadelphia, 1866.
Isham, Asa B. *Prisoners of War.* Cincinnati, 1890.
Jones, Charles C. *The Dead Towns of Georgia.* Savannah, 1878.
Jones, Katharine M. *When Sherman Came.* New York, 1964.
Luvaas, Jay. *The Military Legacy of the Civil War.* Chicago, 1959.
Massey, Mary E. *Bonnet Brigades.* New York, 1966.
Pringle, Elizabeth A. *Chronicles of Chicora Wood.* New York, 1922.
Rhodes, J.F. *"Who Burned Columbia?" American Historical Review,* Vol. 7 (1901–02).
Ridley, Bromfield L. *Battles and Sketches of the Army of Tennessee.* Mexico, Mo., 1906.
Rodgers, Robert L. *An Historical Sketch of the Georgia Military Institute.* Atlanta, 1890.
Ryan, Daniel J. *The Civil War Literature of Ohio.* Cleveland, 1911.
Turner, Ann. *Guide to Indiana Civil War Manuscripts.* Indianapolis, 1965.
Wells, Charles F. *The Battle of Griswoldville.* Macon, Ga., not dated.
White, George. *Historical Collections of Georgia.* New York, 1854.

Newspapers

Augusta (Ga.) *Constitutionalist*
Boston Journal
Chicago Tribune
Columbus (Ga.) *Daily Times*
Fayetteville (N.C.) *Observer*
London Herald
London *Times*
New York Herald
The New York Times
New York Tribune
New York World
Richmond Sentinel
Savannah News

Magazines

British Army & Navy Gazette
Harper's Weekly

Index

A

B

D

E

F

G

H

Q

R

S

T

About the Author

BURKE DAVIS, the author of more than thirty books, is best known for his Civil War narratives, including *To Appomattox,* a Literary Guild selection. His numerous biographies include three of Confederate commanders: *They Called Him Stonewall; Gray Fox: R. E. Lee & the Civil War;* and *Jeb Stuart, the Last Cavalier.* His work on *Sherman's March* covered more than ten years, spent chiefly in gathering hundreds of eyewitness accounts, many of them obscure, forgotten or previously unpublished. Mr. Davis is the father of two young novelists, Angela Davis-Gardner and Burke Davis III. A native of North Carolina, he now lives in Williamsburg, Virginia.

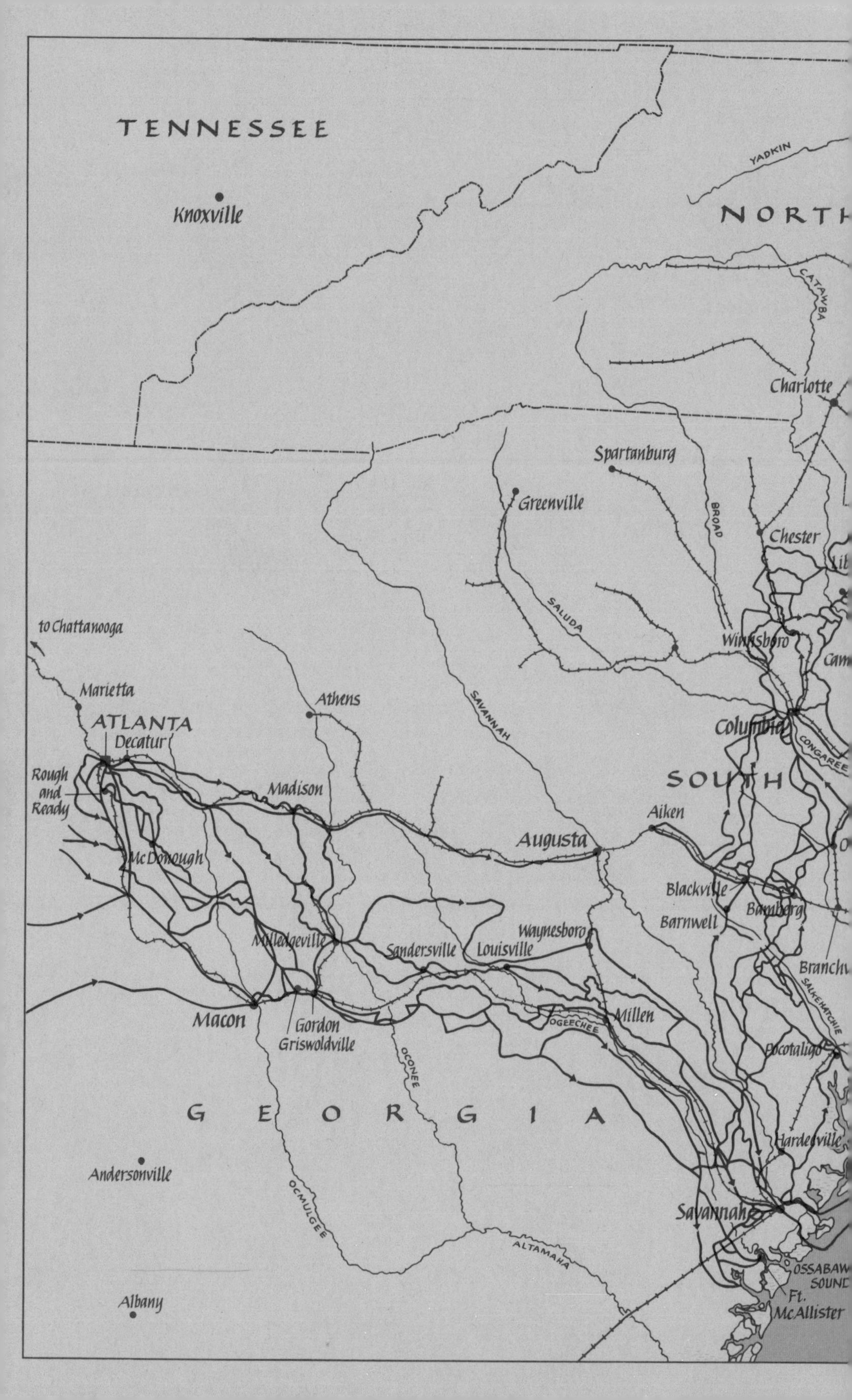
TENNESSEE
Knoxville
NORTH
YADKIN
CATAWBA
Charlotte
Spartanburg
Greenville
BROAD
Chester
SALUDA
Winnsboro
to Chattanooga
Marietta
Athens
ATLANTA
Decatur
SAVANNAH
Columbia
CONGAREE
Rough and Ready
Madison
SOUTH
Aiken
Augusta
McDonough
Blackville
Bamberg
Barnwell
Waynesboro
Milledgeville
Sandersville
Louisville
Branchville
SALKEHATCHIE
Macon
Gordon
Griswoldville
OGEECHEE
Millen
Pocotaligo
OCONEE
GEORGIA
Hardeeville
Andersonville
OCMULGEE
Savannah
ALTAMAHA
OSSABAW SOUND
Ft. McAllister
Albany